Revisiting Classical Economics

T0300076

The financial crisis, and the economic crisis that followed, triggered a crisis in the subject of economics as it is typically being taught today, especially in macroeconomics and related fields. A renewed interest in earlier authors, especially the classical economists from Adam Smith to David Ricardo and John Maynard Keynes, developed. This book may also be seen as a response to this interest. What can we learn from the authors mentioned, that we could not learn from the mainstream?

This volume contains a selection of essays which deepens and widens the understanding of the classical approach to important problems, such as value and distribution, growth and technical progress, and exhaustible natural resources. It is the fourth collection in a row and reflects an on-going discussion of the fecundity of the classical approach.

A main topic of the essays is a comparison between the classical approaches with modern theory and thus an identification of what can be learned by elaborating on the ideas of Smith, Ricardo and Marx above and beyond and variously in contradiction to certain mainstream views. Since the work of Piero Sraffa spurred the revival of classical economic thought, his contributions are dealt with in some detail. The attention then focuses on economic growth and the treatment of exhaustible resources within a classical framework of the analysis.

Heinz D. Kurz is Professor of Economics at the University of Graz, Austria, and Chairman of the *Graz Schumpeter Centre*.

Neri Salvadori is Professor of Economics at the University of Pisa, Italy, and Chairman of *CICSE* (*Centro Ineruniversitario per lo Studio sulla Crescità e lo Sviluppo Economico*).

Routledge Studies in the History of Economics

Revisiting Classical Economics

Studies in long-period analysis

**Heinz D. Kurz and
Neri Salvadori**

Routledge
Taylor & Francis Group

LONDON AND NEW YORK

First published 2015
by Routledge
2 Park Square, Milton Park, Abingdon, Oxon OX14 4RN

and by Routledge
52 Vanderbilt Avenue, New York, NY 10017

First issued in paperback 2020

Routledge is an imprint of the Taylor & Francis Group, an informa business

British Library Cataloguing in Publication Data
A catalogue record for this book is available from the British Library

Library of Congress Cataloguing in Publication data
Kurz, Heinz D.
  Revisiting classical economics : studies in long-period analysis / Heinz D. Kurz and Neri Salvadori.
    pages   cm
  1. Classical school of economics.   I. Salvadori, Neri.   II. Title.
  HB94.K873 2014
  330.15'3–dc23
  2013050067

ISBN 13: 978-0-367-66942-3 (pbk)
ISBN 13: 978-0-415-73290-1 (hbk)

Typeset in Times New Roman by
Out of House Publishing

Contents

Figures

Tables

Contributors

Simone D'Alessandro is Assistant Professor at the University of Pisa, Italy. His main research interests involve distribution of income and wealth, development economics, ecological economics, non-linear dynamics, ecological sustainability and growth.

Christian Gehrke is Associate Professor of Economics at the University of Graz, Austria. His fields of interest are the theory of growth and distribution, the analysis of structural change and the history of economic thought.

Rodolfo Signorino is Associate Professor of Economics at the Law Faculty of the University of Palermo, Italy. He has published in the areas of Classical and Sraffian economics and the methodology of economics. He is also the author of a two-volume intermediate textbook, *Istituzioni di Economia Politica*.

Acknowledgements

We are grateful to the following publications for allowing us to reproduce articles which originally appeared in their pages: *Economics Systems Research* for 'Input-output analysis from a wider perspective: a comparison of the early works of Leontief and Sraffa'; *Production, Distribution and Trade: Alternative Perspectives: Essays in Honour of Sergio Parrinello*, A. Birolo, D. Foley, H.D. Kurz (eds.), London: Routledge, 2010, for 'Spurious "margins" versus the genuine article'; *Journal of Economic Methodology* for 'Piero Sraffa: economic reality, the economist and economic theory – an interpretation'; *Sraffa or an Alternative Economics*, G. Chiodi, L. Ditta (eds.), New York: Palgrave Macmillan, 2008, for 'On a proof of Sraffa´s' and for 'On the collaboration between Sraffa and Besicovitch: the "proof of gradient" '; *The Return to Keynes*, B. Bateman, T. Hirai, C.M. Marcuzzo (eds.), Cambridge (MA) and London: The Belknap Press of Harvard University Press, 2010, for 'Keynes, Sraffa, and the latter´s "secret skepticism" '; *History of Political Economy* for 'Sraffa on von Bortkiewicz: reconstructing the classical theory of value and distribution'; *Economic Development and Social Change*, G. Stathakis, G. Vaggi (eds.), London: Routledge, 2006, for 'Endogenous growth in a stylised "classical" model'; *Journal of Economic Behavior & Organization* for 'Pasinetti versus Rebelo: two different models or just one?'; *A History of Economic Theory: Essays in Honour of Takashi Negishi*, A. Ikeo, H.D. Kurz (eds.), London: Routledge, 2009, for 'Ricardo on exhaustible resources, and the Hotelling Rule'; *The Evolution of Economic Theory: Essays in Honour of Bertram Schefold*, V. Caspari (ed.), London: Routledge, 2011, for 'Exhaustible resources: rents, profits, royalties and prices'. Publication details and dates of all these articles are given in the text.

1 Revisiting Classical economics

An introduction

Heinz D. Kurz and Neri Salvadori

This volume is the fourth in a series of collections of essays written by the two of us, by one of us alone, or by one or the two of us with some other author. The previously published collections of essays were

- *Understanding 'Classical' Economics. Studies in Long-period Theory* (1998);
- *Classical Economics and Modern Theory. Studies in Long-period Analysis* (2003) and
- *Interpreting Classical Economics. Studies in Long-period Analysis* (2007).

Each collection reflects the discussions we were and still are involved in regarding the characteristic features of the Classical economists' approach to economic problems, and its resumption in modern times, which in important respects differs markedly from the later marginalist or neoclassical approach. In the course of time these discussions have both deepened and widened, which can be seen at a glance by comparing the contents of the four volumes. An important development concerns the growing reference to Piero Sraffa's insights into Classical economic thought as they are contained in his hitherto unpublished papers and correspondence. This involves doctrinal questions such as to what extent Sraffa built upon, or deviated from the analyses of the physiocrats, David Ricardo or Karl Marx; the relationship of his approach in terms of simultaneous equations to the general equilibrium analyses of authors such as Vilfredo Pareto; the difference between Sraffa's concept of 'physical real cost' and Alfred Marshall's 'real cost'; and so on. Then there is the problem of which kind of methodology Sraffa had endorsed and what view he held of the relationship between observer, reality and theory. Another question concerns the extension of the discussion to particular problems Sraffa dealt with in *Production of Commodities by Means of Commodities* (Sraffa 1960) only in passing, especially the problem of exhaustible resources and the problem of the pattern of utilisation of durable instruments of production. Both problems are discussed within the analytical framework of a choice of technique. Then there is the question of how Sraffa's work relates to that of other economists who wrote broadly at around the same time in a partly similar vein, especially Ladislaus von Bortkiewicz and Wassily Leontief. Finally there is the problem of

scrutinising critically alternative theories or economic models against the background of the Classical approach.

Several of the chapters in this collection have grown out of controversies
we were involved in. On several occasions the late Mark Blaug had criticised
our Sraffa-inspired interpretation of the nature and genuine significance of the
Classical economists' contributions, especially David Ricardo, and had put forward an alternative interpretation. Scrutinising carefully the latter we arrived at
the conclusion that his alternative consisted essentially in a variant of the one we
had endorsed and that therefore there was more heat than fire in his attacks on
us. A second controversy deserves to be mentioned. In this collection we publish
for the first time two papers one or the two of us had written several years ago in
response to papers published by Giancarlo de Vivo and Giorgio Gilibert on the
origins of Sraffa's production equations in his 1960 book. The two authors had
argued with different degrees of circumspection and firmness that the origin must
have been Marx's schemes of simple reproduction contained in volume II of *Das
Kapital*. De Vivo presented his view at a conference organised by Massimo Pivetti
in Rome in 1998; an Italian version of his paper was published in 2000 and an
English one in 2003 (De Vivo 2000, 2003). One of us (Kurz) was a discussant of
the paper at the conference and argued in some detail why he disagreed with de
Vivo's reconstruction. Both of us (Kurz and Salvadori) shared a serious concern
about the tenability of De Vivo's argument and took into consideration the possibility of writing a joint piece refuting it. Before we completed this paper, one of
us (Kurz) was informed by Pierangelo Garegnani that Giorgio Gilibert had given
a seminar in Rome on the origin of Sraffa's equations and that he, Garegnani, felt
that the new interpretation, which saw the roots of Sraffa's equations to be Marx's
schemes of reproduction, looked rather convincing to him. Kurz expressed his
astonishment and urged Garegnani to arrange for the paper to be shown to him.
He was then sent a copy of the proofs of the piece, which had already been sent
to the printer. Kurz checked the evidence put forward by Gilibert and concluded
that it did not support the case under consideration. He told Garegnani about his
findings on the phone and alerted him to the fact that the publication of interpretations of parts of Sraffa's papers by members of the editorial team, which would
be disputed by other members, might cause trouble for the editorial project. Such
a concern had been expressed by Garegnani himself on various occasions and had
made him ask members of the editorial team to try to sort out conflicting views of
the material and at any rate hold back disputable interpretations till after the editorial project was completed. In the phone conversation Garegnani told Kurz that
he might be right to some extent, but that Gilibert might have a point. Kurz then
jotted down swiftly what he found wrong with Gilibert's argument. After having
read the notes sent to him in 2003, Garegnani got back to Kurz and told him that
he was now convinced that Gilibert's interpretation cannot be sustained: the evidence against it was overwhelming.[1]

The question then was what to do. In late 2003 Kurz developed his notes into
a paper entitled 'Sraffa's equations "unveiled"? A comment on Gilibert'. He sent
it to Garegnani and confidentially also to a few other scholars. He was convinced

that it would be necessary to quickly bring it out in order to make readers aware of what spoke against Gilibert's interpretation. However, Garegnani asked Kurz not to publish his piece, but wait till after the edition was out, which would request only two to three more years. Kurz eventually agreed in the interest of avoiding tensions within the editorial team, which might have slowed down the project further. He now thinks that this was an error. As a consequence of the postponement of the publication of the paper by Kurz on Gilibert we stopped finalising our joint paper on De Vivo. We publish these papers here for the first time in order to document what we think contradicts De Vivo's and Gilibert's interpretations. Re-reading our old pieces on the occasion of preparing this collection of essays has convinced us that what we had written then still holds now.

The material in this volume is subdivided in five parts.

Part I is dedicated to 'Classical Economics and Modern Theory' and has two chapters.

Chapter 2 compares Wassily Leontief's PhD thesis in Berlin, published in 1928, and Sraffa's work in Cambridge in 1927–8 on his equations of production as reconstructed from his unpublished papers. Both authors were keen to move away from subjectivist explanations of relative prices and income distribution and explained them instead in terms of the observable amounts of commodities produced and used up during a year as means of production or means of subsistence in the support of workers. Given the system of production actually in use and the real wage rate, the rate of return on capital and relative prices are determined. The amount of capital in the system, a value magnitude, is determined at the same time as the rate of return and prices and cannot generally be taken as given as in long-period marginalist theory. Sraffa, as is well known, kept elaborating the Classical approach by dealing also with such intricate problems as fixed capital, scarce natural resources and joint production proper, whereas Leontief's interest soon shifted towards applying the new tool of input-output analysis to practical problems. He thereby embraced ideas in the theory of value that were incompatible with his earlier views and are difficult to sustain.

Chapter 3 is the long version of a reply to Mark Blaug's attack on what he called 'Sraffian economics'. (The short version was published in *History of Political Economy*; see Kurz and Salvadori 2011.) It is argued that none of the criticisms levelled at Sraffa's resumption of the Classical approach and the contributions of those adopting it stands up to close examination. Blaug also attributed views to us (and other authors) we (they) never advocated. And he contended that 'Sraffian' authors have not dealt with certain important problems, although the literature he refers to proves the opposite. He mistakes the mathematical form of an argument for its content. The use of simultaneous equations in Sraffa he misinterprets as reflecting a version of Walrasian general equilibrium theory. Surprisingly he no longer maintains that there is a fundamental difference between his own interpretation of the Classical economists and that of the 'Sraffians': it is only 'a question of emphasis', he opines. We argue that Blaug's sharp counterposition of rigour and relevance of a theory is a red herring: a concern with rigour must not be misread as a lack of interest in the relevance of the analysis.

Part II is 'On Sraffa's Contribution' and has four chapters.

Chapter 4 reflects upon Sraffa's warning that 'Caution is necessary ... to avoid spurious "margins" for the genuine article' (Sraffa 1960: v) against the background of certain propositions put forward by Christian Bidard. It is argued that the existence of what Bidard calls 'marginal equalities' does not provide any support for the marginalist explanation of wages or the rate of profits. The fact that the rate of profits equals the derivative of the relationship that can be built between the value of national income as function of the value of capital, both calculated at a given rate of profits, should not come as a surprise. Calling such a derivative 'the marginal productivity of capital appropriately defined' must not be mistaken to mean that the rate of profits is *determined* by some marginal productivity of capital. With the latter being ascertained in terms of a *given* and known rate of profits, there is no causal relation leading from the marginal productivity to the rate of profits. In fact the contrary direction would be more appropriate.

In Chapter 5 Neri Salvadori and Rodolfo Signorino develop a rational reconstruction of an important aspect of Sraffa's methodology: his view of the relationship between the observer or theorist, economic reality and the economic theory designed to analyse this reality. They focus attention on Sraffa's published work on pure economics and argue that while in his 1925 and 1926 papers Sraffa puts forward some observations about economic reality and apparently takes them as self-evident, in his 1960 book he takes care to first clearly identify the object of his inquiry and then decides the best way to analyse it.

Chapter 6 was published as a comment to Lippi (2008). Lippi delivered a paper at the Conference 'Sraffa or an Alternative Economics' (Rome, Italy, 2003) arguing, among other things, that the algorithm in section 37 of Sraffa's book does not need to converge to the desired eigenvalue and eigenvector. Salvadori was surprised and looked for an example. When he found an example, it became clear that a further assumption was required and that Sraffa was not so wrong after all.

Chapter 7 deals with Sraffa's relationship with Keynes, focusing attention on Sraffa's reception of *The General Theory*. While Sraffa approved of Keynes's critical intention with respect to the marginalist theory of output and employment, based on Say's law, he was disenchanted with its execution. It was not only Keynes's occasional sloppiness he had difficulties in coping with. In important respects he found that Keynes's new theory exhibited several loose ends and contradictions. He was particularly critical of Keynes's liquidity preference theory, as we can see from two manuscript fragments Sraffa had apparently composed shortly after the publication of Keynes's magnum opus, but which he apparently never showed to Keynes. He also felt that Keynes had granted conventional theory too much and had not succeeded in fully 'escaping habitual modes of thought'.

Part III deals with various aspects of the development of Sraffa's thoughts that culminated in the publication of his 1960 book and has four chapters.

Chapter 8 deals with a further aspect of the collaboration between Abram S. Besicovitch, the Cambridge mathematician and one of Sraffa's 'mathematical friends', and Sraffa. The latter consulted Besicovitch in the 1940s and 1950s whenever he had problems with proving some of the propositions that eventually entered his 1960 book. Up until now we have tackled in a series of papers a number of instances of Sraffa requesting the assistance of Frank Ramsey, Alister Watson and Besicovitch with intricate problems, when he was not sure, whether the argument he had forged was correct or whether it could be presented in a more effective way; see Kurz and Salvadori (2001, 2004). These papers have been reprinted in earlier collections of our essays and the reader is welcome to consult them. In Chapter 8 we deal with the mathematical property of the system relating to the dependence of relative prices in single-product systems on the general rate of profits. In his papers Sraffa discussed this problem under the heading 'proof of the gradient'.

Chapter 9 reproduces a paper by Christian Gehrke and Heinz D. Kurz on Sraffa's notes on three contributions by Ladislaus von Bortkiewicz, especially the latter's 'Wertrechnung und Preisrechnung im Marxschen System' (Value and price calculation in the Marxian system) (Bortkiewicz 1906–7). Sraffa came across these papers only in 1943. One of his notebooks contains extensive excerpts from and critical comments on Bortkiewicz's papers. The notes are of particular importance because they were written shortly after Sraffa had resumed his re-constructive work in 1942, after having abandoned it for more than a decade because of the Ricardo edition to which the *Royal Economic Society* had appointed him in 1930. By the time he came across Bortkiewicz's notes he had already solved several problems in an attempt to explain profits, rents and the relative prices supporting a given distribution of income in terms of the concept of a social surplus. With a given real wage, conceived of as an 'inventory' of commodities, the costs of production were *physical real costs*. He approved of what he called 'Bortkiewicz's dictum' and 'dogma', that is, the theory of value must be able to show the general cause of interest in conditions of a *given* system of production, setting aside a choice of technique and technical progress. Sraffa had accomplished precisely this in terms of his equations with a surplus in the late 1920s. But he criticised Bortkiewicz for not adopting a circular flow perspective on production, as in the physiocrats and Marx, but sticking to an Austrian conceptualisation of it as a one-way avenue leading from primary inputs to final outputs. Such a framework removed from one's eyes the fact that the maximum rate of profits of the economic system, corresponding to zero wages, is finite and not infinite. The chapter throws light on the relationship of Sraffa's analysis and the analyses especially of Ricardo and Marx.

The last two chapters in this part deal with the origin of Sraffa's production equations. As mentioned above, they were written at the turn of the year 2003 and are here published for the first time. Chapter 10 examines critically Giorgio Gilibert's contention 'that the reproduction schemes are the obvious starting point for the analytical path followed by Sraffa'. The pieces of evidence Gilibert put forward in support of his contention are carefully scrutinised and it is shown that they do not support his case. In fact, they might even be said to support the opposite case, namely that Sraffa did not start from Marx's schemes of reproduction, but developed his equations in an original way, taking up the concept of physical real cost he had encountered in William Petty and the physiocrats.

Chapter 11 examines critically Giancarlo de Vivo's view of the origin of Sraffa's equations. The chapter may thus be considered a twin of Chapter 10, because Gilibert's view is similar to De Vivo's, who had first contended that Sraffa's equations derive from Marx's schemes of reproduction. De Vivo was, however, less sure about his interpretation and with respect to the equations Sraffa had discussed with Frank Ramsey in 1928 pointed out that the magnitudes referred to in them might 'stand for quantities, not values', as Gilibert was to insist. Sraffa left no doubt that the 'things' he spoke of were 'the quantities of things respectively used in production (i.e. consumed) and produced', that is, the quantities of the means of production and the means of subsistence consumed productively on the one hand and gross outputs on the other.

We thus find no evidence from Sraffa's unpublished papers that would support the two authors' interpretations, but evidence to the contrary. We conclude in both cases that the interpretation of the path towards *Production of Commodities by Means of Commodities* put forward cannot be sustained. At the same time we provide implicitly an interpretation of the path Sraffa took that is firmly rooted in, and supported by, Sraffa's papers. See in this context also Chapter 2, Kurz and Salvadori (2005) and Kurz (2012).

Part IV deals with 'Growth and Distribution' and has two chapters.

Chapter 12 provides a formalisation in terms of a simple model of some propositions by David Ricardo. We deal especially with his view that the rate of profit and real wages can be supposed to fall together if with the extension of production of corn to less and less fertile lands the rate of capital accumulation declines (and there is no technical progress counteracting this tendency). This decline is accompanied by a falling rate of growth of the 'demand for hands', that is, agricultural labourers, which is taken to bring about, via a falling real wage rate, a fall in the rate of population growth. Also in this model the growth rate of the system is endogenously determined, as it is generally in the Classical authors.

Chapter 13 by Simone D'Alessandro and Neri Salvadori compares Pasinetti's famous formalisation of the 'Ricardian system' and one of the simplest models developed within the 'new' growth literature, Rebelo's model. Indeed both models share the same structure in the sense that they consist of the same set of equations, even if the interpretation given to these equations and to the symbols involved may be different. This exemplifies the thesis that many endogenous growth models have a 'Classical' flavour since they abandon one of the characteristic features of all neoclassical theories, that is, income distribution is determined by demand and supply of factors of production.

Part V turns to the problem of 'Exhaustible Resources' and contains three chapters that have all been written in an ongoing debate about how to tackle this problem within a Classical approach to the theory of value and distribution.

Chapter 14 expounds Ricardo's treatment of the problem of exhaustible resources against the background of a discussion of the difference between rent and profits: what Ricardo calls profits comprise, indeed, what we nowadays call royalties. The chapter illustrates also the role that capacity constraints in the exploitation of mines play in Ricardo's analysis and how these constraints may be compatible with the constancy of the price of the extracted mineral, while the price of the natural resource *in situ* increases over time at a rate that is equal to the competitive rate of profits. In the case contemplated the Hotelling Rule does not imply that *all* prices need to change over time.

Chapter 15 develops the argument in terms of a little model and a numerical illustration, which bring together the approaches of Ricardo and Hotelling and show that, each seen in isolation, they deal with different 'worlds', that is, are based on different assumptions regarding the system contemplated, where each reflects different aspects of the problem as a whole. Therefore the two approaches are compatible with one another, as the model shows.

Chapter 16 pays tribute to Sergio Parrinello's pioneering work in extending Sraffa's analysis to the problem of exhaustible resources (Parrinello 1983). Parrinello's paper triggered a discussion, to which contributed several scholars working in the Classical tradition, including us. What are the characteristic features of the Classical approach and how does it differ from the conventional neoclassical one? In the course of the discussion Parrinello changed his view somewhat and in his most recent contribution endorses the formulation of the problem as it can be derived from Sraffa's book. In our response to Parrinello and others we show that the analysis of exhaustible natural resources of Ricardo and then Sraffa in terms of profits and differential rents and that of Hotelling in terms of royalties are not incompatible with one another, but capture different aspects of the problem at hand. These aspects can be jointly studied in terms of a single formalisation of the problem of exhaustible resources. This takes into account two facts. The first one was emphasised by Adam Smith and Ricardo who observed that typically several deposits of the resource have to be worked in order to meet effectual demand, giving rise to rents paid to the proprietors of the non-marginal deposits. The second fact concerns the exhaustibility of the resource and involves a rise in its *in situ* price at the current rate of interest.

References

Bortkiewicz, L. v. (1906–7). Wertrechnung und Preisrechnung im Marxschen System. Pts. 1, 2, and 3. *Archiv für Sozialwissenschaft und Sozialpolitik*, 23: 1–50; 25:10–51, 445–88. Translation of parts 2 and 3 as 'Value and price in the Marxian system' in *International Economic Papers*, 2: 5–60.

De Vivo, G. (2000). Produzione di merci a mezzo di merci: note sul percorso intellettuale di Sraffa, in Pivetti, M. (ed.), *Piero Sraffa. Contributi per una biografia intellettuale*, Rome: Carocci.

De Vivo, G. (2003). Sraffa's path to *Production of Commodities by Means of Commodities*: an interpretation. *Contributions to Political Economy*, 22(1): 1–25.

Kurz, H.D. (2012). Don't treat too ill my Piero! Interpreting Sraffa's papers. *Cambridge Journal of Economics*, 36(6): 1535–69.

Kurz, H.D. and Salvadori, N. (2001). Sraffa and the mathematicians: Frank Ramsey and Alister Watson, in Cozzi, T. and Marchionatti, R. (eds), *Piero Sraffa's Political Economy: A Centenary Estimate*, London: Routledge, pp. 254–84. Reprinted in Kurz, H.D. and Salvadori, N. (eds), *Classical Economics and Modern Theory: Studies in Long-period Analysis*, London: Routledge, 2003, pp. 187–217.

Kurz, H.D. and Salvadori, N. (2004). On the collaboration between Sraffa and Besicovitch: the cases of fixed capital and non-basics in joint production, in *Atti dei Convegni Lincei*, Rome: Accademia Nazionale dei Lincei, pp. 255–301. Reprinted in Kurz, H.D. and Salvadori, N. (eds), *Interpreting Classical Economics: Studies in Long-period Analysis*, London: Routledge, 2007, pp. 159–200.

Kurz, H.D. and Salvadori, N. (2005). Representing the Production and Circulation of Commodities in Material Terms: On Sraffa's Objectivism. *Review of Political Economy*, 17(3): 413–441.

Kurz, H.D. and Salvadori, N. (2011). In favor of rigor and relevance. A reply to Mark Blaug. *History of Political Economy*, 43(3): 607–16.

Lippi, M. (2008). Some observations on Sraffa and mathematical proofs, in Chiodi, G. and Ditta, L. (eds), *Sraffa or an Alternative Economics*, New York: Palgrave Macmillan, pp. 243–52.

Parrinello, S. (1983). Exhaustible natural resources and the classical method of long-period equilibrium, in Kregel, J. (ed.), *Distribution, Effective Demand and International Economic Relations*, London: Macmillan, pp. 186–99.

Sraffa, P. (1960). *Production of Commodities by Means of Commodities. Prelude to a Critique of Economic Theory*, Cambridge: Cambridge University Press.

Notes

1 According to entries in his diary, Kurz also contacted Gilibert to inform him about his disagreements. And he talked to De Vivo in the Wren in Cambridge about what he felt was wrong with Gilibert's and also De Vivo's position in this regard.

Part I
Classical economics and modern theory

2 Input–output analysis from a wider perspective

A comparison of the early works of Leontief and Sraffa†

Heinz D. Kurz and Neri Salvadori

Introduction

> Input–output analysis is a practical extension of the classical theory of general interdependence which views the whole economy of a region, a country and even of the entire world as a single system and sets out to describe and to interpret its operation in terms of directly observable basic structural relationships.
>
> (Leontief, 1987*, p. 860)

According to this statement, input–output analysis is based exclusively on magnitudes that are directly observable and that can be measured, using the ordinary instruments for measurement in economics. This objectivist concern is already present in Leontief's Berlin PhD thesis, his 1928 paper 'Die Wirtschaft als Kreislauf' (Leontief, 1928, an abridged English translation of which was published as 'The economy as a circular flow', Leontief, 1991*),[1] and permeates his entire work. In the 1928 essay, the objectivist approach to economic phenomena is counterposed with the then dominant Marshallian analysis and its stress on subjective factors. Marshall, it should be recalled, had tried to patch over what was a major breach with the objectivist tradition of the English classical economists, especially David Ricardo and Robert Torrens. He did this in terms of completely re-defining the received concept of 'real cost'. While originally this was meant to capture the materials (means of production and means of sustenance in the support of workers) used up in the production of a commodity, or the amount of labour actually bestowed upon it, Marshall used it to refer to 'the exertions of all the different kinds of labour that are directly and indirectly involved in making it; together with the abstinences or rather the waitings required for saving the capital used in making it' (Marshall, [1890] 1970, p. 282). Apparently, Leontief was not impressed by Marshall's re-definition and he was also not convinced by Marshall's insistence that prices could be determined only with reference to the forces of 'demand' and 'supply', conceived of as functional relationships between the

† Reproduced with permission from *Economic Systems Research*, 18(4) December 2006.

price of a commodity and the amount demanded or supplied, as is famously exemplified by Marshall's analogy with the two blades of a pair of scissors. Indeed, one of the main messages of Leontief's 1928 paper was that relative prices can be determined exclusively in terms of the observable amounts of commodities that are respectively produced and used up during a year – without any reference to demand and supply.

This was an important finding of Leontief's maiden paper. Unfortunately, he did not pursue much further the line of thought upon which it was based. Concerned with applying the new tool of input–output to practical problems made him put on one side, and eventually lose sight of, certain properties of the economic system. This applied first and foremost to the problem of value and distribution and the role the physico-economic scheme of production played with regard to it. While at the centre of interest in his 1928 essay, this problem disappeared from the scene, or rather was eventually replaced by *given* 'value added' coefficients in Leontief's price equations (see Leontief, 1941). The difficulty with this approach is that the magnitudes of value added per unit of output in the different industries cannot generally be determined prior to, and independently of, the system of prices. In this conceptualization the constraint binding changes in the distributive variables shaped by the system of production in use, and the dependence of relative prices on income distribution – facts stressed by Leontief in his 1928 paper – are removed from the scene.

Value and distribution were already set aside as part and parcel of the analytical problem at hand in Leontief's seminal 1936 paper on 'Quantitative input–output relations in the economic system of the United States' (Leontief, 1936*). Leontief introduced his study in the following terms: 'The statistical study presented in the following pages may be best defined as an attempt to construct, on the basis of the available statistical materials, a *Tableau Economique* of the United States for the year 1919' (Leontief, 1936*, p. 105).

Giving his study the name of *Tableau Economique* is indeed appropriate. As is well known, François Quesnay's original *Tableau* contains a summary account of national production, distribution and consumption during a given year, in the mid eighteenth century, for France. Most importantly for our purpose, it takes the distribution of the surplus product, or *produit net*, and the corresponding prices to be given and known. However, it is clear that the given distribution of the net product exclusively in terms of rents to landlords[2] and the given prices must satisfy the constraints imposed by the given system of production, which distinguishes only between two production sectors of the economy, primary production (agriculture, mining, forestry, etc.), or *la classe productive*, and manufacturing, or *la classe stérile*. In his 1936 paper, Leontief follows Quesnay closely in that he also takes distribution and prices to be given and reflected in the available national accounting system. He is actually forced to do so, because there is no statistical description of the production process of the economy during a year in purely material terms. The available 'description of the flow of commodities and services as it enters the given enterprise (or household) through one end and leaves it by the other' (Leontief, 1936*, p. 106) is typically in money terms. In this perspective, the wider theoretical concerns of Leontief's 1928 paper no longer play a role. The concern with applying the tool of input–output to practical problems in the way with which we are familiar is effected at the cost of narrowing its analytical scope.

Clearly, the analytical potentialities and practical usefulness of an approach that starts from a description of the production process of the economy as a whole in material terms – a 'circular flow' – go beyond conventional input–output analysis. To see this we may start from Paul Samuelson's (1991*) commentary on the abridged English version of Leontief's 1928 paper, because in it Samuelson places Leontief's contribution in a wider theoretical context. Samuelson observed that a historian of science 'would expect that somewhere a Leontief and a Sraffa would be independently discovering at about the same time the theory of input–output'. In a footnote he added that simultaneously John von Neumann perfected his model of a two-person zero-sum game which led him towards his famous model of balanced economic growth (von Neumann, [1937] 1945). Samuelson commented: 'good things in science often come in three [*sic*]'. He continued with regard to Leontief s essay: 'A new embryo contains the future organism, but not even the most discerning eye can see in the constellation of early cells the beautiful baby that is to come.' He went on:

> In embryo, when all mammals begin superficially alike, the semblance is much greater. Therefore, the Sraffian paradigms that remained forever innocent of empirical investigation started out more closely resembling the 1928 Leontief formulations than did the ultimate 1960 classic, *The Production of Commodities by Commodities*. Oddly, the 1928 non-mathematical Italian began more with algebra and formal mathematics than did the *wunderkind* of mathematical economics.
>
> (Samuelson, 1991*, pp. 177–178)[3],[4]

Samuelson concluded:

> The present article [Leontief's 1928 paper] contains no matrix, much less a determinant. It is, so to speak, primarily taxonomic and topological. The pioneer is carving our [*sic*] a new language, prior to composing a scientific poem in that language.
>
> (Samuelson, 1991*, p. 178)

We agree with Samuelson that the contributions of Leontief, Sraffa and von Neumann share important common features.[5] These concern both the method and content of the analysis. At the same time there are notable differences. In this chapter we focus attention on the early contributions of Leontief and Sraffa. We are especially interested in finding out why 'in embryo' the semblance of the two is much greater than in maturity. In other words, we reflect upon the development of input–output analysis from Leontief's 1928 essay to his 1936 and later contributions and compare them with Piero Sraffa's early work on the theory of production. Since the opening of Sraffa's papers at Trinity College Library in Cambridge, UK, we have been able to study in detail Sraffa's independent, but parallel attempt at elaborating an economic approach that proceeds exclusively in terms of magnitudes that can be observed and measured. Also, Sraffa saw his analysis as rooted in the contributions of the classical economists from William Petty to David Ricardo and he too equated his scheme with the *Tableau Economique*. However, while in the years 1927–1928 Leontief and Sraffa may be said to have been independently pursuing similar lines of thought, they soon afterwards, apparently again without knowing of each other's work, parted company, with Leontief turning to the practical application of a stripped-down version of the new instrument, and Sraffa relentlessly seeking to solve the intricate problems the approach posed in the course of its elaboration.

The composition of this chapter is as follows. In the next section we provide a summary account of crucial features of the classical economists' approach to the problem of value and distribution as it emerges from Piero Sraffa's studies in the late 1920s. The third section then turns briefly to Leontief's 1928 paper and shows how closely it is related to the classical approach to the theory of production, distribution and value. The fourth section provides a summary account of Sraffa's work in the period 1927–1931. In it, Sraffa managed to solve several of the problems that the approach was confronted with, some of which had been mentioned but not fully answered by Leontief in his maiden paper. In the short fifth section it will be argued that, due to his premature abandonment of his original line of research, Leontief later proceeded essentially in an eclectical way. In particular, when confronted with the time-honoured problem of value and distribution he developed a concept of prices and distribution that sits uncomfortably with the rest of his scheme. The sixth section draws some conclusions.

This chapter and the paper by Kurz and Salvadori (2000) can be seen as complementary to each other. The latter is concerned with the prehistory of input–output analysis and therefore covers essentially only authors whose contributions predate the publication of Leontief's seminal papers; Sraffa (1960) is therefore only mentioned in passing. The present chapter compares instead Leontief s 1928 essay with the hitherto unpublished manuscripts and working notes of Piero Sraffa that were composed at around the same time. Interestingly, both Leontief and Sraffa were disenchanted with the marginalist doctrine as it had been handed down by Alfred Marshall. They despised the subjectivist character of the explanation of value and distribution given and explicitly sought to elaborate an objectivist alternative to it. Both authors saw their own work as firmly rooted in the contributions of the physiocrats and the English classical political economists. There is no evidence known to us that the two authors knew of each other's similar endeavours and there is every reason to think that no such evidence exists. We are thus confronted with the fact that two major economists of the twentieth century developed, independently of each other, similar approaches to the problem of production. These were meant to revolutionize the subject in the traditional sense of the word as overcoming the ruling doctrine of the time by returning to an earlier one which, as Sraffa (1960, p. v) was to write, 'has been submerged and forgotten since the advent of the "marginal" method'. This return necessitated shedding the weaknesses of the doctrine's earlier formulations, which were at least partly responsible for its premature abandonment and replacement by the marginalist one, and elaborating on its strengths. The question then is how far Leontief and Sraffa got in this regard in the late 1920s and early 1930s, that is, whether they succeeded in providing a coherent approach to the problems under consideration that was faithful to their objectivist outlook on economic phenomena.

Circular flow and physical real costs

Input–output analysis has its roots in the classical economists from William Petty via Richard Cantillon and the Physiocrats to Robert Torrens and David Ricardo and to authors working in the classical tradition, such as Karl Marx, Vladimir K. Dmitriev, Ladislaus von Bortkiewicz and Georg von Charasoff. Since we have elsewhere dealt with the prehistory of input–output analysis (see Kurz and Salvadori, 2000), we may directly turn to some characteristic features of the early classical economists' view of the economic system and the analytical challenges it poses.

The arguably most important and closely intertwined features of the starting point of the classical approach to the theory of production, distribution and value are the following.

(1) Production consists essentially in a *transformation of matter and energy into other forms of matter and energy;* this process is subject to the laws of science (especially physics, chemistry and biology).
(2) Production involves destruction, and the real cost of a commodity consists first and foremost in the commodities necessarily destroyed in the course of its production. This leads to the concept of *physical real cost.*
(3) For the reason just given there is no such thing as production carried out by unassisted labour: *it is impossible to produce something out of nothing.*
(4) Production is essentially a *circular flow*: commodities are produced by (means of) commodities.
(5) Production typically generates a *social surplus.* The surplus refers to those quantities of the different commodities that are left over after the necessary means of production are used up and the means of subsistence in the support of labourers have been deducted from the gross outputs produced during a year.

Features (1) and (3) are well expressed by James Mill's famous dictum that man cannot create matter, man can only decompose and recompose it, change its form and move it (Mill, [1821] 1826, p. 107). They also help us to explain the *objectivist* nature of the analysis of the classical authors or, as William Petty put it in 1690, its 'physician's outlook', the upshot of which is to express oneself only 'in Terms of *Number, Weight* or *Measure* … and to consider only such Causes, as have visible foundations in Nature' (Petty, 1986, p. 244). Given this starting point, economics had to be elaborated in full recognition of the laws of science. Without too much of an exaggeration one can indeed say that in their analyses the classical economists tried to respect what nowadays are known as the laws of thermodynamics.

The perhaps clearest expression of the physical real cost approach, feature (2), has been put forward by James Mill in his *Elements of Political Economy*, first published in 1821. Mill insisted that, in the last instance, '*The agents of production are the commodities themselves* …They are the food of the labourer, the tools and the machinery with which he works, and the raw materials which he works upon' (Mill, [1821] 1826, p. 165, emphasis added).

This feature also invites one to draw an analogy between a product that obtains as the result of the productive consumption or 'destruction' of necessary quantities of means of production and means of subsistence, on the one hand, and a chemical reaction conceived of as a balance of the weights of inputs and outputs.[6] In both cases the balance expresses conservation of matter and energy. Sraffa traced the objectivist or natural science point of view back to William Petty and the Physiocrats. In the Physiocrats, he pointed out, 'il valore sia una quantita intrinseca degli oggetti, quasi una qualita fisica o chimica [let value be an intrinsic quantity of objects, a sort of physical or chemical property]' (D3/12/12: 7).[7] And with regard to Adam Smith's doctrine of 'natural value' he emphasized that the Scotsman was concerned with 'that physical, truly natural relation between commodities' (D3/12/11: 83). He also used the term 'physical value' of products and insisted that it '*is* equal to what has been consumed' (D3/12/1: 5; see also D3/12/10: 54).

The idea expressed in feature (4) can be traced back to William Petty and Richard Cantillon and was most effectively expressed by François Quesnay ([1759] 1972) in the *Tableau Economique*. The different parts of an economy are typically interdependent – they form a connected system of production – and therefore cannot generally be analysed independently of one another. A *general analysis* is needed; a partial analysis will typically not do. Such an analysis of general economic interdependence was in fact for the first time provided by Quesnay. Both Leontief and Sraffa pay tribute to him because of this fact.

Feature (5) raises a number of important issues and is the source of major conceptual and analytical problems that constituted (and still constitute) formidable stumbling blocks to economists. First, in systems characterized by the conservation of matter (and energy) the question is, in what sense is it possible to have a surplus? Second, once this question is satisfactorily answered, how is this surplus distributed amongst different claimants, and what are the implications of different distributions with respect (a) to the properties of the given system of production in use and (b) the forces at work that transform the system over time? The former problem leads directly to the classical analysis of the relationship between income distribution and relative prices, the latter to the analysis of the relationship between income distribution on the one hand and capital accumulation and economic growth and development on the other.

It is this rich picture of the economic system elaborated by the classical authors and those working in their tradition that allows one to adopt a wider perspective from which one may assess input–output analysis conceived as 'a practical extension of the classical theory of general interdependence'. Before doing this we show that there are some remarkable parallels between Leontief's 1928 essay and Sraffa's work in the late 1920s. We begin with a brief summary account of some of the ideas contained in Leontief's essay.

Input–output analysis, Mark I: Leontief's essay of 1928

In his essay 'Die Wirtschaft als Kreislauf' Leontief put forward a two-sectoral input–output system. Throughout his investigation he assumed single production and constant returns to scale; scarce natural resources are mentioned only in passing. In much of the analysis it is also assumed that the system of production (and consumption) is indecomposable. Much of his analysis focuses on the case of a stationary system characterized by constant technical coefficients. He tabulated the 'relations of production' in the following way (Leontief, [1928] 1991, [p. 194]):

$$aA + bB \rightarrow A \tag{1a}$$

$$(1-a)A + (1-b)B \rightarrow B \tag{1b}$$

where A and B give the total quantities produced of two, possibly composite, commodities, and a and b [$(1-a)$ and $(1-b)$] give the shares of those commodities used up as means of production and means of subsistence in the first (second) sector.

Leontief premised his analysis on the conviction that economics should start from 'the ground of what is objectively given' (Leontief, 1928, p. 583); economic concepts are said to be meaningless and potentially misleading unless they refer to magnitudes that can be observed and measured. He adopted explicitly a 'naturalistic' or 'material' perspective ([p. 211] p. 622). The starting point of the marginalist approach, *homo oeconomicus*, he considered inappropriate because it is said to give too much room to imagination and too little to facts (pp. 619–620). Economic analysis should rather focus on the concept of circular flow which expresses one of the fundamental objective features of economic life. A careful investigation of its 'technological' aspects is said to be an indispensable prerequisite to any kind of serious economic reasoning.

Leontief then distinguished between 'cost goods' and 'revenue goods'; the latter satisfy final demand. The concept of revenue good indicates that the economy is taken to produce a surplus over and above what is consumed productively. He suggested (p. 585) that the process of production should be described in terms of three sets of 'technical coefficients': (i) 'cost coefficients', that is, the proportion in which two cost goods participate in the production of a good; (ii) 'productivity coefficients', that is, the total quantity produced of a good in relation to the total quantity used up of one of its inputs; and (iii) 'distribution coefficients', that is, the proportion of the total output of a certain good allotted to a particular group of property income receivers.

Leontief stressed that because of the circular character of production 'a complete elimination of a factor of production from the given system is in principle impossible'. He added: 'Of course, the size of the "capital factor" can be reduced to any chosen level by referring back to even earlier periods of production' ([p. 211] p. 622). The reference is to what became known as the method of reduction to dated quantities of labour (see Sraffa, 1960, chapter VI). This reduction, Leontief stressed, has nothing to do with a historical regress ([p. 192 fn] p. 596, fn. 6).

Most important for the purpose of this chapter, Leontief left no doubt that the physical scheme of production contemplated also held the key – or, to be more precise, one of the (two) keys – to an investigation of exchange relationships. The latter, he stressed, had to fulfil some 'general conditions' imposed by 'the framework of a circular flow' ([p. 193] p. 598). It deserves to be emphasized that the corresponding concept of value is explicitly qualified as one that refers to the 'exchange relation *deduced from all the relationships ... analysed so far*' ([p. 193] p. 598; emphasis added). Leontief thus expressed clearly the fact that the exchange ratios under consideration flow directly from the interdependent structure of the system of production in use.

A part of the (surplus) product of each sector is taken to be appropriated by a so-called ownership group:

> In the general circular flow scheme, income from ownership is of course considered alongside other cost items without the slightest direct reference to how it originates (the phenomenon of ownership). It is the task of the theory of interest to investigate these fundamental relationships.
>
> ([p. 196] p. 600)

Leontief's argument resulted in setting up price equations that reflect not only the socio-technical conditions of production, but also the rule that fixes the distribution of the surplus product. This rule is the second key to a determination of relative prices. Only if both the system of production and the sharing out of the surplus between different claimants in terms of wages, profits (or interest) and rents is known, can relative prices be determined. Two 'keys' are required in order to solve the problem of value and distribution.

There is compelling evidence that Leontief was very clear about this. Counting unknowns and equations, he found that without fixing the distribution of the surplus the number of variables exceeds the number of equations by one. This led him to the idea of investigating the impact of hypothetical variations of one of the unknowns on the levels of the others: 'One may vary at will the exchange proportions and consequently the distribution relationships of the goods without affecting the circular flow of the economy in any way' ([p. 194] pp. 598–599). In other words, the same physical input–output schema can accommodate different price systems reflecting different distributions of income. He related this finding to the classical economists who are explicitly said to have advocated a 'surplus theory' of value and distribution ([p. 209] p. 619). Hence the exchange ratios of goods reflect not only 'natural', that is, essentially technological, factors, but also 'social causes'. For example, assuming free competition, as the classical economists did in much of their analysis, the surplus is distributed in terms of a uniform rate of return on capital across all industries of the economy. With this specification, the general rate of profit together with relative prices can be determined in terms of the system of production in use and given real wages. 'But this is the "law of value" of the so-called objective value theory' ([p. 196] p. 601), Leontief insisted.

These are remarkable propositions. They show that the young Leontief was possessed of a deep understanding of the classical economists' approach to the problem of value and distribution. Comparing his view of the classical economists with the one expressed in the received interpretations of a Marshall, Edwin Cannan or Jacob Hollander testifies to Leontief's astounding originality and profundity. There is of course reason to think that Leontief's perspective on the classical authors was at least partly shaped by the supervisor of his PhD thesis in Berlin, the eminent economic theorist and statistician Ladislaus von Bortkiewicz; see, in particular, von Bortkiewicz (1906–1907 and 1907). As we shall see in the following section, Leontief had independently arrived at a view that is very similar to the one Sraffa elaborated at around the same time. In particular, Leontief had clearly understood that the classical approach provided a coherent explanation of value exclusively in material terms and could entirely do without any reference to labour values. It constituted an analysis that was fundamentally different from the marginalist one and avoided the concepts of demand and supply functions which had no objective contents and to which nothing corresponded in the real world.

A few years later Leontief presented his input–output approach as a development of 'general equilibrium theory' which, at the time, could be expected to be identified with the Walras–Pareto–Cassel theory.[8] See, in this context, the interpretation provided by Gilibert (1981, 1991). Leontief's alleged 'conversion' to neoclassicism remains somewhat of a riddle, not least because scrutiny shows that it is more apparent than real.

We now turn to the work Sraffa carried out in the period 1927–1931. As his unpublished papers document in great detail, there were several stumbling blocks he had to remove on the way to developing a coherent theory of value and distribution exclusively in objectivist terms (quantities of materials, labour, etc.). These included, *inter alia*, the problems of how to deal with (i) durable instruments of production, (ii) scarce natural resources, such as land, and (iii) joint production. Here we set aside these problems, which played an important role in Sraffa's work in the period under consideration, and focus attention instead on the more basic ones he tackled at the beginning of this period. This limitation allows us to concentrate on what is common to Sraffa and Leontief in the late 1920s.

Sraffa's early work on the theory of production, distribution and value

Physical concepts were widely discussed by economists in the late nineteenth and at the beginning of the twentieth century. Economists thus responded to developments in the sciences, especially John Dalton's elaboration of the 'atomic theory' in chemistry. This theory was based on two laws: (i) the Law of the conservation of mass; and (ii) the Law of definite proportions. The latter stated that in a given chemical compound, the elements are always combined in the same proportion by mass. The first Law met largely with approval amongst economists which, however, did not necessarily mean much. More surprisingly, even the second Law appealed to some economists. It was discussed, for example, by Pantaleoni (1894, pp. 99 *et seq.*), whose work Sraffa had meticulously studied while still in Italy. When he was lecturing at the University of Perugia, Sraffa in 1925 criticized the adoption of this law in economics. He came back to his criticism whilst preparing his lectures on advanced theory of value he was supposed to give in Cambridge from Michaelmas term 1927–1928, but which he then postponed for a year. He insisted that the Law does not carry over from chemistry to economics essentially for two reasons. First, workers can subsist in different ways and yet produce the same kind of commodity. (Similarly, they can subsist in the same way and yet produce different kinds of commodities.) Second, one and the same commodity can be produced using different methods of production which request the productive consumption of different means of production.

The laws of science could thus not simply be adopted by economists, rather they had to be adapted judiciously to the economic field and its specific nature. The fundamental questions Sraffa faced were: was an objectivist or material-based approach to the theory of production, distribution and value at all possible? Could property incomes such as profits and rents be explained exclusively in terms of magnitudes that can be observed and measured, or did one have to have recourse to subjectivist concepts such as utility and disutility, as conventional (marginalist) theory maintained? These questions Sraffa began to answer from November 1927 onward in terms of the elaboration of several sets of 'equations', each of which was designed to address, and solve, a particular problem. He followed a growing order of complexity of the problems studied.

First equations: production without a surplus

Sraffa quite naturally first analysed an economy that produces just enough, neither more, nor less, to recover the necessary means of production used up in the process of production and the necessary means of subsistence in the support of workers – a situation reflected in what he called his 'first equations'. He emphasized that this amounts to considering workers' remuneration 'as amounts of fuel for production' (D3/12/7: 138) and identified the situation as the realm of *pure necessities*, or 'natural economy'.[9] In this case the concept of physical real costs applied in an unadulterated way. The means of subsistence in the support of workers are an indispensable part of physical real costs, because only their (recurrent) consumption 'enables' workers to perform their function. The periodic destruction of such commodities is a necessary condition the economic system has to meet in order to realize a 'self-replacing state', but it is not also sufficient. The system must be able to restore periodically the initial distribution of resources in order for the (re) productive process to continue unhampered. With a division of labour and in the absence of a central coordination of economic activities, this coordination must be achieved in terms of interdependent markets. Commodities must be exchanged for one another at the end of the uniform period of production. But which exchange ratios guarantee the repetition of the process? Sraffa showed that the sought ratios, or what in his interpretation Ricardo had called 'absolute' values, were uniquely determined by the socio-technical conditions of production and could be ascertained by solving a set of linear homogeneous production equations. Whether actual markets led up to the same solution was a different question.

We may illustrate Sraffa's reasoning in terms of a document dated winter 1927, which contemplates the 'no surplus' case of an economy composed of three industries:

$$\left.\begin{array}{l} A = a_1 + b_1 + c_1 \\ B = a_2 + b_2 + c_2 \\ C = a_3 + b_3 + c_3 \end{array}\right\} \text{ where } \begin{array}{l} A = \sum a \\ B = \sum b \\ C = \sum c \end{array}$$

These are homogeneous linear equations. They have infinite sets of solutions, but the solutions of each set are proportional. These proportions are univoche {unique}.

These proportions we call ratios of Absolute values. They are purely numerical relations between the things A, B ... They are not necessarily the ratios, in which exchange will actually take place in any community in which the quantities of things respectively used in production (i.e. consumed) and produced satisfy those equations: such actual ratios of exchange are also conditioned by such things as legal institutions, etc, which vary in different organisations of society and which are 'arbitrary', i.e. irrelevant, from our present point of view.

(D3/12/5: 2)

The above equations may be read in different, yet mutually compatible ways. First, they can simply be read as a tabulation of the productive operations carried out, with A, B and C as the gross outputs of the three industries and a_i, b_i and c_i as the amounts of the three inputs consumed in industry i ($i = 1$, 2, 3). A second way of reading them becomes perhaps clearest when we draw a parallel between Sraffa's equations and the representation of chemical reactions, since Lavoisier in the late eighteenth century, as algebraic equations, with the names of the substances expressing the equality of constituents and compounds. Obviously, an expression of the type '$2H_2O = 2H_2 + O_2$' may even be regarded as a proper algebraic equation when interpreted as follows: the mass of two molecules of water is equal to the mass of two molecules of hydrogen plus the mass of one molecule of oxygen. In this interpretation H_2O is not just a symbol for water, but has a quantitative aspect: it is the mass of a molecule of water. Similarly, an expression of the type '$A = a_1 + b_1 + c_1$' could be interpreted both as a tabulation of a production process (and in this case it is not an algebraic equation) and as an algebraic equation stating: the value of the output of the first industry, A, equals the sum of the values of its inputs, a_1, b_1, and c_1.

Yet in order to determine the values of the three kinds of commodities, the above equations are of little use. They had to be replaced by equations of the following type:

$$Ap_1 = a_1 p_1 + b_1 p_2 + c_1 p_3$$
$$Bp_2 = a_2 p_1 + b_2 p_2 + c_2 p_3$$
$$Cp_3 = a_3 p_1 + b_3 p_2 + c_3 p_3$$

where p_i is the 'absolute value', or price, of one unit of commodity i ($i = 1$, 2, 3). This Sraffa did in early 1928. He was clear that only two of the equations could be independent of one another. Hence, setting the price of one of the commodities (or of a bundle of commodities) equal to unity allows one to determine the prices of the remaining two commodities in terms of it.

Before we proceed, the following observations are apposite. First, there is a close parallel between Leontief's claim that the exchange ratios of commodities can be 'deduced from all the relationships' describing the conditions of production in the economy and Sraffa's above demonstration. Indeed, relative prices (or 'absolute values') can be ascertained exclusively in terms of the physical input–output quantities given: there is no need to have recourse to demand and supply schedules and the like. As Sraffa stated in a related note: 'It is clear at once that these technical relations of production leave no room to play with: the values are rigidly fixed, and neither preferences nor … [the punctuation mark is Sraffa's] can have any influence unless they change these relations. – It must be noted that they do not represent only the cost of production: they equally show the use, or disposal, of each product' (D3/12/2: 31). Second, Sraffa emphasized that a system of such algebraic equations is non-contradictory *only* in the case in which there is no surplus (see, for example, D3/12/6: 16 and D3/12/2: 32–35). The with-surplus case Sraffa tackled almost in parallel with the no-surplus case in the winter of 1927–1928.

Second equations: production with a surplus and given real (commodity) wages

Systems with a surplus are the object of what Sraffa called his 'second equations'. More precisely, the latter deal with a system of production that produces a surplus over and above the necessary physical real costs, including the means of sustenance of workers, and in which the surplus is distributed according to a uniform rate of interest on the value of capital invested. Sraffa, thus, at first retained the earlier assumption of given real wages in commodity terms in each of the different industries. Therefore, both in his first and second equations Sraffa felt no need to invoke, and then define, the concept of 'labour': all that mattered were physical real costs, that is, amounts of commodities used up in the course of production. In his 1960 book Sraffa aptly spoke of 'the methods of production and productive consumption' (Sraffa, 1960, p. 3).

There is, however, a crucial difference between the no-surplus and the with-surplus case: 'When we have got surplus, natural economy stops' (D3/12/11: 42) and social and institutional factors become important. Technically this is reflected in the fact that 'the equations become contradictory' (D3/12/6: 16). Materially, 'the "absolute values" have no more the appeal to commonsense of restoring the initial position – which is required if production has to go on' (D3/12/6: 10). Indeed, in the with-surplus economy, a whole range of exchange ratios is, in principle, compatible with the condition of self-replacement (see D3/12/6: 9). Sraffa stressed that 'within those limits value will be indeterminate'. And: 'It is therefore necessary to introduce some new assumption, which in substance will amount to determine … according to which criterion the surplus is distributed between the different industries' (D3/12/6: 16). With free competition, and focusing attention on the case of only circulating capital, the surplus is distributed in terms of a uniform rate of interest on the value of the 'capital' advanced in the different industries. Obviously, with heterogeneous material inputs (means of production and means of subsistence) the value of capital cannot be ascertained independently of, but only *simultaneously* with, the prices of commodities.

By mid 1928 Sraffa had managed, with the help of his colleague and friend Frank Ramsey, to establish that a solution existed and what it was (see Kurz and Salvadori, 2001, pp. 262–264). The system he and Ramsey discussed on 26 June 1928 was the following one:

$$v_a A = (v_a a_1 + v_b b_1 + c_1)r$$
$$v_b B = (v_a a_2 + v_a b_2 + c_2)r$$
$$C = (v_a a_3 + v_b b_3 + c_3)r$$

(see D3/12/2: 29). Here v_i is the value (or price) of one unit of commodity i ($i = a, b$), with the third commodity serving as standard of value, and r is the interest factor (= 1 + interest rate); the meaning of the other magnitudes should be evident. Ramsey transformed the linear homogeneous system into its canonical form and set the determinant equal to zero in order to ascertain the non-trivial solutions.

An investigation of the with-surplus system and given commodity wages yielded the following result. The rate of interest and relative prices are determined exclusively in terms of the given physical input–output scheme. All that matters are the amounts of the different commodities produced and the amounts of them used up, where obviously we now have $A \geq \sum_i a_i$, $B \geq \sum_i b_i$, and $C \geq \sum_i c_i$, and where at least with regard to one of the commodities the strict inequality sign applies. Hence in this respect there is a close parallel between the no-surplus and the with-surplus cum given-commodity-wages case. In a draft of parts of the preface of his book, probably written in the 1950s, Sraffa maintained that this point of view 'implies replacing the notion that "commodities are produced by factors of production" with the other one that "*commodities are produced by commodities*"', which in turn amounted to 'replacing the idea that the process of production has a beginning and an end with that that it is a circular one – an idea first introduced by the Tableau economique' (D3/12/7: 2; emphasis added). And when in the second half of the 1950s Sraffa began to put together his book, for a while he thought of giving it the title 'Outline of an Economic System, or, The Production of Commodities by Commodities' (see D3/12/80: 2). Thus, Sraffa for a while actually tinkered with the idea of giving his book the title Samuelson attributed to it. With regard to his first and second equations this would indeed have been appropriate. (Things are somewhat different with regard to his 'third equations'; see further down.)

Sraffa constructed simple numerical examples in order to illustrate his finding, including the following one with two industries:

$$17V = (6V + 10)r$$
$$23 = (5V + 4)r$$

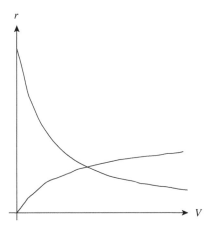

Figure 2.1 The relationship between V and r

(D3/12/8: 26). Here V is the value of one unit of the first product in terms of the second and r is again the interest factor. Sraffa calculated that r will be approximately equal to 1.582 and V equal to 2.108.[10] Sraffa also represented graphically the relationships between V and r given by the two equations and identified the solution of the system as the intersection of the two curves. (See also D3/12/7: 60, 96–100, and 173 together with the corresponding diagram in 57.) Figure 2.1 illustrates the case under consideration.

Next, Sraffa turned to the vexed problem that had already bothered a great deal David Ricardo, and after him many other authors including Karl Marx and Knut Wicksell: how does the rate of interest, and do relative prices, change consequent upon a change in wages, given the system of production? Answering this question implied disclosing the mathematical properties of a given system of production as regards the distributional alternatives it allows for and the corresponding price vectors supporting these alternatives.

Third equations and Ricardo's 'proportional wages'

The study of the impact of a hypothetical variation in wages on the rate of interest and relative prices, given the system of production, Sraffa carried out in terms of what he called his 'third equations'. Following Ricardo's lead (see *Works*, Vol. I, p. 50), he did this first in terms of a redistribution of the surplus product away from profits and towards wages in proportion to the original vector of the surplus product. This assumption allowed him to conceive of the redistribution of the surplus in straightforward physical terms and yet advocate a share concept of surplus wages that is independent of relative prices. He demonstrated that an increase in wages implied a decrease in the rate of interest and in general a change in relative prices. However, for obvious reasons, he was not satisfied with the idea of variable surplus wages with a constant commodity composition. If workers could spend some of their wages on beef, it makes no sense to assume that they consume only bread.

He saw that Ricardo had also allowed for a participation of workers in the surplus product and was especially fascinated by the way Ricardo had done this analytically in terms of what Sraffa called 'proportional wages', which had allowed him to circumnavigate the problem just mentioned. He credited Ricardo with the proposal that a *share* concept of wages was appropriate in the new situation. More specifically, Ricardo had insisted that what could be taken as a given magnitude in the theory of value and distribution is 'the proportion of the annual labour of the country ... devoted to the support of the labourers' (Ricardo, *Works*, Vol. I, p. 49; see also pp. 274–275 and 420). As Sraffa swiftly noted, Ricardo's labour-based share concept was subsequently adopted by Marx in terms of a given 'rate of surplus value', S/V, that is, the ratio between the portion of the net (labour) value added that goes to capital owners, or surplus value, S, and the portion that goes to workers, or variable capital, V. While Sraffa also adopted a share concept, unlike Ricardo (and Marx) he defined wages as a proportion of the national income evaluated in terms of normal prices.

The germs of Sraffa's work in this regard can be traced back to the latter part of the first period of his constructive work (1927–1931), but it was only as a consequence of his work on the Ricardo edition in the 1930s that he understood more clearly the new conceptualization of real wages as proportional wages Ricardo had adopted in the *Principles* (see also Sraffa, 1951, p. lii). In particular, Sraffa became aware of the fact that Ricardo's argument was not meant to be limited to the case of a given economy at a given time but was designed to cover in at least one important respect also the development of the economy *over time*. More specifically, Ricardo's demonstration of the inverse relationship between the rate of profits and wages was seen to encompass the case in which the productivity of labour changes. It was on the basis of the new wage concept (and on the premise that the social capital consisted only of, or could be reduced to, wages) that Ricardo had felt he could assert what may be called his 'fundamental proposition on distribution': that the *rate* of profits depends *on proportional wages*, and on nothing else (see Kurz, 2006).

There was only one further step to be taken in order to arrive at the price equations one encounters in Sraffa (1960, chap. III). While Ricardo (and Marx) had consistently assumed wages to be paid *ante factum*, that is, at the beginning of the (uniform) production period, and thus as belonging to the capital advanced in each industry, Sraffa, after some deliberation, decided to treat wages as paid *post factum*, that is, at the end of the production period and thus out of the product. He admitted that this was a hard choice because of the undeniable ever-present element of subsistence in wages, but compared with the alternatives at hand it was the least unsatisfactory one. In familiar matrix notation, we get the following system of price equations:

$$\mathbf{p} = (1+r)\mathbf{A}\mathbf{p} + w\mathbf{l}$$

where **p** is the *n*-dimensional vector of prices, **A** is the matrix of technical coefficients regarding means of production, **l** is the vector of direct labour coefficients, *r* is now the rate of profits or rate of interest (and no longer the interest factor) and *w* is the wage. In order to be able to interpret *w* as the share of wages in national income, some normalizations are needed (see Sraffa, 1960, chap. III). Most important, it is only now that Sraffa needed a concept of the quantity of 'labour' on the basis of which wages are calculated. In order to render heterogeneous labour commensurable, Sraffa followed the classical economists and had recourse to given wage differentials: quantities of different kinds of labour are aggregated via the relative wage rates of those different kinds of labour (see Kurz and Salvadori, 1995, chap. 11).

What is important to note is the following. Once a standard of value (or *numéraire*) is fixed and the share of wages (or, alternatively, the rate of interest) is given, prices and the rate of interest (or, alternatively, the share of wages) can be determined. However, as soon as prices are ascertained so is the value of the net product of the system, the value of the capital employed in each industry and in the economy as a whole, etc. In other words, the 'value added' is known. This value added depends on prices and therefore on income distribution.

Input–output analysis, Mark II: Leontief's post-1928 contributions

While Leontief conceived of his early contribution as firmly rooted in the classical tradition, he called his input–output method developed in the 1930s and 1940s 'an adaptation of the neo-classical theory of general equilibrium to the empirical study of the quantitative interdependence between interrelated economic activities' (Leontief, 1966, p. 134). Scrutiny shows, however, that in his input–output analysis he preserved the classical concept of circular flow and did not, as is maintained by some interpreters, adopt the Walras–Cassel view of production.[11] In the second edition of *The Structure of American Economy*, published in 1951, he even explicitly rejected the view of production as a one-way avenue that leads from the services of the 'original' factors of production: land, labour and capital – the 'venerable trinity' – to final goods (Leontief, 1951, p. 112). Unlike the theories of Walras and Cassel, in Leontief there are no given initial endowments of these factors. This is why we said earlier that the change is more apparent than real.[12]

In order to understand the real difference between his later and his earlier approach we have to turn to the way in which Leontief within the new input–output framework determined prices.[13] Obviously, attention has to focus on the so-called 'open' model. Leontief proposed a set of 'value-added price equations'. The price each productive sector is assumed to receive per unit of output equals the total outlays incurred in the course of its production. These outlays comprise the payments for material inputs purchased from the same or other productive sectors plus the 'value added'. Surprisingly, the latter is assumed to be *given* from the outside. Assuming a closed economy without a government, the latter represents the sum total of payments to the owners of productive factors: wages, rents, interest and profits. The main problem with this approach is that the magnitudes of value added per unit of output in the different sectors cannot generally be determined prior to and independently of the system of prices. Another way of putting it is that in this formulation two things are lost sight of: the constraint binding changes in the distributive variables, and the dependence of relative prices on income distribution – facts well understood and for perfectly good reasons, it seems, stressed by Leontief in his 1928 paper.[14]

Concluding remarks

The chapter compares the analytical structure of the approach Leontief adopted in his maiden paper published in 1928 with that of Sraffa in his early work on his equations of production in 1927 and 1928. It is argued that the two approaches are very similar and explain relative prices and the distribution of the social surplus essentially in the same way. Both focus attention on physical real costs of production and thus base their argument on 'what is objectively given' (Leontief) in an economy. This approach, whose roots both trace back to the classical economists, is counterposed to the demand and supply approach of the marginalist authors, especially Alfred Marshall. The important lessons the two authors drew from their analyses is that information about the quantities of commodities produced and actually used up, or the physico-economic system of production of the system as a whole, plus information about the rule according to which the surplus is distributed is sufficient in order to determine relative prices: no other data are needed or could have a place in the argument.

Whereas the starting point of the two authors was very similar, the paths they followed afterwards diverged. While Sraffa with untiring effort generalized the argument to the cases of fixed capital, scarce natural resources, joint production and a choice of technique, Leontief applied the new tool of input–output to practical problems. This made him set aside, and eventually lose sight of, certain important analytical findings contained in his 1928 essay. In particular, Leontief henceforth no longer took into account the fact that the 'value added' in each industry is endogenously determined in terms of the system of production in use and the rule fixing the sharing out of the product between the different claimants, typically workers and capital owners. Leontief instead assumed *given* 'value added' coefficients in his 'value-added price equations' (see Leontief, 1941). The difficulty with this procedure is that the magnitudes of value added per unit of output in the different industries can only be known when distribution and prices are known. Therefore, one might say that Leontief's price determination in terms of given value-added coefficients involves a regression compared with his earlier analysis.

Acknowledgements

Paper given on the occasion of the 15th International Input–Output Conference in Beijing, China, 27 June–1 July, 2005. We are grateful to Olav Bjerkholt, Ann Carter, Thijs ten Raa and other colleagues for useful observations and discussions subsequent to the presentation of the paper in Beijing and Ian Steedman and three anonymous referees for valuable comments on an earlier version of the paper. It goes without saying that any errors and misconceptions are entirely our responsibility.

Notes

References

Bortkiewicz, L. v. (1906–1907) Wertrechnung und Preisrechnung im Marxschen System, *Archiv für Sozialwissenschaft und Sozialpolitik*, 23 (1906), pp. 1–50, 25 (1907), pp. 10–51 and 445–488.

Bortkiewicz, L. v. (1907) Zur Berichtigung der grundlegenden theoretischen Konstruktion von Marx im 3. Band des 'Kapital', *Jahrbücher für Nationalökonomie und Statistik*, 34, pp. 319–335.

Garegnani, P. (2004) Di una svolta nella posizione teorica e nella interpretazione dei classici in Sraffa nei tardi anni 20, in: *Atti dei Convegni Lincei 200*, pp. 159–194 (Roma: Accademia Nazionale dei Lincei).

Gilibert, G. (1981) Isnard, Cournot, Walras, Leontief. Evoluzione di un modello, *Annali della Fondazione Luigi Einaudi*, 15, pp. 129–153.

Gilibert, G. (1991) La scuola russo-tedesca di economia matematica e la dottrina del flusso circolare, in: G. Beccatini (Ed.) *Le scuole economiche*, pp. 387–402 (Turin: Utet).

Kurz, H.D. (2006) The agents of production are the commodities themselves. On the classical theory of production, distribution and value, *Structural Change and Economic Dynamics*, 17, pp. 1–26.

Kurz, H.D. and Salvadori, N. (1995) *Theory of Production. A Long-period Analysis* (Cambridge: Cambridge University Press).

Kurz, H.D. and Salvadori, N. (2000) 'Classical' roots of input–output analysis: a short account of its long prehistory, *Economic Systems Research*, 12, pp. 153–179.

Kurz, H.D. and Salvadori, N. (2001) Sraffa and the Mathematicians: Frank Ramsey and Alister Watson, in: T. Cozzi and R. Marchionatti (Eds) *Piero Sraffa's Political Economy. A Centenary Estimate*, pp. 254–284 (London: Routledge).

Kurz, H.D. and Salvadori, N. (2004) Von Neumann, the Classical economists and Arrow–Debreu: some notes, *Acta Oeconomica*, 54, pp. 39–62.

Kurz, H.D., Dietzenbacher, E. and Lager, C. (Eds) (1998) *Input–output Analysis*, 3 vols (Cheltenham, UK: Edward Elgar).

Leontief, W. (1928) Die Wirtschaft als Kreislauf, *Archiv für Sozialwissenschaft und Sozialpolitik*, 60, pp. 577–623.

Leontief, W. (1936) Quantitative input and output relations in the economic systems of the United States, *Review of Economics and Statistics*, 18, pp. 105–125.

Leontief, W. (1941) *The Structure of American Economy* (Cambridge, MA: Harvard University Press).

Leontief, W. (1951) *The Structure of American Economy, 1919–1939: An Empirical Application of Equilibrium Analysis* (White Plains, NY: International Arts and Sciences Press). (Second enlarged edition of Leontief, 1941.)

Leontief, W. (1966) *Input–Output Economics* (New York: Oxford University Press).

Leontief, W. (1987) Input–Output analysis, in: J. Eatwell, M. Milgate and P. Newman (Eds) *The New Palgrave. A Dictionary of Economics*, vol. 2, pp. 860–864 (London: Macmillan).

Leontief, W. (1991) The economy as a circular flow, *Structural Change and Economic Dynamics*, 2, pp. 177–212.

Marshall, A. (1970) *Principles of Economics*, 1st edn 1890, 8th edn 1920, reset and reprinted 1947 (London: Macmillan).

Mill, J. (1826) *Elements of Political Economy*, 1st edn 1821, 3rd edn 1826 (London: Henry G. Bohn).

Neumann, J. von (1945) A model of general economic equilibrium, *Review of Economic Studies*, 13, pp. 1–9. (English translation of German original published in 1937.)

Pantaleoni, M. (1894) *Principii di economia pura*, 2nd edn (Firenze: Barbera).

Petty, W. (1986) *The Economic Writings of Sir William Petty*, edited by C.H. Hull (New York: Kelley). (This is a reprint – in one volume – of the original two volumes published in 1899, Cambridge: Cambridge University Press).

Quesnay, F. (1972) *Quesnay's Tableau Economique* [1759], edited by M. Kuczynski and R.L. Meek (London: Macmillan).

Ricardo, D. (1951–1973) *The Works and Correspondence of David Ricardo*, 11 volumes, edited by Piero Sraffa with the collaboration of M.H. Dobb (Cambridge: Cambridge University Press). (In the text referred to as *Works*, volume number.)

Samuelson, P.A. (1991) Leontief's 'the economy as a circular flow': an introduction, *Structural Change and Economic Dynamics*, 2, pp. 177–179.

Sraffa, P. (1951) Introduction, in: Ricardo (1951), *Works*, Vol. I, pp. xiii–lxii.

Sraffa, P. (1960) *Production of Commodities by Means of Commodities. Prelude to a Critique of Economic Theory* (Cambridge: Cambridge University Press).

Steedman, I. (2000) Income distribution, foreign trade and the value-added vector, *Economic Systems Research*, 12, pp. 221–230.

Notes

1 Papers by Leontief (and by Samuelson) whose years of publication carry an asterisk (*) are reprinted in Kurz *et al.* (1998).

2 Quesnay also mentions interest on fixed capital, but interest plays at most a secondary role in the *Tableau*.

3 The title of Sraffa's book in Samuelson's quote is not fully accurate: the correct title is *Production of Commodities by Means of Commodities*. However, for reasons that will become clear below, Sraffa for a while contemplated the possibility of adopting the title given by Samuelson.

4 Of the three scholars mentioned, in our view only von Neumann deserves to be called a 'wunderkind' of mathematical economics.

5 We have commented on this fact in several of our own contributions; see, in particular, Kurz and Salvadori (1995, chap. 13; 2000; 2004).

6 As we shall see below, Sraffa at first wrote down systems of equations in which apparently heterogeneous things were added up and equated with one another (see on this aspect Garegnani, 2004).

7 References to Sraffa's papers which are kept at Trinity College Library, Cambridge, follow the catalogue prepared by Jonathan Smith, archivist. Unless otherwise stated, all emphases are in the original, where words or passages Sraffa underlined are italicised by us. Sraffa frequently abbreviated 'and' by '+'; we shall use the word instead of the symbol. Since in his texts Sraffa used both round and square brackets, all additions by us will be bracketed by {and}. We are grateful to Jonathan Smith and the staff of Trinity College Library for continuous assistance while working on the Sraffa papers.

8 In *The Structure of American Economy*, first published in 1941, Leontief characterized the volume as an 'attempt to apply the economic theory of general equilibrium' to an empirical study of economic interrelations. Interestingly, he added that a better term than economic equilibrium would be 'general interdependence' (Leontief, 1951, p. 3). Léon Walras is mentioned only when Leontief introduced the important technical assumption of fixed coefficients underlying his empirical analysis (Leontief, 1951, pp. 37 and 201; the first page reference is not included in the index of the book). However, since apart from Walras only John Maynard Keynes, Vilfredo Pareto, Francois Quesnay and the German historicist Gustav Schmoller are mentioned, several readers appear to have implied that the reference to general equilibrium theory pointed in the direction of the analyses of Walras and Pareto. Things are not left in the open in other works of Leontief, in which a connotation with neoclassical theory is clearly spelled out; see, for example, the reference to 'neo-classical theory of general equilibrium' in Leontief (1966, p. 134).

9 The same assumption of given 'necessities of life' paid out of the capital advances at the beginning of the uniform period of production also underlies von Neumann's model (1945, p. 2). For a discussion of the latter and a comparison with the classical approach to value and distribution on the one hand and intertemporal equilibrium theory of Arrow–Debreu on the other, see Kurz and Salvadori (2004).

10 Actually V is closer to 2.107.

11 For a characterization of the Walras–Cassel point of view, see, for example, Kurz and Salvadori (1995, chapter 13, subsection 7.1).

12 For a comparison of Leontief's approach and that of Walras, and the different traditions to which the two belong, see Kurz and Salvadori (2000, pp. 173–174); see also Gilibert (1981, 1991).

13 For Leontief's closed and open models, see Kurz and Salvadori (1995, pp. 393–7)

14 See also Kurz and Salvadori (2000, pp. 173–174) and especially Steedman (2000).

3   In favour of rigour and relevance: a reply to Mark Blaug*

Heinz D. Kurz and Neri Salvadori

Mark Blaug has written another paper in which he attacks 'Sraffian economics'. He characterizes his piece as 'a new version of an earlier effort (Blaug, 1999), [that] extends and hopefully deepens the argument' (Blaug 2009, 219 n. 2).[1] A careful scrutiny of the paper shows that Blaug reiterates once again his previous criticisms, adds a few new ones, but does not enter into a serious discussion of the replies to his earlier efforts (see Garegnani 2002 and Kurz and Salvadori 2002a; 2003, chapter 2). Answering him in detail would necessitate repeating again our counter-arguments. We spare the readers this and ask them to consult our earlier replies to Blaug. Instead, we provide an overall assessment of Blaug's various attacks on 'Sraffians' and draw readers' attention to a significant change in direction in his recent one. In addition we refute a number of contentions and remarks by Blaug.

Our comment is composed as follows. We begin with a characterization of Blaug's respective efforts. Next we refute his contention that Sraffa's analysis is a species of Walrasian general equilibrium theory). The third section then shows that he is wrong in contending that 'Sraffians' have not dealt with a number of problems tackled by the classical authors. Finally we scrutinize and reject his contention that 'Sraffian economics' is not fruitful economics. We conclude with an obvious plea for rigour *and* relevance.

A general assessment of Blaug's repeated attacks

As regards Blaug's various criticisms of the 'Sraffian' view, the following observations are apposite.

1. Blaug has already been given the opportunity in *History of Political Economy* to answer his critics; see Blaug (2002). Apparently, he feels that

* We are grateful to Tony Aspromourgos, Pierangelo Garegnani, Christian Gehrke, Geoff Harcourt, Gary Mongiovi and Luigi Pasinetti for valuable comments on an earlier draft of this paper. Any remaining misconceptions are, of course, our responsibility. A shorter version of this paper was published in *History of Political Economy*; see Kurz and Salvadori (2011). The present version appeared as MPRA Paper No. 20530 on 4 February 2010.

his rejoinder was not effective. This is hardly surprising because Blaug did not attempt to counter the objections of his critics.

2. Scrutiny of his new effort reveals that the situation has not changed. Once again Blaug merely reiterates his previous criticisms, adds a few new ones, but neglects to answer his critics. He seems to feel that repeating his story often will render it credible.

3. The attentive reader will notice that Blaug has changed the direction of his critique. Originally his main concern was that of a historian of economic thought who had to watch over the faithfulness of the interpretations of earlier authors. He criticized Sraffa and his followers for having 'misunderstood' the classical economists, especially David Ricardo (see the title of Blaug 1999). Now the reader is told after several pages of criticizing 'Sraffians' that the difference between his and their interpretation of the classical economists is only 'a question of emphasis' (232). Much ado about a trifle? In our comment on his alternative conceptualization of the characteristic features of the classical theory of value and distribution in Blaug (1999) we concluded that 'Blaug in the end endorses a special version' of the Sraffian interpretation (Kurz and Salvadori 2002a, 234; 2003). He now fully confirms our judgement.

4. While his new paper shows Blaug on the retreat in the field of the history of economic thought, he is on the advance in the field of contemporary economics, broadly speaking. He puts forward a new criterion in terms of which he wishes to evaluate the existing research traditions, fields and approaches by asking, which of them arrive at 'socially and politically relevant conclusions' (219); whether 'Sraffian economics' is relevant 'to our understanding of the real world and ... to the major concerns of modern economists' (221); and whether it is relevant 'to the policy concerns of modern economists' (224). How to approach such difficult questions?

5. Blaug's key to an answer is found in the following postulate: 'There is a trade-off in economics (and elsewhere) between rigor and relevance: the more we achieve deductive certainty in our arguments, the less likely it is that we will achieve socially and politically relevant conclusions' (219). This trite contradistinction is popular with some economists (and especially with undergraduates). It is typically invoked by those who emphasize the relevance of what they are doing but do not insist on the rigour with which it is done.

6. Unless the contradistinction is taken in a practical, common-sense fashion, it is of no use at all. This is demonstrated by Blaug's subsequent disquisition (220–222). He arrives at the conclusion that 'neither rigor nor relevance seems quantifiable even in ordinal rather than the more demanding cardinal terms' (221) and that a 'quantitative incommensurability hangs over the trade-off between rigor and relevance' (222). After having debunked the scaffolding designed to give solidity to his overall construction, he concludes: 'Still, we may agree that there is a spectrum of qualitative alternatives in that trade-off that ranges from much rigor

and little relevance to little rigor and much relevance' (222). Yet what Blaug wants the reader to agree to is not this abstract and vague proposition, but rather a concrete and specific version of it: 'The trade-off between rigor and relevance is pervasive throughout economics and it is avoided only in one or two extreme examples. The point of my paper is that Sraffian economics is not one of these' (224). If there are only one or two exceptions to the rule, as Blaug contends, we may assume that he is at odds not only with 'Sraffian economics', but with economics in general, setting aside the exceptions.

7. This becomes clear in his paper. Comparing the space devoted to 'Sraffian economics' on the one hand and to other traditions or fields or approaches in economics on the other, by far the larger part of the paper deals with issues that have no direct or clear bearing on 'Sraffian economics'. Blaug passes (mostly negative) judgements on, inter alia, Social Choice Theory, General Equilibrium Theory, the Coase Theorem, Public Choice Theory, Evolutionary Economics, Institutional Economics, Game Theory, Mechanism Design Theory, Austrian Economics, Radical Economics and Marshallian Partial Equilibrium Analysis. Much of contemporary economics he considers to be as irrelevant as 'Sraffian economics' when it comes to understanding the capitalist system and elaborating policy conclusions. In the light of this, we wonder what prompted Blaug to choose the title of his piece.

8. Given Blaug's seeming disenchantment with much of modern economics, it is perplexing to see that he wishes to assess 'Sraffian economics' in terms of 'the major concerns of modern economists' (221). Has he not emphasized that these concerns are largely dubious or misleading and at least 'irrelevant'? To the extent to which they meet with his approval, because they are 'policy concerns', is it enough to observe whether an analysis leads to 'socially and politically relevant conclusions'? Should one not also, and indeed first and foremost, be concerned with the quality of such conclusions, whether they manage to realize the sought objectives, what these objectives are, whose interests they further and whose not, etc.? It is ironic to see Blaug assess alternative economic analyses in terms of a criterion that lacks any qualitative dimension, and this in the midst of a deep economic crisis in which, as *The Economist* wrote, the reputation of mainstream economics 'has taken a beating' and some of the policy recommendations of modern macroeconomics and of finance theory are seen as a source of the trouble.[2] To be relevant (in Blaug's sense) may simply mean to be wrong and harmful. What matters is not, as Blaug writes, whether an economic analysis generates 'socially and politically relevant conclusions', but rather whether these conclusions are broadly right or precisely wrong. On this problem Blaug's paper offers nothing.[3]

9. This brings us to one of Blaug's main convictions which we consider to be fundamentally mistaken. He characterizes Walrasian general

equilibrium theory (GET) as 'undoubtedly rigorous but, alas, totally irrelevant: it has no empirical content and is incapable of answering any practical question that an economist might want to pose' (222). Alas, things are quite different, at least as regards simplified versions of the theory. So-called computable general equilibrium models have been (and still are) fashionable among large parts of the economics profession and have exerted considerable influence on economic policy. For the past two decades macroeconomics has been under the spell of the rational expectations paradigm. The macroeconomic models used by many central banks, governmental research departments and international institutions involved in advising on economic policy matters are of the 'Dynamic Stochastic General Equilibrium' (DSGE) variety (see De Grauwe 2008). These models assume that agents are rational and understand the world in all its complexities. They are typically representative agent models in which the agent is taken to successfully maximize utility over an infinite time horizon.[4] How could this agent and thus the economic system as a whole ever err and get into trouble? All systemic problems and risks have been assumed away. In these models there is no room for manias, bubbles and crashes. The problem of the distribution of wealth and income is effectively put on one side, since it makes no difference whether the representative agent gets his or her income in terms of wages or profits. It is on the basis of such models that policy recommendations have been formulated and put in place in many countries and by international institutions, such as the International Monetary Fund. It is hard to imagine that the 'relevance', in Blaug's sense, of the species of GET under consideration has escaped his attention. If it hasn't, will he still cling to his conviction that generating policy advice is invariably a good thing?

10. A word should be said about the term 'Sraffian' or 'neo-Ricardian economics' Blaug uses. It was first coined by Marxist economists to distinguish Sraffa's approach to the theory of value and distribution, which explains relative prices and income distribution strictly in terms of quantities of commodities and labour, from the Marxist one, which starts from labour values (Rowthorn 1974). In some contributions the term was used in a derogatory manner contending that like marginalist (or 'neoclassical') theory it was a variant of 'vulgar' economics, dealing with 'appearances' only. Marginalist economists in turn occasionally applied the term to the analyses of those critics who, in the Cambridge controversies in the theory of capital, attacked marginalism, especially its long-period version, showing it to be logically flawed (see, for example, Kurz and Salvadori 1995, ch. 14).[5]

Sraffa saw his 1960 book as setting the classical approach to the theory of value and distribution, shedding the weaknesses of earlier formulations and building on their strengths. As he explained in a document contained in a folder dated 'End of November 1927' in his unpublished manuscripts, titled 'Principio':

> I shall begin by giving a short 'estratto' [extract] of what I believe is the essence of the classical theories of value, i.e. of those which include W. Petty, Cantillon, Physiocrats, A. Smith, Ricardo and Marx. This is not the theory of any one of them, but an extract of what I think is common to them. I state it of course, not in their own words, but in modern terminology, and it will be useful when we proceed to examine their theories to understand their portata [delivery capacity] from the point of view of our present inquiry. It will be a sort of 'frame', a machine, into which to fit their own statements in a homogeneous pattern, so as to be able to find what is common in them and what is the difference with the later theories.
>
> (D3/12/4: 12)[6]

The later theories to which Sraffa refers were different variants of demand and supply analysis, or marginalist theory. They include the general equilibrium analyses of Walras and Pareto and the partial equilibrium analysis of Marshall. As we know from Sraffa's papers, both published and unpublished, he was convinced neither by the contributions of Marshall, Walras and Pareto nor by later temporary and intertemporal equilibrium models elaborated by J. R. Hicks and others.

11. Blaug, who claims to be concerned with 'historical' reconstructions and despises 'rational' ones, puts forward a hollow exemplar of the latter when trying to support his contention that 'Sraffian economics is general equilibrium theory' (229). He writes: 'It is no accident [!] that Sraffa's book was published in the heyday of general equilibrium theory when it served everyone [!] as the model of rigorous economics' (229). If Blaug was concerned with an historical reconstruction of the case under consideration, he needs to spend some time in Trinity College Library, Cambridge (UK), as we did, in order to study Sraffa's papers and library and find out when Sraffa had arrived at which results, and why. He would then see that his above speculation as well as many other statements he put forward concerning Sraffa's contributions are without foundation; they are pure fiction. Historians of economic thought ought to be aware of the usefulness of archival work.

12. Blaug nowhere defines precisely what he means by a 'Sraffian' but uses the attribute to suit his case. For instance, on p. 229 Ian Steedman is 'a writer deeply sympathetic to the Sraffian enterprise', but on p. 234 he turns into a fully fledged 'Sraffian'. Luigi Pasinetti, one of Sraffa's major students, is said to have 'veered away from the Sraffian camp with his own approach to growth theory (Pasinetti 1981)' (234). Had Blaug read the preface of the book, he would know that Pasinetti considers his own analysis a development of Sraffa's approach.[7] A similarly problematic judgement is passed on Paolo Sylos-Labini. In order to give credibility to his (in itself

rather strange) complaint that 'Sraffians' have not contributed to certain themes or fields in economics, Blaug re-labels some authors: in case X has/has not contributed to field Y, he or she is not/is a 'Sraffian'. We are reminded of the old joke in which a pupil is orally examined by his biology teacher about elephants and answers that elephants have four feet like mice and then goes on to talk about mice.

13. Blaug repeatedly contradicts himself. A case in point is the following one. A few pages after he had stated apodictically that 'Sraffian economics … is irrelevant to our understanding of the real world' (221) he stresses that 'A book like Bowles, Edwards, and Roosevelt's Understanding Capitalism (2005) attractively [!] combines Sraffian ideas [!] on "the production and reproduction of the surplus product" and the profit rate as the driving force of capitalism' (237). How is it possible that something which is 'irrelevant to our understanding of the real world' at the same time provides the basis for 'understanding capitalism'? Blaug cannot be accused of being overly concerned with consistent arguments. Several other examples of this sort could be added.

14. For someone who insists that reconstructing the ideas of some other authors should be faithful to what these authors have written (a concern we share), Blaug is in places surprisingly careless. Three examples must suffice. In the context of a discussion of the problem of the gravitation of market prices to their 'natural' or normal levels, he contends that while Kurz and Salvadori point out 'that little is known about the dynamic behaviour of even simple linear production models; nevertheless, they express the hope that the problem will be "settled in the foreseeable future" (Kurz and Salvadori 1998[a], 20)' (229 n. 20). The reader who checks the source mentioned will not find this statement. Has Blaug got the page wrong? No, in the entire book the reader won't find the statement quoted. Has Blaug perhaps confounded some of our books? Yes, he has, but things are worse still. The only passage we are aware of having written that can be related to Blaug's criticism is contained in a book published in 1995. After having pointed out the extreme complexity of the issue at hand ('gravitation') and the dependence of the results obtained on the specific conditions assumed, we conclude: 'It should then be clear that there is no fear that the issue of gravitation will be settled in the foreseeable future' (Kurz and Salvadori 1995, 20).[8] Hence we say exactly the opposite of what Blaug contends we are saying. This is not only annoying but also raises doubts about the seriousness of the entire enterprise. What is the relevance of a critique that lacks the elementary rigour of not misrepresenting (let alone reversing) the view of the people criticized? Misconstruction is an error surely worse even than historically unfaithful reconstruction?

Another case of misrepresenting our view is to be found in footnote 22. There Blaug asserts that 'my definition [of rational reconstruction] is identical to Lakatos's' (231 n. 22). This he considers enough to criticize the analysis we provided in order to clarify Lakatos's concept of 'rational reconstruction' and how we use this concept (Kurz and Salvadori 2002a, section 2). With no evidence to support his accusation he contends that 'the difficulty is that Kurz and Salvadori do not believe [!] that they are reconstructing anything: they are merely expressing what the classical economists themselves would have said if they had known about simultaneous equations' (231 n. 22). A look at section 2 in our 2002 reply to Blaug shows that Blaug's criticism is unwarranted. As Keynes wrote in his debate with Hayek, we wonder whether Blaug has

> read [our] book[s] with that measure of 'good will' which [authors are] entitled to expect of a reader. Until he can do so, he will not see what [we] mean or know whether [we] are right. He evidently has a passion which leads him to pick on [us], but we are left wondering what that passion is.
>
> (Keynes, *CW*, Vol. XIII, 243)

Finally, the following case of misrepresentation of Marshall (1890) and Sraffa (1925, 1926) may be mentioned. Blaug asserts: 'Marshall thought that increasing returns to scale external to firms but internal to industries ... would be compatible with a perfectly competitive market structure' (235). Interestingly, Blaug uses almost the same wording as Sraffa, who, in section 3 of the 1925 paper, reconstructed rigorously Marshall's theory of the decreasing cost (i.e. increasing returns) industry and then explained, in section 5, that, in order to be rigorous, Marshall's presentation of increasing returns industries requires an extra assumption, *not* found in Marshall. 'It is necessary', Sraffa insisted, 'that the advantages of increased production in the industry considered should not have repercussions in any way on the other industries.' To this he added the condition that must be met in order for this to be true: 'The economies of large scale production must be "external" from the point of view of the individual firms, but "internal" from the point of view of the industry' (Sraffa 1925, English translation, 362). Sraffa then refers the reader to Marshall's *Industry and Trade* (1919, 188) where it is maintained that this situation is extremely rare in reality, which implies that the ability of Marshall's theory to explain reality is very limited. Blaug, on the contrary, presents a Marshall who in the *Principles* had allegedly already been conscious of the problem Sraffa raised and who, like Samuelson (1971) much later, had drawn the attention to a case in which partial equilibrium analysis arrives rigorously at the same result as general equilibrium analysis!

Sraffa's analysis – a 'species of Walrasian GET'?

In his 1999 paper Blaug (1999, 229) contended that the Sraffian interpretation of the classical economists 'reads Smith and Ricardo and Marx through

Walrasian-tinted glasses.' Now he writes 'that Sraffian economics is quite simply a species of Walrasian GET' (226–227). We have already argued in the previous section (see observation 10) above that this view cannot be sustained. Here we draw attention to some serious misunderstandings on Blaug's part.

The first concerns the necessary ingredients of a theory. According to Blaug,

> A telltale sign of Sraffa's indebtedness to Walrasian GET is his careful separation of endogenous and exogenous variables, or variables that are explained within the theory and variables that are taken as given and explained, if at all, outside the theory.
>
> (230)

Does Blaug think that the separation of endogenous and exogenous variables is not required in general and that it is a peculiar feature of only a subset of theories? Would Blaug draw attention to *any* theory, economic or other, that does not distinguish between variables that are explained or determined by the theory and variables that are taken as given? In his paper Blaug expresses anew how fond he is of Marshall's partial equilibrium analysis (241). As we asked in Kurz and Salvadori (2003, 16 n. 7): Does he wish to claim that Marshall's analysis does not have this separation? Marshall's partial equilibrium approach to a single market is no different in regard to this issue: there are two endogenous variables, the market price of the commodity under consideration and the quantity traded, and there are two types of exogenous variables, the parameters of the demand function and those of the supply function. We cannot believe that it is really necessary to explain such elementary things to our critic. Since *any* theory is based on a separation between endogenous and exogenous variables, and since Blaug does not provide any other criterion to distinguish between theories, applying his logic means that *all* theories could be said to be 'indebted' to or to be 'quite simply a species of Walrasian GET' – clearly an absurd statement.

Blaug also mistakes the *form* of an argument for its *substance* (see also Kurz and Salvadori 2002a, 226). He thinks that any economic theory that is formulated in terms of simultaneous equations (or inequalities) is *ipso facto* a version, or 'species', of Walrasian theory. This is a misconception. The mathematical form of an argument is one thing, the content of the argument another. The determinants of the general rate of interest (or profits) contemplated by Walras and Ricardo (and by modern reformulations of their theories), for example, are very different. Most importantly, whereas in Ricardo the competitive rate of return is seen to depend on real wages (or the share of wages), which in the context of ascertaining this rate and relative prices for a given system of production are taken to be an independent magnitude, in Walras it depends on the given endowment of the economy of productive factors, including capital goods.[9] What matters when distinguishing between theories is *which* endogenous variables are explained or determined by means of *which* exogenous variables, and precisely *how* this is done. Blaug has overlooked the important part of the problem, the *content* of a theory, because of an ill-conceived preoccupation with the mere *mathematical form* in which it is presented.

Having said this, the following should be pointed out. Walras (but not modern Walrasian GET; see Kurz and Salvadori 2004) was concerned with explaining the competitive (uniform) rate of profits and thus with a long-period problem. Since *any* long-period theory has to satisfy Sraffa's price equations, it is no surprise that some version of Sraffa's equations may be found in Walras's analysis (Walras 1954). This is the case in the part of the *Elements* devoted to what Walras called 'capitalization'.[10] For the full story, see Kurz and Salvadori (2002b; see also Kurz and Salvadori 1995, 23–25 and 439–441). Clearly, Walras's principal criticism of Ricardo (a criticism already put forward by William Stanley Jevons and rightly refuted by Knut Wicksell) cannot be sustained: Ricardo did *not* commit the elementary error of trying to determine two unknowns with a single equation. There is no underdeterminacy in Ricardo's analysis of value and distribution. As regards Sraffa's equations, these investigate the relationships that must hold between prices and the distributive variables, given the system of production in use. The equations themselves do not yet constitute an explanation of income distribution. Something more is needed, as, for example, in Ricardo a theory of how the real wage rate (or rather the share of wages) is determined, or in Sraffa the proposition that the rate of profits can be considered as 'susceptible of being determined from outside the system of production, in particular by the level of the money rates of interest' (Sraffa 1960, 33).

Themes in classical economics allegedly not dealt with by 'Sraffians'

As we noted in the first section above (observation 3), Blaug now plays down differences in interpreting the classical economists between him and the 'Sraffians' as 'a question of emphasis' (232). This is fair enough, and we, at least, can easily live with it. However, some of his related statements cannot pass without comment. In this section we rebut Blaug's contention that 'Sraffians' have not dealt with a number of problems the classical economists were concerned with. In the following section we rebut his contention that 'Sraffians' have nothing to say on important contemporary problems. Blaug prides himself with having a comprehensive knowledge of the 'Sraffian' literature. However, as will be seen his knowledge is incomplete and many of his charges are unfounded.

Before we turn briefly to the evidence that contradicts Blaug's contentions, the following remark is apposite. His accusation that 'Sraffians', including us, do not deal with every problem the classical authors have been concerned with is peculiar. First, we never claimed that this was our intention. Second, Blaug omits to tell the reader why it should have been our intention. Third, it is not an especially fruitful task, because several problems have already been solved or were of only short-lived historical interest.[11] We took up what we consider to be fruitful ideas and concepts possessed of a great explanatory potential.[12]

'Sraffians', including us, have dealt with many more aspects of classical (and non-classical) economics than Blaug seems to be aware of. Several of our publications and works we edited have escaped his attention, and those of our writings to which he refers he apparently has not read with sufficient care, because otherwise he could not make some of his allegations.[13] A few examples must suffice.[14] In footnotes we add some randomly chosen references to the writings of other 'Sraffians' that contradict Blaug's respective claims. Many more could of course be given, but space constraints prevent us from doing it.

Blaug contends that many important issues in classical economics are not addressed by 'Sraffians'. These include the following.

(a) *Foreign trade* (225). Not true: see Kurz (1992) on Adam Smith's 'vent-for-surplus' argument on foreign trade. 'Sraffian historians of economic thought' are said to 'hardly [!] mention Ricardo's doctrine of comparative advantage' (232). Not true: see Kurz and Salvadori (1995, 152 and the literature referred to there) and Kurz and Salvadori (1998b, entries on 'Autarky versus trade', 'Comparative advantage', 'Foreign trade', 'Specialization and trade' and 'Vent for surplus').[15]

(b) *Malthusian law of population* (225). Not true: see Kurz and Salvadori (1998b, entry on 'Malthus, Thomas Robert'; 2002a; 2003, chapter 2; 2006; 2007, chapter 2). In another place Blaug opines: 'But the most astonishing lacuna in the Sraffian characterization of classical economics is the downplaying of the importance of the Malthusian theory of population' (231). No one could sensibly dispute that the law of population plays a role in Ricardo's writings: the fact is obvious. Much less obvious is precisely *what* importance Ricardo attached to it, when and why. Blaug just states the simple fact mentioned. This is not good enough. First, there are several statements in Ricardo (some of which we have cited in Kurz and Salvadori 2002a, 234) that squarely contradict the law, and that are typically ignored by some interpreters, including Blaug. They show clearly that Ricardo was not the ardent advocate of the law that Blaug portrays him to be. Second, in discussions with Malthus on the theory of value and distribution it was convenient for Ricardo to accept the law, because it provided him with a firm basis to stand on in terms of a fixed real wage rate. The rate of profits could then be determined residually. Third, the analytical structure of Ricardo's surplus-based approach to the problem of value and distribution is entirely independent of the law: The rate of profits is determined residually irrespective of whether wages are at some subsistence level or above it. We made these points in our 2002 reply to Blaug's earlier criticism. He neither answered them in his rejoinder (Blaug 2002) nor in his most recent paper. This is a genuine 'astonishing lacuna'.

(c) *Falling rate of profit.* 'Sraffian economists maintain a steadfast silence on the problem [of the cause of the declining rate of profit] and deliberately so. ... [T]hey fail in any way, however, to demonstrate that the rate of profit will decline with the continuous accumulation of capital' (226). And later in his paper he accuses us of being 'even more unfair [!] to Marx [than to Ricardo] in saying nothing [!] about the technological causes of the falling rate of profit ..., which was the lynchpin of Marx's pessimistic predictions about the fate of capitalism' (231). Not true: see Kurz (1978, 1998), Salvadori (1981), Kurz and Salvadori (1995, 248, 402 and 474; 1998b, entries on 'Accumulation of capital', 'Falling rate of profits', 'Marx, Karl', 'Marx, Karl, as an interpreter of the Classical economists', 'Mathematical formulations of Marxian economics', 'Profits'; 2006) and Gehrke and Kurz (2006, 119 *et seq.*).[16]

Blaug presents Ricardo as a technological pessimist, who believed in the overwhelming importance of the Malthusian law in combination with diminishing returns in agriculture and who saw the stationary state as just around the corner. He insists that 'the contention that [Ricardo] was centrally concerned, nay obsessed, with the threat posed by the rising marginal cost of growing wheat to feed workers is a point of total agreement among historians of economic thought' (225). This interpretation does not do justice to Ricardo. As early as in *The Essay on Profits* of 1815 he expressed the view that there are no signs pointing in the direction of a deceleration of capital accumulation in the foreseeable future: 'we are yet at a great distance from the end of our resources, and ... we may contemplate an increase of prosperity and wealth, far exceeding that of any country which has preceded us' (Ricardo, *Works* IV, 34). This view is confirmed in a letter to Hutches Trower of 5 February 1816, in which he concluded from the fall in grain prices since 1812 that 'we are happily yet in the progressive state, and may look forward with confidence to a long course of prosperity' (Ricardo, *Works* VII, 17). And in his entry on the 'Funding System' for volume IV of the *Supplements to the Encyclopædia Britannica*, published in September 1820, he stressed that 'the richest country in Europe is yet far distant from that degree of improvement', that is, the stationary state, and that 'it is difficult to say where the limit is at which you would cease to accumulate wealth and to derive profit from its employment' (Ricardo, *Works* IV, 179).

(d) *Economic growth.* 'Sraffian economics has nothing whatever to say about [economic growth in Adam Smith]' (226). Not true: see, in particular, Kurz (1997), Kurz and Salvadori (2003, chs 6 and 7; 2008); see also Salvadori (2003). We are said to 'utterly [!] bypass the central message of [Ricardo's *Principles*] about the depressing effect of diminishing returns in agriculture on the general rate of economic growth' (231). Not true: see Kurz (1978, 1997, 1998), Kurz and Salvadori (1992; 1998b, entries on 'Growth'; 2006) and the discussion under item (c).[17]

(e) *Division of labour*. Blaug insists that we 'totally [!] ignore the opening three chapters of *The Wealth of Nations* on the division of labor' (231). Not true: see Kurz and Salvadori (1995, 17–18; 1998b, 'Accumulation of capital', 'Division of labour', 'Smith, Adam'; 2003, chs 6 and 7).

(f) *Say's Law of Markets*. 'Sraffians' are said to 'hardly [!] mention Ricardo's vigorous defense of Say's Law of Markets' (232). Not true: see Gehrke and Kurz (2001) and Kurz and Salvadori (1998b, entries on 'Effective demand', 'Limiting and regulating principles', 'Say, Jean-Baptiste', 'Say's law', 'Supply and demand').

This should suffice to dispel Blaug's contention that 'Sraffians' did not deal with these problems.

'Sraffian economics' – fruitful or not?

Blaug contends that 'Sraffian economics' is barren and irrelevant 'to our understanding of the real world and ... to the major concerns of modern economists' (221), and that it has nothing to say on economic policy matters. However, since he also believes that from a classical perspective useful things can be said about the real world and since he now overall endorses Sraffa's interpretation of the classical economists, it would indeed be surprising could he consistently entertain this dismissive stance throughout his paper. As we have seen, he cannot and in fact contradicts himself (see observation 13 in the first section). However, he nevertheless tries to convey the impression that 'Sraffians' have nothing to say on the economic problems of today. To do this, he has to ignore large parts of the existing literature. A look into such easily accessible journals as (in alphabetical order) the *Cambridge Journal of Economics*, *Contributions to Political Economy*, *Metroeconomica* or the *Review of Political Economy*, not to speak of numerous monographs and articles published in books, would have exposed him to a great many works dealing inter alia with applied and policy oriented work, including such topics as effective demand and economic growth, taxation, the pension system, fiscal retrenchment, monetary policy, the economics of disarmament, employment policy, health care, environmental policy, the economics of waste management, the situation of Indian agriculture, etc. Blaug who on various occasions has prided himself with being particularly well read would not even have had to muster the energy to collect easily available information himself. He could have simply consulted Tony Aspromourgos's survey article (Aspromourgos 2004), which provides more than two hundred references to the literature and contains a detailed and highly informative account of the Sraffa-inspired extant economic literature at the beginning of the new millennium, on which problems and by whom.[18] And he might have had a look at the April 2007 issue of the *Review of Political Economy*, which contains a symposium on precisely this question of the practical implications of Sraffa's resumption of the classical approach. What are we to make of Blaug's sweeping statements that ignore the relevant literature?

Concluding remarks

None of Blaug's criticisms stands up to close examination. He attributes views to us (and to other authors) we (they) never advocated. He contends that 'Sraffian' authors have not written about certain problems, while referring to writings which show precisely the opposite. He commits a number of elementary blunders and mistakes the mathematical form of an argument for its content. He variously contradicts himself in the paper. He puts forward bold statements that are contradicted by the facts.

Interestingly, he no longer maintains that there are fundamental differences between the 'Sraffian' interpretation of the classical economists and his own interpretation; the differences, he surmises, are only 'a question of emphasis'. A careful investigation of Blaug (1958) shows how much the young Blaug was indebted to Sraffa's interpretation of Ricardo. It seems that the mature Blaug has come close to where he once started from.

As regards Blaug's contradistinction of rigour and relevance, it is obvious that an economic analysis that rightly wishes to gain respect should seek to be *both* rigorous *and* relevant. The classical approach to economics, we are convinced, is on the right track.

References

Aspromourgos, Tony. 2004. Sraffian Research Programmes and Unorthodox Economics. *Review of Political Economy* 16.2: 179–206.

Blaug, Mark. 1958. *Ricardian Economics: An Historical Study*. New Haven, CT: Yale University Press.

Blaug, Mark. 1999. Misunderstanding Classical Economics: The Sraffian Interpretation of the Surplus Approach. *HOPE* 31.2:213–236.

Blaug, Mark. 2002. Kurz and Salvadori on the Sraffian Interpretation of the Surplus Approach. *HOPE* 34.1:237–240.

Blaug, Mark. 2009. The Trade-Off between Rigor and Relevance: Sraffian Economics as a Case in Point. *HOPE* 41.2:219–247.

Bowles, Samuel, Richard Edwards and Frank Roosevelt. 2005. *Understanding Capitalism*. New York: Oxford University Press.

Caminati, Mauro and Fabio Petri, eds. 1990. *Convergence to Long-Period Positions*. Special issue of *Political Economy. Studies in the Surplus Approach*, 6.

De Grauwe, Paul. 2008. DSGE-Modelling: When Agents are Imperfectly Informed. ECB Working Paper No. 897. Available at SSRN: http://ssrn.com/abstract=1120763

Garegnani, Pierangelo. 1987. Surplus Approach to Value and Distribution. In J. Eatwell, M. Milgate and P. Newman (eds), *The New Palgrave Dictionary of Political Economy*. London: Macmillan, vol. 4, 560–574.

Garegnani, Pierangelo. 2002. Misunderstanding Classical Economics? A Reply to Blaug. *HOPE* 34.1:241–254.

Gehrke, Christian and Heinz D. Kurz. 2001. Say and Ricardo on Value and Distribution. *European Journal of the History of Economic Thought* 8.4.

Gehrke, Christian and Heinz D. Kurz. 2006. Sraffa on von Bortkiewicz: Reconstructing the Classical Theory of Value and Distribution. *HOPE* 38.1:91–149.

Keynes, John Maynard. 1973 ssq. *The Collected Writings of John Maynard Keynes*. 32 vols, managing eds A. Robinson and D. Moggridge, London: Macmillan. In the text referred to as *CW*, volume number and page number.

Kurz, Heinz D. 1978. Rent Theory in a Multisectoral Model. *Oxford Economic Papers* 30:16–37.

Kurz, Heinz D. 1992. Adam Smith on Foreign Trade: A Note on his 'Vent-for-Surplus' Argument. *Economica* 59:475–81.

Kurz, Heinz D. 1997. What Could the 'New' Growth Theory Teach Smith or Ricardo?. *Economic Issues* 2.2:1–20. Reprinted in Kurz and Salvadori (2003).

Kurz, Heinz D. 1998. Marx on Technological Change: The Ricardian Heritage. In R. Bellofiore (ed.), *Marxian Economics. A Reappraisal*, vol. 2. Houndmills, Basingstoke and London: Macmillan, 119–138.

Kurz, Heinz D. and Neri Salvadori. 1992. Morishima on Ricardo: A Review Article. *Cambridge Journal of Economics* 16:227–247.

Kurz, Heinz D. and Neri Salvadori. 1995. *Theory of Production. A Long-period Analysis*. Cambridge: Cambridge University Press.

Kurz, Heinz D. and Neri Salvadori. 1998a. *Understanding 'Classical' Economics. Studies in Long-Period Theory*. London and New York: Routledge.

Kurz, Heinz D. and Neri Salvadori, eds. 1998b. *The Elgar Companion to Classical Economics*. Two vols. Aldershot (UK): Edward Elgar.

Kurz, Heinz D. and Neri Salvadori. 2002a. Mark Blaug on the 'Sraffian Interpretation of the Surplus Approach'. *HOPE* 34.1:225–236.

Kurz, Heinz D. and Neri Salvadori. 2002b. One Theory or Two? Walras's Critique of Ricardo. *HOPE* 34.2:365–398.

Kurz, Heinz D. and Neri Salvadori. 2003. *Classical Economics and Modern Theory. Studies in Long-Period Analysis*. London and New York: Routledge.

Kurz, Heinz D. and Neri Salvadori. 2004. Von Neumann, the Classical Economists and Arrow-Debreu: Some Notes. *Acta Oeconomica* 54.1:39–62.

Kurz, Heinz D. and Neri Salvadori. 2006. Endogenous Growth in a Stylised 'Classical' Model. In G. Stathakis and G. Vaggi (eds), *Economic Development and Social Change. Historical Roots and Modern Perspectives*. London and New York: Routledge, 106–124.

Kurz, Heinz D. and Neri Salvadori. 2007. *Interpreting Classical Economics. Studies in Long-Period Analysis*. London and New York: Routledge.

Kurz, Heinz D. and Neri Salvadori. 2008. New Growth Theory and Development Economics. In Amitava Krishna Dutt and Jaime Ros (eds), *International Handbook of Development Economics*. Cheltenham (UK): Edward Elgar, 207–222.

Kurz, Heinz D. and Neri Salvadori. 2011. In Favor of Rigor and Relevance: A Reply to Mark Blaug. *HOPE* 43.3: 607–616.

Marshall, Alfred. 1890. *Principles of Economics*. 8th edn 1920. Reprint, reset. London: Macmillan, 1977.

Marshall, Alfred. 1919. *Industry and Trade. A Study of Industrial Technique and Business Organization*. London: Macmillan & Co.

Pasinetti, Luigi L. 1981. *Structural Change and Economic Growth. A Theoretical Essay on the Dynamics of the Wealth of Nations*. Cambridge: Cambridge University Press.

Pasinetti, Luigi L. 2007. *Keynes and the Cambridge Keynesians: A 'Revolution in Economics' to be Accomplished.* Cambridge: Cambridge University Press.

Ricardo, David. 1951 ssq. *The Works and Correspondence of David Ricardo.* 11 volumes. Edited by Piero Sraffa with the collaboration of Maurice H. Dobb. Cambridge: Cambridge University Press. In the text referred to as *Works*, volume number and page number.

Rowthorn, Robert. 1974. Neo-Classicism, Neo-Ricardianism and Marxism. *New Left Review* I.8:63–87.

Salvadori, Neri. 1981. Falling Rate of Profit with a Constant Real Wage: An Example. *Cambridge Journal of Economics* 5:59–66.

Salvadori, Neri, ed. 2003. *The Theory of Economic Growth: A 'Classical' Perspective.* Cheltenham (UK): Edward Elgar.

Samuelson, Paul A. 1971. An Exact Hume-Ricardo-Marshall Model of International Trade. *Journal of International Economics* 1:1–18. Reprinted in R. C. Merton (ed.), *The Collected Scientific Papers of Paul A. Samuelson*, vol. 3, 1972, Cambridge, MA: The MIT Press, 356–373.

Schefold, Bertram. 1976. Different Forms of Technical Progress. *Economic Journal* 86:806–819.

Sraffa, Piero. 1925. Sulle relazioni fra costo e quantità prodotta. *Annali di Economia* 2:277–328. English translation by John Eatwell and Alessandro Roncaglia in Luigi L. Pasinetti (ed.), *Italian Economic Papers*. Bologna: Il Mulino and Oxford: Oxford University Press, 1998, 323–363 and in Heinz D. Kurz and Neri Salvadori (eds), *The Legacy of Piero Sraffa*. Cheltenham (UK): Edward Elgar, 2003, vol. 1, 3–43.

Sraffa, Piero. 1926. The Laws of Returns under Competitive Conditions. *Economic Journal* 36:535–550.

Sraffa, Piero. 1960. *Production of Commodities by Means of Commodities.* Cambridge: Cambridge University Press.

Steedman, Ian. 1977. *Marx after Sraffa.* London: New Left Books.

Walras, Léon. 1954. *Elements of Pure Economics.* London: George Allen & Unwin. English translation by W. Jaffé of the definitive edition of Léon Walras, *Eléments d'économie politique pure*, 1874. Lausanne: Corbaz. 5th and definitive edn Paris: F. Richon, 1924.

Notes

1 In the following all isolated page numbers refer to Blaug (2009).

2 See the cover story of the 18 July 2009 issue of *The Economist* entitled 'Modern Economic Theory. Where it went wrong – and how the crisis is changing it', p. 11.

3 As 'Sraffians' have not been involved in shaping the policies that led to the current worldwide economic problems, there is little fear that Blaug will put the blame on them.

4 So-called 'New-Keynesian' versions of the DSGE model adopt the same basic framework, but add price and wage stickiness to it.

5 We note that according to Blaug 'Sraffians scored a great victory in the Cambridge capital theory controversies' (237).

6 References to Sraffa's hitherto unpublished manuscripts and correspondence follow the catalogue prepared by Jonathan Smith, archivist of the Wren Library, Trinity College, Cambridge (UK).

7 Luigi Pasinetti kindly sent us a letter in which he insisted:

> Blaug is of course wrong in asserting that I veered away from Sraffa. I always considered my multi-sector analysis (cum vertically integrated sectors) a development of Sraffa's approach (as now is much more clearly argued in my latest CUP book – *Keynes and the Cambridge Keynesians* [Pasinetti 2007] –, which Blaug should be advised to read before pronouncing any negative judgement on my relations with Sraffa). Blaug is also wrong in asserting that no empirical research followed.

For explicit statements of how Pasinetti sees the relationship between his own analysis and Sraffa's, see Pasinetti (2007, 278 and 302–304).

There is a substantial literature on empirical work on vertically integrated sectors and, for example, on the high tech content of various commodities and the international competitiveness of industries.

8 To avoid a possible misunderstanding, the observation that rates of profit never seem to deviate 'too much' from one another has prompted us to start from the 'stylized fact' of a uniform rate of profits in much of our work (Kurz and Salvadori 1995, 21). For a discussion of the problem at hand and arguments in favour of gravitation, see Caminati and Petri (1990) and especially Garegnani's contribution therein.

9 For a detailed discussion of Walras's misunderstanding and criticism of Ricardo, see Kurz and Salvadori (2002b).

10 Walras's failure to elaborate a coherent long-period analysis in his treatment of 'capitalization' was a main motive of Erik Lindahl, J. R. Hicks and Friedrich August von Hayek to abandon the long-period method in favour of intertemporal and temporary equilibrium analyses, which, in turn, paved the way towards modern GET. For a summary account of the relevant literature on this development, see Kurz and Salvadori (1995, ch. 14).

11 Blaug calls Kurz and Salvadori (1998a) 'the most detailed Sraffian history of classical economics to date' (230). This is a surprising description, because the volume contains just a selection of previously published papers of ours. It is not, and was never meant to be, a comprehensive history of classical economics. Blaug's generous description appears to have a single purpose: it allows him, or so he thinks, to point out that several important themes are absent from the volume. Given the nature of the book this should not come as a surprise. Blaug criticizes books for what they do not contain and authors for what they have not written. Shouldn't the object of criticism be what books actually contain and what authors actually have written? Had Blaug been interested in a fairly comprehensive account of classical economics in which all the problems mentioned by him are dealt with, he might have referred to the two volumes of *The Elgar Companion to Classical Economics* we edited (Kurz and Salvadori 1998b). While in his 1999 paper he referred extensively to the *Companion*, in his 2009 paper he does not even mention it.

12 We note incidentally that there is something strange in Blaug's attitude towards our work. On the one hand he is keen to convey the impression that our work on the classical authors is misleading, on the other hand he deplores the fact that we have not written more on them.

13 Selections of our essays are collected in three easily accessible volumes; see Kurz and Salvadori (1998a, 2003, 2007).

14 We refer to publications and a work edited by us that are in English and easily accessible.

15 Ricardo's approach to trade theory has been investigated in a number of papers by Sergio Parrinello, Stanley Metcalfe and Ian Steedman, and Ian Steedman alone; see the references in Aspromourgos (2004).

16 See also Schefold (1976), Steedman (1977) and Garegnani (1987).
17 Blaug seems to have also overlooked the large and swiftly growing literature that combines a classical perspective on production, value and distribution with Keynes's principle of effective demand within a growth context, and which shows that effective demand matters not only in the short, but also in the long run. To this literature contributed Pierangelo Garegnani, Amit Bhaduri and Steven Marglin, and Amitava K. Dutt, to mention but a few scholars.
18 In the meantime many more contributions have been published. In preparation of this reply we have sent letters to many people whom Blaug would in all probability dub 'Sraffians' of sorts. They kindly sent us detailed information especially about papers and books published during the past few years that deal with applied and policy related problems. We should like to express our gratitude to them. Due to space constraints we cannot provide the details of their valuable responses to our letter.

Part II
On Sraffa's contribution

4   Spurious 'margins' versus the genuine article[*]

Heinz D. Kurz and Neri Salvadori

Introduction

In the Preface to his book, Piero Sraffa expressed a warning concerning the use of the concept of 'margin' in economic theory. He wrote:

> Caution is necessary ... to avoid mistaking spurious 'margins' for the genuine article. Instances will be met in these pages which at first sight may seem indistinguishable from examples of marginal production; but the sure sign of their spuriousness is the absence of the requisite kind of change. The most familiar case is that of the product of the 'marginal land' in agriculture, when lands of different qualities are cultivated side by side: on this, one need only refer to P. H. Wicksteed, the purist of marginal theory, who condemns such a use of the term 'marginal' as a source of 'dire confusion'.
>
> (Sraffa, 1960, pp. v–vi; the reference is to Wicksteed, 1914)

As the debate after the publication of Sraffa's book showed, this warning was appropriate, but unfortunately has not always been respected. The result is that the debate would have provided Wicksteed with additional cases to chastise because the term 'marginal' is used in a way that is anew the source of 'dire confusion'.

In this chapter we deal with one such case. For reasons that become clear in the sequel, the starting point of our reasoning is chapter 21, 'The marginal equalities', of Christian Bidard's book *Prices, Reproduction, Scarcity* (Bidard, 2004). Indeed, the present chapter is essentially a comment on it. We proceed in the following way. We begin with a discussion of a famous numerical example provided by Garegnani (1970). Bidard has criticized the example as not dealing with heterogeneous capital at all. In our view this criticism is unfounded. In order to show this the salient features of

[*] Reproduced with permission from A. Birolo, D. Foley and H. D. Kurz (eds), *Production, Distribution and Trade: Alternative Perspectives: Essays in Honour of Sergio Parrinello*, London: Routledge, 2010.

Garegnani's example are emphasized by means of counterposing it with another example taken from Kurz and Salvadori (1995) (the second section). In the third section we turn to a brief critical account of a contribution by Sato (1974), who argued that reswitching is unimportant because it can be ruled out by assumptions that in Sato's judgement are 'weak' in some sense. It is then argued that Bidard in chapter 21 of his book based his argument as to the absence of reswitching on what he calls 'differentiability hypothesis'. While he does not clearly define the concept, it appears to be clear that his reasoning is similar to Sato's (the fourth section). Next we deal with a proposition by Bidard concerning the concept of the 'marginal productivity of capital'. We stress in particular that the finding of an equality between the rate of profits and the marginal productivity of capital, appropriately defined, implies nothing whatsoever as regards the determination of the level of the rate of profits. 'Marginal equalities' must not be mistaken for substantive explanations of economic phenomena, that is, they must not be taken for the 'genuine article', as Sraffa said (the fifth section). The final section concludes.

Before we enter into our argument, the following remark is apposite. The problem of discriminating between spurious margins and the genuine article was present throughout the years of existence of the Trieste Summer School, organized by Sergio Parrinello in cooperation with Pierangelo Garegnani and Jan Kregel. The school was of great importance to many of those who participated in it. It provided a stimulating environment and led to fruitful discussions and it brought people together. As a matter of fact, the two authors of this chapter met for the first time in the summer of 1981 on the occasion of the annual summer school. It was shortly afterwards that we began our collaboration, which has continued up until today. Sergio Parrinello in his capacity as main organizer of the meetings served not only as the medium that brought us together, he and other friends were also involved in many of the discussions we had over the years. If our approach to and understanding of economic problems happen to have improved over time, then this is partly due to the exchanges we had with him and his support for what we were doing. Parrinello's contribution to our intellectual development could hardly be called 'marginal'.

In defence of Garegnani (1970)

In section 5 of Chapter 21 Bidard (2004, pp. 244–8) investigates a famous example by Garegnani (1970) and criticizes it on the basis of what he calls a 'WS analysis', where W stands for Walras or Wicksell and S for Sraffa (see Bidard, p. 240). Alas, Bidard's analysis is difficult to sustain. This can be clarified with reference to some problems posed in Kurz and Salvadori (1995, pp. 160–2). These problems, couched in the form of exercises, were constructed in order to alert the reader of our book to the kind of difficulties that concern us here.

For the reader's convenience the Appendix of this chapter reprints the three related exercises. Here is a summary account of their rationale. The first exercise presents Garegnani's numerical example. The second gives an example which might at first sight appear to be similar to it, but which is actually totally different. In fact, in the former exercise there is an infinite number of commodities, one of which is a consumption good and all the others are capital goods. However, in the latter there are just two commodities: a consumption good and a capital good. In the former exercise for each capital good there is only one process to produce that capital good (by labour and itself) and only one process to produce the consumption good by using that capital good (and labour). Since there is an infinite number of capital goods this means that there is also an infinite number of processes to produce the consumption good (each by means of a different capital good) and an infinite number of processes producing capital goods, one for each of them. In the latter exercise there is an infinite number of processes to produce the consumption good using the same capital good and an infinite number of processes producing that capital good by labour and itself. Further, the two examples are built in such a way that the technology appears to be the same, but with a different meaning of the symbols used. The difference consists in the fact that in the former example there is only one index, whereas in the latter there are two indexes. This is so because in the former example a process producing the consumption good by means of a specific capital good can be operated if and only if the unique process producing that capital good by the capital good itself and labour is also operated, whereas in the latter example a process producing the consumption good can be operated if and only if any process producing the unique capital good by itself and labour is also operated. The third exercise consists just in asking the reader to compare the two previous exercises and thus to develop the argument summarized here, stressing the fact that whereas in the second exercise there is a single capital good, in the first there are many capital goods, indeed an infinite number of them. Therefore 'capital' is heterogeneous in the first exercise and homogeneous in the second.

It appears to have escaped Bidard's attention that the examples of the two exercises contain valid descriptions of possible technologies (which, however, are not identical). Instead he thinks that only the second one (i.e. the one using two indexes) contains such a description. This becomes clear when he writes:[1]

> Garegnani is not a faithful Sraffian: in his numerical example, the methods used in both industries depend on one parameter only ($u = v$ by *definition*), therefore the choices of methods are not independent and there is no basis for the wage-maximization property. Nor is he a faithful Walrasian, for the same reason: the differentiability hypothesis presumes a sufficient number of degrees of freedom on the isoquant, not only a 'derivative'; this is why an apparent reswitching is found in his calculations.
>
> (Bidard, 2004, p. 247)

As against this it has to be stressed that Garegnani uses a single index in his calculations, because he deliberately and explicitly chose to rest his argument on an assumption regarding technology that allows for an infinite number of capital goods. As a consequence, the reswitching he found is not at all 'apparent'. The title of Garegnani's essay 'Heterogeneous Capital, ...' already draws the attention to a fact which Bidard appears to have overlooked. In his version of Garegnani's example 'capital' is *not* heterogeneous. This is all the more surprising because Garegnani left no doubt that his example started *explicitly* from the kind of technology introduced by Samuelson (1962), who had analysed an 'economy' in which for each method to produce the 'single consumption good *A*' there is 'a capital good $C^{(\alpha)}$ specific to the method', as the following quotation shows:

> The economy Samuelson assumes in his article is one where production takes place in yearly cycles and where a *single* consumption good *A* exists, obtainable by a number of alternative 'systems of production', α, β, γ, etc. Each 'system', e.g., consists of two 'methods of production': a method for the direct production of A by means of fixed quantities $l_a^{(\alpha)}$ of labour, and $C_a^{(\alpha}$ of a capital good $C^{(\alpha)}$ *specific to the method*; and the method for producing $C^{(\alpha)}$ by $l_c^{(\alpha)}$ of labour and $C_c^{(\alpha}$ of itself.
>
> (Garegnani, 1970, p. 408, emphasis added)[2]

The idea of introducing two indexes in order to eliminate reswitching is not new: it was used already by Sato (1974) a few years after the publication of Garegnani's essay in a paper mentioned in the References of Bidard's book.[3] It is perhaps useful to scrutinize in some detail Sato's approach to the problem under consideration and then assess Bidard's argument against this background.

Why Sato's assumptions cannot be considered as weak

Sato (1974) introduced a 'Technology Frontier' (TF), which is the set of all efficient techniques available in a given state of technical knowledge. The TF represents a functional relationship among the production coefficients. Sato argued that reswitching can occur only if there are not many techniques available from which cost-minimizing producers can choose and that 'when techniques are available more abundantly than assumed in the usual discussion of this phenomenon, we are not likely to observe the strict coming back of any particular technique' (Sato, 1974, p. 365). From this Sato concluded that with a sufficiently large number of technical alternatives we may ignore the phenomenon of reswitching.

Throughout his analysis Sato assumed explicitly that the TF is continuous and twice differentiable. He contended that this assumption 'is made only for mathematical convenience' (Sato, 1974, p. 364) and thus does not in the least prejudice the results obtained. Yet this is not the case. As Salvadori (1979) has shown, because of this assumption Sato's results amount to a restatement of results already known at the time when he published his paper concerning technological assumptions which suffice to rule out reswitching. Sato's claim that if there are sufficiently many technical alternatives, then we can ignore reswitching, is just an unproven contention. As a matter of fact, it would not even suffice to have an infinite number of technical alternatives: these must rather be arranged in a very special way in order to obtain continuous differentiability and strict convexity. Let us briefly clarify the issue at hand.[4]

Sato assumed a state of technical knowledge analogous to the one studied by Samuelson (1962) and Garegnani (1970): for every technique T, there is one capital good (which can be different for different techniques) and a consumption good (which is the same for all techniques), so that each technique T is defined by its input matrix:

$$T = \begin{bmatrix} \alpha & \beta \\ a & b \end{bmatrix}$$

where α (capital) and β (labour) are the unit production coefficients of the consumption good and a (capital) and b (labour) are the unit production coefficients of the capital good. He then normalized the physical magnitude of capital by putting $b = 1$. This allowed him to define a technique by the vector $T = (a, \beta, \alpha)$ so that the whole technology can be represented by the function

$$\alpha = \psi(a, \beta).$$

This function Sato called the 'Technology Frontier' (TF). The description of technology through a 'Technology Frontier' is in itself not restrictive. In particular, if the domain of TF is finite or countable, it represents the usual case of a finite or countable set of techniques (once dominated techniques have been eliminated); if it is a curve on the plane (a, β), it represents the case of the continuous set of techniques as studied, for example, by Garegnani (1970); if it is a portion of the plane (a, β), it represents the case studied by Sato, which requires two indexes instead of just one. What is restrictive is the assumption entertained by Sato (1974, pp. 362–4) that

> $\psi(a, \beta)$ is everywhere continuously differentiable with respect to both a and β and strictly convex.[5]

In fact, if this is so, for each $\bar{a}$ – which means for each process to produce a capital good, since b has been normalized and equals 1 – the function $\alpha = \psi(\bar{a}, \beta)$ can be interpreted as the unit isoquant of a production function, which, because of the assumptions employed by Sato, is also convex and continuously differentiable. As a consequence, it is possible to apply the proof used by Burmeister and Dobell (1970, p. 273) to demonstrate that reswitching cannot occur. This is not what Sato does, since he arrives at his non-reswitching theorem directly, without recognizing that the assumptions he had adopted 'only for mathematical convenience' had effectively transformed the problem in a different and already known one in which reswitching was successfully ruled out.

Consider the wage frontier as the envelope of partial wage frontiers, each of which is defined by a given $\bar{a}$ and an infinite number of processes defined by the unit isoquant $\alpha = \psi(\bar{a}, \beta)$. If the technique $\bar{T} = (\bar{a}, \bar{\beta}, \bar{\alpha})$ pays the largest wage rate at a given rate of profits r^* among all techniques such that $a = \bar{a}$, then

$$\frac{w_{\bar{T}}(r^*)}{p_{\bar{T}}(r^*)} = -(1+r^*)\frac{\partial \psi}{\partial \beta}\bigg|_{a=\bar{a},\beta=\bar{\beta}}$$

where $w_{\bar{T}}(r)/p_{\bar{T}}(r)$ is the wage rate in terms of the price of the capital good for technique $\bar{T} = (\bar{a}, \bar{\beta}, \bar{\alpha})$. If the same technique is on the same partial wage frontier at $r = r^{**} \neq r^*$, then it is also true that

$$\frac{w_{\bar{T}}(r^{**})}{p_{\bar{T}}(r^{**})} = -(1+r^*)\frac{\partial \psi}{\partial \beta}\bigg|_{a=\bar{a},\beta=\bar{\beta}}$$

which is impossible since $w_{\bar{T}}(r)/p_{\bar{T}}(r)$ is a decreasing function of r and $\partial\psi/\partial\beta$ for $a = \bar{a}$, and $\beta = \bar{\beta}$ is a negative constant (with respect to r). Hence on the wage frontier we can have a reswitching of a partial wage frontier, but not the reswitching of a technique.

It is immediately checked that if the function $\psi(a, \beta)$ is convex, but not strictly convex, then the same technique can contribute to a partial wage frontier over a whole range, and, as a consequence, reswitching of partial wage frontiers allows for a reswitching of techniques. Therefore it is by no means sufficient to assume that 'techniques are available more abundantly than assumed in the usual discussion of this phenomenon'![6]

We are now in a position to scrutinize Bidard's view against the background of Sato's argument and in full recognition of the latter's deficiencies.

Bidard's view and his 'differentiability hypothesis'

In his book Bidard stresses variously that it is important for an author to be as clear and rigorous as possible in order to avoid ambiguity of expression, which is a source of misunderstanding and misinterpreting. Happily, in his book he mostly succeeds in following this laudable (and highly demanding!)

principle. But there are exceptions to this. Chapter 21 carries several state-ments that are rather vague; in particular, Bidard nowhere defines in a clear-cut way what exactly he means by the 'differentiability hypothesis' which plays an important role in the chapter. We tried hard to understand his reasoning and have arrived at the following conclusion: His contention that reswitching is excluded when the differentiability hypothesis holds amounts essentially to a restatement of Sato's argument. In case our interpretation happens to hold true, and we found nothing in Bidard's book that contradicts it, then his contention suffers from the same shortcoming as Sato's: if only one of the assumptions of strict convexity and continuous differentiability is not met, then the contention cannot be sustained.

Let us have a closer look at Bidard's reasoning. He writes:

> The reswitching phenomenon ... has been at the centre of the Cambridge debates, because it clearly undermines the logical foundations of the neoclassical aggregate production function. It may occur in the presence of finitely many methods or a continuum of methods. Why not under the *differentiability hypothesis* (note that differentiability requires a high enough dimension of the space of methods, in order to allow a mar-ginal change of one input without changing the other inputs)? A simple economic argument is: given a technique within the family of available techniques, the marginal productivity of labour is well defined by local comparisons. So is the associated wage ... The use of the same technique at two levels of the rate of profit would imply that the wage would be the same, which contradicts the w–r trade-off.
>
> (Bidard, 2004, p. 240; emphasis added)

This formulation directs us to Bidard's differentiability hypothesis. Alas, no definition of it is provided in chapter 21 (or, as far as we can tell, in the rest of the book). Yet there is reason to think that what he intended with the hypothesis is this. For each commodity i any input vector $(l_i, a_{i1}, a_{i2}, \ldots, a_{in})$ satisfying a smooth and convex isoquant

$$1 = F^i(l_i, a_{i1}, a_{i2}, \ldots, a_{in}) \tag{1}$$

is technically feasible and the smoothness and convexity properties imply that there is an infinite number of such vectors.

In terms of this assumption it is immediately shown that the technique (necessarily unique) which can pay the largest wage rate for a given rate of profits r^*, $(\mathbf{A}^*, \mathbf{l}^*)$, whatever is the numeraire, is also the technique which sat-isfies the condition

$$wdl_i + (1+r^*)\sum_{k}^{n} da_{ik} p_k = 0 \tag{2}$$

where dl_i, da_{i1}, da_{i2}, ... , da_{in} are any scalars such that

$$\left.\frac{\partial F^i}{\partial l_i}\right|_{A=A^*,l=l^*} dl_i + \sum_k^n \left.\frac{\partial F^i}{\partial a_{ik}}\right|_{A=A^*,l=l^*} da_{ik} = 0 \tag{3}$$

and $(p_1, p_2, \cdots, p_n)^T = \mathbf{p} = w[I-(1+r^*)A^*]^{-1}\mathbf{1}^*$. As a consequence

$$(1+r^*)\left.\frac{\partial F^i}{\partial l_i}\right|_{A=A^*,\, l=l^*} = \left.\frac{\partial F^i}{\partial a_{i1}}\right|_{A=A^*,\, l=l^*}\frac{w}{p_1}$$

$$= \left.\frac{\partial F^i}{\partial a_{i2}}\right|_{A=A^*,\, l=l^*}\frac{w}{p_2} = \dots = \left.\frac{\partial F^i}{\partial a_{in}}\right|_{A=A^*,\, l=l^*}\frac{w}{p_n} \tag{4}$$

In order to obtain equation (2) we start from equation

$$\frac{p_i}{w} = (1+r^*)\sum_k^n a_{ik}\frac{p_k}{w} + l_i \tag{5}$$

and obtain

$$d\frac{p_i}{w} = (1+r^*)\sum_k^n a_{ik}d\frac{p_k}{w} + (1+r^*)\sum_k^n da_{ik}\frac{p_k}{w} + dl_i$$

and since (A^*, l^*) is the technique which can pay the largest wage rate at the rate of profits r^* whatever is the numeraire, $d(p_i/w) = d(p_k/w) = 0$. Hence equation (2) is obtained. Equations (4) can also be written as

$$\left.\frac{\dfrac{\partial F^i}{\partial l_i}}{\dfrac{\partial F^i}{\partial a_{ih}}}\right|_{A=A^*,\, l=l^*} = \frac{w}{(1+r^*)p_h}\ \forall h \tag{6a}$$

$$\left.\frac{\dfrac{\partial F^i}{\partial a_{ih}}}{\dfrac{\partial F^i}{\partial a_{ik}}}\right|_{A=A^*,\, l=l^*} = \frac{p_h}{p_k}\ \forall h,k \tag{6b}$$

which can be interpreted as the usual relationship which in equilibrium must hold between the slope of the isoquant and the relative prices of the inputs.

Since function $F^i(l_i, a_{i1}, a_{i2}, \ldots, a_{in})$ in (1) is homogeneous of degree one, we have

$$1 = \frac{\partial F^i}{\partial l_i} l_i + \sum_k^n \frac{\partial F^i}{\partial a_{ik}} a_{ik}$$

which, because of equations (6a), becomes

$$\frac{w}{\left. \dfrac{\partial F^i}{\partial l_i} \right|_{A=A^*, l=l^*}} = w l_i^* + (1+r^*) \sum_k^n a_{ik}^* p_k$$

and because of (5)

$$\left. \frac{\partial F^i}{\partial l_i} \right|_{A=A^*, \, l=l^*} = \frac{w}{p_i} \tag{7}$$

Finally, from (6a) for $h = i$ and (7) we obtain

$$\left. \frac{\partial F^i}{\partial a_{ii}} \right|_{A=A^*, \, l=l^*} = 1 + r^* \tag{8}$$

and from (8) and (6b) for $k = i$ we obtain

$$\left. \frac{\partial F^i}{\partial a_{ih}} \right|_{A=A^*, \, l=l^*} = \frac{(1+r^*) p_h}{p_i} \forall h$$

which can be interpreted as the equilibrium condition stating the equality between the marginal productivity of an input and the price of that input in terms of the output.

These are well known facts which, to the best of our knowledge, no 'Sraffian', 'Post-Sraffian' or 'Neo-Sraffian' has ever contested (or should contest), and in fact Bidard provides no evidence to the contrary. Bidard does not claim that his differentiability hypothesis is new; it has, in fact, been exhaustively explored and used by Burmeister and Dobell in chapter 9 of their book (Burmeister and Dobell, 1970, especially p. 273).[7] We have argued in the above that Sato's Non-reswitching theorem amounts to a theorem by Burmeister and Dobell. The same applies to Bidard's Non-reswitching theorem.

The above procedure exposes a number of properties of the cost-minimiz-ing techniques in the case in which the special assumption holds which Bidard (supposedly) wishes to express with his differentiability hypothesis. It can also be used to determine the cost-minimizing techniques for a *given* rate of profit in the same conditions. In this context it has to be stressed that these equilibrium properties or equalities provide no support whatsoever to the received marginalist attempt to *explain* the rate of profits in terms of the 'marginal productivity' or 'relative scarcity' of a factor called 'capital'.[8] We shall come back to this fact in the following section.

Now, in chapter 21 Bidard is not on the look-out for an explanation of the rate of profit. His observation concerning the circumstances in which reswitching can be ruled out is not accompanied by any doubts as to the possibility of a rising 'demand for labour curve', which contradicts conventional theory. In fact, in section 3 of the chapter Bidard shows by means of a neat numerical example that a rising demand for labour schedule can obtain; he also stresses that an example is all that is needed in order to rebut the conventional view that the demand for labour is inversely related to the real wage rate. Of course, more could be said in this regard. Mas-Colell (1989), for example, showed that given any set of pairs of consumption levels per capita and levels of the rate of profits satisfying a simple restriction Mas-Colell calls 'Golden Rule Restriction', a 'well-behaved' technology with two capital goods can be found having precisely this set as 'the steady-state comparative static locus', that is as the relationship between consumption per unit of labour and the rate of profits.

Since we agree with what is stated in section 3 of chapter 21 we turn immediately to section 4, which is devoted to the concept of the marginal productivity of capital.

The marginal productivity of capital

Section 4 of Chapter 21 concludes with the statement of a Theorem:

> *Theorem 2.* When adequately measured, the marginal productivity of capital is equal to the rate of interest.
>
> (p. 243)

The meaning of the statement is not clear and may give rise to misunderstandings and thus confusion. Substantially it says that we can define the concept of 'marginal productivity of capital' in such a way that it equals the rate of profits. This is not a new finding. Indeed, what Bidard proves in the section is well known. The problem is that it may be read as meaning something totally different. Therefore, as we learned already, 'caution is necessary … to avoid mistaking spurious "margins" for the genuine article'. In the case under consideration we are indeed facing the case of a spurious margin.

The readers will remember that the so-called Cambridge debate about the marginal productivity of capital started in 1956 with a paper by Joan Robinson, that is, four years before the publication of Sraffa's book (Robinson, 1956).

The argument developed by Joan Robinson, while obviously and admittedly inspired by Sraffa, was not based on Sraffa's own construction, but on something else. The description of the technology advocated by Joan Robinson was in terms of what she called 'productive curve' and 'pseudo-production function'.[9] A productive curve is a sort of production function but presupposes a *given* rate of profits. This allows one to measure capital in terms of the product where for each technique the relative prices specific to that technique are used. (For a recent formalization of the argument, see Salvadori, 1996.) Once this is done, the cost-minimizing techniques at the given rate of profits turn out to be those (possibly only one) which satisfy the condition that the derivative of the productive curve with respect to capital is equal to the given rate of profits. Of course, for each level of the rate of profits we can carry out the same exercise and arrive at a 'family of productive curves', which can be represented by the function

$$y = F(k,r) \tag{9}$$

while the cost-minimizing techniques are characterized by the condition

$$\frac{\partial F(k,r)}{\partial k} = r \tag{10}$$

and the relationship between k and y implicitly defined by equations (9) and (10) is what Joan Robinson called 'pseudo-production function'.

Therefore, the controversy is not about whether the marginal rule plays, or does not play, a role, but rather whether the derivative of the pseudo-production function is, or is not, equal to r. In fact, what Bidard calls 'marginal productivity of capital' is the derivative of income with respect to capital when not only the rate of profit, but also the prices are taken as *given* and are equal to those of the cost-minimizing technique at the given rate of profit. What Bidard has proved is well known and to the best of our knowledge has never been disputed.

The so-called pseudo-production function, that is, the locus of k and y for which there is an r satisfying both equations (9) and (10), is in fact not a function as also Joan Robinson recognized: it is a correspondence. However, if (k^*,y^*) is a point of this locus, and if at this point $\partial^2 F/\partial k \partial r \neq 1$, then a segment of this locus including point (k^*,y^*) can be represented as a differentiable function. Moreover

$$\frac{dy}{dk} = r + \frac{\partial F}{\partial r} \frac{\dfrac{\partial^2 F}{\partial k^2}}{1 - \dfrac{\partial^2 F}{\partial k \partial k}}$$

Obviously $dy/dk = r$ if either

$$\frac{\partial F}{\partial r} = 0 \tag{11}$$

or

$$\frac{\partial^2 F}{\partial k^2} = 0 \tag{12}$$

(or both). It is possible to prove (see Salvadori, 1996) that equation (11) holds in the following cases: (i) the capital and the product consist of the same commodity; (ii) the derivative of the function of the value of capital in terms of r for the technique used in that point equals zero in that point, even if not in general; (iii) the rate of profits equals the growth rate. Equation (12) holds (iv) when two techniques are cost-minimizing at that r. These four cases are well known to those that have studied the reswitching debate. Case (i) has been investigated by Samuelson (1962), Bhaduri (1969) and mainly Garegnani (1970). Case (ii) is Ng's counter example (see Harcourt, 1972, pp. 149–50). Case (iii) is related to the 'golden rule of accumulation': Bhaduri (1966) maintained that it was proved by von Weizsäcker (with no reference); Harcourt (1972, p. 149) referred to Pearce (1962), Koopmans (1965), Bhaduri (1966), Harcourt (1970) and Nell (1970) and maintained that the formulation presented by himself is due to Laing (with no reference). Case (iii) has also been investigated by Garegnani (1984). Case (iv) has been investigated by Solow (1967, 1970), whose interpretation of the result under consideration has been criticized by Pasinetti (1969, 1970).

The debate between Solow and Pasinetti just mentioned is also relevant in the present context. At the time Robert Solow thought to be able to escape the criticism levelled at the marginalist theory of capital and distribution by adopting Irving Fisher's concept of 'rate of return' and by replacing the stock concept of capital by the flow concept of investment. However, as Luigi Pasinetti succeeded in demonstrating, Solow was mistaken: the concept showed no way out of the impasse in which marginalist long-period theory found itself. In his paper 'Switches of technique and the "rate of return" in capital theory', published in 1969, Pasinetti stated the fact of the equality of the marginal product of capital, measured in value terms at given prices, and the rate of profits, but added that this must not be misunderstood as providing any support whatsoever for the marginalist theory. A finding such as the one presented in equation (10) or, in Solow's case, the use of 'rate of return' as a synonym for 'rate of profits' apparently contribute nothing to an explanation of the rate of profits. Pasinetti added:

> The idea which had been basic to marginal capital theory was another and deeper one. The idea was that, even at the simplest stage of a

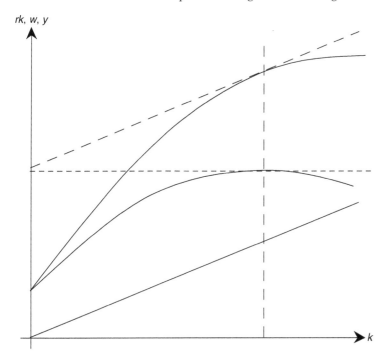

Figure 4.1 rk, w and y as functions of k for given r, g, and the consumption basket

stationary economic system, there exists something – to be called the 'rate of return' – *which can be defined autonomously and independently of the rate of profit*; something which is higher or lower according to whether the existing 'quantity of capital' is lower or higher, and as such represents a general technical property of the existing 'quantity of capital'. Such a thing would justify and *explain* the rate of profit. It is this idea which has been shown to be an illusion; for, in general, such a thing does not exist.

> (Pasinetti, 1969, p. 529; second emphasis in the original)

We conclude this section by making use of a diagram for illustrative purposes. In Figure 4.1 we put rk, w and y as functions of k. Since $y = w + rk$, the value of k where w assumes its maximum level coincides with the value of k where $y = w + rk$ has the slope r. How are these curves built? Consider a given growth rate g, a given consumption basket $\mathbf{c}$ and a given rate of profits r^*, then for each technique α we can determine the wage rate w_α and the capital per head k_α. We insert into the w-k plane all these points, and the frontier of the convex hull of all these points is the w function plotted in the diagram. Since $r = r^*$ is given, the other two curves are immediately obtained. The fact that

$$\frac{\partial y}{\partial k} = r$$

is equivalent to

$$\frac{\partial w}{\partial k} = 0$$

is an obvious fact, but it does not add anything to the determination of r, which in this construction is, and has to be, given from the outside.

Concluding remarks

The chapter scrutinizes some of the propositions contained in chapter 21, 'The marginal equalities', of Bidard (2004, pp. 237–52). In it Bidard maintains that 'the debates about marginal equalities and capital theory have an ideological emphasis which, on the whole, has been detrimental to the post-Sraffian stream of thought' (ibid., pp. 237–8). He exemplifies his contention as follows:

> A typical unfortunate argument is: 'A comparison between the Euler identity $Q = F(K, L) = F'_K K + F'_L L$ and the accounting equality $Q = rK +wL$ shows the logical equivalence between the two relations $F'_K = r$ and $F'_L = w$. Since the theory of capital proves that the first equality is wrong, the real wage rate is not equal to the marginal productivity of labour.' We stress, on the contrary, that under a differentiability hypothesis, the Sraffa models imply the equality between the wage and the marginal productivity of labour. Though we do not claim that this is Sraffa's own position, we consider that it would be inconsistent to study the model and not to mention one of its necessary consequences (Bellino 1993 is an exception).
>
> (ibid., p. 238)

This passage and Bidard's subsequent argument elicit the following remarks. First, unfortunately Bidard does not tell the reader who, if anyone, has put forward the statement in quotation marks. (We are not aware of anyone who has expressed such an opinion.) Second, there is reason to assume that Bidard has misinterpreted Garegnani's famous numerical example (Garegnani, 1970). The example was explicitly designed to discuss the case with heterogeneous capital goods. We conclude that Bidard's criticism of Garegnani is unwarranted. Third, Bidard refers to a differentiability hypothesis (ibid., pp. 238 and 240) but does not define it. However, the hypothesis is designed to clarify an important theoretical problem. As Bidard stresses:

> note that differentiablity requires a high enough dimension of the space of methods, in order to allow a marginal change of one input without changing the other inputs.
>
> (ibid., p. 240)

This remark is added in parenthesis to the contention that by means of the differentiability hypothesis the reswitching of techniques can effectively be ruled out (ibid., p. 240).

It is our contention that Bidard's argument is very similar to an argument put forward by Sato in 1974. Sato contended that 'when techniques are available more abundantly than assumed in the usual discussion of this phenomenon, we are not likely to observe the strict coming back of any particular technique' (Sato, 1974, p. 365). We think that it is safe to assume that Bidard's notion of 'a high enough dimension of the space of methods' is designed to express essentially the same thing.

Does this mean that in order to rule our reswitching that the 'Technology Frontier', to use Sato's term, has to be strictly convex, or continuously differentiable, or both? Sato apparently thought that he could do without the assumption that the Technology Frontier is continuous and twice differentiable. In fact he insisted that this assumption 'is made only for mathematical convenience' (ibid., p. 364). However, his contention cannot be sustained. The unobtrusive assumption does the job, a result well-known at the time, since it had been established as early as 1970 in a widely read textbook on economic growth by Burmeister and Dobell (1970, p. 273). Sato's argument and *a fortiori* Bidard's suffer from the same shortcoming: reswitching is effectively ruled out only by the twin assumptions of strict convexity and continuous differentiablity. If one of them is not met, then the no-reswitching contention falls to the ground.

Whether economic theory is well advised to rest its case entirely on the twin assumptions of strict convexity and continuous differentiablity is, of course, another matter. Bidard does not appear to think that it should. At any rate, an economic theory based on these two assumptions can hardly be called general. We are also not aware of empirical evidence according to which economists are well advised to adopt the two assumptions. It follows that reswitching cannot be ruled out in general. However, if one adopts the two assumptions for whichever purpose, then certain implications follow, whether these are mentioned or not. Why 'it would be inconsistent to study the model and not to mention one of its necessary consequences', as Bidard stresses, is not clear to us.

The real issue is whether the fact that there are 'marginal equalities' provides any support for the marginalist explanation of the real wage rate or the rate of profits. This is definitely not so, and Bidard in some passages makes it very clear that it is not. The fact that the rate of profits equals the marginal productivity of capital, *appropriately defined*, should not come as a surprise. It should especially not be mistaken to mean that the rate of profits *is determined* by the marginal productivity of capital. If the latter is ascertained in terms of a given and known rate of profits, the marginal equality under consideration cannot be taken to involve a causal relation leading from the marginal productivity to the rate of profits. (The contrary direction would be more correct.) As Pasinetti had pointed out a long time ago, the idea underlying marginal productivity theory, that one could 'justify and *explain* the rate of profit' in terms of the marginal productivity of 'capital' 'has been shown to be an illusion; for, in general, such a thing does not exist' (Pasinetti, 1969, p. 569, emphasis in the original).

Beware of spurious 'margins'!

Appendix

8.23. (Calculus) (Garegnani, 1970) Let $U = \{u \in \Re \mid 0 \leq u \leq 1.505\}$ be a set of indices. Let us assume that for each $u \in U$ there is a commodity, called *u*-commodity, which can be utilized either to produce itself or to produce a further commodity called corn. Corn is the only commodity required for consumption. Finally, for each u there exist the processes defined by Table 4.1, where $x = 27e^{-2u}$, $y = \sqrt[10]{u^{11}}$, and e is the base of natural logarithms.

Explore this technology and show that

(i)   this economy can be analysed within the framework of Subsection 3.3, but it cannot be analysed within the frameworks of Subsections 3.2 and 3.4;
(ii) as r rises from 0 to 0.13 the *u*-commodity which is utilized to produce corn will vary continuously from the 0-commodity to the 1.505-commodity;
(iii) as r rises from 0.13 to the maximum admissible level in the economy, 0.2, the *u*-commodity which is utilized to produce corn will vary continuously from the 1.505-commodity to the 0-commodity;
(iv) there is no switch point in the sense that for no level of the rate of profits two distinct techniques are cost-minimizing.

[Hint: for each u the *w-r* relationship is

$$w = \frac{1-(5+y)r}{(5+y)+[x-(5+y)^2]r};$$

the envelope is found by setting the derivative with respect to u equal to zero; in doing this it is convenient to recall that $x' = -2x$ and $y' = (11y/10u)$, where x' and y' are the derivatives of x and y with respect to u.]

8.24. (Calculus) There exist two commodities, corn and iron. Only corn is required for consumption. Let $U = \{u \in \Re \mid 0 \leq u \leq 1.505\}$ and $Z = \{z \in \Re \mid 0 \leq z \leq 2\}$ be two sets of indices. Let us assume that for each $u \in U$ there is a process producing corn and for each $z \in Z$ there is a process producing iron defined in Table 4.2 where $x = 27e^{-2u}$, $y = \sqrt[10]{u^{11}}$.

Explore this technology and show that

(i)   this economy can be analysed within the framework of Subsections 3.3 and 3.4, but it cannot be analysed within the framework of Subsection 3.2;

Table 4.1 The input–output coefficients of Exercise 8.23

	material inputs				outputs	
	corn	u-commodity	labour		corn	u-commodity
(u)	0	$\dfrac{x}{6+y}$	$5+y-\dfrac{x}{6+y}$	$\rightarrow$ 1		0
(2u)	0	$\dfrac{5+y}{6+y}$	$\dfrac{1}{6+y}$	$\rightarrow$ 0		1

Table 4.2 The input–output coefficients of Exercise 8.24

	material inputs				outputs	
	corn	iron	labour		corn	iron
(u)	0	$\dfrac{x}{6+y}$	$5+y-\dfrac{x}{6+y}$	$\rightarrow$ 1		0
(z)	0	$\dfrac{5+z}{6+z}$	$\dfrac{1}{6+z}$	$\rightarrow$ 0		1

(ii) whatever value r takes in the interval [0, 0.2], where $r = 0.2$ is the maximum admissible r, iron is produced with the process corresponding to $z = 0$;

(iii) there is r^*, $0.15 < r^* < 0.16$, such that as r rises from 0 to r^* the process operated to produce corn will vary continuously from that corresponding to $u = 0$ to that corresponding to $u = 1.505$;

(iv) whatever value r takes in the interval $[r^*, 0.2]$, corn is produced with the process corresponding to $u = 1.505$;

(v) there is no switch point, in the sense that for no rate of profits are two distinct techniques cost-minimizing.

[Hint: since iron is the unique basic in all techniques prove point (ii) by taking iron as the numeraire. The wage frontier is then

$$w = 1 - 5r.$$

Prove that the cost-minimizing technique is that which minimizes the price of corn in terms of iron. Show that the relation between u and r for $0 \le r \le r^*$ is the locus

$$r = \frac{11y(6+y)^2}{55y(6+y)^2 + 6(120u + 20uy + 11y)x},$$

which is increasing in the relevant range and such that when $u = 1.505$, $r = r^*$.]

8.25. Compare the results of exercises 8.23 and 8.24.

Acknowledgements

An earlier version of this chapter was given on the occasion of a round table entitled 'Prices, Reproduction, Scarcity' held on 11th March 2005 at the Università Cattolica del Sacro Cuore, Milan. We are grateful to the participants of the round table and especially Enrico Bellino, Christian Bidard and Sergio Parrinello for valuable comments on the earlier version.

References

Bhaduri, A. (1966). The Concept of the Marginal Productivity of Capital and the Wicksell Effect, *Oxford Economic Papers*, 18: 284–8.

Bhaduri, A. (1969). On the Significance of Recent Controversies on Capital Theory: A Marxian View, *Economic Journal*, 79: 532–9.

Bidard, Ch. (2004). *Prices, Reproduction, Scarcity*, Cambridge: Cambridge University Press.

Burmeister, E. and Dobell, A. R. (1970). *Mathematical Theories of Economic Growth*, London: Macmillan.

Garegnani, P. (1970). Heterogeneous Capital, the Production Function and the Theory of Distribution, *Review of Economic Studies*, 37: 407–36.

Garegnani, P. (1984). On Some Illusory Instances of 'Marginal Products', *Metroeconomica*, 37: 143–60.

Harcourt, G. C. (1970). G. C. Harcourt's Reply to Nell, *Journal of Economic Literature*, 8(1): 44–5.

Harcourt, G. C. (1972). *Some Cambridge Controversies in the Theory of Capital*, Cambridge: Cambridge University Press.

Koopmans, T. C. (1965). On the Concept of Optimal Economic Growth, in *Pontificiae Academiae Scientiarum, Scripta varia*, Amsterdam: North-Holland: 225–87.

Kurz, H. D. and Salvadori, N. (1995). *Theory of Production*, Cambridge: Cambridge University Press.

Mas-Colell, A. (1989). Capital Theory Paradoxes: Anything Goes, in G. R. Feiwel (ed.), *Joan Robinson and Modern Economic Theory*, London: Macmillan: 505–20.

Nell, E. J. (1970). A Note on Cambridge Controversies in Capital Theory, *Journal of Economic Literature*, 7: 41–4.

Pasinetti, L. L. (1969). Switches of Techniques and the 'Rate of Return' in Capital Theory, *Economic Journal*, 79: 508–31.

Pasinetti, L. L. (1970). Again on Capital Theory and Solow's 'Rate of Return', *Economic Journal*, 80: 428–31.

Pearce, I. F. (1962). The End of the Golden Age in Solovia: A Further Fable for Growthmen Hoping to be 'One Up' on Oiko, *American Economic Review*, 52: 1088–97.

Robinson, J. V. (1956). *The Accumulation of Capital*, London: Macmillan.

Salvadori, N. (1979). The Technological Frontier in Capital Theory: A Comment, *Economic Notes*, 8(1): 117–24.

Salvadori, N. (1996). 'Productivity curves' in *The Accumulation of Capital*, in M. C. Marcuzzo, L. L. Pasinetti and A. Roncaglia (eds), *The Economics of Joan Robinson*, London and New York: Routledge: 232–48.

Samuelson, P. A. (1962). Parable and Realism in Capital Theory: The Surrogate Production Function, *Review of Economic Studies*, 29: 193–206.

Sato, R. (1974). The Neo-Classical Postulate and the Technological Frontier in Capital Theory, *Quarterly Journal of Economics*, 88: 353–84.

Sraffa, P. (1960). *Production of Commodities by Means of Commodities. Prelude to a Critique of Economic Theory*, Cambridge: Cambridge University Press.

Solow, R. (1967). The Interest Rate and Transition between Techniques, in C. H. Feinstein (ed.), *Socialism, Capitalism and Economic Growth, Essays presented to Maurice Dobb*, Cambridge: Cambridge University Press: 30–9.

Solow, R. (1970). On the Rate of Return: Reply to Pasinetti, *Economic Journal*, 80: 423–8.

Wicksteed, P. H. (1914). The Scope and Method of Political Economy, *Economic Journal*, 24: 1–23. Presidential Address to Section F of British Association, Birmingham, 1913.

Notes

1 Instead of index z as in the appendix below he uses index v, where $z = \sqrt[10]{v^{11}}$.

2 In his article Garegnani sometimes refers to a single technique of this example as a 'two commodity system', which in itself is not wrong because in a single technique only two commodities are involved. It would be unfortunate if an inaccurate reading were to prompt the reader to interpret the example as if there were just two commodities not in a single technique only (or what Garegnani calls a 'system'), but in the technical alternative available to the economy as a whole.

3 We were unable to locate any reference to Sato's paper in Bidard (2004); at any rate neither Sato's name nor his concept of 'Technology Frontier' are to be found in the book's author or subject index.

4 For a more detailed discussion, see Salvadori (1979).

5 Sato (1974, pp. 362–3) shows that if the function is concave somewhere only the convex parts are relevant, and this seems to justify at least partially his assumptions, but what he needs in order to avoid reswitching is not just convexity, but *strict convexity*, and not differentiability almost everywhere, but *differentiability everywhere*.

6 It goes without saying that Sato's above formulation is surprisingly unrigorous.

7 The book is, however, not contained in the References of Bidard (2004).

8 It has also been argued that such an assumption is dangerous because it prompts one to think that two techniques that are close to one another as regards small variations in the rate of profits are also similar with respect to the kinds and quantities of capital goods they employ. Yet there is no reason for this supposition.

9 Initially she called this curve 'real-capital-ratio curve', but then she changed to the other name which she borrowed from Solow.

5 Piero Sraffa: economic reality, the economist and economic theory*

An interpretation

Neri Salvadori and Rodolfo Signorino

Introduction

As is well known, Piero Sraffa never published extensive discussions of episte-
mological or methodological issues. Yet, in recent years, partly as a response
to growing interest in economic methodology, several scholars have tried to
outline rational reconstructions of some aspects of Sraffa's logic of scientific
research in economics. To mention just a few: Lunghini (1975), Roncaglia
(1978) and Marion (2005) have deeply analysed the relationship between
Sraffa and Wittgenstein; Davis (1988, 1993, 1998, 2002) has highlighted the
Gramscian roots of Sraffa's critique of methodological individualism both
in Marshallian economics and in Wittgenstein's logical atomism (see also
Signorino 2001a for an analysis of Sraffa's unpublished manuscripts at this
regard); Mongiovi (1996) has investigated the relationship between the 1925
and 1926 papers and the 1960 book against the background of the classical
method of logical separation of the analysis of output from that of price;
Salvadori (2000) has reconstructed Sraffa's strategy of research on the role of
demand; Salanti and Signorino (2001) have traced some elements of continuity and some of discontinuity in Sraffa's overall contribution to economics
from a methodological point of view; Kurz and Salvadori (2004, 2005) have
analysed the role of objectivism in Sraffa's thought.

In this chapter we concentrate on a specific and hitherto neglected aspect
of Sraffa's implicit methodology: the threefold relationship between 'economic reality', 'the economist' and 'economic theory'. By 'economic reality'
we mean the collection of human agents and material objects which constitute the human process of production and reproduction of commodities. By
'the economist' we mean the human agent who observes, classifies and analyses economic reality. By 'economic theory' we mean the main intellectual
product emerging from the economist's effort to analyse the economic reality
under investigation.

Our main results may be summarized as follows. In his published works
of the 1920s and early 1930s Sraffa appears to consider economic reality *as*

* Reproduced with permission from *Journal of Economic Methodology*, 14(2) 2007. www.
tandfonline.com

if it existed independently of the activity of observation and classification carried out by economists. Furthermore, he makes several empirical claims about economic reality *as if* they were self-evident or, at least, easily verifiable. Whereas Sraffa acknowledges that an element of human arbitrariness is unavoidable within economic theorizing, he also stresses that different *quæsita* may require different 'points of view' in the sense that, given a specific theoretical problem, one specific 'point of view' may prove to be best suited to analyse and solve the problem at hand. This implies the necessity of the choice of the 'point of view' by an economist. This choice is relevant in so far as this choice determines the portion of economic reality which can be consistently described by the theory elaborated by the economist in question. From this perspective, Sraffa appears to be an advocate of a method of analysis which some philosophers of science call 'piecemeal theorising' (Salanti and Signorino 2001 and Signorino 2005). With respect to *Production of Commodities by Means of Commodities* (*PC* hereafter) our investigation shows that there is a methodological continuity in Sraffa's work, running from his early papers on the Marshallian theory of value through to his 1960 book. Such a methodological continuity may be obscured by the fact that in *PC* Sraffa's 'style of argumentation' is radically different from that adopted in his previous contributions. As is well known, in *PC* Sraffa's remarks on the structural properties of economic reality are sparse, indirect and extremely general. Notwithstanding the fact that with the lapse of time Sraffa becomes more guarded when he speaks of economic reality, we claim that Sraffa does not change his mind on the relationship between economic reality and the economist/observer and on the importance of choosing the point of view best suited to solve the given problem selected by the economist. What matters to Sraffa is to detect what different economists/observers can consistently say about a given object or to build the analytic tools required to discover a given property of the object.

This is perhaps the place to stress that we are not making nor intend to make binding claims on Sraffa's ontology. While Sraffa's ontology concerns his vision about 'reality' as an object which does or does not exist independently of its 'observer', Sraffa's methodology concerns the rules the economist must abide by in the process of elaboration of economic theory. Though interrelated, these two levels of analysis should be kept distinct. To consider the economic reality as something that exists independently from the activity of observation and classification carried out by the economist is certainly not an ontological position that is unique to Sraffa; nor is the belief that the perspective of the investigator is, in some sense, relevant to the shaping of the economic theory. In particular, many Marshallian economists would have shared basically the same assumption about an independent reality (Signorino 2000a, 2000b, 2001b). We claim that a characteristic of Sraffa's methodology, not shared by the majority of his contemporaries, is how Sraffa makes use of these elements in his critical writings and in the elaboration of his own theory. As we show in the chapter, in some crucial passages of his argument Sraffa introduces and compares different observers with specific analytical attitudes and investigates how these attitudes may be useful to or detrimental for grasping some specific aspects of the object under investigation. This procedure explains why Sraffa is particularly attentive in separating the elements which are part of the object under analysis and those which depend on the special theoretical lenses used by the observer: in our view Sraffa's implicit assumption is that theoretical lenses are indeed required for the investigation to be carried out and therefore an effort is to be made in order to choose which are the best ones in the given situation. The differences we notice in this regard between the young Sraffa and the mature one lie mainly in that in the later writings the distinction between the object of analysis and the perspective of the observer is more explicit. Our exclusive concern with Sraffa's methodology explains why we do not attempt to reconstruct what exactly Sraffa means when he speaks of a 'point of view'. Such a question is an intricate one and may involve a circularity problem: to the extent that a 'point of view' has any coherent structure at all, it is already informed by a theory of some sort – an embryonic theory perhaps, but a theory nonetheless. In short, economic theory is shaped by the economist's point of view, but the point of view must on some fundamental level be grounded in a theoretical framework. In this chapter we consider the different points of view chosen by different economists as exogenous and we focus on (i) Sraffa's assessment of the economic theory which may be consistently elaborated from a given point of view; and (ii) Sraffa's comparison of the results achieved from different standpoints.

Finally, we want to stress that the analysis we propose in this chapter may help furthering our understanding of Sraffa's economics since (i) it helps give unity to the many lines of criticism Sraffa directed against marginalist economics during his long intellectual carrier; and (ii) it helps to show the intimate relationship existing between the *pars destruens* and the *pars construens* of Sraffa's overall theoretical contribution.

In this chapter we have deliberately chosen to focus on Sraffa's published material and, among the published works, only on the theoretical contributions, setting aside his historiographical and applied contributions. Nevertheless in some cases we quote from Sraffa's unpublished papers just to confirm that the unpublished material we had the opportunity to consult supports, or is at least consistent with, the line of interpretation we provide here. A first obvious reason for our choices is that of manageability. A further reason for the former choice is that we intend to analyse the wording that Sraffa chose with deliberation and care. Analysis of this kind on material that an author has written just for himself could be misleading. We think that an investigation such as that presented here must be rooted in the material that the author has chosen to publish, even if we acknowledge that Sraffa's silence on economic methodology implies that a rational reconstruction of Sraffa's logic of scientific research in economics involves an unavoidable element of conjecture. As to the latter choice, a further reason is the following. We are aware of the fact that a threefold relationship of the kind we analyse here may be discovered also in Sraffa's historiographical and applied works. For example, it would be interesting to investigate the threefold relationship between Ricardo's texts, the interpreter of Ricardo and the interpretation of Ricardo's economics. We thought it best first to establish our point on Sraffa's theoretical contributions.

We are perfectly aware that, since the opening of Sraffa's manuscripts at the Wren Library of Trinity College (Cambridge, UK), his published contributions to economic theory can be assessed in the light of the huge amount of preparatory material he collected from the early 1920s. Moreover, the unpublished material may include some explicit statements concerning the issues dealt with here. An investigation of Sraffa's manuscripts on the issues dealt with here will be the subject of future work.

The structure of the chapter is as follows. In the second and third sections we concentrate on the works of the 1920s and early 1930s. In the second section we propose a rational reconstruction of the concept of economic reality and of the ability of the economists to appraise it. In the third section we tackle the 'problem of the arbitrariness of the economist', its genesis and its possible boundaries. The fourth section analyses in detail *PC*. We highlight the way Sraffa defines the various objects to be analysed and the different points of view from which they can be observed and how he modifies his theoretical schemes in accordance with the different structural properties of the objects under investigation. The final section concludes.

The relationship between economic reality and the economist in the 1920s and early 1930s

Careful reading of the texts of the 1925–6 papers and of the 1932 exchange with Hayek shows that Sraffa makes continuous reference to economic reality. In 'Sulle relazioni fra costo e quantità prodotta' (1925 [1998]) Sraffa speaks of 'objective circumstances inherent in the various industries' (p. 324) and of 'objective conditions of the economic system studied' (p. 357). Moreover, Sraffa frequently uses expressions like 'experience' (p. 325), 'commonly observed fact' (p. 343), 'general fact' (p. 331), 'reality' and 'concrete reality' (pp. 330, 340, 344, 347, 350, 361, 362 and 363). Similarly, in 'The laws of returns under competitive conditions' Sraffa (1926) makes use of expressions like 'in fact' (p. 538), 'in reality' (pp. 540 and 541 fn 1), 'the reality of things' (p. 543), 'the actual conditions of industry [in the different industries]' (pp. 540 and 542), 'the actual process of determining the price and the quantity produced' (p. 544), 'real conditions' (p. 541), 'the actual state of things' (p. 542) and 'everyday experience' (p. 543). Finally, in his 1932 'Rejoinder' to Hayek Sraffa writes that 'Nobody could believe that anything that logically follows from such [Hayek's] fantastic assumptions is true *in reality*' (p. 250; emphasis added).

Moreover, the texts of the 1925–6 and 1932 papers provide extensive evidence of Sraffa making empirical claims about economic reality even in the absence of hard empirical data. Some of these claims have for Sraffa a status of certainty, while others only have a probabilistic nature. A few examples must suffice. In relation to the objective characteristics of a given plot of land, Sraffa writes that 'the proposition that the productivity of a given piece of land is to a large extent independent of whether or not another piece of land is cultivated is *both true and obvious*' (1925 [1998]: 335; emphasis added). On the contrary, in relation to external economies, Sraffa writes that in his view 'it seems *probable* that there must be very few cases indeed of external economies which can be introduced as a consequence of a variation – not a very large one – in the size of an industry' (1998 [1925]: 363; emphasis added). The 1926 paper contains several expressions like 'seldom' (pp. 540 and 542) 'great frequency' (p. 542) 'it is not easy ... to find' (p. 543), 'it is not likely to be found' (p. 548), 'it is extremely unlikely' (p. 549), 'it will generally be found' (p. 550).[1] In the same vein, in his 1932 review of Hayek's *Prices and Production* Sraffa defines as 'platitudes' (p. 44) his views of money as 'a store of value, and the standard in terms of which debts, and other legal obligations, habits, opinions, conventions, in short all kinds of relations between men, are more or less rigidly fixed'. Similarly, in his rejoinder to Hayek Sraffa defines his argument on the permanence of capital accumulated by means of forced saving as 'an appeal to common sense' (p. 249).

The evidence provided above shows that in his published works of the 1920s and early 1930s Sraffa describes economic reality (i) *as if it* had given structural properties which do not depend on the activity of observation and classification carried out by the economist (economic theory is crafted by the economist while economic reality is not); and (ii) *as if* the structural properties of economic reality could be appraised by economists who, on a few occasions, are able to make quantitative judgements on them. We use the 'as if' clause to underline the fact that we are not making binding claims on Sraffa's ontology, as mentioned in the first section. Points (i) and (ii) may be due to the fact that the gist of Sraffa's criticism of Marshall and Hayek is that their theories apply only to a set of cases that rarely if ever exist in reality. In order for the criticism to be persuasive, the characterization of reality that is inconsistent with Marshall's and Hayek's theories must be straightforward and widely shared. In short, the criticism is compelling only to the extent that Sraffa's description of reality cannot be refuted.

Yet, we claim the relevance of the choice of the 'point of view' adopted by the economist for Sraffa: different 'points of view' allow economists to elaborate different economic theories characterized by different theoretical domains.[2] The gist of Sraffa's 1925–6 criticism of Marshallian economics is just that the point of view chosen by Marshallian economists allows them to elaborate an economic theory whose theoretical domain is limited to industries which employ factors specific to the industry itself and industries whose scale economies are external to firms and internal to the industry. Similarly, the essence of Sraffa's 1932 criticism of Hayek is that his theory, even if

purged from its logical blunders, can deal only with a 'neutral money economy', that is an economy where money is just a 'medium of exchange' and
not also a 'store of value', and thus an economy which behaves exactly as a
barter economy.

Sraffa acknowledges that the economist has to carry out a few discretionary
choices in the process of elaboration of economic theory. Sraffa's acknowl-
edgement of the problem of the arbitrariness of the economist raises (at least)
two orders of questions:

(i) What exactly is the source of the 'arbitrariness' of the economist?
(ii) How does one cope with the problem of the arbitrariness of the econo-
     mist, that is, what are, if any, its admissible boundaries?

The following section is devoted to answering the above questions.

The 'arbitrariness' of the economist and its boundaries in the 1920s and early 1930s

The expression 'point of view' or 'standpoint' recurs 25 times in the 1925
paper (pp. 323, 324, 326, 327 fn 11, 330, 330 fn 14, 334, 337 fn 32, 338, 342,
344 fn 49, 346, 349, 350, 351 fn 64, 355, 356, 362 and 363), 13 times in the
1926 paper (pp. 536, 538, 539, 540, 542, 543, 544, 547, 548 and 548 fn 2) and
twice in the 1932 paper (pp. 45 and 47). The expression 'arbitrariness' and its
derivatives appear on 12 occasions in the 1925 paper (pp. 324, 327, 336, 337,
338, 349, 354, 357 and 358), not at all in the 1926 paper and twice in the 1932
paper (pp. 50 and 51).

The problem of the arbitrariness of the economist lies at the very heart of
Sraffa's 1925–6 critique of the Marshallian theory of value and its inability to
classify real world industries into the three 'boxes' of constant, increasing and
diminishing returns. In the opening section of the Italian paper, Sraffa asks
(rhetorically) whether

> the failing cannot be found in the very nature of the criterion according
> to which the classification should be conducted. In particular, it remains
> to be seen whether the *fundamentum divisionis* is formed by objective cir-
> cumstances inherent in the various industries, or, instead, is dependent on
> the point of view of the person acting as observer; or, to put it another
> way, whether the increasing and decreasing costs are nothing other than
> different aspects of one and the same thing that can occur at the same
> time, for the same industry, so that an industry can be classified arbitrarily
> in one or the other category according to the definition of 'industry' that
> is considered preferable for each particular problem, and according to
> whether long or short periods are considered.
>
> (Sraffa 1998 [1925]: 324)

Similarly, in the final section of the same paper, Sraffa writes:

> [the hypotheses of decreasing and increasing productivity], rather than referring to different phenomena, represent different aspects under which the same phenomenon can be considered. That is to say that the applicability of one or of the other group depends, in many cases, not so much on the objective conditions of the economic system studied, as on the nature of the problems that we propose to study in respect to it. The element of arbitrariness that is thus introduced into the criterion that should guide us in a classification of industries according to the manner of the variation of cost, is evident in the choice of the characteristic that is to be taken as the basis of a definition of 'industry'.
>
> (Sraffa 1998 [1925]: 357)

The aim of the 1925 paper is to show the tension, existing within the Marshallian theoretical framework, between an object, economic reality and its structural properties, and the point of view chosen by a subject, the economist/observer. Such a tension obliges Marshallian economists to introduce some further assumptions, such as external–internal scale economies, within their theoretical framework. As a consequence, the theoretical domain of Marshallian theory is drastically reduced:

> The fact that the 'external economies' peculiar to an industry, which make possible the desired conciliation between scientific abstraction and reality, are themselves a purely hypothetical and unreal construction, is something that is often ignored.
>
> (Sraffa 1998 [1925]: 347)

The same argument is used by Sraffa in the 1926 paper to criticize the ability of the Marshallian theory of value, based on the assumption of perfect competition and the method of partial equilibrium, to analyse an economic reality characterized by scale economies:

> Here again we find that in reality the economies of production on a large scale are not suitable for the requirements of the supply curve: their field of action is either wider or more restricted than would be necessary. ... The only economies which could be taken into consideration would be such as occupy an intermediate position between these two extremes; but it is just in the middle that nothing, or almost nothing, is to be found. Those economies which are external from the point of view of the individual firm, but internal as regards the industry in its aggregate, constitute precisely the class which is most seldom to be met with.
>
> (Sraffa 1926: 540)

Finally, the same method of criticism is employed by Sraffa in his 1932 review of Hayek's *Prices and Production* (1931). Sraffa highlights the many contradictions, existing within the Hayekian theoretical framework, between the *asserted* object under investigation and the peculiar point of view chosen by Hayek. We have stressed the word 'asserted' because Sraffa claims that Hayek progressively shifted his analytical focus in the course of his book from the accumulation of capital in a monetary economy, the asserted object, to the statement that only a constant money policy does not distort the voluntary decisions of agents. It is true that Sraffa's review emphasizes Hayek's logical blunders, though Sraffa was of the opinion that the basic flaws of Hayek's theory originate with its 'subjective' method. (A possible explanation of Sraffa's chosen style of exposition is that Sraffa was aware of the risk of annoying his readers with an explicit methodological discussion: see Signorino 2001a in this regard.) Nonetheless, as already noted by Lawlor and Horn (1992: 23–4) Sraffa was well aware that *Prices and Production* contains both methodological prescription and positive analysis and, accordingly, he put under fire both Hayek's chosen framework and Hayek's use of his own framework.

According to our reconstruction of Sraffa's implicit methodology, the problem of the arbitrariness of the economist within economic theorizing derives from the freedom of the economist/observer to select her point of view. Sraffa's methodology involves at its normative level a kind of consistency requirement between the choice of the problem to solve and the choice of the point of view from which to tackle the selected problem. (As we show in the following section, this aspect of Sraffa's methodology becomes particularly evident in *PC*.) This requirement is manifest in a passage of the 1926 paper and in the final sentence of the 1930 rejoinder to Robertson. In the 1926 paper Sraffa writes:

> What is important is to ascertain how the various forces at work can be grouped in the most homogeneous manner, so that the influence of each of them on the equilibrium resulting from their opposition may be more readily estimated.
>
> (Sraffa 1926: 544)

The 'various forces at work' and the 'equilibrium resulting from their opposition' constitute the economic reality investigated by the economist. The arbitrariness of the economist lies in the choice of the scheme of classification, that is to say, the way the economic forces may be grouped. Since different schemes may be selected, the criterion to follow for Sraffa, at least in the 1920s, is that of simplicity, 'the most homogeneous manner', which obliges the economist to choose the scheme best suited to highlight the influence of each force on the equilibrium position. In the same vein, in his 1930 rejoinder to Robertson Sraffa stresses that the point of view chosen by Marshallian economists is not the best suited to solve the theoretical *quæsita* raised by themselves. The theoretical domain of Marshallian theory, once reconstructed in a logically consistent way, turns out to be too narrow:

> Reduced within such restricted limits, the supply schedule with variable costs cannot claim to be a general conception applicable to normal industries; it can prove a useful instrument only in regard to such exceptional industries as can reasonably satisfy its conditions.
>
> (Sraffa 1926: 540)

According to Sraffa, the Marshallian theory may gain logical consistency only by making recourse to unrealistic assumptions. Thus it proves to be unfit to hit the theoretical targets announced by the same Marshallian economists:

> I am trying to find what are the assumptions implicit in Marshall's theory; if Mr Robertson regards them as extremely unreal, I sympathise with him. We seem to be agreed that the theory cannot be interpreted in a way which makes it logically self-consistent and, at the same time, reconciles it with the facts it sets out to explain.
>
> (Sraffa 1930: 93)

Here it is possible to find an echo of Poincaré's methodology according to which the choice between different scientific explanations of the same natural phenomenon should be conducted according to the criterion of simplicity. Indirect confirmation of this parallel between Sraffa's and Poincaré's methodologies comes from the analysis of Sraffa's papers at the Wren Library. Kurz points out that

> apparently, Sraffa studied intensively Jules Henri Poincaré's *La Science et l'Hypothèse* (1902) and François Simiand's *La Méthode Positive en Science Économique* (1912), which is reflected in many annotations and underlinings in the two books. ... Sraffa apparently agreed with Poincaré's proposition that the axioms of geometry are neither synthetic judgements a priori nor experimental facts. They are rather conventions. Our choice from among all conventions at our disposal is first and foremost guided by experimental facts. In addition there is the necessity of avoiding contradictions. In this way the postulates of a theory may be rigorously true despite the fact that they were abstracted from experimental laws which are only approximative. Poincaré concludes that it makes no sense to ask, for example, whether Euclidian geometry is right or wrong. One should rather ask whether it is the most convenient.
>
> (Kurz 2004)

The relationship between economic reality and the economist in *PC*

In the Preface to *PC* Sraffa introduces one object of analysis, 'the properties of an economic system' which 'do not depend on changes in the scale of production or in the proportions of factors', and two observers of that object. The former observer is introduced as (i) 'anyone accustomed to think in terms of the equilibrium of demand and supply', the latter as (ii) the scholar adopting the 'standpoint ... of the old classical economists from Adam Smith to Ricardo'.

According to Sraffa, observers (i) and (ii) adopt two different attitudes towards the object under investigation. Such differences have a direct bearing on the observer's ability to comprehend it. Observer (i) 'may be induced' by the symmetrical theory of value to interpret a model in which demand conditions play no explicit analytical role in price determination as a model based on an implicit assumption of constant returns to scale. Observer (ii) appears to be better equipped than observer (i) to perform the task of studying the properties of the object under investigation:

> In a system in which, day after day, production continued unchanged in those respects, the marginal product of a factor (or alternatively the marginal cost of a product) would not merely be hard to find – it just would not be there to be found.
>
> (Sraffa 1960: v)

In our view, the reason why Sraffa is so eager to establish a tight connection between a well-defined object and a specific point of view, the classical one, is that he aims to highlight the constraints to which the observer is (consciously or unconsciously) tied in the moment she selects a given point of view. For Sraffa marginalist observers are *obliged* by their theory of value to study the properties of an economic system which depend on the (infinitesimal) changes in the proportion of factors of production or in the scale of production:

> The marginal approach *requires* attention to be focused on change, for without change either in the scale of an industry or in the 'proportions of the factors of production' there can be neither marginal product nor marginal cost.
>
> (Sraffa, 1960: v; emphasis added)

Moreover, Sraffa's emphasis that in an economic system in which production continues unchanged day after day the marginal product of a factor or the marginal cost of a commodity is not 'there to be found' may be interpreted as a warning for his readers: marginal products and marginal costs are theoretical objects and not observable objects. In fact, even in a stationary state the observer could calculate the marginal product of a factor or the marginal cost of a commodity provided that infinitesimal changes *were* assumed (coun-terfactually); but obviously no observer could experience them. Things are different with respect to what Wicksteed called 'spurious margins': 'The most familiar case is that of the product of the "marginal land" in agriculture, when lands of different qualities are cultivated side by side' (Sraffa, 1960: v). In this case two different objects are experienced by the observer and the difference between the two objects defines the increments implicit in the con-cept of margin. This concept of margin was actually introduced by classical economists. Sraffa reminds us that 'P.H. Wicksteed, the purist of marginal theory ... condemns such a use of the term "marginal" as a source of "dire confusion"' (*ibid.*).

Production and prices

Sraffa describes technology by listing industries and each industry is consid-ered as fully described by the list of inputs and the list of outputs. Where do these data come from? Sraffa is silent about this. However, even a quick explo-ration of the unpublished manuscripts clarify that these data are supposed to have been directly observed:

> The significance of the equations is simply this: that if a man fell from the moon on the earth, and noted the amount of things consumed in each factory and the amount produced by each factory during a year, he could deduce at which values the commodities must be sold, if the rate of inter-est must be uniform and the process of production repeated. In short, the equations show that the conditions of exchange are entirely determined by the conditions of production.
>
> (D3/12/7: 87; quoted by Kurz and Salvadori 2004: 1546)

> This paper deals with an extremely elementary problem; so elementary indeed that its solution is generally taken for granted. The problem is that of ascertaining the conditions of equilibrium of a system of prices and the rate of profits, independently of the study of the forces which may bring about such a state of equilibrium. Since a solution of the second problem carries with it a solution of the first, that is the course usually adopted in modern theory. The first problem however is susceptible of a more general treatment, independent of the particular forces assumed for the second; and in view of the unsatisfactory character of the latter, there is advantage in maintaining its independence.
>
> (D3/12/15: 2; quoted by Kurz and Salvadori 2005: 433)

Yet the act of observation would have provided the observer with a body of data larger than that actually contemplated by Sraffa. Thus we claim that the data have been screened and weighed by the observer, Sraffa, who has made use of his discretionary power of selection.

The basic feature of the object analysed in Chapter I of *PC* is that

> nothing has been added by production to the possessions of society as a whole: ... each commodity, which initially was distributed between the industries according to their needs, is found at the end of the year to be entirely concentrated in the hands of its producer.
>
> (p. 3)

Straightforward scrutiny shows that (p. 3):

> There is a unique set of exchange-values which if adopted by the market restores the original distribution of the products and makes it possible for the process to be repeated; such values spring directly from the methods of production. In the particular example we have taken, the exchange-value required is 10 qr. of wheat for 1 t. of iron.

It is noteworthy that Sraffa here makes use of a hypothetical sentence, that is to say, he does not affirm the existence in the economy under study of a law which ensures that those exchange values would actually rule intersectoral transactions. A possible explanation is that the reader 'accustomed to think in terms of the equilibrium of demand and supply' when confronted with such a law might be induced to think that the observer is silently introducing some assumptions concerning individual behaviour in the market place. Instead Sraffa emphasizes that, independently of any assumption on individual behaviour, those prices will actually rule intersectoral transactions if that society is to survive. With a different set of prices that society cannot reproduce itself. In order to determine the prices there is no need to investigate either the behaviour of the agents or their preferences.

Given the properties of the object under study, the observer has no need to introduce any assumption concerning individual behaviour into her theoretical scheme. Despite the fact that individual behaviour is part of the observed object, the introduction of any assumption about it implies a number of choices by the observer and therefore may introduce what Sraffa would call an arbitrary element: given the properties of the object under investigation, the only assumption needed is that individual agents do not make choices whose consequences may threaten the requirements for systemic reproduction. Such an assumption may be taken for granted. In fact Sraffa, as observer, focuses attention on economic systems which actually survive (p. 5 n1):

> Systems which are incapable of doing so [being brought to a self-replacing state] under any proportions and show a deficit in the production of some commodities over their consumption even if none has a surplus do not represent viable economic systems and are not considered.

In Chapter II of *PC* Sraffa introduces an economy which 'produces more than the minimum necessary for replacement and there is a surplus to be distributed' (p. 6). The observer-Sraffa remarks: 'the system becomes self-contradictory'. This 'contradiction', however, is not inherent in the object under observation. Thus Sraffa's remark amounts to a warning concerning the observer and her theoretical schemes: the observer would fall into a contradiction if she analysed the object 'production with a surplus' by means of the same analytical tools used for the object 'production for subsistence'. A different theoretical scheme is needed.[3] In our view Sraffa's warning is justified by the fact that at least two substantive differences exist between the object of Chapter I and the object of Chapter II: the existence of a surplus, in fact, determines the necessity for the observer (i) to choose a rule for the distribution of the surplus; and (ii) to distinguish between basic commodities and non-basic commodities.

In Chapter I, with no surplus to be distributed, the observer who seeks to solve the problem of price determination has no analytical decision to take: her arbitrariness is bounded by the fact that prices are uniquely determined by technology. By contrast, in Chapter II there is a surplus to be distributed and prices are determined in accordance with the rule on the distribution of the surplus. Hence, the observer is to make use of her freedom by choosing a hypothesis on the rule according to which the surplus is distributed. Obviously, the observer's choice is discretionary but should not be arbitrary in the sense that the chosen assumption on distribution of the surplus must be in accordance with the (political, legal, etc.) institutions and social norms which, in a given historical period, characterize the economy under investigation.

Actually Sraffa provides two alternative schemes to analyse the object 'production with a surplus'. In the former (sections 4–7) wages are regarded 'as consisting of the necessary subsistence of the workers and thus entering the system on the same footing as the fuel for the engines or the feed for the cattle' (p. 9). In the latter (sections 8–11) the subsistence wages assumption is dropped. As a matter of fact, many other alternatives are possible. The basic point is how the surplus is distributed. Only once such a question is answered is it possible to determine the prices and one distributive variable.

Sraffa's first choice is to add 'the rate of profits (which must be uniform for all industries) as an unknown' to be determined jointly with prices (p. 6). Sraffa does not explain why such a rate 'must' be uniform. But the whole heritage of the classical tradition, not contradicted, in this respect, by the neoclassical economists, may justify this silence.

After Sraffa has introduced in sections 4–7 this possible choice of the rule of distribution of the surplus, he abandons it and introduces another one, which is then followed in the whole book (except in Chapter XI on land, where it is modified to insert further recipients of surplus: the owners of natural resources which are used in production and are in short supply). The abandonment is justified since wages 'besides the ever-present element of subsistence, … may include a share of the surplus product' (p. 9). If workers can get part of the surplus, two distributive variables have to be determined and the result of adding the wage as one of the variables is that the number of these now exceeds the number of equations by one and the system can move with one degree of freedom; and if one of the variables is fixed the others will be fixed too.

(p. 11)

The introduction of workers as recipients of surplus is certainly a change in the object to be studied: it may be taken for granted that an economy where workers do not participate in the distribution of surplus and an economy where workers do participate are characterized by different (political, legal, etc.) institutions and social norms and thus they must be reckoned as different objects. Sraffa analyses the consequences stemming from such a change (p. 10):

> The drawback of this course is that it involves relegating the necessaries of consumption to the limbo of non-basic products. This is due to their no longer appearing among the means of production on the left-hand side of the equations: so that an improvement in the methods of production of necessaries of life will no longer directly affect the rate of profits and the prices of other products. Necessaries however are essentially basic and if they are prevented from exerting their influence on prices and profits under that label, they must do so in devious ways (*e.g.* by setting a limit below which the wage cannot fall; a limit which would itself fall with any improvement in the methods of production of necessaries, carrying with it a rise in the rate of profits and a change in the prices of other products).[4]

Another, even more relevant consequence of the change is supplied in section 44 (p. 33):

> The choice of the wage as the independent variable in the preliminary stages was due to its being there regarded as consisting of specified necessaries determined by physiological or social conditions which are independent of prices or the rate of profits. But as soon as the possibility of variations in the division of the product is admitted, this consideration loses much of its force. And when the wage is to be regarded as 'given' in terms of a more or less abstract standard, and does not acquire a definite meaning until the prices of commodities are determined, the position is reversed. The rate of profits, as a ratio, has a significance which is independent of any prices, and can well be 'given' before the prices are fixed. It is accordingly susceptible of being determined from outside the system of production, in particular by the level of the money rates of interest.

This paragraph has been commented upon elsewhere by one of us in a way that is clearly pertinent to this chapter:

The fact that workers' demand cannot be defined on the basis of physiological or social conditions does not imply, according to Sraffa, the necessity of an analysis of the determinants of it. In the traditional Classical
analysis the role of workers' consumption is that of determining the real
wage rate (i.e., one of the distributive variables) from outside the relations
among prices that must hold if commodities are to be reproduced. This
role can be played, Sraffa argues, by the rate of profits, which, 'as a ratio',
is a pure number 'and can well be "given" before the prices are fixed'. It
is remarkable that an important aspect of the analysis emerges as a consequence of a difficulty of the *observer*, rather than as an *observed aspect*
of reality.

(Salvadori 2000: 186)

As already mentioned, beside the necessity to choose the distribution rule,
Sraffa highlights another consequence of the distinction between the object
'production for subsistence' and the object 'production with a surplus': the
distinction between basic commodities and non-basic commodities. Such a
distinction cannot be made in the case of production for subsistence because
in that case either non-basics cannot be produced or, if they are, production with a surplus can be obtained by not producing them. The asymmetry
between these two kinds of commodities derives from the structural properties of the object.[5] Evidence supporting our interpretation is provided by
the content of a letter, dated 4 June 1962, to Peter Newman where Sraffa
replies to some conclusions reached by Newman in his 1962 article on *PC* (see
Sraffa 1962). In particular, Sraffa counteracts Newman's criticism according
to which the distinction between basic and non-basic commodities depends
on the level of aggregation of the system arguing that 'aggregation is the *act
of the observer*, whilst the distinction is based on a difference in *objective properties*' (Sraffa 1962: 13; emphasis added).[6]

A 'preliminary survey' and the complete analysis

It is in Chapters III–VI of *PC* that we may recognize that in the 1960 book
Sraffa adopts the following analytical strategy: first he describes accurately
the salient features of the object he wants to investigate and then he provides
the results which can be obtained on the basis of the assumptions he has
introduced and the concepts he has forged. In short, Sraffa takes great pains
over showing the tight relationship between his theoretical achievements and
the specific standpoint he has chosen.

The main aim of Chapter III is to provide a 'preliminary survey' (p. 15) of
price movements consequent upon changes in distribution on the assumption
that the methods of production remain unchanged. The results presented in
this chapter are those which can be obtained by the observer without any special theoretical tool. The complete analysis of these movements is presented
in Chapter VI. Sraffa chooses to split the analysis of price movements into

two chapters: Chapter III and Chapter VI. This procedure shows clearly that Sraffa takes care to separate what can consistently be said about the object under investigation *without* making use of the analytical tool represented by the Standard commodity from the results that *require* the use of such a tool, elaborated in Chapters IV and V. Despite the relevance of it, this story is not told here since it has been extensively investigated by one of us on another occasion. The interested reader may consult Kurz and Salvadori (1993).

Joint production

In dealing with joint production Sraffa is confronted with difficulties not encountered in the analysis of single production. The two ways out of these difficulties consist of either (i) setting an assumption on the properties of the observed object; or (ii) providing a more careful interpretation of the object under consideration. Our analysis reveals also that Sraffa prefers to be close to common sense whenever this is possible.

Joint products were referred to by major marginalist authors, in particular Jevons (1965 [1871]: 200), see also John Stuart Mill (1965 [1848]: 583), as phenomena which cannot be analysed without a theory of demand. Their argument is the following: with joint production the number of production processes operated will generally fall short of the number of products whose prices have to be ascertained. Hence there is a problem of underdeterminacy. Before Sraffa the solution was actually found by Frederik Zeuthen (Zeuthen 1933: 15; see also Kurz and Salvadori 1995: 241–2). What concerns us here is mainly the path followed by Sraffa to propose the solution, rather than the solution itself.

Sraffa begins this discussion with an explicit reference to the problem of underdeterminacy in the familiar case in which two products are produced by a single process and states: 'The conditions would no longer be sufficient to determine the prices. There would be more prices to be ascertained than there are processes, and therefore equations to determine them' (p. 43). 'In these circumstances', Sraffa continues, 'there will be room' either 'for a second, parallel process which will produce the two commodities by a different method and ... in different proportions' or for the production of 'a third commodity by two distinct processes' which use the two jointly produced commodities 'as means of production in different proportions'. Such further processes 'will not only be *possible* – [they] will be *necessary* if the number of processes is to be brought to equality with the number of commodities so that the prices *may be determined*' (p. 43; emphasis added). Then Sraffa assumes 'that the number of processes should be equal to the number of commodities' (p. 44).[7] Once again an assumption on the properties of the object is introduced because otherwise the observer cannot do her job.

Further, Sraffa is aware of the fact that prices do not need to be definite and positive and, once again, he uses assumptions on the observed objects to solve the problem. Productive processes must be 'subject ... to the general

requirement of the resulting equations being mutually independent and having at least one system of real solutions: which rules out, for example, pro-
portionality of *both* products and means of production in the two processes'.
Sraffa continues:

> However (and this is the only economic restriction), while the equations
> may be formally satisfied by negative solutions for the unknowns, only
> those methods of production are practicable which, in the *conditions*
> *actually prevailing* (i.e. at the given wage or at the given rate of profits) do
> not involve other than positive prices.
>
> (p. 44; emphasis added)

Note that whereas in analysing single production prices are *proved* to be
positive, in analysing joint production prices are *assumed* to be positive. The
observed data are such as to allow positive prices at 'the conditions actually
prevailing'.

Thus section 50 of *PC* is devoted to the introduction of two assumptions
and to arguments concerning their plausibility. Both assumptions concern the
'conditions actually prevailing', i.e. the observations from which the data are
obtained by the observer. A similar way out is used again in dealing with the
positivity of prices *outside* the 'conditions actually prevailing'.

Since prices cannot be proved to be positive in general it is not true that 'if
the prices of all commodities are positive at any one level of the wage between
1 and 0, no price can become negative as a result of the variation of the wage
within those limits' (p. 59). The solution provided by Sraffa is the following.

> This conclusion is not in itself very startling. All that it implies is that,
> although *in actual fact* all prices were positive, a change in the wage might
> create a situation *the logic of which* required some of the prices to turn
> negative: and this being unacceptable, those among the methods of pro-
> duction that gave rise to such a result *would be discarded* to make room
> for others which *in the new situation* were consistent with positive prices.
>
> (p. 59; emphases added)

Sraffa's suggested way out of the impasse arising from the negativity of the
price of a joint product outside the 'conditions actually prevailing' is tan-
tamount to the assumption that there is always one or several processes of
production which, if adopted, make the phenomenon of negative price disappear.[8] The prices relative to a given technique and a given rate of profits do
not need to be non-negative, but the prices of a cost-minimizing technique
at a given rate of profit are non-negative, provided that an appropriate reasonable assumption is introduced. Once again the way out of a difficulty is
obtained by means of an assumption on the observed data.

Let us now analyse a case in which an assumption on observed data cannot do the job. Sraffa remarks that the multipliers defining the Standard

commodity do not need to be positive (p. 47). The way out of the difficulty cannot be an assumption regarding the observation. The Standard commodity, in fact, is a construction of the observer and not an aspect of the observation. But precisely this property gives the solution in section 56. Some components of the Standard commodity need to be negative, but

> there is fortunately no insuperable difficulty in conceiving as real the negative quantities that are liable to occur among its components. These can be interpreted, by analogy with the accounting concept, as liabilities or debts, while the positive components will be regarded as assets.
>
> (p. 48)

This is the reason why '[w]e must therefore in the case of joint-products be content with the system of abstract equations, transformed by appropriate multipliers, without trying to think of it as having a bodily existence' (p. 48).

Comparing sections 50 and 56 gives us a way to interpret an aspect of the methodology used by Sraffa. In section 50 'conditions actually prevailing' are dealt with and these can be assumed to be such that a plausible property (non-negative prices) is obtained. In section 56 an abstract object is dealt with and if this can have a property which would not be plausible if applied to a concrete object, a deeper interpretation is put forward to argue that such a property is not required. In fact Sraffa maintains:

> a Standard commodity which includes both positive and negative quantities can be adopted as money of account without too great a stretch of the imagination provided that the unit is conceived as representing, like a share in a company, a fraction of each asset and of each liability, the latter in the shape of an obligation to deliver without payment certain quantities of particular commodities.
>
> (p. 48)

Let us now analyse an argument which allows us to highlight the role of common sense in Sraffa's arguing. We accomplish this task by comparing the choice of the 'maximum rate of profit' in section 64 with the analogous choice in Chapter V for single product systems. In Chapter V Sraffa had maintained that there may be as many as k candidates for the role of the Standard commodity. However, there cannot be more than one with non-negative entries. This procedure is not applicable to joint production:

> In deciding which, among the j possible sets of values, is the one relevant to the economic system, we can no longer rely on there being, as the obvious choice, a value of R to which corresponds an all-positive Standard commodity; for in a system of joint production all may include negative quantities among their components.
>
> (p. 53)

Sraffa then reconsiders the matter from the standpoint of the single-products system and finds

> that while an all-positive Standard *appeals to commonsense*, its superiority is due at least as much to its being at the same time (as was shown in § 42) the one that corresponds to the lowest possible value of R. And we shall see that the possession of this last property is by itself sufficient to make the Standard net product that is endowed with it (no matter whether all-positive or otherwise) the one eligible for adoption as unit of wages and prices.
>
> (ibid.; emphasis added)

Therefore the mentioned argument from Chapter V was not the main reason for the choice, even if the choice would not have been changed if the main reason were used. A formally more appropriate procedure would have been to make the choice on the basis of the argument developed for joint production and then to prove that in the case of single production all coefficients relative to basics are positive, the others being nought. But in the analysis of single production Sraffa prefers to justify the choice of the multipliers defining the Standard commodity on the basis of their positivity because it has the advantage to 'appeal to commonsense'. We may conclude this point by asserting that Sraffa investigates more deeply an issue only when this is needed and in his exposition prefers to be close to common sense whenever this is possible.

Final remarks

In this chapter we have analysed Sraffa's main contributions to pure economics in order to elaborate a rational reconstruction of an aspect of Sraffa's implicit methodology which has not been duly investigated so far. We refer to the threefold relationship between 'economic reality', 'the economist/observer' and 'economic theory', that is, the collection of human economic agents and material objects which constitute the subject field of economic theorizing, the human being who observes, classifies and analyses economic reality, and the main intellectual product emerging from the economist's effort to analyse the economic reality under investigation, respectively.

We have shown that in the 1925–6 and 1932 papers Sraffa plainly makes several empirical claims about economic reality *as if they* were self-evident or at least easily verifiable; while in the 1960 book Sraffa appears more concerned with the theoretical difficulties inherent both in the identification of the objects of his inquiry and the way(s) to analyse them. In particular, we have emphasized how Sraffa takes care to define (i) the salient features of the object he wants to investigate; (ii) the point of view chosen by himself and by others; (iii) the consequent assumptions and tools which can be used; and finally (iv) what can consistently be said about the object, given the point of view he has chosen and the assumptions he has introduced. We have also highlighted the role of the appealing to common sense in Sraffa's way of presenting his results. Moreover, we have investigated the role which, for Sraffa, the economists' arbitrariness plays in shaping economic theory and we have highlighted the constraints which, for Sraffa, should bind it.

Acknowledgements

We would like to thank without implicating Heinz D. Kurz, Maria Cristina Marcuzzo, Nerio Naldi, Alessandro Roncaglia, Annalisa Rosselli and two anonymous referees of the *Journal of Economic Methodology* for their detailed comments and suggestions.

References

Davis, J. (1988) 'Sraffa, Wittgenstein and neoclassical economics', *Cambridge Journal of Economics* 12: 29–36, reprinted in J. Wood (ed.) *Piero Sraffa: Critical Assessments*, 1995, London: Routledge.

Davis, J. (1993) 'Sraffa, interdependence and demand: the Gramscian influence', *Review of Political Economy* 5: 22–39, reprinted in J. Wood (ed.) *Piero Sraffa: Critical Assessments*, 1995, London: Routledge.

Davis, J. (1998) 'Sraffa's early philosophical thinking', *Review of Political Economy* 10: 477–91.

Davis, J. (2002) 'Gramsci, Sraffa, Wittgenstein: philosophical linkages', *European Journal of the History of Economic Thought* 9: 382–99.

Jevons, W. S. (1871) *The Theory of Political Economy*, London: Macmillan.

Jevons, W. S. (1965) *The Theory of Political Economy*, reprint of Jevons (1871), New York: Kelley.

Kurz, H. D. (2004) 'Sraffa's early studies of the production of commodities by means of commodities: towards an "atomic analysis"', mimeo, Graz.

Kurz, H. D. and Salvadori, N. (1993) 'The "Standard commodity" and Ricardo's search for an "invariable measure of value"', in M. Baranzini and G. Harcourt (eds) *The Dynamics of the Wealth of Nations: Growth, Distribution and Structural Change. Essays in Honour of Luigi Pasinetti*, New York: St Martin Press, pp. 95–123.

Kurz, H. D. and Salvadori, N. (1995) *Theory of Production. A Long-period Analysis*, Cambridge, New York and Melbourne: Cambridge University Press.

Kurz, H. D. and Salvadori, N. (2001) 'Sraffa and the mathematicians: Frank Ramsey and Alister Watson', in T. Cozzi and R. Marchionatti (eds) *Piero Sraffa's Political Economy: A Centenary Estimate*, London and New York: Routledge, pp. 254–84.

Kurz, H. D. and Salvadori, N. (2004) '"Man from the moon": on Sraffa's objectivism', *Economies et Societés, Histoire de le pensée économique* 35: 1545–57.

Kurz, H. D. and Salvadori, N. (2005) 'Representing the production and circulation of commodities in material terms: on Sraffa's objectivism', *Review of Political Economy* 17: 413–41.

Lawlor, M. S. and Horn, B. (1992) 'Notes on the Sraffa–Hayek exchange', *Review of Political Economy* 4: 317–40, reprinted in H. D. Kurz and N. Salvadori (eds) *The*

Legacy of Piero Sraffa, 2 Vols, 2003, Cheltenham and Northampton: Edward Elgar.

Lunghini, G. (1975) 'Teoria economia ed Economia politica: note su Sraffa', introduction to G. Lunghini (ed.) *Produzione, Capitale e distribuzione*, Milan: Isedi, xi–xxviii.

Marion, M. (2005) 'Sraffa and Wittgenstein: physicalism and constructivism', *Review of Political Economy* 17: 381–406.

Mill, J. S. (1965) [1848] *Principles of Political Economy with Some of Their Applications to Social Philosophy*, ed. J. M. Robson, Toronto: University of Toronto Press.

Mongiovi, G. (1996) 'Sraffa's critique of Marshall: a reassessment', *Cambridge Journal of Economics* 20: 207–24, reprinted in H. D. Kurz and N. Salvadori (eds) *The Legacy of Piero Sraffa*, 2 Vols, 2003, Cheltenham and Northampton: Edward Elgar.

Roncaglia, A. (1978) *Sraffa and the Theory of Prices*, New York: John Wiley and Sons.

Salanti, A. and Signorino, R. (2001) 'From 1925/1926 articles to 1960 book: some notes on Sraffa's not so implicit methodology', in T. Cozzi and R. Marchionatti (eds) *Piero Sraffa's Political Economy: A Centenary Estimate*, London and New York: Routledge, pp. 165–86.

Salvadori, N. (2000) 'Sraffa on demand: a textual analysis', in H. D. Kurz (ed.) *Critical Essays on Piero Sraffa's Legacy in Economics*, Cambridge: Cambridge University Press, pp. 181–97.

Signorino, R. (2000a) 'The Italian debate on Marshallian (and Paretian) economics and the intellectual roots of Piero Sraffa's "Sulle relazioni fra costo e quantita prodotta": a note', *History of Economic Ideas* 8: 143–57.

Signorino, R. (2000b) 'Method and analysis in Piero Sraffa's 1925 critique of Marshallian economics', *European Journal of the History of Economic Thought* 7: 569–94, reprinted in H. D. Kurz and N. Salvadori (eds) *The Legacy of Piero Sraffa*, 2 Vols, 2003, Cheltenham and Northampton: Edward Elgar.

Signorino, R. (2001a) 'Piero Sraffa on utility and the subjective method in the 1920s: a tentative appraisal of Sraffa's unpublished manuscripts', *Cambridge Journal of Economics* 25: 749–63.

Signorino, R. (2001b) 'An appraisal of Piero Sraffa's "The laws of returns under competitive conditions"', *European Journal of the History of Economic Thought* 8: 230–50, reprinted in H.D. Kurz and N. Salvadori (eds) *The Legacy of Piero Sraffa*, 2 Vols, 2003, Cheltenham and Northampton: Edward Elgar.

Signorino, R. (2005) 'Piero Sraffa's *Lectures on the Advanced Theory of Value 1928– 1931* and the rediscovery of the classical approach', *Review of Political Economy* 17: 359–80.

Sraffa, P. (1925) 'Sulle relazioni fra costo e quantita prodotta', *Annali di Economia* 2: 277–328. The references are to the English translation, Sraffa (1998).

Sraffa, P. (1926) 'The laws of returns under competitive conditions', *Economic Journal* 36: 535–50, reprinted in H. D. Kurz and N. Salvadori (eds) *The Legacy of Piero Sraffa*, 2 Vols, 2003, Cheltenham and Northampton: Edward Elgar.

Sraffa, P. (1930) 'A criticism' and 'Rejoinder' (contributions to the Symposium on 'Increasing Returns and the Representative Firm'), *Economic Journal* 40: 89–93.

Sraffa, P. (1932) 'Dr. Hayek on money and capital' and 'A rejoinder', *Economic Journal* 42: 42–53 and 249–51.

Sraffa, P. (1960) *Production of Commodities by Means of Commodities. Prelude to a Critique of Economic Theory*, Cambridge: Cambridge University Press, Italian edition: *Produzione di Merci a Mezzo di Merci. Premesse a una Critica della Teoria Economica*, Torino: Einaudi.

Sraffa, P. (1962) 'Letters to Newman', reprinted in H. D. Kurz and N. Salvadori (eds), *The Legacy of Piero Sraffa*, 2 Vols, 2003, Cheltenham and Northampton: Edward Elgar.

Sraffa, P. (1998) 'On the relations between cost and quantity produced', in L. L. Pasinetti (ed.) *Italian Economic Papers*, Vol. III, Bologna: il Mulino and Oxford: Oxford University Press, pp. 323–63, reprinted in H. D. Kurz and N. Salvadori (eds) *The Legacy of Piero Sraffa*, 2 Vols, 2003, Cheltenham and Northampton: Edward Elgar, English translation of Sraffa (1925).

Zeuthen, F. L. B. (1933) 'Das Prinzip der Knappheit, technische Kombination und ökonomische Qualität', *Zeitschrift für Nationalökonomie* 4: 1–24.

Notes

1 The same attitude surfaces in private correspondence. In a letter to Keynes, dated 6 June 1926, Sraffa writes: 'of course, in reality the connection between cost and quantity produced is obvious' (quoted in Roncaglia 1978: 12).

2 Sraffa's archive at Cambridge reveals that Sraffa from the 1920s onwards cultivated a deep interest in the contemporary developments in the fields of natural sciences (especially physics and mechanics) and philosophy of science. He extensively read Bridgman, Poincaré, Russell, Whitehead, etc. In particular, quantum physics may have been a source of inspiration for Sraffa. As remarked by Kurz,

> quantum physics introduced the possibility that the observer's mind affects the reality he sees. Quantum theory tells us that nothing can be measured or observed without disturbing it, so that the role of the observer is crucial in understanding any physical process.
>
> (Kurz 2004)

3 The exploration of the Sraffa Papers in the Wren Library shows that this was also the intellectual path followed by Sraffa himself in 1927. The equations explored in Chapter I are called 'first equations' and Sraffa discovers that those equations cannot be used when there is a surplus since otherwise the equations are 'contradictory' (D3/12/2: 32–5) and 'the problem is overdetermined' (D3/12/ 11: 17, see Kurz and Salvadori 2001: 262).

4 As stressed by Sraffa, to rescue necessaries from the limbo of non-basic products it would be necessary to

> separate the two component parts of the wage [subsistence and share of the surplus] and regard only the 'surplus' part as variable; whereas the goods necessary for the subsistence of the workers would continue to appear, with the fuel, *etc.*, among the means of production(pp. 9–10)

Sraffa just hints in this direction but he prefers to stick to the more traditional notion of wages as being wholly variable (see Roncaglia 1978: Ch. II).

5 Sraffa is highly concerned with the empirical relevance of these concepts as is witnessed by the attention he pays to pick up concrete objects from the economic reality. Sraffa, in fact, first introduces commodities which 'are not used ... in the production of others' (p. 7). Such commodities cannot play any role in the determination of 'the price-relations of the other products and [of] the rate of profits'

(pp. 7–8). Then the same argument is extended to commodities which 'are merely used in their own reproduction, either directly (e.g. racehorses) or indirectly (e.g. ostriches and ostrich-eggs) or merely for the production of other [non-basics] (e.g. raw silk)' (p. 8).

6 Moreover, in the course of the same letter, in relation to the possibility of some non-basic commodities fetching negative prices Sraffa writes: 'how rare (if any) such cases must be *in the real world*. … I certainly failed to discover any faintly realistic example of this which I could use, and had to invent those "beans"' (*ibid.*; emphasis added). The wording of this letter clearly shows how, in private correspondence, the mature Sraffa refers to economic reality in a way which is close to that used in his early papers.

7 See Salvadori (2000) for a detailed analysis of the way followed by Sraffa to justify this assumption.

8 This assumption, peculiar as it may seem at first sight, is however no less *ad hoc* than the assumption of free disposal. In fact, the latter is equivalent to the assumption that for each process producing a given product there exists another process which is exactly identical to the first one except that the product under consideration is *not* produced.

6 On a proof of Sraffa's[*]

Neri Salvadori

Introduction

Marco Lippi (2008) has argued that proofs by Sraffa (1960) are not complete and that some of them are circumvoluted. He has also argued that conclusions obtained in Part I of Sraffa's book are correct and that flaws in the conclusion would have been detected by Sraffa, whereas better equipped authors failed because they lacked intuition. I will not comment on these arguments, because I substantially agree with him.[1] I rather want to shed light on one of the examples analyzed by Lippi concerning the proof of the existence of the Standard commodity. Lippi has argued that the algorithm in section 37 of Sraffa's book is not precisely stated and that it does not need to converge to the desired eigenvalue and eigenvector. The first part of the proposition was also sustained by Alister Watson at the proof-reading stage of Sraffa's book (cf. Kurz and Salvadori, 2001, pp. 272–3). But the second part has escaped the attention of all commentators before Lippi. Indeed examples can be found in which an algorithm corresponding to the description provided by Sraffa converges to a vector which is not an eigenvector and it is certainly to Lippi's credit to have uncovered the problem.

   The problem I want to discuss here is not whether the proof by Sraffa can be completed or not. It can, of course. Lippi provides a complete proof in an appendix of his paper by using a very special algorithm from among all the algorithms corresponding to the description of section 37. Another special algorithm has been provided, without a proof, by Kurz and Salvadori (2001, p. 284). Instead I want to investigate what are the properties that an algorithm needs to have in order to obtain a complete proof. The fact that Sraffa has not chosen a particular algorithm makes us think that he was convinced that any algorithm would do the job. This is wrong, but, as we will see, any algorithm satisfying an extra assumption does actually do the job. Therefore one might say that Sraffa was not so wrong after all. In the next section I provide the intuition that underlies my argument. In the third section I put forward a

* Reproduced with permission from Guglielmo Chiodi and Leonardo Ditta (eds.), *Sraffa or an Alternative Economics*, New York: Palgrave Macmillan, 2008.

formal presentation of the proof. The fourth section illustrates the argument in terms of an example in which the algorithm converges to a vector which is not an eigenvector.

The intuition

Let $\mathbf{A} = \begin{bmatrix} a_{ij} \end{bmatrix}$ be a square irreducible nonnegative matrix. It is well known that

$$\rho = \min_{x>0} \max_{j} \frac{\sum_{i=1}^{n} x_i a_{ij}}{x_j}$$

is the eigenvalue of maximum modulus of matrix $\mathbf{A}$. Further, since for each positive scalar α

$$\min_{x>0} \max_{j} \frac{\sum_{i=1}^{n} (\alpha x_i) a_{ij}}{(\alpha x_j)} = \min_{x>0} \max_{j} \frac{\sum_{i=1}^{n} x_i a_{ij}}{x_j} = \rho$$

we have

$$\rho = \min_{x>0, \sum_i x_i l_i = \beta} \max_{j} \frac{\sum_{i=1}^{n} x_i a_{ij}}{x_j}$$

for any given positive vector $\mathbf{l} = \begin{bmatrix} l_1, l_2, ..., l_n \end{bmatrix}^T$ and positive scalar β. Sraffa tried to find the vector

$$\mathbf{x} = \arg\min_{x>0, \sum_i x_i l_i = \beta} \max_{j} \frac{\sum_{i=1}^{n} x_i a_{ij}}{x_j}$$

starting from any feasible vector[2] $\mathbf{x}_0 \in \left\{ \mathbf{x} > \mathbf{0} \,\middle|\, \mathbf{x}^T \mathbf{l} = \beta, \mathbf{x}^T [\mathbf{I} - \mathbf{A}]^{-1} \geq \mathbf{0}^T \right\}$ and then building up an algorithm based on two sequences: $\{\mathbf{x}_t\}$ and $\{\lambda_t\}$, where

$$\lambda_t = \lambda(\mathbf{x}_{t-1}) = \max_{j} \frac{\mathbf{x}_{t-1}^T \mathbf{A} \mathbf{e}_j}{\mathbf{x}_{t-1}^T \mathbf{e}_j}$$

so that $\mathbf{x}_{t-1}^T [\lambda_t \mathbf{I} - \mathbf{A}] \geq \mathbf{0}^T$ and $\mathbf{x}_{t-1}^T [\lambda_t \mathbf{I} - \mathbf{A}] \neq \mathbf{0}^T$, and $\mathbf{x}_t$ $(t > 0)$ is a vector such that $\mathbf{x}_t > \mathbf{0}$, $\mathbf{x}^T \mathbf{1} = \beta$ and $\mathbf{x}_t^T [\lambda_t \mathbf{I} - \mathbf{A}] > \mathbf{0}^T$. Sequence $\{\lambda_t\}$ is decreasing and bounded from below, thus it is convergent. Then the algorithm is certainly convergent. If the sequence $\{\lambda_t\}$ converges to $\min_{x>0, \sum_i x_i l_i = \beta} \lambda(\mathbf{q})$, then the eigenvalue of maximum modulus and the corresponding eigenvector have been found.

As Alister Watson, Kurz and Salvadori (2001) and Lippi (2008), among others, have remarked, the algorithm is not well defined since there are infinitely many ways to define $\mathbf{x}_t$. Completing the definition of the algorithm means to define a function $\phi(\mathbf{q})$ such that $\mathbf{x}_t = \phi(\mathbf{x}_{t-1})$, each t. In order to be more precise we introduce the sets

$$R = \left\{ \mathbf{q} \in \mathfrak{R}^n \,\middle|\, \mathbf{q} \geq 0, \, \mathbf{q}^T \mathbf{1} = \beta, \, \mathbf{q}^T [\mathbf{I} - \mathbf{A}] \geq \mathbf{0}^T \right\} \tag{1}$$

$$R^* = \left\{ \mathbf{q} \in \mathfrak{R}^n \,\middle|\, \exists \rho \geq 0 \,:\, \mathbf{q} \geq 0, \, \mathbf{q}^T \mathbf{1} = \beta, \, \mathbf{q}^T [\rho \mathbf{I} - \mathbf{A}] = \mathbf{0}^T \right\} \tag{2}$$

$$S = R - R^* \tag{3}$$

and the set of functions

$$Z(S_0) = \left\{ \phi \,:\, S_0 \to R \,\middle|\, \forall \mathbf{q} \in S_0 \,:\, \phi(\mathbf{q}) \in S_0 \cup R^*, \lambda(\mathbf{q})\phi(\mathbf{q}) - \mathbf{A}^T \phi(\mathbf{q}) > \mathbf{0} \right\},$$

where S_0 is any subset of S. Each function of the set $Z(S_0)$ defines a different algorithm which corresponds to Sraffa's description.

If function $\phi(\mathbf{q})$ has a fixed point in S, then sequence $\{\mathbf{x}_t\}$ may converge on the fixed point of function $\phi(\mathbf{q})$. As a consequence sequence $\{\lambda_t\}$ may converge to a number which does not even need to be close to $\min_{q \in R} \lambda(\mathbf{q})$. In this case the algorithm converges to a scalar and a vector which are not the eigenvalue of maximum modulus and the corresponding eigenvector. This argument suggests that the required condition which ensures that the algorithm depicted by Sraffa does converge on the eigenvalue of maximum modulus and the corresponding eigenvector is that the function $\phi(\mathbf{q})$ does not have a fixed point in S. This is immediately obtained if function $\phi(\mathbf{q})$ has the mentioned inequality properties in the whole S and, therefore, the set of functions to be considered is restricted to

$$Z = Z(S) = \left\{ \phi \,:\, S \to R \,\middle|\, \forall \mathbf{q} \in S \,:\, \phi(\mathbf{q}) \geq 0, \, \lambda(\mathbf{q})\phi(\mathbf{q}) - \mathbf{A}^T \phi(\mathbf{q}) > \mathbf{0}, \, \mathbf{1}^T \phi(\mathbf{q}) = 1 \right\} \tag{4}$$

In the following section I will show that any algorithm defined by a continuous function in set (4) converges to the eigenvalue of maximum modulus and corresponding eigenvector.

The proof

In providing this proof we cannot use the Perron-Frobenius Theorem, since the proof itself can be considered an alternative proof of this theorem. Nonetheless we need a number of statements which are connected with the Perron-Frobenius Theorem. For this reason I first give three lemmas. I will use the proofs provided by Kurz and Salvadori (1995, Mathematical Appendix) or a modified version of them when obliged by the different framework.

Lemma 1. Let **A** be a nonnegative square matrix. If there is a real number μ and a vector **x** such that $\mathbf{x} \geq 0$, $\mathbf{x} \not> 0$, and $\mu\mathbf{x}^T \geq \mathbf{x}^T\mathbf{A}$, then matrix **A** is reducible.

Proof. See Kurz and Salvadori (1995, p. 516, Lemma A.3.7).   □

Lemma 2. Let **A** be an irreducible nonnegative square matrix and let **q** be a nonnegative vector such that $\mathbf{q}^T(\lambda I - \mathbf{A}) \geq 0$ for a given scalar λ, then

(i) $\mathbf{v}^T(\lambda I - \mathbf{A}) \geq 0^T \Rightarrow \mathbf{v} \geq 0$;
(ii) matrix $(\lambda I - \mathbf{A})$ is invertible and its inverse is positive.

Proof. Because of Lemma 1, $\mathbf{q} > 0$. Then, assume that statement (i) does not hold, i.e., that there is a vector $\mathbf{v} \not\geq 0$ such that $\mathbf{v}^T(\lambda I - \mathbf{A}) \geq 0^T$ and let h be such that

$$0 > \frac{\mathbf{v}^T e_h}{\mathbf{q}^T e_h} \leq \frac{\mathbf{v}^T e_i}{\mathbf{q}^T e_i} \quad \text{each } i$$

then

$$\mathbf{w} := \left[\mathbf{v} - \frac{\mathbf{v}^T e_h}{\mathbf{q}^T e_h}\mathbf{q}\right] \geq 0$$

and

$$\mathbf{w}^T(\lambda I - \mathbf{A}) \geq 0^T$$

Hence contradiction: Lemma 1 implies that vector **w** is positive, whereas its h-th element equals zero. This proves statement (i). If **v** is a solution to the equation

$$\mathbf{x}^T(\lambda I - \mathbf{A}) = 0^T \tag{5}$$

then also $-\mathbf{v}$ is a solution, and, by statement (i), both **v** and $-\mathbf{v}$ are non-negative. Therefore $\mathbf{v} = 0$ and equation (5) has no nontrivial solution. Hence matrix $(\lambda \mathbf{I} - \mathbf{A})$ is invertible. Finally, each row of such inverse is nonnegative as a consequence of statement (i) and it is actually positive as a consequence of Lemma 1 and of the fact that a row of an inverse matrix cannot be nought.   □

Lemma 3. Let $\mathbf{A}$ be an irreducible nonnegative $n \times n$ matrix. Then

$$\mathbf{I} + \mathbf{A} + \mathbf{A}^2 + \ldots + \mathbf{A}^{n-1} > \mathbf{0}.$$

Proof. See Kurz and Salvadori (1995, pp. 518–19, Theorem A.3.8).   □
We can now introduce sets (1), (2), (3), and (4). In order to show that set (4) is not empty, we provide here three examples. Example 1 is the mentioned special function used by Kurz and Salvadori (2001). Example 3 is the mentioned special function used by Lippi (2008).

Example 1. $\phi(\mathbf{q}) = \left[\dfrac{\beta}{\mathbf{q}^T \left[\mathbf{I} - \mathbf{A} \right]^{-1} \mathbf{1}} \mathbf{q}^T \left[\mathbf{I} - \mathbf{A} \right]^{-1} \right]^T$

Example 2. $\phi(\mathbf{q}) = \left[\dfrac{\beta}{\mathbf{q}^T \left[\mathbf{I} + \mathbf{A} + \mathbf{A}^2 + \ldots + \mathbf{A}^{n-1} \right] \mathbf{1}} \mathbf{q}^T \left[\mathbf{I} + \mathbf{A} + \mathbf{A}^2 + \ldots + \mathbf{A}^{n-1} \right] \right]^T$

Example 3. $\phi(\mathbf{q}) = \left[\dfrac{\beta}{\mathbf{b}^T \left[\lambda(\mathbf{q})\mathbf{I} - \mathbf{A} \right]^{-1} \mathbf{1}} \mathbf{b}^T \left[\lambda(\mathbf{q})\mathbf{I} - \mathbf{A} \right]^{-1} \right]^T$ where $\mathbf{b}$ is a

given positive vector.
Lemma 3 is all we need in order to show that in the third example $\phi(\mathbf{q})$ is defined in R and that $\lambda(\mathbf{q})\phi(\mathbf{q}) - \mathbf{A}^T \phi(\mathbf{q}) > \mathbf{0}$ in S. Similarly, Lemma 2(ii) and the equality $\left[\mathbf{I} - \mathbf{A} \right]^{-1} \mathbf{A} = \mathbf{A} \left[\mathbf{I} - \mathbf{A} \right]^{-1}$ is all we need in order to prove the same in the first example. Lemma 2(ii) is all we need in order to show that in the second example $\phi(\mathbf{q})$ is defined in S and that $\lambda(\mathbf{q})\phi(\mathbf{q}) - \mathbf{A}^T \phi(\mathbf{q}) > \mathbf{0}$ there. The functions of all the examples are continuous in S.
   It is immediately recognized that set (1) is closed and bounded and that set (3) is bounded but it is closed if and only if set (2) is either empty or not enclosed in set (1). We want to prove that set (2) consists of one element and this element is positive and is in set (1). Let us first prove that if R * is not empty, then it consists of one element and this element is positive. Then we will prove that the set S is not closed and therefore R * is not empty and its unique element is in R.

Lemma 4. If $R^* \neq \varnothing$ then $R^* = \{\mathbf{q}^*\}$ and $\mathbf{q}^* > \mathbf{0}$.

Proof. Let $\lambda_1, \lambda_2, \mathbf{q}_1, \mathbf{q}_2$ be such that

$$\mathbf{q}_1 \geq \mathbf{0}, \quad \mathbf{q}_1^T \mathbf{1} = \beta, \quad \mathbf{q}_1^T \left(\lambda_1 \mathbf{I} - \mathbf{A} \right) = \mathbf{0}^T$$

$$\mathbf{q}_2 \geq \mathbf{0},\ \mathbf{q}_2^T \mathbf{1} = \beta,\ \mathbf{q}_2^T\left(\lambda_2\mathbf{I}-\mathbf{A}\right)=\mathbf{0}^T$$

Then $\mathbf{q}_1 > \mathbf{0}$ because of Lemma 1. Let us first assume that $\lambda_1 < \lambda_2$. Then $\mathbf{q}_1^T\left[\lambda_2\mathbf{I}-\mathbf{A}\right]=\left(\lambda_2-\lambda_1\right)\mathbf{q}_1^T > \mathbf{0}^T$ and matrix $\left(\lambda_2\mathbf{I}-\mathbf{A}\right)$ is invertible because of Lemma 2(ii). Hence a contradiction and $\lambda_1 = \lambda_2$. Let φ be a scalar such that vector $\mathbf{q}_1 - \varphi\mathbf{q}_2$ is nonnegative with at least one zero element. If $\mathbf{q}_1 - \varphi\mathbf{q}_2$ is semipositive, it is positive because of Lemma 1, since $\left(\mathbf{q}_1 - \varphi\mathbf{q}_2\right)^T\left(\lambda_1\mathbf{I}-\mathbf{A}\right)=\mathbf{0}^T$. Hence $\mathbf{q}_1 - \varphi\mathbf{q}_2 = \mathbf{0}$. Thus $\mathbf{q}_1 = \mathbf{q}_2$ since $\mathbf{q}_1^T\mathbf{1} = \beta = \mathbf{q}_2^T\mathbf{1}$.   □

Let us now define the sequence $\{\mathbf{q}_i\}$ such that $\mathbf{q}_0 \in S$ and

$$\mathbf{q}_{t+1} = \begin{cases} \mathbf{q}_t & \text{if } \lambda\left(\mathbf{q}_t\right)\mathbf{q}_t - \mathbf{A}^T\mathbf{q}_t = 0 \\ \phi\left(\mathbf{q}_t\right) & \text{if } \lambda\left(\mathbf{q}_t\right)\mathbf{q}_t - \mathbf{A}^T\mathbf{q}_t \neq 0 \end{cases}$$

Obviously, for each $\phi(\mathbf{q}) \in Z$ and for each vector $\mathbf{q}_0 \in S$ we have a different sequence.

Theorem 1. $R^* \neq \varnothing$ and for each sequence defined by a pair $\left(\phi(\mathbf{q}),\mathbf{q}_0\right)$ such that the function $\phi : S \to R$ is in Z and is continuous in S

$$\lim_{i\to\infty}\mathbf{q}_i = \mathbf{q}^*$$

Proof. Since $\lambda\left(\phi(\mathbf{q})\right) < \lambda(\mathbf{q})$ the sequence $\{\lambda(\mathbf{q}_i)\}$ is decreasing and since it is bounded from below it is convergent. Let $\bar{\lambda} = \lim_{i\to\infty}\lambda(\mathbf{q}_i)$. Since the set S is bounded, we can extract a convergent (sub)sequence $\{\mathbf{q}_{s_i}\}$ from sequence $\{\mathbf{q}_i\}$. Let $\bar{\mathbf{q}} = \lim_{i\to\infty}\mathbf{q}_{s_i}$. If $\bar{\mathbf{q}} \in S$, then $\lambda\left(\phi(\bar{\mathbf{q}})\right) < \lambda(\bar{\mathbf{q}}) = \bar{\lambda}$. However, since functions $\phi : S \to R$ and $\lambda : S \to \Re$ are continuous in S and since every sequence extracted from a convergent sequence converges to the same limit:

$$\lambda\left(\phi(\bar{\mathbf{q}})\right) = \lambda\left(\phi\left(\lim_{i\to\infty}\mathbf{q}_{s_i}\right)\right) = \lim_{i\to\infty}\lambda\left(\phi\left(\mathbf{q}_{s_i}\right)\right) = \lim_{i\to\infty}\lambda\left(\mathbf{q}_{s_i+1}\right) = \lim_{i\to\infty}\lambda\left(\mathbf{q}_i\right) = \bar{\lambda}$$

Hence a contradiction and $\bar{\mathbf{q}} \notin S$. Then $\bar{\mathbf{q}}$ is in the boundary of S but not in S. Hence S is not closed, $R^* = \{\mathbf{q}^*\}$, $\mathbf{q}^* \in R$, and $\bar{\mathbf{q}} = \mathbf{q}^*$. All the convergent sequences extracted from sequence $\{\mathbf{q}_i\}$ converge to the same vector $\mathbf{q}^*$. Then also the sequence $\{\mathbf{q}_i\}$ is convergent and $\lim_{i\to\infty}\mathbf{q}_i = \mathbf{q}^*$. Finally we get that

$$\bar{\lambda} = \lambda(\mathbf{q}^*) = \rho.$$ □

An example

Let

$$
\mathbf{A} = \begin{bmatrix} 0 & h \\ k & 0 \end{bmatrix}, \quad \mathbf{1} = \begin{bmatrix} \frac{1}{2} \\ \frac{1}{2} \end{bmatrix}, \beta = 1 \quad 0 < h < k < 1
$$

It is easily calculated that the eigenvalue of maximum modulus of matrix $\mathbf{A}$ is $\sqrt{hk}$ and that the left eigenvector associated with this eigenvalue normalized as above is

$$
\begin{bmatrix} \dfrac{2\left(k - \sqrt{hk}\right)}{k - h} & \dfrac{2\left(\sqrt{hk} - h\right)}{k - h} \end{bmatrix}
$$

It is easily recognized that

$$
R = \left\{ \mathbf{q} \in \Re^2 \;\middle|\; \frac{2k}{1+k} \le q_1 \le \frac{2}{1+h}, \; q_2 = 2 - q_1 \right\}
$$

Finally, let us consider the function

$$
\phi(\mathbf{q}) = \begin{bmatrix} \dfrac{1}{1 - 2\varepsilon} \end{bmatrix} + \varepsilon \mathbf{q} \tag{6}
$$

with

$$
0 < \varepsilon < \frac{1}{2} - \frac{1}{2}\sqrt{\frac{h}{k}} \tag{7}
$$

From inequalities (7) we obtain the inequality

$$
\frac{1}{1 - \varepsilon} < \frac{2\left(k - \sqrt{hk}\right)}{k - h}
$$

from which we obtain[3] that $\lambda(\mathbf{q})\phi(\mathbf{q}) - \mathbf{A}^T \phi(\mathbf{q}) > 0$ for each $\mathbf{q} \in S_1$, whereas this property does not hold for $\mathbf{q} \in S_2$, where

$$
S_1 = \left\{ \mathbf{q} \in S \;\middle|\; q_1 < \frac{1}{1 - \varepsilon} \right\}
$$

$$S_2 = \left\{ q \in S \;\middle|\; \frac{1}{1-\varepsilon} \le q_1 < \frac{2\left(k - \sqrt{hk}\right)}{k-h} \right\}$$

Further, it is easily verified that $q \in S_1 \Rightarrow \phi(q) \in S_1$. Therefore each element of any sequence defined by the conditions

$$q_0 \in S_1, q_{t+1} = \begin{cases} q_t & \text{if } \lambda(q_t)q_t - A^T q_t = 0 \\ \phi(q_t) & \text{if } \lambda(q_t)q_t - A^T q_t \neq 0 \end{cases}$$

satisfies the conditions stated by Sraffa, but

$$\lim_{i \to \infty} \lambda(q_i) = (1 - 2\varepsilon)k > \sqrt{hk}$$

$$\lim_{i \to \infty} q_i = \begin{bmatrix} \dfrac{1}{1-\varepsilon} \\ \dfrac{1-2\varepsilon}{1-\varepsilon} \end{bmatrix} \neq \begin{bmatrix} \dfrac{2\left(k - \sqrt{hk}\right)}{k-h} \\ \dfrac{2\left(\sqrt{hk} - h\right)}{k-h} \end{bmatrix}$$

The last limit is the unique fixed point of function (6).

Conclusion

In this chapter I have investigated what are the properties that the algorithm mentioned in section 37 of Sraffa's (1960) book needs to have in order to obtain a complete proof.

Acknowledgments

I would like to thank Marco Lippi for useful discussions during the Conference and in the following months and Heinz Kurz for his valuable comments on previous versions of the chapter.

References

Kurz, H. D. and Salvadori, N. *Theory of Production. A Long Period Analysis*, (Cambridge: Cambridge University Press, 1995).
Kurz, H. D. and Salvadori, N. Sraffa and the Mathematicians: Frank Ramsey and Alister Watson, in T. Cozzi and R. Marchionatti (eds.), *Piero Sraffa's Political Economy. A Centenary Estimate*, (London and New York: Routledge, 2001) 254–84.

Lippi, M. Some Observations on Sraffa and Mathematical Proofs, in G. Chiodi and L. Ditta (eds.), *Sraffa or an Alternative Economics*, (New York: Palgrave Macmillan, 2008) 243–52.

Sraffa, P. *Production of Commodities by Means of Commodities*, (Cambridge: Cambridge University Press, 1960).

Notes

1 The reader of Sraffa's Preface will probably recall that after thanking A. S. Besicovitch, Frank Ramsey, and Alister Watson "for invaluable mathematical help," Sraffa added:

> It will be only too obvious that I have not always followed the expert advice that was given to me – particularly with regard to the notation adopted, which I have insisted on retaining (although admittedly open to objection in some respects) as being easy to follow for the non-mathematical reader.

Sraffa, it might be conjectured, would in all probability have had no qualms with some of Lippi's remarks and simply stressed his concern with the non-mathematical reader.

2 From a mathematical point of view, the condition $\mathbf{x}^T [\mathbf{I} - \mathbf{A}]^{-1} \geq \mathbf{0}^T$ is not required, but Sraffa was actually interested in matrices $\mathbf{A}$ such that $\rho < 1$, and I will follow him in this respect.

3 If $q_1 \leq 2\left(k - \sqrt{hk}\right)(k - h)^{-1}$, then $\lambda(\mathbf{q}) = k(2 - q_1)q_1^{-1}$. Further $\lambda(\mathbf{q})\mathbf{e}_1^T \phi(\mathbf{q}) - \mathbf{e}_1^T \mathbf{A}^T \phi(\mathbf{q}) > 0$ if and only if $q_1 < (1 - \varepsilon)^{-1}$ where as $\lambda(\mathbf{q})\mathbf{e}_2^T \phi(\mathbf{q}) - \mathbf{e}_2^T \mathbf{A}^T \phi(\mathbf{q}) > 0$ for $q_1 \leq 2\left(k - \sqrt{hk}\right)(k - h)^{-1}$, provided that inequalities (7) hold.

7 Keynes, Sraffa, and the latter's "secret skepticism"*

Heinz D. Kurz

Introduction

The relationship between Keynes and Sraffa was very close in some respects and quite the converse in other respects. Keynes was deeply impressed by Sraffa's breadth and depth of knowledge, his sharpness and intellectual brilliance, and he found his younger Italian colleague a truly likeable person. There are numerous documents that express vividly their close personal relationship, which grew into friendship (see Ranchetti 2005). Without Keynes's continuous support up until his premature death in 1946, it is difficult to imagine how Sraffa would have fared in an environment like Cambridge, given the peculiarities of his character, his meticulosity, and even his pedantry. Thanks to Keynes, Sraffa could pursue his work without much interference. Keynes, it seems, had full trust in Sraffa's intellectual capabilities and made no serious effort to direct his research. He allowed Sraffa to follow his course and develop his truly novel ideas, which were eventually born into an environment that was not prepared for them and had difficulties absorbing them. Sraffa was and remained a loner amongst the economics profession in Cambridge. Highly respected and even feared by his colleagues, he was hardly ever fully understood (see Marcuzzo 2002; Ranchetti 2002). Sraffa knew how much his critical and constructive work contradicted the received wisdom in Cambridge and elsewhere. Apart from some early attempts at communication, he was reluctant to let his colleagues know what precisely his work was all about, which difficulties he had encountered, which results he had got, and when. Sraffa kept his cards very much to himself and typically disclosed them only in the moment in which he was absolutely sure that what he had to offer was both new and sound. Unlike Keynes, he was horrified by the vision of circulating half-baked ideas and leaving it to others to straighten them out. It is telling that apart from Maurice Dobb, Sraffa discussed his work typically

* Reproduced with permission from B. Bateman, T. Hirai, and M.C. Marcuzzo (eds.), *The Return to Keynes*, Cambridge (MA) and London: The Belknap Press of Harvard University Press, 2010.

only with mathematicians: in the late 1920s with Frank Ramsey and in the 1940s and 1950s with Abram S. Besicovitch and Alister Watson.[1]

Sraffa was well aware of how much he owed to Keynes's steadfast support and throughout his life was loyal to the man who had brought him to Cambridge and who looked after him so well. However, there is every reason to believe that the two minds hardly ever fully met when it came to economic theory (see Ranchetti 2005). The two scholars had high esteem and respect for one another, but they followed different lines of thought. They were both engaged in a project destined to provide an alternative to contemporary mainstream economics, but they did not directly join forces in this regard. They approached the project from different points of view, and they reached different conclusions as to how to best challenge a doctrine they considered problematic, if not outright wrong.

Since apart from a few instances, on which more below, Sraffa never wrote down in a comprehensive way how he viewed Keynes's achievements as an economic theorist and what he thought in particular of the *General Theory*, we can only indirectly infer from Sraffa's writings, published and unpublished, his assessment of Keynes's work. While Keynes was critical of several of Marshall's views, his thinking was nevertheless to a considerable extent "Marshallian" and remained so. At the same time, he considered Say's law to be the characteristic feature of classical economics and a main obstacle to an understanding of persistent unemployment and depressive tendencies in the economy. Sraffa, in contrast, had convinced himself that the Marshallian symmetrical theory of value and distribution could not be sustained and that the old classical approach to the theory of value was the right starting point of a probing into the laws of production and distribution. The two scholars therefore were at cross-purposes right from the beginning of their encounter and cooperative relationship, despite the fact that both shared a critical orientation toward orthodox economics. We might perhaps say that in Sraffa's view Keynes never managed to free himself fully from the straightjacket of marginalist economics: Keynes's new doctrine of effective demand, while containing some radically new elements, was thwarted by the remnants of the old theory in it (see Garegnani 1978, 1979). This theory sees a tendency toward full employment, brought about by the "forces" of demand and supply in the various markets, including the "labor market." Because of these remnants of orthodoxy, Keynes's partly revolutionary intellectual message could be tamed and his construction reabsorbed, or so it seemed, into the mainstream, which turned out to be highly elastic with regard to new ideas that at first sight look incompatible with it, namely, the so-called Neoclassical Synthesis.

Sraffa had concluded his rejoinder to D. H. Robertson in the 1930 *Economic Journal* symposium on "Increasing Returns and the Representative Firm" with the following words:

We seem to be agreed *that the* [Marshallian] *theory cannot be interpreted in a way which makes it logically self-consistent and, at the same time, reconciles it with the facts it sets out to explain.* Mr. Robertson's remedy is to discard mathematics, and he suggests that my remedy is to discard the facts; perhaps I ought to have explained that, in the circumstances, I think it is Marshall's theory that should be discarded.

(Sraffa 1930, p. 93; emphasis added)

Sraffa's wish did not come true. Keynes and with him most Cambridge economists clung to Marshallian concepts, making use, in particular, of the Marshallian demand-and-supply apparatus. Seen from Sraffa's point of view, this meant that their analyses were flawed. A careful scrutiny would invariably bring the flaws into the open. As regards Keynes's contributions, Sraffa's criticism concerned especially the following:

1. The idea expressed in the *Treatise* that the price level of consumption goods and that of investment goods can be considered as determined independently of one another, and the related idea that the price level of the latter is determined exclusively by the propensity of the public to "hoard" money.
2. The "marginal efficiency of capital" schedule in the *General Theory*, which carried over the concept of a given order of fertility of different qualities of land to the ordering of investment projects.
3. The view that the banking system can control the money supply and that therefore the quantity of money in the system can be considered exogenous.
4. The argument put forward by Keynes to substantiate his view that the liquidity preference of the public prevents the money rate of interest from falling to a level compatible with a volume of investment equal to full employment savings.

While some elements of Sraffa's criticism derived directly from his involvement in discussions of the "Circus," other elements derived from his parallel critical work on the foundations of the received marginalist theory of value and distribution and his endeavor to elaborate an alternative to it.

In this chapter, I deal with the four problems mentioned. In order to better understand Sraffa's objections, we repeatedly have to summarize findings in his parallel work to the extent to which they are pertinent to the issues at hand. It deserves to be mentioned already at this point that while Sraffa was critical of several of Keynes's ideas and concepts, his objections were not meant to undermine Keynes's critical project as such. They were instead destined to knock out elements that could not be sustained and thus eliminate weaknesses of the analysis.

The composition of this chapter is as follows: the second section deals with Sraffa's explicit criticism of Keynes's analysis around his so-called Fundamental Equations in the *Treatise*. While this theme is in itself of little importance, not least because Keynes himself later recanted his respective views, it allows us to introduce some of Sraffa's early theoretical findings, which form the background of his objections also to later ideas of Keynes. The third section turns to Keynes's view that investment projects can be ordered independently of the level of the rate of interest according to their marginal efficiencies of capital. This idea is but another expression of what Sraffa dubbed the "monotonic prejudice" that permeates much of marginalist analysis and which can be sustained only in exceptionally special cases. A truly "general theory," which Keynes aspired to elaborate, had to dispense with this "prejudice." In the fourth section, I turn to Sraffa's critical account of Friedrich August Hayek's monetary overinvestment theory of the business cycle. In it, Sraffa used the concept of "commodity rate of interest," which Keynes then picked up in the *General Theory* in an attempt to counter Hayek's objection that the *Treatise* lacked a proper capital theoretic foundation. The subsequent section addresses Sraffa's criticism of Keynes's liquidity preference theory contained in his annotations in his personal copy of the *General Theory* and two manuscript fragments that Sraffa appears to have composed shortly after the book had been published, but which he apparently had never shown to anybody. The final section then draws some conclusions.

Determination of price levels in the *Treatise*

Using a famous formulation of Keynes, we may say that in the late 1920s and early 1930s both Keynes and Sraffa were involved in a "struggle of escape from habitual modes of thought and expression" (CWK 7, p. xxiii). While Keynes focused on the problem of money and output as a whole, Sraffa focused on the problem of value and distribution.

Sraffa had put forward his criticism of Marshall's partial equilibrium theory in two essays published in the mid-1920s (Sraffa 1925, 1926), which had impressed the scientific community.[2] Yet, as regards an alternative construction, the two papers contain little, except for a few hints in which direction to search. It was in the winter of 1927–1928 that Sraffa experienced a breakthrough in terms of his "systems of equations," which foreshadow his later work (Sraffa 1960, chaps. 1 and 2). Keynes, meanwhile, was working in broadly the same period on "a novel means of approach to the fundamental problems of monetary theory," as he wrote in his preface to the *Treatise* with reference to books III and IV of the work (CWK 5, p. xvii). He was not happy with the outcome and called it "a collection of material rather than a finished work" (CWK 5, p. xviii). The reason was that "The ideas with which I have finished up are widely different from those with which I began … There are many skins which I have sloughed still littering the pages … I feel like someone who has been forcing his way through a confused jungle" (CWK 5, p. xvii).

The original novelty of the *Treatise* was the "Fundamental Equations" for the value of money in book III. They were designed to tackle

> The real task of such a [monetary] theory [which] is to treat the problem
> dynamically, analysing the different elements involved, in such a manner
> as to exhibit the causal process by which the price level is determined, and
> the method of transition from one position of equilibrium to another.
>
> (CWK 5, p. 120)

The quantity theory of money in its various forms, Keynes insisted, was ill
adapted for this purpose. He then proposed to break away from the conventional method of starting from a given quantity of money irrespective of the
uses to which it is put. Instead he started from the flow of aggregate earnings
or money income and "its twofold division (1) into the parts which have been
earned by the production of consumption goods and of investment goods
respectively, and (2) into the parts which are *expended on* consumption goods
and on savings respectively" (CWK 5, p. 121; Keynes's emphasis). He maintained that if the two divisions (1) and (2) are in the same proportions, then
the price level of consumption goods will equal their respective costs of production. If not, price level and costs will differ from one another, giving rise
to (extra, or windfall) profits or losses in the consumption sector.

The price level of consumption goods is said to be "solely determined by
the disposition of the public towards 'saving'" and "*entirely independent of the
price level of investment goods*" (CWK 5, pp. 129 and 123; emphasis added).
The latter is said to depend on the public's choice between "bank deposits"
and "securities." This is motivated in terms of the observation that the decision to hold the one or the other relates "not only to the current increment to
the wealth of individuals, but also to the whole block of their existing capital"
(CWK 5, p. 127). And while in a footnote on the same page Keynes tells the
reader that in the present context he uses the term "investing" not in the sense
of "the purchase of securities" but in the sense of "the act of the entrepreneur
when he makes an addition to the capital of the community," he nevertheless
identifies the price level of newly produced investment goods with the price
level of securities. He concludes that the "actual price level of investments is
the resultant of the sentiment of the public [i.e., whether it is 'bearish' or 'bull-
ish'] and the behaviour of the banking system," or "by the disposition of the
public towards hoarding money" (CWK 5, pp. 128 and 129–130).

In the period from January 1930 to 1932, Sraffa exchanged a couple of notes
with Keynes in which he raised objections to which Keynes then answered.[3]
Sraffa's objections concerned inter alia the propositions just mentioned,[4] and,
at a deeper level, Keynes's view of the determinants of profits. Sraffa disputed
Keynes's confounding of securities and fixed capital items "under the ambiguous name of 'new investment goods'" (Sraffa's Papers D1/71).[5] This was misleading: in the short run, the (market) prices of new machines depend on the
demand of firms that are intent upon expanding (or reducing) their productive
capacity, and the prices of securities depend on the demand of investors in
financial markets; whereas in the long period, the prices of machines are regulated by their costs of production (inclusive of profits at a normal rate) and

those of securities by the rate of interest. It is misleading to identify the price level of newly produced capital goods with that of securities. If in the short run savings exceed investment, then this will have only a small effect on the prices of consumer goods, but it will have a large effect on the price of securities: "in reality the price of [consumer goods] is as sticky as the price of securities is fluid; it would be hard to find two more typical instances of an imperfect, and of a perfect, market" (Sraffa's Papers Dl/71). Keynes was wrong in assuming that the effect of a fall in consumption demand would be an immediate and proportional fall in price, whereas an increased demand for securities would not appreciably raise their price.[6] Keynes also overlooked the fact that a rise in the price of securities is a source of profits (equal to premiums) that would compensate firms for any losses due to a fall in consumption prices.

Contrary to Keynes's view, the price levels relating to industries producing investment and consumption goods were not independent of one another. Sraffa's respective objection has at its background the analysis of systems of equations of production he had started to elaborate from November 1927 until 1930 when he had to focus all his energy on preparing the edition of David Ricardo's works and correspondence on behalf of the Royal Economic Society.[7] In a system characterized by a circular flow of commodities, Keynes's distinction lacks precision, because one and the same type of commodity may be used both as an investment and as a consumption good. How can the price of such a commodity be determined in two radically different and independent ways?

More important, the two kinds of industries are typically intimately intertwined. In his papers of the 1920s, Sraffa had not taken into account the fact that in modern industrial systems, commodities are produced by means of commodities. He had defended this neglect by pointing out that "the conditions of simultaneous equilibrium in numerous industries" are far too complex and that "the present state of our knowledge ... does not permit of even much simpler schema being applied to the study of real conditions" (Sraffa 1926, p. 541). "The process of diffusion of profits throughout the various stages of production and of the process of forming a normal level of profits throughout all the industries of a country," he had then surmised, was "beyond the scope of this article" (Sraffa 1926, p. 550). It was precisely this problem that Sraffa began to tackle after he had moved to Cambridge in 1927 (see Kurz and Salvadori 2005; Kurz 2006). By the time he was confronted with Keynes's "Fundamental Equations," which dealt with a closely related problem, he had already established a number of important results.

In a simple numerical example of 1928, there are two industries, the first producing an investment and the second a consumption good. Sraffa tabulated production as follows:

$$17v = (6v + 10)r$$

$$23 = (5v + 4)r$$

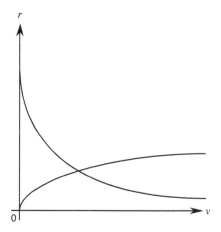

Figure 7.1 Simultaneous determination of interest rate and relative price

Here, 17 (23) units of the first (second) commodity are produced by means of 6 (5) units of the first and 10 (4) units of the second commodity; v is the value of one unit of the capital good in terms of the means of subsistence, and r is the interest factor ($= 1 +$ interest rate). Sraffa calculated r (≈ 1.582) and v (≈ 2.108), represented graphically the relationships between v and r given by the two equations, and identified the solution of the system as the intersection of the two curves (see Figure 7.1).

Next Sraffa turned to a problem that had bothered economists since the early years of the discipline and that bothered also Keynes: how does the rate of return on capital change consequent upon a change in real wages caused, e.g., by a change in the price of the consumption good, given money wages and given the system of production in use? Answering this question implied disclosing the mathematical properties of a given system of production as regards the distributional alternatives it allows for and the corresponding price vectors supporting these alternatives. Sraffa stressed that it is "as clear as sunlight" that a change in income distribution generally affects the price of the intermediate product relative to the consumption good, and that with a fall in real wages the general rate of return on capital would increase (see, for example, Sraffa's Papers D3/12/7, p. 95). In terms of Figure 7.1, a change in the real wage rate would involve a shift of the two curves and with them a shift of their point of intersection.

Against this background, it should come as no surprise that Sraffa objected to Keynes that "the price of investment goods is determined *in the same way* as that of consumption goods, and a change in the demand for either may give rise (or fail to give rise) to profits or losses" (Sraffa's Papers Dl/72/3; emphasis added). Keynes understood that his position could not be sustained and abandoned the idea.

Before we continue, it should be stressed that in terms of his systems of equations, Sraffa had established that the rate of return and relative prices generally depend on two sets of data: (a) the system of production in use, that is, the methods of production actually employed to produce given levels of output, and thus on physical real costs; and (b) the wages share.

We now turn to Keynes's view of the inducement to investment in chapter 11 of the *General Theory*. There Keynes puts forward his concept of the "marginal efficiency of capital." Could this concept be sustained vis-à-vis Sraffa's theoretical findings?

The "marginal efficiency of capital" schedule

Keynes essentially adopted the internal rate of return method when dealing with investment projects from which a manufacturer may choose:

> I define the marginal efficiency of capital as being equal to that rate of discount which would make the present value of the series of annuities given by the returns expected from the capital-asset during its life just equal to its supply price.
>
> (CWK 7, p. 135)

(This method has serious shortcomings, which, however, need not concern us here.) Keynes goes on to argue that the various projects may be ordered according to their marginal efficiencies and then suggests to aggregate them, "so as to provide a schedule relating the rate of aggregate investment to the corresponding marginal efficiency of capital in general which that rate of investment will establish" (CWK 7, p. 136). This he calls the "investment demand schedule," which he confronts with the current rate of interest. He concludes: "the rate of investment will be pushed to the point on the investment demand-schedule where the marginal efficiency of capital in general is equal to the market rate of return" (CWK 7, pp. 136–137).

Keynes rests his argument on the dubious partial equilibrium method: he assumes that the schedule and the money rate of interest are independent of one another. Yet, if one was to depend on the other, or if they were interdependent, the argument in its present form would break down. Several commentators, including Pasinetti (1974), have emphasized that Keynes's argument consists of an adaptation of the classical doctrine of extensive diminishing returns to the theory of investment. This doctrine (see, e.g., Kurz 1978) typically assumes that the different qualities of land can be brought into an *order of fertility*, with the first quality exhibiting the lowest unit costs of production of, say, corn; the second quality, the second lowest unit costs; and so on. In competitive conditions, with a rise in "effectual demand" (Adam Smith), the different qualities of land will be taken into cultivation according to this order. The different qualities of land can also be ranked according to the rent they yield per acre; this ranking is known as the *order of rentability*. It has commonly been assumed that both orders are independent of income distribution and that they coincide.

In the late 1920s, Sraffa showed that this is true only in exceedingly special cases. In general, both orders depend on the rate of interest and do not coincide (see also Kurz and Salvadori 1995, chap. 10). Sraffa established this result in the course of an analysis of the problem of the choice of technique of cost-minimizing (profit-maximizing) producers. He first studied the problem of which qualities of land from a set of alternatives will be cultivated in order to match effectual demand. In around mid-1929, he demonstrated that the order of fertility depends on the rate of interest. Hence, different qualities of land cannot generally be ordered monotonically with respect to that rate: with a change in it, the order will typically change as well.[8] The reason for this is that different methods of production employed in cultivating different qualities of land typically use different capital goods, or the same capital goods in different proportions, relative to labor. Since relative prices of (capital) goods will generally change with a change in the rate of interest, relative costs of production and thus the cheapness of methods will also change. A particular quality of land that at one level of the rate of interest is cost-minimizing at a higher (lower) level may be dominated by another quality of land. It may even "come back" at a still higher (lower) level. A similar result Sraffa then established with respect to a pure capital goods model, focusing attention both on circulating and fixed capital.[9]

Sraffa's findings have a direct bearing on Keynes's investment demand schedule and his closely related view as regards the long-period relationship between the overall capital-labor ratio and the rate of return on capital. Both as regards the short and the long period, Keynes had fallen victim to the "monotonic prejudice" (see Gehrke and Kurz 2006). As regards the former, with a change in the rate of interest it cannot be presumed that the ranking of investment projects will remain the same, because both expected gross revenues and costs will generally be affected by the change. The ranking of investment projects in a descending order of marginal efficiency is thus no less dependent on the rate of interest than the ranking of different qualities of land in terms of "fertility." As regards the long period, there is no presumption that an increase in the capital-labor ratio is invariably accompanied by a decrease in the marginal efficiency of capital in general, as Keynes contended (see, e.g., CWK 7, p. 136).[10]

Sraffa's findings are indisputable. As Mas-Colell (1989) stressed, the relationship between the capital-labor ratio and the rate of return on capital can have almost any shape whatsoever. This implies that the "demand function" for capital in terms of the rate of interest need not be downward sloping in the perhaps only point in which it cuts the given "supply function" of capital (which we may, for simplicity, take to be a straight vertical line). The resulting equilibrium, while unique, would be unstable. We may ask with Marshall, what is the explanatory power of such an equilibrium?

We now turn to Sraffa's assessment of Keynes's liquidity preference theory. In order to get a better grasp of it, we must, for the reasons given earlier, first deal briefly with Sraffa's criticism of Hayek's "Austrian" theory of the business cycle (see Kurz 2000; see also Ranchetti 2002).

Sraffa's criticism of Hayek

In the 1930s, upon the request of Lionel Robbins of the London School of Economics, Friedrich August Hayek assumed the role of a main adversary of Keynes's explanation of unemployment and economic crises in the *Treatise* (Hayek 1931b, 1932b). Hayek advocated instead an explanation of the phenomena that built upon the works of Ludwig von Mises, Eugen von Böhm-Bawerk, and Vilfredo Pareto. When Sraffa was confronted with Hayek's argument, he knew already that its theoretical core – Böhm-Bawerk's theory of capital and interest – was shaky (see Gehrke and Kurz 2006). Therefore, Sraffa must have been amused when, in Hayek's rejoinder to Keynes's reply to his criticism in *Economica*, Hayek maintained that the main weakness of Keynes's argument was its lack of a proper capital theoretic foundation and that Keynes was well advised to adopt Böhm-Bawerk's theory (Hayek 1931a).

Keynes appears to have accepted the criticism but not the proposal, presumably because Sraffa had informed him about the deficiencies of Böhm-Bawerk's capital theory. Was there another option available to make good the lacuna? Keynes appears to have convinced himself that there was indeed such an option and that it revolved around the concept of commodity rate of interest. I am aware of no evidence that Sraffa himself played any role in this. Had he in advance been informed about Keynes's idea, he would in all probability have expressed his reservation. The concept was, of course, already known to Keynes from his work on foreign currency markets and portfolio decisions and his development of the interest rate parity theorem.[11] It had played a role in the *Tract on Monetary Reform* published in 1923 (CWK 4), which Sraffa translated into Italian and published in 1925, and was referred to in the *Treatise*. Last, but not least, it was an indispensable tool in Keynes's, Kahn's, and Sraffa's dealings on the Stock Exchange.[12] However, in the *General Theory*, the concept of commodity rate of interest assumed an entirely new status, elevated to the role of providing a choice- and capital-theoretic foundation of Keynes's theory of investment behavior, both real and financial. Given its uttermost importance in the central chapter 17 of the *General Theory* and Keynes's explicit wish to relate his analysis to Sraffa's, it appears to be appropriate to deal carefully with how Sraffa defined the concept and put it to work in his criticism of Hayek.

Confronted with Hayek's attack, Keynes found himself in an impasse because he was not familiar with the main building blocks of Hayek's argument. Sraffa, who had studied the contributions of Böhm-Bawerk and Pareto, came to Keynes's defense. First, he took issue with Hayek's claim that the possibility of a difference between own rates of interest and thus a divergence of some rates from the "equilibrium" or "natural" rate is a characteristic of a money economy that is absent in a barter economy (1932, p. 49). With reference to Wicksell's definition (Wicksell 1898, pp. 93ff.) that interest is the surplus in real units of the exchange of physically homogeneous goods across time, Sraffa emphasized that

> If money did not exist, and loans were made in terms of all sorts of commodities, there would be a single rate which satisfies the conditions of equilibrium, but there might be at any moment as many "natural" rates of interest as there are commodities, though they would not be "equilibrium" rates. The "arbitrary" action of the banks is by no means a necessary condition for the divergence; if loans were made in wheat and farmers (or for that matter the weather) "arbitrarily changed" the quantity of wheat produced, the actual rate of interest on loans in terms of wheat would diverge from the rate on other commodities and there would be no single equilibrium rate.
>
> (Sraffa 1932, p. 49)

Next Sraffa illustrated his argument in terms of two economies, one with and the other without money. In both economies, loans can be made in terms of all goods for which forward markets exist. Assume that a cotton spinner at time t borrows a sum of money M for θ periods hence in order to buy on the spot market a certain quantity of cotton at price p^t which he at the same time sells on the forward market θ periods later at a price $p^{t+\theta}$. This means that the cotton spinner in fact borrows cotton for θ periods. Sraffa expounds:

> The rate of interest which he pays, per hundred bales of cotton, is the number of bales that can be purchased with the following sum of money: the interest on the money required to buy spot 100 bales, plus the excess (or minus the deficiency) of the spot over the forward prices of the 100 bales.
>
> (Sraffa 1932, p. 50)

If we let $i_{t,\theta}$ be the money rate of interest for θ periods, then we have

$$M = (1+i_{t,\theta})p^t - p^{t+\theta}.$$

The commodity rate of interest of cotton between t and $t+\theta$, $\rho_{t,\theta}$, is then given by the amount of cotton that can be purchased by this sum of money at the given forward price, i.e.,

$$\rho_{t,\theta} = \frac{M}{p^{t+\theta}} = \frac{(1+i_{t+\theta})p^t - p^{t+\theta}}{p^{t+\theta}} = \frac{(1+i_{t+\theta})p^t}{p^{t+\theta}} - 1.$$

Sraffa explained:

> In equilibrium the spot and forward price coincide, for cotton as for any other commodity; and all the "natural" or commodity rates are equal to one another, and to the money rate. But if, for any reason, the supply and the demand for a commodity are not in equilibrium (*i.e.* its market price exceeds or falls short of its cost of production), its spot and forward prices diverge, and the "natural" rate of interest on that commodity diverges from the "natural" rates on other commodities.
>
> (ibid.)

Therefore, out of equilibrium, there is not only one "natural rate," as Hayek had wrongly maintained, but there are many natural rates. Sraffa added that "under free competition, this divergence of rates is as essential to the effecting of the transition [to a new equilibrium] as is the divergence of prices from the costs of production; *it is, in fact, another aspect of the same thing*" (ibid.; emphasis added).

Using classical terminology, what we have here is the well-known problem of the so-called gravitation of "market prices" toward their normal or "natural" levels, where the latter are determined in the way Sraffa had analyzed in his systems of equations (see the second section above). Sraffa illustrated the basic idea underlying this process of gravitation in the following way:

> immediately some [commodities] will rise in price, and others will fall; the market will expect that, after a certain time, the supply of the former will increase, and the supply of the latter fall, and accordingly the forward price, for the date on which equilibrium is expected to be restored, will be below the spot price in the case of the former and above it in the case of the latter; in other words the rate of interest on the former will be higher than on the latter.
>
> (ibid.)

In a long-period position of the economy, and setting aside different degrees of risk, etc., all rates will be equal, and their common level depends, as we have seen, on the physical real costs of production and the given rate of interest.[13]

Keynes was very pleased with Sraffa's performance, not only because it had effectively countered the assault on his intellectual project launched by Lionel Robbins and his circle, but also because it had drawn his attention to a concept upon which Keynes thought he could erect his novel edifice. Most important, perhaps, it allowed him, or so he thought, to drive home the main message of the *General Theory*, that it is the downward rigidity of the money rate of interest that is the source of all the trouble.

As we see from his library and his as-yet unpublished papers, Sraffa did not think highly of Keynes's respective argument. I proceed in two steps. First I summarize Sraffa's annotations in chapter 17 of his working copy of the

General Theory. Then I deal briefly with two short manuscript fragments that were found in his working copy after he had passed away in 1983 (see Kurz 1996; Ranchetti 2002).

Sraffa's criticism of Keynes's liquidity preference theory

Sraffa's annotations in chapter 17

Sraffa scrutinized Keynes's chapter essentially in the same manner he had previously scrutinized Hayek's book, asking whether the concepts used were well defined, whether the argument was developed without contradictions, and whether it mimicked the essential features of the reality it purported to analyze. Since according to Sraffa the theory of liquidity preference "involves *all* the functions considered in the system: it is, in fact, Keynes's system!," the latter stood or fell with it.

Keynes starts the chapter by pointing out "that the *rate of interest on money* [emphasis added] plays a peculiar part in setting a limit to the level of employment." Wherein lies "the peculiarity of money as distinct from other assets" (CWK 7, p. 222)? Keynes defines the money rate of interest à la Wicksell and adds that with regard to all durable goods there is an analogue to the money rate of interest: "Thus for every durable commodity we have a rate of interest in terms of itself, a wheat-rate of interest, a copper-rate of interest, a house-rate of interest" (pp. 222–223). In a footnote he adds: "This relationship was first pointed out by Mr Sraffa, *Economic Journal*, March 1932, p. 50" (p. 223n).

At any given moment of time, these rates will generally not be equal to one another: the ratio between spot and future price will be "notoriously different" between different commodities:

> This, we shall find, will lead us to the clue we are seeking. For it may be that it is the *greatest of* the own-rates of interest ... which rules the roost ...; and that there are reasons why it is the money-rate of interest which is often the greatest (because, as we shall find, certain forces, which operate to reduce the own-rates of interest of other assets, do not operate in the case of money).
>
> (pp. 223–224; Keynes's emphasis)[14]

Why is this so? Surprisingly, Keynes approaches the question by defining the own rates of different commodities not in terms of expected changes of prices but in terms of three characteristics that supposedly can all be translated into interest rate equivalents. These are

1. the "yield or output q ... by assisting some process of production or supplying services to a consumer";
2. the costs of holding the object or "carrying cost c"; and

3. the "liquidity premium" l, expressing the amount, in terms of the object, its proprietor is willing to part company with for the "potential convenience or security" associated with the "power of disposal over an asset during a period" (p. 226).[15]

Keynes concludes:

> It follows that the total return expected from the ownership of an asset over a period is equal to its yield minus its carrying cost plus its liquidity-premium, i.e. to $q - c + l$. That is to say, $q - c + l$ is the own-rate of interest of any commodity, where q, c and l are measured in terms of itself as the standard.
>
> (p. 226)

Sraffa remarks in the margin of this passage: "this contradicts definitions of pp. 222–223."

It is only now that Keynes turns explicitly to the determination of the *expected returns of* different assets. We ought to know, he writes, "what the *changes in relative values* during the year are expected to be" (p. 227; emphasis added). Sraffa comments dryly that this should have been done right at the beginning, when defining the own rates.

Next Keynes assumes that the expected rates of increase (or decrease) of the prices of houses and of wheat, expressed in money, are a_1 and a_2 percent and goes on to say:

> It will also be useful to call $a_1 + q_1$, $a_2 + q_2$ and l_3, which stand for the same quantities reduced to money as the standard of value, the house-rate of money interest, the wheat-rate of money interest and the money-rate of money-interest respectively. With this notation it is easy to see that the demand of wealth-owners will be directed to houses, to wheat or to money, according as $a_1 + q_1$, $a_2 + q_2$ or l_3 is greatest.
>
> (p. 227)

In the margin of this passage, Sraffa puts a big question mark. Indeed, as he had made clear in his criticism of Hayek, the expected changes in prices fully express differences in the "yield" of different assets, as perceived by the market. How could Keynes's summing up over the a's and q's *not* involve double counting?

Sraffa spots immediately that the usual choice of *money as standard of value* has an important implication: "The point is, that in the case of the rate of the article chosen as standard, *the effect upon it of the expected depreciation is concealed*" (emphasis added). This is a crucial point, which Keynes apparently had lost sight of and which had seriously misled him. For example, if an increase in the amount of money happens to lead to a fall in the value of money, then this would imply an increase in the "money-rate of wheat interest," a fact that, unfortunately, Keynes does not take into account. The same objection reappears in several forms.

Next Keynes brings in the marginal efficiency of capital and compares it with the rate of interest. Sraffa comments: "'Marginal efficiency' and 'the' rate of interest are obscure: the former is not defined in this context and the latter has two definitions on p. 227." It is at any rate misleading what Keynes says, because the rate of interest of an object, whose actual price exceeds cost of production, is according to the definition given on pp. 222–223 (relatively) *high*, not low.

Keynes then expounds his view in terms of the three-assets example. Since in equilibrium the own rates, expressed in the same numeraire, must be equal, one gets the following result: with the own rate of money being constant, "it follows that a_1 and a_2 must be rising. In other words, the present money-price of every commodity other than money tends to fall relatively to its expected future price" (p. 228). Sraffa comments that exactly the opposite follows: "this will *lower*, not raise, their rates of interest." Keynes simply got it wrong.

On the following page, Keynes insists that it is "that asset's rate of interest which declines most slowly as the stocks of assets in general increase, which eventually knocks out the profitable production of each of the others" (p. 229). In the margin, Sraffa asks whether here Keynes should have referred to the concept of marginal efficiency of capital.

In the third section of the chapter, Keynes argues that the elasticity of production of money is zero and its elasticity of substitution close to zero or zero. Sraffa is obviously not convinced by this and spots a few more contradictions. Keynes's view that if wages were not relatively rigid, "the position might be worse rather than better" (p. 232), prompts Sraffa to the sarcastic remark: "as usual, heads I win, tails you lose."

However, Sraffa vividly expresses his agreement with Keynes's proposition that "The conception of what contributes to 'liquidity' is a partly vague one" (p. 240) by underlining the sentence and adding exclamation marks in the margin.

Looking at Sraffa's annotations, one cannot escape the impression that in his judgment the chapter was a mess, confused, and confusing. This impression is confirmed by two manuscript fragments to which we now briefly turn (see Sraffa's Papers I 100).

Two manuscript fragments

Sraffa's criticism concerns especially the following elements:

1. The concept of liquidity that Keynes uses is vague and ambiguous.
2. There is no reason to presume that liquidity is always a good thing for each and every agent.
3. Keynes advocates different concepts of commodity rate of interest that are not compatible with one another.

4. Keynes erroneously admits Fisher's effect for all commodities, except money.

With regard to the second element, Sraffa observes that the inverse relationship between holding cash and the rate of interest, i.e., the liquidity preference curve, is reminiscent of the usual *marginal utility curve:* "liquidity is always an advantage, though diminishing." Yet this is not generally true, Sraffa objects. While for some agents it may be the case in a particular situation, for others it may be quite otherwise. Banks, for example, must remain solvent and liquid, but they must also make profits. Since their income consists almost exclusively of interest, they must, with a lower rate of interest, get less liquid in order to keep up their income. Therefore, Sraffa concludes, it is generally impossible to say that there is a definite relationship between the quantity of money and the rate of interest. There is no such thing as *the* liquidity preference curve.

Sraffa insists that advantages associated with carrying an asset have nothing to do with its commodity rate. People who borrow money or any other asset typically do this not in order to carry what is being borrowed until the expiration of the contract but in order to buy with it other things. What is being borrowed is not what is wanted to be kept but the standard in which the debt is fixed. Therefore, it is irrelevant whether a person pays in money or wheat and whether what is borrowed is a durable or a perishable good. Sraffa concludes "that K. has in the back of his mind two wrong notions, which have entirely misled him," namely, (a) that commodities are borrowed to be kept until the end of the loan and (b) that only durables can be borrowed.

There remains, however, the fact that a large quantity of money (cash) and a low rate of interest often go together, which gives the curve a certain plausibility. Yet, Sraffa insists, "causation is the other way round": it is a low rate of interest that is responsible for a large quantity of money, not a large quantity of money that causes a low rate of interest. Attention ought to focus on those who demand loans (investors) and not on those who provide them with liquid funds. Keynes's theory of liquidity preference with its emphasis on the supply of loans, Sraffa concludes, is similar to the old long-period theory of the supply of savings that is elastic with respect to the rate of interest placed into a short-period setting.

The commodity rate of interest, Sraffa insists, depends exclusively on expected price changes and is thus defined with respect to the forward price of a commodity. There are two ways in which the commodity rates of interest can become uniform again: either via changes in prices and/or via changes in production. Surprisingly, Keynes accepts both possibilities for all commodities other than money. This becomes clear when we consider, for example, the case in which agents develop a large propensity to hoard money. Due to the ensuing depressive tendencies in the economy, commodity prices will tend to fall. This implies a rise in the value of money. An expected increase in the value of money implies, however, a lower "own rate of money interest," to use Keynes's peculiar concept. Sraffa emphasizes that "therefore the money rate will be *lower than* other rates and not higher."[16] Sraffa adds that this is "Fisher's effect, which K. admits for all commodities except money." The reference is obviously to Irving Fisher (1892, 1907), who first elaborated the concept of own rates.[17] Sraffa concludes: "Thus in the K. case, the result [on rates of interest], is opposite to K.'s conclusion."

In chapter 17, Keynes did not reason correctly and got entangled in a maze of contradictions. Liquidity preference theory, i.e., "Keynes's system," is logically incoherent. Its basic notion is but another expression of the marginal utility of hoarding, which is but a particular aspect of marginal theory. Keynes who with one foot had managed to escape received modes of thought with his other foot was still tightly tied to them.

Concluding remarks

Sraffa approved of Keynes's critical intention but was disenchanted with its execution. It was not only Keynes's occasional sloppiness Sraffa found difficult to cope with. In important respects, he felt that Keynes had granted too much to received economic theory. Keynes's new theory exhibited several loose ends and contradictions and retained in new garb marginalist concepts that Sraffa deemed untenable.

It is ironic to see that the distinguishing feature of what today is known as "Neo-Keynesian" and "New Keynesian" theory is the premise of sticky prices: Keynes is interpreted as an imperfectionist. While there are traces of imperfectionism to be found in his magnum opus, in the central part of it he assumes fully flexible prices. Keynes's analysis therefore cannot be accused of lacking generality because of an alleged assumption of price rigidities. The problem, rather, is whether his explanation of a lower boundary to the money rate of interest (in combination with an inverse investment-interest relation) vis-à-vis flexible prices stands up to close examination. According to Sraffa, it does not. Keynes's argument suffers in particular from neglecting the implications of flexible prices via the value of money for the level of the "own rate of money interest." However, Keynes's failure must not be taken to be orthodox theory's triumph. In Sraffa's view, Keynes failed because in his analysis the orthodox elements overwhelm the truly novel ones.

Sraffa developed his criticism of Keynes from an approach that also considers (long-period) prices as fully flexible. This does not mean, however, that the conventionally invoked "forces of demand and supply" can be expected to generally bring about a full employment equilibrium. The irony is that Sraffa established these findings in terms of an elaboration of the classical approach to the theory of value and distribution. This approach, coherently developed, actually effectively undermines Say's law – the law for which Keynes had thought he could put classical analysis on one side. Keynes, keen to free himself of "habitual modes of thought and expression," was only partly successful.

Acknowledgments

This chapter is based on a paper given at the conference "Keynes's Economics and His Influences on Modern Economics," held at Sophia University, Tokyo, March 14–15, 2007. 1 am grateful to the participants of the conference, especially Richard Arena, Bob Dimand, Cristina Marcuzzo, Nerio Naldi, and Yosh Ono, for valuable comments and suggestions. The view that Sraffa was "secretly skeptical" of Keynes's new ideas was first expressed by Joan Robinson (1978, p. xii).

References

Barens, I. and Caspari, V. (1997). "Own-Rates of Interest and Their Relevance for the Existence of Underemployment Equilibrium Positions," in G. C. Harcourt and P. A. Riach (eds.), *A "Second" Edition of The General Theory*, Volume 1, London and New York: Routledge, 283–303.

De Cecco, M. (2005). "Sraffa's Lectures on Continental Banking: A Preliminary Appraisal," *Review of Political Economy*, 17:3. Reprinted in Kurz, Pasinetti and Salvadori (2008), 185–194.

Fisher, I. (1892). *Mathematical Investigations in the Theory of Value and Prices*, New Haven: Transactions of the Connecticut Academy, Vol. IX, July 1892.

Fisher, I. (1907). *The Rate of Interest*, New York: Macmillan.

Garegnani, P. (1978). "Notes on Consumption, Investment, and Effective Demand: I," *Cambridge Journal of Economics*, 2, 325–353.

Garegnani, P. (1979). "Notes on Consumption, Investment, and Effective Demand: II," *Cambridge Journal of Economics*, 3, 63–82.

Gehrke, C. and Kurz, H. D. (2002). "Keynes and Sraffa's 'Difficulties with J.H. Hollander,' A Note on the History of the RES Edition of *The Works and Correspondence of David Ricardo*," *European Journal of the History of Economic Thought*, 9:4, 644–671.

Gehrke, C. and Kurz, H. D. (2006). "Sraffa on von Bortkiewicz: Reconstructing the Classical Theory of Value and Distribution," *History of Political Economy*, 38:1, 91 –149.

Harrod, R. F. (1951). *The Life of John Maynard Keynes*, London: Macmillan.

Hayek, F. A. (1931a). "Reflections on the Pure Theory of Money of Mr. J.M. Keynes," part I, *Economica*, 11, 270–295.

Hayek, F. A. (1931b). *Prices and Production*, London: Routledge & Sons.

Hayek, F. A. (1932a). "Reflections on the Pure Theory of Money of Mr. J.M. Keynes," part II, *Economica*, 12, 22–44.

Hayek, F. A. (1932b). "Money and Capital: A Reply," *Economic Journal*, 42, 237–249.

Keynes, J. M. (1971–1989). *The Collected Writings of John Maynard Keynes*, D. Moggridge (ed.), London: Macmillan.

Kurz, H. D. (1978). "Rent Theory in a Multisectoral Model," *Oxford Economic Papers*, 30, 16–37.

Kurz, H. D. (1996). "Sraffa und die Keynessche Theorie der Liquiditätspräferenz," *Homo oeconomicus*, 13:3, 363–391.

Kurz, H. D. (2000). "The Hayek-Keynes-Sraffa Controversy Reconsidered," in H. D. Kurz (ed.), *Critical Essays on Piero Sraffa's Legacy in Economics*, Cambridge: Cambridge University Press, 257–301.

Kurz, H. D. (2006). "The Agents of Production Are the Commodities Themselves. On the Classical Theory of Production, Distribution and Value," *Structural Change and Economic Dynamics*, 17, 1–26.

Kurz, H. D. and Salvadori, N. (1995). *Theory of Production. A Long-period Analysis*, Cambridge: Cambridge University Press. (Paperback edn 1997.)

Kurz, H. D. and Salvadori, N. (2005). "Representing the Production and Circulation of Commodities in Material Terms: On Sraffa's Objectivism," *Review of Political Economy*, 17:3, 413–441. Reprinted in Kurz, Pasinetti and Salvadori (2008).

Kurz, H. D., Pasinetti, L. L. and Salvadori, N. (eds.) (2008). *Piero Sraffa: The Man and the Scholar*, London: Routledge.

Marcuzzo, C. (2002). "The Collaboration between J. M. Keynes and R. F. Kahn from the Treatise to the General Theory," *History of Political Economy*, 34:2, 421–447.

Marcuzzo, C. (2008). "Sraffa and Cambridge Economics, 1928–1931," in T. Cozzi and R. Marchionatti (eds.), *Piero Sraffa's Political Economy. A Centenary Estimate*, London and New York: Routledge, 81–99.

Marshall, A. (1920 [1890]). *Principles of Economics*, eighth edn (first edn. 1890), London: Macmillan.

Mas-Colell, A. (1989). "Capital Theory Paradoxes: Anything Goes," in R. Feiwel (ed.), *Joan Robinson and Modern Economic Theory*, London: Macmillan, 505–520.

Morgenstern, O. (1931). "Offene Probleme der Kosten- und Ertragstheorie," *Zeitschrift für Nationalökonomie*, 2, 481–522.

Pasinetti, L. L. (1974). *Growth and Income Distribution. Essays in Economic Theory*, Cambridge: Cambridge University Press.

Ranchetti, F. (2002). "On the Relationship between Sraffa and Keynes," in T. Cozzi and R. Marchionatti (eds.), *Piero Sraffa's Political Economy. A Centenary Estimate*, London and New York: Routledge, 311–331.

Ranchetti, F. (2005). "Communication and Intellectual Integrity. The Correspondence between Keynes and Sraffa," in M. C. Marcuzzo and A. Rosselli (eds.), *Economists in Cambridge. A Study through their Correspondence, 1907–1946*, London: Routledge, 119–137.

Robinson, J. V. (1978). *Contributions to Modern Economics*, Oxford: Blackwell.

Rosselli, A. (2005). "Sraffa and the Marshallian Tradition," *European Journal of the History of Economic Thought*, 12:3. Reprinted in Kurz, Pasinetti and Salvadori (2008, pp. 31–50).

Sraffa, P. (1925). "Sulle relazioni fra costo e quantità prodotta," *Annali di Economia*, 2, 277–328.

Sraffa, P. (1926). "The Laws of Returns under Competitive Conditions," *Economic Journal*, 36, 535–550.

Sraffa, P. (1930). "A Criticism" and "Rejoinder," Symposium on "Increasing Returns and the Representative Firm," *Economic Journal*, 40, 89–93.

Sraffa, P. (1932). "Dr. Hayek on Money and Capital," *Economic Journal*, 42, 42–53.

Sraffa, P. (1960). *Production of Commodities by Means of Commodities*, Cambridge: Cambridge University Press.

Wicksell, K. (1898). *Geldzins und Güterpreise*, Jena: Gustav Fischer.

Notes

1 He showed some of his early findings in 1928 to Keynes and Arthur Cecil Pigou.
2 Sraffa's 1925 paper was praised as a masterpiece by leading authorities in economics; see, for example, Oskar Morgenstern's commendation (Morgenstern 1931). Sraffa's assessment of Marshall's analysis contradicted Keynes's opinion, as reported by Harrod (1951, p. 324), that all that one needed in order to be a good economist was a thorough knowledge of Marshall's *Principles* and a careful daily reading of the *Times*.
3 For a detailed account of the correspondence between Keynes and Sraffa, see Ranchetti (2005, pp. 126–130).
4 He was not the only one who had difficulties with Keynes's postulate of the independence of the two price levels. For Richard Kahn and Joan Robinson's difficulties with it, see Marcuzzo (2002, pp. 427–429).
5 References to Sraffa's Papers kept at Wren Library at Trinity College, Cambridge, follow the catalog prepared by Jonathan Smith, archivist.
6 It is interesting to note that this was precisely the approach Keynes had taken in his "banana parable" in the *Treatise*, a thought experiment whose preliminary result had put him on the path toward the *General Theory*.
7 On the close collaboration between Keynes and Sraffa regarding the Ricardo edition, see Gehrke and Kurz (2002).
8 When in 1942 Sraffa resumed his work on his book, he recapitulated his findings of more than a decade before. In a note composed on November 13 entitled "Order of fertility," he asked:

> Is it possible in our scheme to arrange a series of lands of different qualities in a descending order of 'fertility' that will be valid for all values of (independently of) r [rate of interest] and w [wage rate]? No, it is not possible(Sraffa's Papers D3/12/25, p. l)

He illustrated the dependence of the order of fertility, and of the reversal of his order, in terms of a simple example.
9 This involved an investigation of fixed capital goods and the extensive and intensive dimension of their utilization. In this context, Sraffa studied carefully what Keynes in the *Treatise* had to say about the role of "working" and fixed capital in production (see CWK 5, chap. 8). As Sraffa's hitherto unpublished papers show, he was convinced that the growing importance of durable instruments of production had rendered a great elasticity to the modern economic system, which allowed it to increase and decrease considerably the rate of output in response to varying levels of effective demand. This was possible, for example, by switching between a single- and a double-shift system of capital utilization. Keynes's view in the *General Theory* that employment and real wages are of necessity negatively correlated (see the concept of the "employment function"; CWK 7, chap. 20) was difficult to reconcile with this observation, at least when starting from low levels of employment and capital utilization. As is well known, Keynes partly recanted his earlier view on the matter in his discussion with Dunlop and Tarshis.
10 In the 1960s, the possibility that the capital-labor ratio rises (falls) with a rise (fall) in the rate of profits (and a corresponding fall [rise] in the real wage rate) became known as *capital reversing or reverse capital deepening*; for a discussion of this phenomenon, see Kurz and Salvadori (1995, chap. 14). The discussion sets aside the problem of "inventions," i.e., the fact that new methods of production become available as time goes by. Here it suffices to point out that Keynes's view is not rendered more credible if inventions are taken into account.

11 See the contributions by Marcello de Cecco and Jan Kregel in the book in which the present chapter was first published. For a criticism of the use Keynes made of the concept of own rates of interest, see also Barens and Caspari (1997).

12 One event is worth telling. In late 1937, Keynes and Sraffa had different views as to the development of the price of lard, one of several pig products, and cotton oil, used to feed pigs. Keynes was convinced that the price of lard could be expected to rise and belittled Sraffa's objections by writing in a letter to Kahn: "If Piero [Sraffa] had ever seen a pig, he would know that the live animal cannot be kept in cold storage waiting till its food stuffs are cheaper" (CWK, pp. 22–23). Keynes therefore decided to job from cotton oil into lard. In a letter to Kahn in October 1937, Sraffa explained his point of view, based on an argument about the fattening of pigs, which culminated in the statement: "The less lard there is in stock, the more (with a multiplier) there is under the skin of pigs" (CWK 12, p. 24). Sraffa therefore expected a fall in the price of lard. Kahn reported Sraffa's argument to Keynes, yet to no avail. As Moggridge writes in his comment on the incident: "Keynes persisted in his view. His losses continued, by the end of 1937 totaling £27,210 on lard. He also lost over £17,000 on cotton oil" (CWK 12, p. 24).

13 According to Sraffa, the banking system can control only the money rate(s) of interest and has to leave the decision about the quantity of money and credit in the system to the public. Money is genuinely an endogenous magnitude.

14 Hayek had argued that crises are caused by too low a money rate of interest; Keynes argued exactly the opposite.

15 In this context it is worth mentioning, as de Cecco (2005) pointed out, that in his lectures on continental banking, which Sraffa gave to third year undergraduates in Cambridge in the springs of 1929 and 1930, he introduced the idea that different assets and commodities may be arranged in order of liquidity. According to de Cecco, Keynes in his theory of liquidity preference was in all probability influenced by Sraffa's respective argument, which can be traced back to Sraffa's studies of "forward exchange rates, around 1919, and provided Keynes with data on the lira's forward rates"; see de Cecco in Kurz, Pasinetti and Salvadori (2008, p. 190).

16 Keynes in one place uses the concept of "own rate of money interest," which, with money taken as standard of value, Sraffa comments, is a "hybrid" concept that "indeed has no other use than to patch up the confusion created," but in fact is only there "to make confusion more confounded."

17 Copies of Irving Fisher's books with annotations in Sraffa's hand are in Sraffa's library.

Part III

Production of Commodities by Means of Commodities in its making

8 On the collaboration between Sraffa and Besicovitch: the 'proof of gradient'*

Heinz D. Kurz and Neri Salvadori

Introduction

As is well known, Chapters III–VI of *Production of Commodities by Means of Commodities* explore the results arrived at as regards the model defined in the second part of Chapter II. Whereas the main aim of Chapter III is to provide a 'preliminary survey' (p. 15) of price movements consequent upon changes in distribution without the help of any specific tool, the complete analysis of these movements is presented in Chapter VI, where Sraffa has recourse to the tool elaborated in Chapters IV and V, the Standard commodity. In analysing price movements, Sraffa maintains in section 49, i.e. the very last section of Chapter VI, that 'there is … a restriction to the movement of the price of any product: if as a result of a rise in the rate of profits the price falls, its rate of fall cannot exceed the rate of fall of the wage'. This property is important because if the wage as a function of the rate of profits is decreasing in any numeraire, then it is decreasing in all numeraires. And since the Standard commodity is a numeraire in which the wage as a function of the rate of profits is a decreasing straight line, then

> if the wage is cut in terms of *any* commodity (no matter whether it is one that will consequently rise or fall relatively to the Standard) the rate of profit will rise; and vice versa for an increase of the wage.
>
> (Sraffa, 1960, pp. 38 and 40; Sraffa's italics)

* Reproduced with permission from Guglielmo Chiodi and Leonardo Ditta (eds), *Sraffa or an Alternative Economics*, New York: Palgrave Macmillan, 2008.

We should like to thank Pierangelo Garegnani, literary executor of Sraffa's papers and correspondence, for granting us permission to quote from them. Citations beginning with the letter D followed by a series of numbers refer to Sraffa's papers at Trinity College Library, Cambridge; the format of the citations follows the catalogue prepared by Jonathan Smith, archivist. Unless otherwise stated, all emphases are in the original; we shall use italics when Sraffa used underlinings. He frequently abbreviated *and* by +; we shall use the word instead of the symbol. We are grateful to Jonathan Smith and the staff of Trinity College Library for continuous assistance while working on the Sraffa papers. The views contained in this chapter have not been discussed with all the participants in the project of preparing an edition of Sraffa's papers and correspondence and therefore do not implicate them.

In this chapter we analyse how Sraffa in 1944 elaborated this property and which role Sraffa's 'mathematical friend' Abram S. Besicovitch played in this. In 1944 also the concept of Standard commodity matured[1] jointly with a number of other concepts.[2] All these developments were going on *pari passu*. However, in this chapter we will not deal with the parallel evolution of all the other concepts, including the Standard commodity.

The composition of the chapter is the following. In the second section we summarize briefly the relevant bits of the path Sraffa's work took in the first period devoted to what in December 1927 he called 'la mia teoria' and his 'libro' (D3/12/11: 55) which extended roughly from late 1927 to the end of 1931. The emphasis is on his early attempts to come to grips with the dependence of the rate of profits and relative prices on wages, given the system of production in use. Towards the end of this period Sraffa had essentially elaborated the analytical framework within which he then, upon the resumption of his work in 1942, began to study the various problems he faced in detail. It was clear from an early point onward that the problems were of a nature that required the use of mathematics, especially linear algebra. While Sraffa in the first period of his work had made a few attempts to acquaint himself with the relevant mathematical tools, his command of them was insufficient to have allowed him to effectively tackle the problems he encountered without the assistance of mathematicians. Sraffa was in the lucky position that with Abram S. Besicovitch he found another Trinity fellow that was not only able to provide the missing expertise (at least in the majority of cases in which Sraffa consulted him) but who also willingly did so. The third section turns to the collaboration between the two men, who soon got on friendly terms with one another, on what Sraffa called the 'proof of the gradient', an expression partially adopted from Besicovitch. Their respective collaboration took place in the last three months of 1944. This section focuses on the path that led to the proof of the gradient with regard to single-products systems. Sraffa also attempted to generalize the proof to systems with joint production. While these attempts failed, his work was not entirely futile because he found other properties of the system he had not searched for. In particular, he found another proof of the gradient which we eventually encounter in section 49 of his book. The fourth section deals with a few further notes drafted by Sraffa in 1945 in which he pointed out some of the properties of the system of production that followed from the gradient argument. The final section contains some concluding remarks.

The present chapter is the third in a row in which we investigate Sraffa's collaboration with his 'mathematical friends' (see also Kurz and Salvadori, 2001, 2004). The evidence provided shows that there can be no doubt about the great importance of this collaboration, and especially the one with Besicovitch, for the success of Sraffa's intellectual project. Not for nothing did Sraffa, in the Preface of his book, emphasize: 'My greatest debt is to Professor A. S. Besicovitch for invaluable mathematical help over many years' (Sraffa, 1960, p. vi).

Sraffa's work before autumn 1944

In November 1927 Sraffa began to elaborate his systems of equations. His attention focused first on systems without a surplus. Almost in parallel he studied systems with a surplus and wages fixed in terms of a given inventory of commodities. Some of the mathematical properties of such systems he was able to establish in the first half of 1928, assisted by Frank Ramsey (see Kurz and Salvadori, 2001, pp. 262–4).

Following Ricardo's lead, Sraffa in early 1928 also began to study the implications for the rate of profits and relative prices in the case in which workers participated in the sharing out of the surplus product. He did this first in terms of a redistribution of the surplus product away from profits and toward wages in proportion to the given vector of the surplus product (see, for example, D3/12/7: 93). This allowed him to conceive of the redistribution of the surplus in straightforward physical terms and yet advocate a share con-cept of surplus wages that is independent of relative prices. A share concept had already been introduced by Ricardo who had referred to the portion of any given annual value of the net product (in terms of labour values) paid to the labouring class (see Ricardo, *Works*, Vol. I, pp. 49–50). Sraffa dem-onstrated that an increase in surplus wages implied a decrease in the rate of interest and in general a change in relative prices. Investigating the properties of a system with only two industries, one producing 'consumer goods', the other 'intermediate goods', Sraffa in a document composed in the late 1920s stressed: 'È chiaro come il sole che se cambiano i salari cambiano anche i valori' (D3/12/7: 95).[3] He worked out a number of numerical examples that illustrated the phenomenon.

However, having to solve a set of simultaneous equations for each and every level of wages in order to find the corresponding level of the rate of interest and relative prices was cumbersome and the results not very trans-parent. Sraffa was therefore on the lookout for a second method that would provide a more direct grasp of the essential features of the economic system. It was apparently this concern that made him study, around the turn of 1928, among other things, Eugen von Böhm-Bawerk's *Positive Theory of Capital* (Böhm-Bawerk, 1889, 1959) (see, for example, D3/12/7: 89). Böhm-Bawerk in his book had put forward a concept of production according to which any product could be envisaged as the result of a flow of dated inputs of labour (and other 'original' factors of production) of finite length. Sraffa had come across the idea of reduction already in the writings of Adam Smith and other classical authors, and, in taking up a suggestion of William Petty to reduce the values of commodities to 'food', had elaborated himself some such reduction with regard to his first equations. He now applied the method of reduction to workers' means of subsistence to his with-surplus equations: 'It is necessary therefore to reduce each commodity ultimately to two things, surplus {the rate of interest} and any one commodity (or group of commodities, which are in constant proportion, such as subsistence of workers)' (D3/12/7: 126).

This was basically the stage at which Sraffa had to leave the matter in order to focus attention on the edition of the works and correspondence of David Ricardo, a task to which the Royal Economic Society had appointed him at the beginning of 1930.

When in the summer of 1942 Sraffa resumed work on his constructive task he quickly advanced in a variety of directions. This was not least due to his collaboration with Besicovitch, which appears to have started in June of that year (D3/12/2: 15). In October 1942 Sraffa, upon a suggestion of Besicovitch, adopted the notation we eventually encounter in his 1960 book (see D3/12/23: 1(1–4), 2 and 4). At the time he worked with great dedication and untiring energy on several problems, including the problem of reduction. The most important steps taken by him as seen from the perspective of the present chapter were finding the maximum rate of profits of a given system of single production, R, and the identification of the Standard commodity associated with the system. He knew, in fact, that for a system of k commodities, there existed k solutions for the maximum rate of profits, the set of prices and the multipliers of the Standard system. Sraffa in fact, in 1944, considered each eigenvector (of the input matrix of the means of production) as a 'Standard commodity' and indicated them with letter U (U', U'', ...); see, for instance, D3/12/40: 3–18. These analytical steps mentioned above Sraffa was able to take at the beginning of 1944 (see folder D3/12/36). The Standard commodity's characteristic feature was foreshadowed in several earlier notes and papers, some composed already in the first period. For example, in a paper he had begun to write in February 1931 he contemplated the case in which 'the value of total capital in terms of total goods produced cannot vary [as income distribution changes], since the goods are composed exactly in the same proportions as the capitals which have produced them' (D3/12/7: 157(3)). He was sure that in any real economy this condition was never actually met, but it might perhaps be approximately true. Some twelve years later, in a note composed a few weeks before the discovery of the Standard commodity, he clarified that his earlier proposition was based on the 'statistical compensation of large numbers' (D3/12/35: 28). Henceforth he called the assumption that the value of social capital relative to the social product does not change with a change in distribution 'My Hypothesis'. He had encountered a similar hypothesis in Marx at the beginning of the 1940s, if not earlier, who had characterized a given system of production in terms of a given 'organic composition of capital', that is, the ratio of the labour embodied in the means of production and of living labour expended during a year. The inverse of the organic composition gave the maximum rate of profits compatible with the system. Sraffa had understood that no actual system could ever be expected to satisfy the hypothesis. He therefore had to construct an artificial system that did so. He constructed it out of the equations representing the actual system and was thus able to preserve all the salient features of the latter.

The ground is now prepared for entering into the main theme of this chapter which concerns Sraffa's collaboration with Besicovitch on the 'proof of gradient' and which for the most part took place from October to December 1944.

Sraffa's collaboration with Besicovitch on the 'proof of gradient'

If the rate of profits is given, the price equations and the equation fixing the numeraire are linear and therefore one solution exists for prices and the wage rate. If, on the contrary, the wage rate is given, then the system is not linear and k solutions for the prices and the rate of profits exist, where k is the number of commodities involved. Some of these solutions are real, others are not, and some real solutions have negative values. We know, now, that only one real solution has non-negative prices and wage rate, provided the given wage rate is low enough. This was not known to Sraffa at the time and actually he was looking to find a solution to this problem of multiplicity. When working on this problem on 3 October 1944 he put to himself a different exercise. Instead of giving the wage rate he took the wage as an unknown and considered the equation

$$A_1 p_a = Lw \tag{1}$$

(D3/12/40: 12). Yet this did not really change the problem at hand, since this equation is equivalent to giving the wage using commodity a as numeraire. On 10 October Besicovitch replied to some other questions contained in the same document, but not to this one. A reply to the latter was provided on 12 October: 'k different Systems of Solutions' (D3/12/40: 16). On the same day Sraffa wrote a note in Italian in which he mentions Besicovitch's answer, but with details which are not in the written answer by his friend. There is every reason to think that the reference is to an oral answer accompanying the written one:

> In sostanza, l'unica obbiezione sensata fatta da B., è che se, invece di dare un valore arbitrario a w, introduco l'equazione $A_1 p_a = Lw$ lasciando w variabile, il risultato è: non posso più ottenere l'equazione … $r = R(1 - w)$, e quindi anche prendendo la Standard Commodity per unità, la soluzione non è più unica; ci sono quindi k valori di w.[4]

Two days later he added

> *N. B.* La sostanza dell'obbiezione di B. sembra questa. Per qualsiasi U Lw è una funzione lineare di r. Ma il prezzo della merce a, e quindi $A_1 p_a$ *non* e funzione lineare di r: quindi oscilla col variare di r, e la linea del prezzo $A_1 p_a$ *interseca in k punti* (in k valori di r) la retta che rappresenta Lw: in ciascuno di questi punti il *dato* salario reale è uguale a un *diverso* salario proporzionale (w).[5]

Exploring the unpublished papers we see that after this event Sraffa went back to some of the results he had obtained earlier, annotating them. For instance, on the same day, 14 October, he jotted down a few remarks on the document containing a proof of the existence of 'at most *one* value of *R* to which correspond positive prices and positive multipliers' (D3/12/39: 3), obtained in May of the same year. He also formulated further conjectures about answers to the objection by Besicovitch. However, two weeks later the situation changed dramatically and Sraffa wrote:

> 31 Ottobre 44. Oggi, dopo dieci mesi di resistenza, Besicovich [*sic*] ha finalmente ceduto, ammettendo che il sistema ha una soluzione unica [insertion later in pencil:] ˢnel caso che ogni processo dà un solo prodottoˢ. L'argomento decisivo e stato che la curva del prezzo della merce A non può tagliare più di una volta la retta del salario; perchè il prezzo non può mai cadere (in consequenza di una caduta dell salario) in proporzione maggiore del salario; e ciò perchè il prezzo può essere espresso in termini di una serie (v. sopra). Il caso in questione è quello in cui una data Merce Standard è presa per unità dei prezzi e una merce arbitraria per unità del salario.
>
> (D3/12/40: 28)[6]

Following his hint ('see above'), we find the equation

$$p_a = L_0 w + L_1 w(1+r) + L_2 w(1+r)^2 + \cdots \tag{2}$$

equation (1), and a figure that comes close to Fig. 4 in Sraffa's book (1960, p. 39).

   Probably Sraffa was too emphatic. The 'ten months of resistance' were *not* on the issue under discussion, but on the uniqueness of the Standard ratio and the uniqueness of the Standard commodity. The solution was to be found in another direction than Sraffa had originally thought, a fact that was actually close at hand since May 1944: uniqueness could not be found by manipulating the equations,[7] but by specifying more carefully the desired properties of the sought standard. This Sraffa eventually did by considering the *unique* 'Standard commodity'[8] with non-negative multipliers (all positive for processes producing basics and zero for the others). What Besicovitch recognized on 31 October was that there was a single solution to equation (1). Yet this statement is partially wrong: equation (1) has actually *k* solutions, some real, others not, and among the real solutions some are positive, others not. What *is* unique is a positive solution with a positive wage and non-negative prices. The proof apparently given orally on 31 October was then provided in written form on 2 November. Before the written proof was available to Sraffa, the two met anew on 1 November. Sraffa noted on the back of document D3/12/40: 28:

1.11.44 Bes. ammette che la conclusione rimane valida se, invece della Standard Commodity, si prende come unità di prezzi la merce *A*: poichè si tratta solo di un cambiamento di unità.[9]

The document containing the proof is D3/12/63: 6; it is dated, as mentioned, 2 November 1944. It has a part emphasized by red lines around it which reads:

[Dictated by Besicovitch]
w and *r* vary always in the opposite direction. p_a being capable of being expressed in the form

$$p_a = L_0 w + L_1 w(1+r) + L_2 w(1+r)^2 + \cdots$$

where *L*s are all non-negative, the gradient of p_a is always less than the gradient of *w*. And therefore the equation

$$A_1 p_a = Lw$$

cannot have more than one real root for *r*.

As it is stated, the sentence is not fully correct: p_a is capable of being expressed in the form (2) only for

$$-1 \le r < \frac{1-\lambda}{\lambda},$$

where λ is the eigenvalue of maximum modulus of the matrix of inputs, and therefore what has been proved is not that equation (1) 'cannot have more than one real root for *r*': other real solutions are possible, but they are smaller than −1 or larger than (1 − λ)/λ.

Another remark concerns the fact that the proof is based on a difference in the slopes of *w* and p_a. To indicate such slopes Besicovitch used the mathematical term 'gradient'. Sraffa used the term when characterizing the proof under consideration in his unpublished writings, but he did not use it in his book. This may be seen as justifying the title of the present chapter.

Immediately after this issue had been settled with respect to systems with single production, Sraffa, on 3 November, tried to generalize the result to joint production. He started to write a long document (D3/12/40: 19–27) which he continued on 4, 5, 7, 9, and 10 November. This was just the first of a number of attempts. Eventually he understood that the result cannot be carried over to joint production (cf. Sraffa, 1960, pp. 61–2). The earlier parts of the document were also shown to Besicovitch on 4 November and Sraffa noted in the margin of D3/12/40: 22: '4.11.44 Bes. says this is *wrong*'.

On 12 November Sraffa wrote a paper (D3/12/40: 33–36) in which he put down in clean form the whole result with regard to single production. He drew also two diagrams (D3/12/40: 33 and 35). In one the Standard commodity serves as numeraire, whereas in the other commodity *a* serves as numeraire: in the former the *w-r* relationship is a straight line and the A_1p_a-*r* relationship has ups and downs, whereas in the latter the A_1p_a-*r* relationship is a horizontal line and the *w-r* relationship is decreasing, but with alternate concavities; Sraffa remarks: 'Since the two curves have been transformed proportionally, they can have no more intersections than they had before' (D3/12/40: 35). Sraffa extends the same argument also to the case in which wages are paid *ante factum* (D3/12/40: 36). On the same and the following days he tried to extend the result. He asked: What happens if $A_1 = 0$? After some deliberation he arrived at the following remark (D3/12/40: 40) on 14 November:

> In the System
>
> $$\left.\begin{array}{l}(A_a p_a + \cdots + K_a p_k)(1+r) + L_a w = A p_a \\ \cdots \\ (A_k p_a + \cdots + K_k p_k)(1+r) + L_k w = K p_k\end{array}\right\}$$
>
> make $p_b = 1$
> and $A_1 p_a = Lw$
> Now suppose we make $A_1 = 0$, does it follow that $w = 0$? No, because p_a might be ∞. And this is the case, e.g. when *b* is one of the 'other' Standard Commodities, U'', U''' etc.

This is actually the right answer when *a* is a basic commodity and the eigenvalues of basics coincide with the eigenvalues of the whole system, as is usually (and implicitly) assumed by Sraffa. In this note he gets very close to recognizing the reason on the basis of which the appropriate *R* was to be chosen, but this result was effectively obtained only later.

In another note (D3/12/40: 39) dated 12 November he asks himself 'Is labour itself such a commodity?' He answers:

> Suppose we take labour as unit of prices, i.e. make $w = 1$, and we make real wages = A_1. Then in the equation $A_1 p_a = Lw$ we have $wL = 1$ and therefore $A_1 = \dfrac{1}{p_a}$ so that at $A_1 = 0$ it must be $p_a = \infty$.

Once again he found a nice result and his comment on it may clarify why he was not favourable to using labour as standard: 'Note the disastrous effects of taking the "*price* of labour"… as standard'. He continued:

Therefore, whenever we can guarantee that in the equation $A_1p_a = Lw$ at $A_1 = 0$ there cannot correspond $p_a = \infty$ then at $A_1 = 0$ there *must* correspond $w = 0$.

And then, marked with three red lines in the margin, indicating the great importance attached by him to the statement, followed:

> But the most simple way to obtain this result is to take *the same* commodity A as unit of *ps* and w as well as component of the real wage.

The note concludes:

> For in that case $p_a = 1$ at all values of r; and when in the equation $A_1p_a = A_1 = Lw$ we make $A_1 = 0$ w *must* be $= 0$.

Here, too, he was close to recognizing the reason for choosing the appropriate R. Many other attempts he undertook in order to extend the argument were in the direction of joint production, but, as we know, no solution could be found. However, as by-products, Sraffa was able to establish other results concerning joint production. For instance, he recognized that negative prices reflected the presence of 'uneconomical' processes[10] and that

> The remedy would be to give up the unec. process, to use only the other, and give away free the 'neg. price' commodity – all through: in other words, drop it from among the 'commodities' and treat the surviving equation as producing only the other.
>
> (D3/12/63: 65)

This is substantially stating the rule of free goods, which he did not adopt in his book, but which was employed by many of his followers.[11] Finally, on 16 November, he recognized that 'The "Reduction to Labour and Gradient" proof cannot be extended from one-one case to many-one case' (D3/12/63: 45). However, he tried to find other proofs for the single production ('one-one') case which could perhaps be extended to the joint production ('many-one') case. His respective work turned out to be fruitful, but not because it fulfilled the expectations Sraffa appears to have had when embarking on it: While he did not find what he sought to find, he found something else that was useful. In the same document dated 16 November we find some elements of the other proof we encounter in section 49 of *Production of Commodities*:

> There are three elements ⁱvariablesⁱ constituting the price of a product (i.e. on left side):
>
> 1) Lw, rises with w
> 2) $1 + r$, falls with rise of w

3)   price of Const. Cap., may rise or fall with rise of w.

For the price to fall more than in proportion with w it is necessary for (3) to fall *much more* than in proportion with w, so as to annull ⁱcancel entirelyⁱ the contrary effect of (2) and leave something over.

But (3) is the price of a group of other commodities.

Therefore for p_a to fall proportionately more than w, it is necessary for the price of some other commod. to fall more than p_a.

Thus we can arrange the commodities in the order of their gradient, and there will be one (or several) with the maximum gradient. But this is impossible, since it could only be due to other commodities (its means of production) having a gradient greater than the maximum.

On 4 December Besicovitch went back to what he had dictated on 2 November and Sraffa noted on the respective document D3/12/63: 6:

> 4.12.44 This holds for $r \geq -1$. I.e. the function is monotone, therefore not more than one root > -1....
>
> N.B. – B. had a doubt whether when the equations are of even degree there could be only one root: for in that case they must have two or none. But this was dispelled by the consideration that, although the polynomial expressing p_a is of kth degree (and k may be even) the above expression is an infinite series of infinite degree, and that makes it OK.

Thus Besicovitch introduced a first correction, but he did not observe that there is also another boundary, namely that within which the series is convergent. Further, the doubt of the 'N.B.' adjunct is inappropriate even if the number of the terms of the sum were to be finite and this is so exactly for the reason that there is the interval $r < -1$. In fact, because of Descartes' Theorem, the equation in $1 + r$ has only one positive solution for $1 + r$, whereas all other real solutions are negative and all complex solutions have a negative real part since there is only one variation.

On the same day Besicovitch expressed also some further doubts. On a piece of recycled paper (D3/12/63: 5) Besicovitch wrote

$$A_1\{L_0 + L_1(1+r) + L_2(1+r)^2 + \cdots\} = L$$
$$\text{when } A_1, L_0, L_1, \cdots, L \geq 0$$

In order to remind himself of what Besicovitch had said to him, Sraffa added before the formulas by Besicovitch 'The equation $A_1 p_a = Lw$ is equivalent to' and after them '(where w is eliminated, as it occurs on both sides. Therefore the condition "w and r vary always in the opposite direction" is unnecessary [says Bes.])'. Sraffa added also the date and in the margin the fact that the reference is to the document of 2.11.1944 mentioned above (D3/12/63: 6). It is clear what had happened. Besicovitch had got doubts as to the correctness of what he had dictated about one month earlier: since there is no constraint on w, why should this expression make it necessary that 'w and r vary always in the opposite direction'? Also this doubt by Besicovitch was inappropriate. He probably had forgotten that the necessity of the statement 'w and r vary always in the opposite direction' was a consequence of the existence of a single real solution – in the relevant range – of exactly that equation.

On 12 December (D3/12/63: 5) Sraffa summarized the debate with Besicovitch on this point in a *nota bene*, where the N.B. is in red pencil:

N.B. Notare che, in un primo tempo (31.10. e 2.11.44) B. aveva accettato la 'prova del gradient' incondizionatamente. Gli si era affacciato il dubbio che, se l'equazione era di grado pari, doveva avere almeno due soluzioni; e l'aveva risolto dicendo che la Reduction equation è di grado infinito.

Poi, il 4.12.44, (senza ricordarsi l'ultimo punto) ha aggiunto la restrizione che $r \geq -1$.[12]

This makes us think that Besicovitch's other doubt was not considered relevant or that further discussions with no written trace have taken place. This summary was written in order to introduce the following conjecture.

Ora, mi sembra, questa restrizione può essere eliminata se si pone $e^\rho = (1 + r)$, dove $\rho = \log(1 + r)$. Perchè in tal caso a $r = -1$ corrisponde $\rho = -\infty$, e ad $r < -1$ non corrisponde nessun valore *reale* di ρ. In altri termini, alla proposizione 'vi è una sola radice reale $\sigma \geq -1$ per r' si sostituisce l'equivalente 'vi è una sola radice *reale* per ρ.[13]

Obviously, the passage to continuous time does not change things and Sraffa was certainly wrong with his conjecture, but it shows his interest in eliminating a problem that from an economic point of view is totally irrelevant: if negative levels of the rate of profits are irrelevant in a long-period analysis, rates of profits lower than -1 are even more so in this and in other contexts.

Besicovitch's doubts probably prompted Sraffa to try to find an alternative proof such as the one he started to compose on 16 November. On 20 December the proof is clearly laid out in the following document. It is noteworthy that the first line is underlined in bold red, once again indicating the importance of the element at hand.

Other proof of gradient ('commodity' point of view)
in one-one case
Consider the 'elements' composing the cost of production of a commodity.

(a) the labour-term, which falls in proportion to w
(b) the 'means of production' terms. Each of these contains two variables, p and r. Since r rises, if the price of the product has to fall more than w, the price of the means of production must fall more than w, to make up: since they are multiplied by $1 + r$ (which is rising) they can only contribute to the rate of decrease of the price of the product less than their own rate of decrease.

Now consider, among the k products, the one that has (over a given interval) the greatest rate of decrease: its means of production's price has a smaller rate of decrease, and it is further reduced (as it is passed on in the product) through being multiplied by $1 + r$ (increasing). Therefore this product can only obtain its higher rate of decrease from its labour term: but this cannot contribute more than it has, i.e. w, therefore its rate of decrease must be < rate of w.

(D3/12/63: 7)

This gets very close to the wording used in the published version. We may conclude by saying that both proofs we encounter in section 49 were produced in 1944. Besicovitch played an important part in finding the former, but none in finding the latter. As a matter of fact there is no trace that Sraffa even showed the latter to Besicovitch. In the case that he did, which we think can safely be assumed, Besicovitch could be expected to have swiftly approved of it.

The afterglow

While the main issue was settled, Sraffa nevertheless went back to the discussion of the gradient a few times shortly afterwards in attempts to round off the argument by exploring some of its implications. The following document entitled 'Implications of the "Gradient" argument', dated 21 January 1945, is of particular interest, because in it he relates his findings to David Ricardo's analysis which, as we have seen in the second section above, was the starting point of his own probing into the problem under consideration more than fifteen years earlier:

1) In *whatever* commodity wages may be fixed, they will always fall with the rise of the rate of profit. or
2) If labour is taken as measure of prices, the prices of *all* commodities fall {this is clearly a typo; it should obviously read 'rise'} with the rise of rate of profit. or
3) With the rise of the rate of profit some commodities will rise and some will fall – depending on which commodity is taken as standard of prices; but the prices of labour will fall in any case, *independently* of the standard chosen. Cp. Ricardo, Princ., 1st ed., my ed. p. 63 'no commodities whatever are raised in absolute price [in ed 2 "exchangeable value"] merely because wages rise'. In this argument he is supposing 'money to be of

an invariable value; in other words to be always the produce of the same quantity of *unassisted labour.*' [ib., next para; my italics].

The first proposition simply reiterates the fact that there is an inverse relation between the rate of profits and the wage rate, independent of the standard in which wages are expressed. If expressed in terms of national income, then *w* represents the share of wages in national income. With a rise in the rate of profits, given the system of production in use, proportional wages, i.e. the wage share, must of necessity fall. This is a restatement of Ricardo's fundamental theorem concerning income distribution within the context of a circular flow. The second proposition states that prices measured in units of 'labour commanded' are bound to rise as the rate of profits rises. Clearly, the smaller the wage rate, the more labour a given commodity can 'command' or is exchanged for. The third proposition implies that with a rise in the wage rate (a fall in the rate of profits), the exchangeable values of all commodities would fall, expressed in a standard that is produced without any means of production, that is, by 'unassisted labour'. This contradicts a view that was widespread at the time of Ricardo and which Adam Smith had elevated to the level of a scientific truth, namely, that a rise in wages would entail a rise in the prices of all other commodities. Obviously, this view is untenable.

On 21 May 1945 Sraffa put forward the following

> *Proposition:* Total profits must *always* increase with the rise of *r* and fall of *w*, in whatever commodity they are measured.

This proposition cannot be sustained: While profits divided by wages are a rising function of the rate of profits, profits taken by themselves are not unless we use the social product as standard and wages are paid in units of the social product. In this way the value of the social product is fixed, the wage part is decreasing when *r* rises and therefore profits are increasing. Sraffa continued:

> Proof. We have seen that the price of no commodity (in terms of any other [or of the Standard Commodity?]) can fall as fast as *w*, if only circ. cap. is used; and it cannot do so without negative prices, if also fixed capital is used.

We were not able to find in the Sraffa papers the proof that the 'proof of gradient' holds when fixed capital is used, and prices are non-negative. However the proposition is true. Sraffa's final proposition reads:

> But *r*, being a linear function of *w*, rises as fast as *w* falls.
> Therefore, 'the price of any commodity, simple or composite, multiplied by *r*' must always rise with the fall of *w:* And total profits are 'the price of the aggregate means of production multiplied by *r*'.

[?] This would be so if r were $= 1/w$. But is it with $r = R(1 - w)$?]

(D3/12/40: 185)

This proposition is certainly true for sufficiently low levels of the rate of profits, but does not need to be true in general. The sentence in square brackets bears testimony to the fact that Sraffa saw the difficulty, which is certainly solved if $rw = 1$, which, however, is generally not the case.

On 2 June 1945 Sraffa added some further 'Propositions' which he illustrated with the help of a diagram:

From 'Gradient' it follows that the *quantity* of commodity in Real Wage always *falls* with the rise of r, whatever the commodity

- Therefore the aggr. income of workers (*however* measured) falls with rise of r.
- Therefore the aggreg. income of capitalists *always rises* with rise of r however) measured), being the complement of worker's income CA, i.e. $(1 - w)$.
- Therefore the price of the aggregate Const. Cap. of any SubSystem relatively to its product cannot fall as much as the reciprocal of r, with the rise of r. Since at an increased r the price of that Const. Cap. multiplied by r must be equal to a larger quantity of the product.

(D3/12/40: 182)

In the margin of the second proposition Sraffa put a question mark, and for good reason, because the proposition is true, as mentioned above, only if the standard of value is national income (the social product) and workers are actually paid in terms of this standard. In the diagram Sraffa apparently plotted the social product as a line parallel to the abscissa at the level of the maximum level of wages compatible with a non-negative rate of profits. This might be interpreted as implying that in this way he indicated that wages were actually taken to be measured in terms of national income. However, in the rest of the document there is nothing that would remove the uncertainty as to the interpretation of the diagram. To be sure, in order to avoid such uncertainty it would have to be explicitly stated in terms of which commodity (or standard) workers are actually taken to be paid. This problem was probably not seen by Sraffa at the time. In the margin of the third proposition Sraffa put a straight line, indicating approval. However, Sraffa did not insert this result in his book.

The above quotations document well Sraffa's analytical concerns in the 1940s and his vacillations as regards the correctness or otherwise of some of his propositions concerning the properties of the economic system under consideration. It suffices to note that none of the errors contained in the above manuscripts survived and made their way into the book. Sraffa's untiring effort to get his argument right bore fruit.

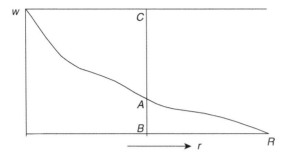

Figure 8.1 Figure drawn by Sraffa in D3/12/40: 182; here redrawn

Concluding remarks

Prices, Sraffa in Chapter III of his book (1960, pp. 12 and 15) insisted, generally do not follow a 'simple rule' and that 'the pattern of price-variations arising from a change in distribution' may be rather 'complex'. In Chapter VI he qualified these statements by pointing out:

> There is however a restriction to the movement of the price of any product: if as a result of a rise in the rate of profits the price falls, its rate of fall cannot exceed the rate of fall of the wage rate.
>
> (p. 38)

This holds true (in single production) independently of the standard in terms of which prices and the wage rate are expressed.

This result was established by Sraffa who was assisted by Besicovitch towards the end of 1944. A first proof of the 'gradient' was provided by Besicovitch at the beginning of November 1944; a different proof was apparently independently elaborated by Sraffa in the second half of December of the same year. We encounter both again in section 49 of Sraffa's book.

References

Böhm-Bawerk, E. V. *Kapital und Kapitalzins. Zweite Abteilung: Positive Theorie des Kapitales*, (Innsbruck: Wagner, 1889; 4th edn, Jena: Fischer, 1921).

Böhm-Bawerk, E. V. *Capital and Interest*, two vols. Translation of the 4th edn of Böhm-Bawerk (1889), (South Holland, Illinois: Libertarian Press, 1959).

Filippini, C. and Filippini, L. 'Two Theorems on Joint Production', *The Economic Journal*, XCII (1982) 386–90.

Kurz, H. D. and Salvadori, N. *Theory of Production. A Long Period Analysis*, (Cambridge: Cambridge University Press, 1995).

Kurz, H. D. and Salvadori, N. 'Sraffa and the Mathematicians: Frank Ramsey and Alister Watson', in T. Cozzi and R. Marchionatti (eds), *Piero Sraffa's Political Economy. A Centenary Estimate*, (London and New York: Routledge, 2001) 254–84. Reprinted in Kurz, H.D. and Salvadori, N., *Classical Economics and Modern Theory. Studies in Long-Period Analysis*, London: Routledge, 2003, 187–216.

Kurz, H. D. and Salvadori, N. 'On the Collaboration between Sraffa and Besicovitch: The Cases of Fixed Capital and Non-Basics in Joint Production', in *Convegno internazionale Piero Sraffa (Roma, 11–12 febbraio 2003)*, (Rome: Accademia Nazionale dei Lincei, 2004) 255–301. Reprinted in Kurz, H.D. and Salvadori, N. *Interpreting Classical Economics. Studies in Long-Period Analysis*, London: Routledge, 2007, 159–200.

Sraffa, P. *Production of Commodities by Means of Commodities*, (Cambridge: Cambridge University Press, 1960).

Notes

1 On 31 January 1955 Sraffa wrote: 'The Standard Commodity is first identified in the packet of small sheets of College notepaper dated 27.1.44 and headed "Hypothesis"'; see D3/12/36: 91, with a clear reference to D3/12/36: 61–67.

2 These include the distinction between basics and non-basics, subsystems and the further elaboration of the reduction to dated quantities of labour.

3 'It is as clear as sunlight that if wages change also values change.'

4 'In substance, the only objection I felt B. was making was that if, instead of attributing an arbitrary value to w, I introduce equation $A_1p_a = Lw$, leaving w variable, the result is: I can no longer obtain the equation... $r = R(1 - w)$, and therefore even if I were to take the Standard Commodity as unity, the solution is no longer unique; there are k values of w.'

5 '*N.B.* The substance of B.'s objection seems to be the following. For whichever U Lw is a linear function or r. But the price of commodity a, and therefore A_1p_a, is not a linear function of r: therefore it oscillates as r varies, and the curve of the price A_1p_a *intersects in k points* (k values of r) the straight line that represents Lw: in each one of these points the *given* real wage is equal to a different proportional wage (w).'

6 '31 October 44. Today, after ten months of resistance, Besicovich [*sic*] has finally given in, admitting that the system has a unique solution in the case in which each process gives only a single product. The decisive argument is that the curve of the price of commodity A cannot cut the wage line more than once; because the price can never fall (in consequence of a fall in the wage) in a larger proportion than the wage; and this is so because the price can be expressed by means of a series (see above). The case under consideration is the one in which a given Standard Commodity is taken as the unit of prices and an arbitrary commodity as wage unit.'

7 Besicovitch insisted with Sraffa as to this aspect on 10 October 1944: 'anyhow by manipulating with your equations only you cannot single out a value of r' (D3/12/40:13).

8 The inverted commas are required since we are using the language Sraffa used at the time and not the one used in the published book: In 1944 a 'Standard commodity' was any composite commodity made up in a proportion to an eigenvector; in 1960, the 'Standard commodity' is unique since it is the composite commodity made up in a proportion to the unique non-negative eigenvector normalized by the condition that the direct and indirect labour required to produce them equals unity.

9 '1.11.44 Bes. admits that the conclusion remains valid when instead of the Standard Commodity one takes as unit of prices commodity A: because what is at issue is only a change of unit.'

10 In modern parlance we would say 'dominated processes'; see Filippini and Filippini (1982).

11 The rule of free goods is alluded to in a note on joint production contained in a folder (D3/12/11: 25) dated November 1927.

12 'N.B. Note that B. had first (31.10. and 2.11.44) unconditionally accepted the 'proof of the gradient'. Then faced the doubt that when the equation was of even degree, it had to have at least two solutions; and this he solved by saying that the Reduction equation is of infinite degree.

   Then, on 4.12.44, (without remembering the last point) he added the restriction that $r \geq -1$.'

13 'It seems to me now that this restriction could be eliminated if one puts $e^\rho = (1 + r)$, where $\rho = \log(1 + r)$. Because in this case there corresponds to $r = -1: \rho = -\infty$, and to $r < -1$ there corresponds no *real* value of ρ. Put differently, to the proposition 'there is only a single real root $\sigma \geq -1$ for r' one substitutes the equivalent 'there is only a single *real* root for ρ'.'

9 Sraffa on von Bortkiewicz: reconstructing the classical theory of value and distribution*

Christian Gehrke and Heinz D. Kurz

Among Piero Sraffa's unpublished papers is a notebook with extensive excerpts from and critical comments on three contributions of Ladislaus von Bortkiewicz: "Der Kardinalfehler der Böhm-Bawerkschen Zinstheorie" (1906), "Zur Zinstheorie. II. Entgegnung" (1907b), and "Wertrechnung und Preisrechnung im Marxschen System" (1906–7).[1] The reading notes and commentaries on Bortkiewicz's three essays were mainly written between January and April 1943, with some additions in December 1945 and June 1955. It was presumably the discussion of Bortkiewicz's contributions in Paul Sweezy's *Theory of Capitalist Development* (1942) that brought them to Sraffa's attention, who up until then appears to have been unaware of them.[2] What will perhaps come as a surprise to some readers is that there are no excerpts from or comments on Bortkiewicz's famous paper "Zur Berichtigung der grundlegenden theoretischen Konstruktion von Marx im 3. Band des *Kapital*" (1907a) in Sraffa's papers.[3] While the three articles mentioned above are the

* Reproduced with permission from *History of Political Economy*, 38(1), 2006.

Earlier versions of this chapter were presented at conferences in Strasbourg in October 2001 and in Salvador de Bahia in September 2002, and on the occasion of a PhD seminar of the DEA at the Université de Paris I–Panthéon-Sorbonne in November 2004. We are grateful to the participants at the conferences for useful discussions and observations. We should like to thank Pierangelo Garegnani, literary executor of Sraffa's papers and correspondence, for granting us permission to quote from them. Citations beginning with the letter D followed by a series of numbers (e.g., D1/91: 5–33) refer to Sraffa's papers at Trinity College Library, Cambridge; the format of the citations follows the catalog prepared by Jonathan Smith, archivist. We have used Sraffa's annotations in his personal copies of various books, which are also in the Wren Library at Trinity College; in our reference list, the catalog numbers of the corresponding items are given in parentheses. Unless otherwise stated, all emphases are in the original. Sraffa frequently abbreviated *and* by + ; we shall use the word instead of the symbol. Since in his texts Sraffa used both parentheses and square brackets, all additions by us to Sraffa's texts and to all other quoted passages (whether by Sraffa or not), will be indicated by curly brackets. We are grateful to Jonathan Smith and the staff of Trinity College Library for continuous assistance while working on the Sraffa papers. We gratefully acknowledge receipt of valuable comments on an earlier draft of this chapter from Gilbert Faccarello, Pierangelo Garegnani, Geoff Harcourt, John King, Gary Mongiovi, Arrigo Opocher, Neri Salvadori, and two anonymous referees. We should like to stress that the views contained in this chapter have not been discussed with the other participants in the project of preparing an edition of Sraffa's papers and correspondence (we are involved in that project as well) and therefore do not implicate them.

only writings of Bortkiewicz from which Sraffa appears to have excerpted, he may well have read other contributions by him.[4] As we shall see below, Sraffa apparently held Bortkiewicz in high esteem because of what he, Sraffa, dubbed "Bortkiewicz's dictum" and his "dogma," which concerned criteria that the theory of value and distribution ought to satisfy. These criteria Sraffa had established independently of him and had actually met in terms of his own analysis of the problems of value and distribution. On the other hand Sraffa accused Bortkiewicz of having put forward misleading interpretations of Ricardo and Marx and of inconsistencies in the 1906–7 article.

The chapter is organized as follows. The first section describes where Sraffa stood in his own constructive and interpretive work when he came across Bortkiewicz's papers in 1943. Without a clear idea of what Sraffa had himself accomplished by that time, it is impossible to understand his response to Bortkiewicz's criticism of Marx and its role in his reconstruction of the classical theory of value and distribution. The second section provides a brief account of Bortkiewicz's essay on the "cardinal error" in Böhm-Bawerk's theory of interest and of Sraffa's comments on it. Sraffa approved of Bortkiewicz's specification of the task of interest theory, a task Sraffa had accomplished (with regard to single production) with his "second equations" relating to an economy with a surplus and given real (i.e., subsistence) wages elaborated toward the end of 1927. The third section turns to Sraffa's detailed notes on Bortkiewicz's "Wertrechnung und Preisrechnung im Marxschen System" ("Value and Price Calculation in the Marxian System"). The emphasis is on alternative conceptualizations of production – as a circular flow or as a unidirectional process – and their implications for the theory of value and distribution. An important issue will be the effects of the accumulation of capital on income distribution and thus the Ricardian and Marxian explanations of a falling tendency of the rate of profits. Sraffa's notes were composed not least with a view to how the earlier authors' doctrines related to the concept of a falling marginal product of capital and what was wrong with it. While we touch upon this important critical task in Sraffa's work, it is far beyond the scope of this chapter to deal with it in depth. Sraffa defended Marx against some of Bortkiewicz's criticisms. He supported especially two elements of Marx's analysis: (1) the circular flow concept of production, which implies that the maximum rate of profits is finite, and (2) his view that over time this rate is bound to fall as capital accumulates, where, in Sraffa's interpretation, Marx's argument invariably refers to the special case in which capital accumulates but there is no technical progress proper ("invention"). Marx is thus seen to closely follow Ricardo, who in a first step had investigated the implications of the accumulation of capital on the rate of profits in conditions of constant technological knowledge. The fourth section assesses the importance of Bortkiewicz's contributions and Sraffa's critical disquisition on them for the latter's overall task of reformulating the classical approach to the theory of value and distribution and providing the basis for a criticism of marginalist theory.

Before we proceed, some specific difficulties we encountered when working on this chapter deserve to be mentioned. Sraffa's notes, including those
on Bortkiewicz, were not meant to be published. They were written in an
attempt to reach clarity on some of the more difficult analytical and interpretive problems he faced in the course of reconstructing the surplus approach to
the theory of value and distribution. These concerned, first, the impossibility
of reducing commodities to finite series of dated quantities of labor in a circular flow framework. However far back one traces the process of production (in logical time), one will never arrive at a stage where labor is employed
without being assisted by produced means of production. This fact has far-
reaching implications and was at the center of some of Sraffa's criticisms of
Bortkiewicz and his admiration for Marx. One of the implications is that the
maximum rate of profits of a given system of production (corresponding to
zero wages) is finite, not infinite. This fact has an immediate bearing on the
second issue we are concerned with: the impact of the accumulation of capital on the general rate of profits. This issue occupied center stage both in
Ricardo's and in Marx's alternative explanations of a falling tendency of the
rate of profits, and it recurred in a somewhat different form in the concept of
the marginal productivity of capital advocated by neoclassical authors. Hence
Sraffa was not only confronted with an intricate analytical problem but also
with intricate problems of interpretation: How did Ricardo formulate his theory, and on the basis of which assumptions did he reach which conclusions,
and was his reasoning sound? Was Marx's discussion of the falling tendency
of the rate of profits premised in the same way as Ricardo's, and if not, could
the differences in results be fully explained in terms of differences in assumptions? How did the marginalist authors frame their problem and how does
their formulation relate to those of Ricardo and Marx? Given the intrinsic
complexity of the problems at hand, it should come as no surprise that none
of the doctrines under consideration is easy to interpret, a fact that is reflected
in competing views on each of them and on the relationship between them
in the literature. Also, Sraffa's understanding of these doctrines, their merits
and demerits, underwent considerable change over time. This is evidenced by
his comments on certain propositions of the authors he dealt with, by his side
remarks in his working notes, and by his annotations in his books.

It hardly needs to be stressed that the various dimensions of the aim of this
chapter pose not only difficult questions of interpretation, but also of presentation. In order to deal with those questions within the confines of a single
chapter, we must expect from our readers some familiarity with the doctrines
of Ricardo, Marx, and Böhm-Bawerk, with Bortkiewicz's assessment of their
achievements and failures, and with Sraffa's *Production of Commodities by
Means of Commodities* (1960) – the point on which Sraffa's critical and constructive work on the classical approach was to converge. His discovery of
Bortkiewicz's "Wertrechnung" (1906–7) occurred at a crucial stage of the
work on his book, shortly after he was able to resume his studies, which he
had to abandon during the 1930s because of his absorption with the Ricardo

editorial project, and soon after he had studied in great depth Marx's *Capital* at the beginning of the 1940s. Bortkiewicz's essay turned out to be the touchstone of Sraffa's own analysis as he had been able to develop it up until then and of his understanding of the classical authors, most notably Ricardo and Marx. The period from January to April 1943 must therefore be regarded as a most vibrant phase in Sraffa's intellectual development. Had Bortkiewicz anticipated in important respects what Sraffa was about to accomplish? Or had Sraffa by the time he came across Bortkiewicz's work already succeeded in reaching a higher standpoint and a deeper understanding of the classical authors? Without a clear view of the outcome of Sraffa's critical disquisition on Bortkiewicz's views, it is difficult to understand the development of his studies in the 1940s and thereafter.

Sraffa's analytical achievements up until the beginning of 1943

To someone not familiar with the state of Sraffa's analytical and interpretive work at the beginning of 1943, many if not most of his comments on and criticisms of Bortkiewicz might be incomprehensible. Therefore we must prepare the ground by first giving a summary account of where Sraffa stood when he was exposed to Bortkiewicz's studies.[5]

Sraffa's sources and program

Sraffa's constructive work can be traced back to the mid-1920s; it gained momentum in the second half of 1927 and developed with accelerating speed until 1931, when it was abruptly stopped because of the Ricardo edition project to which Sraffa had been appointed in early 1930 by the Royal Economic Society. For the following ten years Sraffa's constructive work was basically at a standstill. However, not surprisingly, because of his editorial work his understanding of Ricardo's theory and of the contributions of other classical economists grew remarkably and made him see things not seen or plainly misunderstood in the received interpretations of Alfred Marshall, Edwin Cannan, Jacob Hollander, and others. When at the beginning of the 1940s Sraffa was finally able to get back to his old notes and to continue his constructive work, he did so with a substantially increased knowledge of the classical approach to the theory of value and distribution and the reasons why it had prematurely been abandoned. Sraffa had already been clear for a considerable time that Marx was the last major classicist before the marginalist doctrine rose to predominance. Therefore two questions were close at hand: First, how did Marx's analysis relate to the analysis especially of Ricardo – did it involve analytical progress or, as some commentators (including Bortkiewicz) maintained, regress? Second, what went wrong – why had demand and supply theory, which Sraffa considered to be inherently flawed, managed to prevail over classical theory? This explains why Sraffa would read the recently published reprint of volume 1 of *Capital* (Marx [1867] 1938) while he was in an internment camp on the Isle of Man from 4 July to 9 October 1940. Back in Cambridge he then carefully scrutinized volumes 2 and 3 of *Capital*, which is reflected in several notes and references in Sraffa's papers and in annotations in his books. It is worth mentioning that Sraffa's annotations in his copies of the various editions of *Capital*, especially the French and English ones, typically contain indexes prepared by him on the flyleaves at the ends of the books or on their inside back covers. These indexes were apparently composed at different times, reflecting Sraffa's progressing analytical preoccupations. This can be inferred from Sraffa's handwriting, which changed over time, and from the parallel reflection of the different problems he was concerned with in his working notes.

We now take a brief look at Sraffa's work in the periods 1927–31 and 1942–43. We begin by mentioning a number of aspects that provide the background against which Sraffa started to reformulate the surplus approach to the theory of value and distribution.

Circular flow, physical real costs, and social surplus

Sraffa was deeply interested in and impressed by recent advances in the natural sciences, especially physics, chemistry, and biology. He was fascinated by quantum physics and thermodynamics and was keen to develop an approach in economics in full recognition of the developments in the natural sciences and the laws regarding the physical and chemical world established by them. This met with his materialist and objectivist orientation, which he had brought to Cambridge not least as a fruit of his long discussions with Antonio Gramsci, and which, he felt, was corroborated by recent developments. He studied authors such as Jules-Henri Poincaré, Heinrich Hertz, Arthur Stanley Eddington, Alfred North Whitehead, and Percy Williams Bridgman. In the late 1920s, Sraffa appears to have wanted to adopt a "natural science point of view" and to develop a "purely objective theory" – an "atomic analysis," as he called it in the summer of 1929 (see D3/12/13: 16 (9), 18). His "first equations," developed in November 1927 and which eventually became chapter 1 of *Production of Commodities* (1960), relate to an economic system without a surplus and thus revolve around the concept of balancing inputs and outputs taken as a whole. Close at hand is the analogy between a product that obtains as the result of the "destruction" of necessary quantities of means of production and means of subsistence, on the one hand, and a chemical reaction conceived of as a balance of the weights of inputs and outputs.[6] In both cases the balance expresses conservation of matter. Sraffa traced the objectivist or natural science point of view back to William Petty (see below) and the physiocrats and discerned a close relationship between his equations and François Quesnay's *Tableau économique*. In the physiocrats, he pointed out, "il valore sia una quantità intrinseca degli oggetti, quasi una qualità fisica o chimica {value is an intrinsic quantity of objects, a quasi physical or chemical property}" (D3/12/12: 7). And with regard to Adam Smith's doctrine of "natural value" he emphasized that the Scotsman was concerned with "that physical, truly natural relation between commodities" (D3/12/11: 83). He also used the term "physical value" of products and insisted that it *"is* equal to what has been consumed" (D3/12/1: 5; see also D3/12/10: 54).

Throughout his work Sraffa did not vacillate as regards his main objective: to explain profits and rents, and the relative prices supporting a given distribution of income, in terms of the concept of *social surplus*. The surplus was obtained after the means of production and the means of sustenance (or wages) in the support of the workers necessary to produce given outputs had been deducted from those outputs. With a given real wage, conceived of as an "inventory" of commodities, the costs under consideration were *physical real costs*. Sraffa at the time saw the history of economics as characterized by a gradual degeneration from this concept of cost to that of psychic costs in contemporary marginalism – Marshall's "real cost" (see Garegnani 2004). Keen to lay a solid foundation of fact revolving around the twin concepts of physical real cost and surplus, Sraffa avoided all subjectivist elements. Subjectivism, he was convinced, made it too easy to slip in ideological elements in economics. Cases in point were the "abstinence" and "waiting" theories of interest, which he considered to be outright apologetic. And he was careful to avoid circular reasoning, that is, to explain values in terms of values.[7] As he stressed in a document presumably written in the second half of 1929, echoing a dictum by Petty, relative prices and income distribution had to be ascertained exclusively in terms of "quantities {that} have an objective, independent existence at every or some instants of the natural (i.e. not interfered with by the experimenter) process of production and distribution; they can therefore be measured physically, with the ordinary instruments of measuring number, weight, time, etc." (D3/12/13: 2).[8]

Simultaneous equations

An important further aspect concerns Sraffa's use of simultaneous equations. An approach to the theory of value and distribution that was based on the concept of circular flow could obviously not exploit its full potentialities without the use of simultaneous equations and the mathematics needed to solve them. This is why we see Sraffa from November 1927 onward formulating such systems of equations. In order to find out their properties, he first consulted textbooks of algebra and then sought the assistance of his "mathematical friends" – Frank P. Ramsey in 1928 and Abram S. Besicovitch and Alister Watson in the 1940s and 1950s (see Kurz and Salvadori 2001, 2004b). Sraffa referred to "my equations," and for good reasons. Simultaneous equations were a tool that he had not encountered in the writings of the classical authors, and the fact that these authors had lacked this tool was in no small degree responsible for their inability to fully master the analytical difficulties encountered. At the same time, Sraffa was aware that this tool played an important role in the most advanced version of marginalism – general equilibrium theory – and was extolled by its advocates, especially Vilfredo Pareto, as involving a huge progress compared with earlier economics. Sraffa had been exposed to Pareto's "equazioni dell'equilibrio generale" (Pareto 1906) while still in Italy, and he had referred to general equilibrium theory in his "Sulle relazioni fra costo e quantità prodotta" (1925).[9]

From a philological point of view it is interesting to note that in describing his first sets of equations and their solutions, Sraffa typically used the term *equilibrium*. Although, as Sraffa noted in the course of his studies of the classical authors, the notion of "equilibrium" had also been employed, among others, by Robert Torrens and Marx, it was, of course, in the late 1920s *the* central concept of marginalism. Sraffa therefore appears to have felt almost at once the need to specify the nature and meaning of his equations as opposed to those of marginalist theory. In a document contained in a folder dated by Sraffa "November 1927" that appears to have been composed immediately after he had elaborated his first and second equations, he noted that "I have not clearly defined nor have clearly in mind" the assumptions underlying "the equations from which the equilibrium is determined" (D3/12/11: 67). The following addendum to the passage just quoted suggests that he was intent on defining his equations with regard to those of marginalist theory and especially of contemporary welfare economics championed by A. C. Pigou and Pareto: "Obviously, among these assumptions there must be a definition of the maximum or optimum of some sort, towards which the whole system tends – something comparable to the 'maximum of utility'." This concern with an optimum is then reflected in Sraffa's attempt to find out at which set of (nonnegative) prices compatible with the given equations and a self-replacing state of the economy is the total value of the (net) product a maximum. However, Sraffa quickly saw that this did not lead anywhere and gave up the idea. It then did not take him long to render precise the purpose and meaning of his equations. In a document titled "Man from the Moon," probably written in 1928, he expounded as follows:

> The significance of the equations is simply this: that if a man fell from the moon on the earth, and noted the amount of things consumed in each factory and the amount produced by each factory during a year, he could deduce at which values the commodities must be sold, if the rate of interest must be uniform and the process of production repeated. In short, the equations show that the conditions of exchange are entirely determined by the conditions of production.
>
> (D3/12/7: 87)[10]

As early as the first period of his work Sraffa also began to see that his equations could serve a critical purpose in addition to the constructive one. Since contemporary (i.e., long-period) general equilibrium theory sought to determine the competitive (uniform) rate of interest and the corresponding set of prices, the equilibrium it established necessarily had to satisfy Sraffa's equations. The latter could thus be used to find out, as Sraffa stressed variously and also in a note dated 2 April 1957, "whether there is room enough for the marginal system" (D3/12/46: 32a). A concern with this critical task permeates all three periods of his work.

The whole and its parts

There is an important feature of Sraffa's equations to which we have to turn briefly. This concerns the assumption of given gross outputs. Adopting the method of simultaneous equations did by no means involve adopting Paretian general equilibrium theory. While Sraffa credited Pareto with having improved upon traditional marginalist theory by introducing indifference curves and refining the general equilibrium method, major flaws of the theory had been left untouched.[11] The "forces" the theory contemplated as bringing about a tendency toward equilibrium – "demand" and "supply," conceived of as schedules or functions – were essentially the traditional ones. According to Sraffa, these had no objective contents: nothing corresponded to them in the real world; and they were based on the untenable assumption of continuity. Inequality of income, customs, collective agreements, etc., were of much greater importance than individual utility and disutility or their modern equivalents. Sraffa agreed with methodologists and ethnologists like François Simiand and Bronislaw Malinowski who had argued that the marginalist perspective of *homo economicus* on human nature and society could not be sustained. Some of the difficulties besetting the theory had recently also surfaced in the writings of the more attentive marginalist authors themselves. With reference to the works of Alfred Marshall, Henry Cunynghame, Francis Y. Edgeworth, and A. C. Pigou, Sraffa pointed out that the allowance for *external economies* had undermined the strictly individualistic point of view. Hence, general equilibrium theory was not only confronted with the phenomenon of great complexity, as Pareto had maintained; it was also confronted with a kind of complexity that could not, as a matter of principle, be captured in terms of the individualistic approach. As regards the problem of externalities and demand, Sraffa stressed in a note composed in the summer of 1927 when preparing his lectures on advanced value theory "that it is not sufficient to make {the} utility of one commodity {a} function of all others consumed by {the} individual," but it would have also to be made dependent on the consumption of the "community" as a whole! Sraffa drew the following parallel: "It would be as if in astronomy we said the movement of each star depends upon all the others, but we have not the faintest idea of the shape of the functions!" (D3/12/3: 63).

This raised the question whether the part should be considered as constitutive of the whole, as neoclassical authors assumed, or vice versa. Sraffa, for reasons that should by now be obvious, sided with the latter methodological standpoint and found himself in agreement with the "objectivism" of contemporary natural sciences (see, for example, Whitehead 1926). The view that the whole is constitutive of the part is reflected, inter alia, in Sraffa's assumption of given gross outputs. To take gross outputs as given was clearly dictated by the ubiquitous nature of externalities and by increasing returns that are external to the industry as they had been investigated by Adam Smith in his analysis of the division of labor. This methodological position Sraffa shared with the classical economists and also with John Maynard Keynes.

When Sraffa began his constructive work, his knowledge of the classical authors, although swiftly growing, was not yet very developed. Edwin Cannan's lectures at the LSE and Marshall's *Principles* had exposed him to the conventional interpretation of the classical authors as early and crude demand and supply theorists. In 1927 and 1928 he read the newly published French edition of Karl Marx's *Theorien über den Mehrwert*, the *Histoire* (Marx [1861–63] 1924–25), which contains a radically different perspective on the classical authors. He had already encountered versions of this perspective in the early 1920s while consulting the available Italian literature devoted to the theory of value (e.g., books by Augusto Graziani and Arturo Labriola). Reading the *Histoire* appears to have contributed a fair measure of confidence to Sraffa's growing conviction that there must have been a fundamentally different approach to the theory of value and distribution that had been "submerged and forgotten since the advent of the 'marginal' method" (Sraffa 1960, v). Sraffa also saw that Marx had to be credited with having rediscovered this approach, but for reasons given further down he originally thought that Marx's reconstruction involved a "corruption" of it. Also, in terms of sophistication, modern marginalist theory could not be compared with the demand and supply theories Marx had attacked and dubbed "vulgar economics." The former had to be scrutinized closely in order to see whether and to what extent it had managed to overcome the deficiencies of its "vulgar" predecessors.

Hence Sraffa was confronted with three huge tasks that he specified as early as November 1927 in the following way:

1. Identify the "essence of the classical theories of value" by going back to the writings of Petty, Cantillon, the physiocrats, and the English classical political economists.
2. Reconstruct this "essence" in terms of a formulation that sheds the weaknesses and elaborates on the strengths of its earlier versions.
3. Find out "what is the difference with the later theories" and why the classical theory had been abandoned.

(With respect to these three tasks, see, in particular, D3/12/4: 12.)

Identifying the essence of the classical theories of value

Sraffa at the time was already clear that major classical economists had adopted a strictly "objectivist" point of view. He was particularly impressed by William Petty's "'physician's' outlook," which consisted in expressing himself only

> in Terms of Number, Weight or Measure, …. and to consider only such Causes, as have visible Foundations in Nature; leaving those that depend upon the mutable Minds, Opinions, Appetites, and Passions of particular Men, to the Consideration of others.
>
> (Petty [1899] 1986, 244)

Sraffa saw that, several differences notwithstanding, the contributions of Smith, Ricardo, Marx, and many other authors exhibited a similar orientation and analytical structure and sought to explain all shares of income other than wages in terms of the surplus product within a circular flow framework of the analysis. In Sraffa's interpretation, physical real cost held the key to the classical approach to the problem of value. He saw this view corroborated in the writings of numerous authors. A particularly clear expression of it had been given by James Mill ([1821] 1826, 165), who had insisted that, in the last instance, "the agents of production are the commodities themselves … They are the food of the labourer, the tools and the machinery with which he works, and the raw materials which he works upon."[12] Or, as Sraffa stressed toward the end of 1927, "the sort of 'costs' which determines values is the collection of material things used up in production" (D3/12/7: 106). And, "the fundamental force is physical real cost," which, however, is "seen only in general equilibrium" (D3/12/42: 46). The reference to "general equilibrium" was close at hand, because with the "Production of Commodities by Commodities," as Sraffa for a considerable time intended to title the book he was in the process of composing, echoing Mill's dictum above, the determination of values involved solving a set of simultaneous equations.

It will not have escaped the reader's attention that up until now the concept of "labor" and with it the labor theory of value, which had played a central part in the classical authors and Marx, have not been mentioned. The reason for this is that at the beginning of his constructive work Sraffa was convinced that these stood for the failure of the earlier authors to elaborate a coherent theory of value and distribution. The right starting point, he insisted, was that of Petty, who had singled out workers' means of subsistence, their "food," not labor, as the "ultimate measure of value." Sraffa accused Ricardo and Marx of having "corrupted" the concept of physical real cost (see, for example, D3/12/4: 2). As late as 1929 he still considered labor as "not a quantity at all" and called the concept "metaphysical" (see, for example, D3/12/11: 64). He questioned the special treatment of the labor of a wage earner as compared with that of a slave, a horse, or a machine, as it was advocated by some classical authors and also by Marshall, and maintained that "it is a purely mystical conception that attributes to human labour a special gift of determining value" (D3/12/9: 89). This view was understandable with regard to what Sraffa called his "first" and "second equations" (see below), that is, those relating to an economy without and with a surplus and given *real*, that is, *commodity*, wages, as we encounter them again in Sraffa 1960 (see paragraphs 1–5 of that book). In such a framework, the problem of value and distribution could be dealt with without any need of ever mentioning labor.

Yet, as soon as Sraffa, following Ricardo's lead, turned to the case in which workers participate in the sharing out of the surplus product in his "third equations," a new wage concept was needed – a fact that forced him to reconsider his views on labor. Sraffa was impressed by the way in which Ricardo had attempted to deal with the case under consideration in terms of what Sraffa called "proportional wages," that is, "the proportion of the annual labour of the country ... devoted to the support of the labourers" (Ricardo 1951–73, 1:49).[13] Toward the end of the first period of his constructive work, if not earlier, Sraffa had eventually convinced himself that the classical authors had good reasons to treat labor as an economic quantity in proportion to which wages were paid. Because with workers receiving a share of the surplus product, wages could be given only in some more or less abstract standard and their magnitude could be specified in proportion to the labor (time) performed. And when at around the same time he developed what he called his "second way of approach" to the problem of value in terms of the reduction to dated amounts of wages paid in the production of a commodity or the quantities of labor, the first being simultaneous equations, he was finally possessed of a solid basis from which to assess the merits and demerits of the labor theory of value in a circular flow framework. He saw that to a share of wages equal to unity corresponded a zero rate of interest and relative prices which, using the method of reduction to wages or labor, could be seen to be proportional to the total wages paid or the quantities of labor needed directly and indirectly in the production of the various commodities.

We now turn briefly to Sraffa's equations.

Reconstructing the classical theory of value and distribution

Sraffa's "first equations"

In November 1927 Sraffa began to elaborate his systems of equations. He quite naturally started with an economy that produces just enough, neither more nor less, to recover the necessary means of production used up in the process of production and the necessary means of subsistence in the support of workers – a situation reflected in what he called his "first equations." He emphasized that this amounts to considering wages "as amounts of fuel for production" (D3/12/7: 138) and identified the situation as the realm of *pure necessities*, or "natural economy." In this case the concept of physical real cost applied in an unadulterated way. With respect to value in such conditions, Sraffa insisted that there was no problem of "incentives," the grand theme of marginalism: what mattered were exclusively the material costs of production of a commodity. The means of subsistence in the support of workers were an indispensable part of these physical real costs, because only their (recurrent) consumption "enabled" workers to perform their function. The periodic destruction of such commodities is a necessary condition for the economic system to realize a "self-replacing state," but it is not alone sufficient. The system must be able to restore periodically the initial distribution of resources in order for the (re)productive process to continue unhampered. Commodities must be exchanged for one another at the end of the uniform period of production. But which exchange ratios guarantee the repetition of the process? Sraffa showed that the sought-after ratios, or what Ricardo had called "absolute" values, were uniquely determined by the sociotechnical conditions of production and could be ascertained by solving a set of linear homogeneous production equations.

Sraffa's "second equations"

Next Sraffa in his "second equations" turned to the case in which the system produces a surplus over and above the necessary physical real costs, including subsistence wages. He stressed, "When we have got surplus, natural economy stops" (D3/12/11: 42) and social and institutional factors become important. Technically this is reflected in the fact that "the equations become contradictory" (D3/12/6: 16). Materially, "the 'absolute values' have no more the appeal to commonsense of restoring the initial position – which is required if production has to go on" (D3/12/6: 10). Indeed, in the with-surplus economy a whole range of exchange ratios is, in principle, compatible with the condition of self-replacement (see D3/12/6: 9). Sraffa stressed that "within those limits value will be indeterminate." "It is therefore necessary to introduce some new assumption, which in substance will amount to determine ... according to which criterion the surplus is distributed between the different industries" (D3/12/6: 16). With free competition, and focusing attention on the case of only circulating capital, the surplus is distributed in terms of a uniform rate of interest on the value of the "capital" advanced in the different industries. How is this rate determined? It is determined, Sraffa insisted, *simultaneously* with relative prices and thus the value of capital employed in each industry and in the system as a whole. By June 1928 he had managed, with the help of his friend and colleague Frank Ramsey, to establish that a solution existed and what it was (see Kurz and Salvadori 2001, 262–264). (His respective considerations foreshadow paragraphs 4–5 of his 1960 book.)

Sraffa's "third equations" and Ricardo's "proportional wages"

While in his second equations he retained the assumption of given inventory wages, Sraffa almost in parallel began to investigate the case of a change in wages and its impact on the rate of interest and relative prices, given the system of production, in terms of his "third equations." (His respective considerations foreshadow paragraphs 8–12 of his 1960 book.) He did this first in terms of a redistribution of the surplus product away from profits and toward wages in proportion to the original vector of the surplus product.[14] This assumption allowed him to conceive of the redistribution of the surplus in straightforward physical terms and yet advocate a share concept of surplus wages that is independent of relative prices. He demonstrated that an increase in wages implied a decrease in the rate of interest and in general a change in relative prices. However, for obvious reasons he was not happy with the idea of variable surplus wages with a constant commodity composition: How could the latter be known independently of the prices of commodities? He saw that Ricardo had also allowed for a participation of workers in the surplus product and was especially fascinated by the way Ricardo had done this analytically in terms of proportional wages, which had allowed him to circumnavigate the problem just mentioned. The germs of Sraffa's work in this regard can be traced back to the latter part of the first period of his constructive work, but it was only as a consequence of his work on the Ricardo edition in the 1930s that he understood more clearly the new conceptualization of real wages as proportional wages that Ricardo had adopted in the *Principles* (see also Sraffa 1951, lii). In particular, Sraffa became aware of the fact that Ricardo's argument was not meant to be limited to the case of a given economy at a given time but was designed to cover in at least one important respect also the development of the economy *over time*. More specifically, Ricardo's demonstration of the inverse relationship between the rate of profits and wages was seen to encompass the case in which the productivity of labor changes. It was on the basis of the new wage concept (and on the premise that the social capital consisted only of, or could be reduced to, wages) that Ricardo had felt he could assert what may be called his "fundamental proposition on distribution": that the *rate* of profits depends on *proportional wages*, and on nothing else.

Before we proceed with a summary account of Sraffa's achievements in the first period, it is worth noting that Sraffa upon resuming his work on his book in the summer of 1942 adopted for good a share concept of wages in his third equations, with wages, w, expressed as a proportion of the net product ($1 \geq w \geq 0$). However, at first he retained the Ricardo-Marx assumption that wages as a whole were paid out of the capital advanced at the beginning of the uniform period of production, that is, *ante factum*.[15] It was only toward the end of 1943 that he abandoned the classical assumption and took wages to be entirely paid out of the product. A consequence of this was the replacement of the classical socio-economic distinction between "necessaries" and "luxuries" with the more technical distinction between "basic" and "nonbasic" products.

Relative prices and distribution: the Austrian concept of "period of production" and Sraffa's statistical hypothesis

In the context of an investigation in the late 1920s of how a change in wages affects the rate of interest and relative prices, given the system of production in use, Sraffa saw that solving a set of simultaneous equations for each and every level of wages was cumbersome and the results not very transparent. He was therefore on the lookout for a second method designed to render the properties of the system easier to grasp. The method sought, as we have already noted, was the reduction to dated quantities of labor (or wages appropriately discounted forward). Could the series of dated labor terms be expressed in a compact form, in a single magnitude, that was independent of distribution? As is well known, Eugen von Böhm-Bawerk had thought that this was indeed possible and in his *Positive Theory of Capital* ([1889] 1959) had elaborated such a measure in terms of the "average period of production." Sraffa around the turn of 1928 studied Böhm-Bawerk's attempt and saw that the concept could not be defined independently of the rate of interest. Therefore it could not be used as a primitive technical data, or given, in the theory of value and distribution. However, in studying the impact of a change in distribution on relative prices, it was possible to employ the average period as a measure of the capital-to-labor ratio with which a given commodity was produced at the level of the rate of interest taken as the starting point of the investigation. Sraffa in fact for a while used the concept for this purpose and was even provisionally prepared to accept two doctrines Böhm-Bawerk had advocated. First, with a rise in wages (and the corresponding fall in the rate of interest), consumption goods would fall in price relative to capital goods. This was seen to be an implication of the Austrian unidirectional conceptualization of production which starts with unassisted labor and leads via a finite sequence of intermediate or capital goods to final or consumption goods. Being obtained at the very end of the production process, the latter were generally taken to be produced with a higher capital-to-labor ratio (or average period of production) than capital goods. Second, in the case in which there is a choice of technique, cost-minimizing producers at a lower (higher) rate of interest would invariably adopt that method of producing a given commodity which is associated with a higher (lower) average period of production.

Sraffa soon got doubts as to the validity of these doctrines. In a manuscript he began to write in February 1931 he stated that, contrary to the marginalist proposition, consumption goods were not necessarily produced in a more capital-intensive way than capital goods. In a circular flow framework, the Austrian classification of goods according to their greater or smaller distance from the maturing of the final product made no sense: wheat, for example, was both a means of production (seed) and a consumption good. Sraffa concluded as follows with regard to the sum total of capital goods compared with the sum total of goods produced:

> It may be said that *the value of total capital in terms of total goods produced cannot vary* {as a consequence of a variation of wages and a contrary variation of the rate of interest}, *since the goods are composed exactly in the same proportions as the capitals which have produced them.*
>
> (D3/12/7: 157(3); emphasis added)

Sraffa added that the proposition is "false, but may contain an *element of truth*." Some twelve years later, in a note composed in November 1943, he clarified that his proposition was based on the "statistical compensation of large numbers" (D3/12/35: 28). Henceforth he called the assumption that the value of social capital relative to that of social product does not change with a change in distribution "My Hypothesis" or simply "Hypothesis."

Exploring the "element of truth" mentioned, Sraffa eventually had to abandon the idea that any actual economic system could ever be expected to satisfy the hypothesis. He therefore had to construct an artificial system out of his equations that did so. This he accomplished in late January 1944 in terms of the device of the "Standard commodity" and "Standard system" (see the pages beginning with 61 in D3/12/36).

However, prior to mastering this task, and actually helping him a great deal in this respect, Sraffa at the beginning of the 1940s credits Marx explicitly with a number of important analytical achievements. Since there are no traces of the attributions under consideration to be found in Sraffa's papers relating to the first period of his work, it appears safe to assume that at the time he was not aware of these achievements. His findings must have come as a formidable surprise to him and apparently must have greatly contributed to his growing admiration for Marx, the economic theorist, as distinct from Marx, the materialist philosopher and social critic.

Sraffa on Marx's analytical achievements

Studying carefully Marx's *Capital* (and anew the *Theories of Surplus Value*) at the beginning of the 1940s, Sraffa found that Marx had detected an important error in Ricardo's argument. Marx had approved of Ricardo's new conceptualization of real wages as proportional wages (see Marx [1861–63] 1989, 226–227, 419) and had translated it into the relation between the value of the social surplus product (S) and that of the social variable capital (V), or *rate of surplus value* (S/V).[16] Accordingly, Ricardo's proposition that the level of the general rate of profits is inversely related to proportional wages is equivalent to the statement that its fall (rise) is conditional on a fall (rise) in the rate of surplus value. Marx ([1861–63] 1989, 10) had objected to this that Ricardo had erroneously identified the rate of profits with the rate of surplus value: he had been led to this identification because "in his observations on profit and wages, Ricardo ... treats the matter as though the entire capital were laid out directly in wages." If we take into account nonwage capital – or, more precisely, if we take into account that capital cannot be resolved entirely into direct and indirect wages in a finite number of steps, as Ricardo had been inclined to assume – then his proposition no longer held necessarily true: *the rate of profits can fall (or rise) even if proportional wages remain constant.*

However, as Sraffa noted, Marx had not always been consistent in his own treatment of wages. Notwithstanding his approval and adoption of Ricardo's concept of proportional wages, Marx – especially in his own working notes on the law of the falling tendency of the rate of profits – had freely moved between this concept and the traditional one of real wages conceived of as an inventory of commodities. As will be seen below, in Sraffa's view the existence side by side of these two conceptions, which are not mutually compatible with each other, was a fertile source of confusion and misinterpretation.

While Sraffa had always held Marx in high esteem, at the beginning of the 1940s he saw in detail what in the late 1920s and at the beginning of the 1930s he appears to have seen only vaguely, if at all, namely, that Marx had grappled with similar problems and had made some considerable progress over and above the state in which Ricardo had left the theory of value and distribution. According to Sraffa, Marx's most remarkable and closely related achievements were the following:

1. Marx's representation of a given system of production in terms of his schemes of reproduction shared the same outlook as the circular flow approach of the physiocrats.[17]
2. Closely related to this was Marx's concept of "Constant Capital," which expresses the fact that commodities are produced by means of commodities. This is why, as we shall see, Sraffa defended this concept against Bortkiewicz, who, starting from Dmitriev's "Austrian" representation of production as a linear flow of finite duration, had maintained that the concept was unimportant and could be dispensed with.
3. In terms of his labor-value-based approach, Marx had been able, however imperfectly, to see through the complexities of the system under consideration and establish the fact that the rate of profits was bounded from above. In Marx's conceptualization, the maximum rate of profits that obtained when wages were nil was equal to L/C, that is, the ratio of total living labor expended during a year ($L=V + S$) and social constant capital (C). It was thus equal to the inverse of the "Organic Composition of Capital" of the system as a whole.[18] Sraffa must have been especially flabbergasted when he found out that Marx in terms of what Sraffa called the former's "Value Hypothesis" had presupposed a fact which he, Sraffa, had sought to establish with his statistical "Hypothesis": both postulated that the ratio of social capital to social product was independent of the rate of profits.
4. With the capital-to-output ratio being independent of the way in which the product is shared out between wages and profits, Marx had paved the way to the establishment of the inverse relationship between the *rate* of profits and proportional wages in a circular flow system.

As a reflection of his deeper knowledge and understanding of Marx's contribution, in the 1940s we see Sraffa use such notions as simple reproduction, constant and variable capital, rate of surplus value, and organic composition of capital. However, Marx's concepts are typically not simply adopted, but are adapted to Sraffa's own non-labor-value-based approach. By the end of the first period of his constructive work, Sraffa had understood that relative prices depended in a possibly intricate manner on the distribution of income. However, it was not immediately clear how this dependence could be given a precise expression nor how the distributive variables, the rate of profits and proportional wages, were related. In the early 1940s he saw that by taking the rate of profits as given, which was suggested by considerations that eventually led to the short paragraph 44 of his book, he could render the equations of production linear. The only thing that was missing in order to determine relative prices at each level of the rate of profits was the relationship between the latter and proportional wages. Once this relationship was found, Sraffa could proceed in a familiar way: with a given rate of profits he could determine the corresponding share of wages. These two magnitudes could then be plugged into the equations and the latter could be solved using the mathematical tools Sraffa had acquainted himself with. This explains why he spent so much time on establishing the relation between the two distributive variables.[19] He was able to fully solve the problem for systems with single production in 1944 in terms of the Standard commodity. With wages paid *post factum* and expressed as a proportion of the Standard net product, the sought-after relation between the two distributive variables is linear and, most important, it applies also to the actual economic system.

We are now ready to discuss Sraffa's comments on Bortkiewicz's papers. We begin with Bortkiewicz's criticism of Böhm-Bawerk's theory of capital and interest because it contains a specification of an important criterion that interest theory has to meet, a criterion that Sraffa shared. This discussion prepares the ground for Sraffa's treatment of Bortkiewicz's disquisition on Marx and Ricardo.

Bortkiewicz on the "cardinal error" of Böhm-Bawerk's theory of interest

Böhm-Bawerk's "third ground"

In his paper "Der Kardinalfehler der Böhm-Bawerkschen Zinstheorie," Bortkiewicz (1906) criticized the "Three Grounds" put forward by Böhm-Bawerk in his theory of capital and interest in favor of a positive rate of interest: (1) the differences between wants and provision in different periods of time; (2) the systematic underestimation of future wants and the means available to satisfy them; and (3) the technical superiority of present compared with future goods of the same quality and quantity. Bortkiewicz focused attention on the third ground – according to Böhm-Bawerk ([1889] 1902, 286) the "main pillar" of his theory of interest – which referred to a "purely objective factor" (Bortkiewicz 1906, 945). Was it possible to derive from it a value agio in favor of present goods as the basis of a positive rate of interest?

Bortkiewicz did not think so – he rather considered Böhm-Bawerk's respective argument to contain the "cardinal error" of his entire construction.[20] To show this, he turned to a numerical example in the *Positive Theory of Capital* meant to illustrate the superiority of "more roundabout" processes of production. The example, Bortkiewicz maintained, was misleading because Böhm-Bawerk had given only an incomplete picture of the case under consideration. The example concerns production processes started in consecutive years. Alas, Böhm-Bawerk had assumed without any justification that all processes stop at the end of the process started first. If each process was instead taken to break off after the same number of years as the first one, we arrive at a uniformly staggered system of production. Now the process started first is no longer superior to all other processes with regard to all future time periods, because after its truncation the other processes still generate outputs, whereas the first one no longer does. Without a knowledge of the value relations between the goods obtained at different points in time, the result is a *"non liquet"* (Bortkiewicz 1906, 954). Bortkiewicz concluded that, seen from a purely formal point of view, he (Böhm-Bawerk) did not reason correctly. His argumentation, on which he puts the main weight, suffers from an internal mistake:

> It appears that we need not go beyond the very abstract scheme of v. Böhm-Bawerk to prove that interest cannot be determined, in the way he attempts to (nor, as I believe, in any other way), *from the technical conditions of production.*
>
> (958; emphasis added)

Sraffa excerpted this passage and marked his translation of the last sentence with a straight line in the margin (D1/91: 5): it was precisely this task (i.e., to determine interest exclusively from the technical conditions of production) he had put to himself in 1927–28.

Next, Bortkiewicz had turned to a critical examination of Böhm-Bawerk's discussion of which method(s) of production will be chosen by cost-minimizing producers when there is a choice of technique, and which interest rate and prices would obtain. The discussion was based in the usual marginalist way on the assumption that different "quantities of capital" available to producers involve the adoption of different methods of production. More precisely, "the more capital a producer has at his disposal, the higher the output (per unit of labor employed) he produces." Bortkiewicz added that in this version, which avoided the disputed "average period," Böhm-Bawerk's basic underlying idea "can most likely be advocated." But, Bortkiewicz asked,

> is it allowed, when the question is to explain the phenomenon of interest, to make a comparison between producers who are endowed with capital goods in different quantities? Has not Böhm-Bawerk himself explained to the followers of the productivity theory {the reference is especially to Thünen} that a plus of product obtained through a plus of capital is not as such identical with a plus of value, since as a consequence of a stronger participation of the factor capital in production a cheapening of the product may result?
>
> (959)

Bortkiewicz added that Böhm-Bawerk's objection obviously assumed that the more capitalistic method was universally employed, because otherwise the value of the product could not be regulated by it. As Rudolf Stolzmann (1896) had already pointed out, this had the fatal implication that Böhm-Bawerk's objection now applied also to his own theory. If Böhm-Bawerk was right in maintaining that with the universal use of the more capitalistic method the value of the product was bound to fall, then it was unclear whether this fall left any room for interest. At any rate, as Stolzmann had rightly stressed, interest "can no longer be derived from the difference between the amount of product which can be obtained *without* the capitalistic roundabout, and the amount of product which can be obtained *with* the help of it" (as quoted in Bortkiewicz 1906, 959). Bortkiewicz concluded:

> With these remarks Stolzmann has, I believe, really shown up the weakest point in the Böhm-Bawerkian theory of interest. The objective basis of this theory could in fact be held to be valid if it {were} established, on whatever grounds, *that methods of production of different degrees of productivity are applied side by side*, or, more exactly, must be applied under the condition that each producer follows uncompromisingly the economic principle.
>
> (960; emphasis added)

The italicized part was marked by Sraffa with two vertical lines in the margin (see D1/91: 6).

"Bortkiewicz's dictum" on the "touchstone" of interest theory

In Bortkiewicz's view, Böhm-Bawerk had not succeeded in explaining interest. He had failed not least because of his inability to integrate the theory of interest and the theory of value in a coherent manner. And he had put the problem in a quasi "dynamic" setting where it did not belong. This becomes clear in Bortkiewicz's (1906, 970–971) following remarkable proposition:

> I believe that this can be regarded as *the touchstone of such a theory*: whether it is able to show the general cause of interest also for the case in which not only *no technical progress*, of whichever type, takes place, but also the length of the periods of production appears to be technically predetermined, so that *no choice* is possible between different methods.
>
> (emphases added)[21]

In other words, interest had to be explained in conditions of a *given* system of production – setting aside a choice of technique and technical progress. Sraffa marked this passage in the margin, and in brackets referred to a number of further passages in Bortkiewicz's paper with similar or related statements. As we have seen on p. 153 above, Sraffa in 1927, unaware of the conditions Bortkiewicz had enunciated two decades earlier, met them in terms of his "second equations."[22]

The next entry in Sraffa's notebook is an excerpt of two statements from Bortkiewicz's article "Zur Zinstheorie. II. Entgegnung" (Bortkiewicz 1907b), which is a rejoinder to a critical comment by H. Oswalt (1907) on the "Kardinalfehler" article. The two statements are closely related to the passage quoted above and strike a recurrent theme in Sraffa's papers:

> Now my opinion is that in general the value of goods can only depend upon such technical knowledge as is applied in practice. But the value of goods remains unaffected by knowledge which, on whatever grounds, is not utilized ... The result thus obtained can be summed up in the following brief formula: *for [the determination of] the value of goods there come into consideration only actual methods of production (Ver-wendungsarten), and not merely potential ones.*
> (D1/91: 7; see Bortkiewicz 1907b, 1296–1297, 1299)

Sraffa marked these passages approvingly in the margin and then noted, apparently having looked up the "Critical Excursions" in the *Positive Theory of Capital*,[23] in which Böhm-Bawerk had answered his critics, that the Austrian had misunderstood Bortkiewicz: "And he begs the question by saying that the touchstone of no choice of period cannot be applied to his theory which professes to be based on just such a choice" (D1/91: 7). In Sraffa's papers, Bortkiewicz's insistence on the exclusive relevance in the theory of value of methods that are *actually used* recurs repeatedly as "Bortkiewicz's dictum" (see, for example, D3/12/18: 9). Sraffa had actually stated the same maxim, independently of Bortkiewicz, in a document of October 1929:

> Clearly, we must reduce *all* the data to things that actually happen, excluding inexistent possibilities. Only such things are measurable, and can enter the theory as "knowns," or "constants"; and, in reality, only really happening things can be real causes and determine effects.
> (D3/12/13: 1(2))

In the next entry, dated 21 April 1943, Sraffa takes up Bortkiewicz's "Der Kardinalfehler" again. While Bortkiewicz had requested that the theory of interest must be able to explain the cause of interest also when there is no choice of technique, he had not been of the opinion that the problem of choice has no role to play in it. However, he had maintained, adopting Böhm-Bawerk's (in)famous distinction, that while it is of no import with regard to the *cause* of interest, it plays a role as regards the determination of its *size* (Bortkiewicz 1906, 971). Sraffa commented on this distinction:

> Now if one interprets it as distinguishing between "causes of existence" and "causes of size," it seems frightfully metaphysical. One can start asking, how can "existence" be determined in the abstract, without being a particular, specific, existence determined in its magnitude and its location? etc.

But more probably he means that the total of profits, or proportion of the product, or $1-w$ {w stands for the share of wages in net income} is determined on other grounds, and that the "coefficients" and "alternative methods" can only determine the quantity of capital and thereby the numerical value of the rate of interest.

(D1/91: 8)

Sraffa thus agreed with Bortkiewicz that the "touchstone" of the theory of interest was to show the "general cause of interest" for a *given system of production* in which "no choice is possible between different methods." This specification flew in the face of the marginalist explanation of interest in terms of a hypothetical *change* in the proportion of "factors" of production and thus a change in technique. As Sraffa was to write in the preface of his 1960 book, "In a system in which, day after day, production continued unchanged in those respects, the marginal product of a factor ... would not merely be hard to find – it just would not be there to be found" (v).

Therefore, Sraffa must have been taken aback when Bortkiewicz, who had so clearly and convincingly spelled out the requirements the theory of interest had to meet, toward the end of his paper on Marx and Ricardo opted for incorporating the cost equations into a Walrasian system of equations. However, before we come to this aspect we must first provide a summary account of Sraffa's assessment of Bortkiewicz's views on Marx and Ricardo.

Bortkiewicz on Marx and Ricardo

Preliminary observations

We learned in the first section that Sraffa showed little interest in the problem of the so-called "transformation" of labor values into prices of production, which had bothered Marx and whose approach Bortkiewicz had scrutinized critically. According to Sraffa, the early classical economists had rightly started from physical real costs and were only pushed toward basing their theory of value on labor magnitudes as a consequence of their inability to overcome the analytical difficulties they faced vis-à-vis the circular flow of heterogeneous commodities. The method of simultaneous equations, which would have solved their problem, was not at their disposal. As Sraffa's early work demonstrates impressively, the classical theory of value and distribution could be elaborated without any reference to "labor values."

Sraffa was instead interested in whether Bortkiewicz's essay contained anything that was of help to better understand marginalist theory and its deficiencies. According to Sraffa this was indeed the case. Sraffa's concern with marginalism is particularly obvious in his discussion of the problem of the impact of capital accumulation on the rate of profits. Indeed, the marginalist asks what would be the effect of an infinitesimally small increase in the "quantity of capital" on the rate of profits, given the technical alternatives from which cost-minimizing producers can choose. This perspective is made very clear in a document dated

20 August 1943. Sraffa there assumed "conditions of stationary technical pos-sibilities (i.e. no inventions)." He qualified this assumption as "in itself utterly absurd," but justified it in the following terms: "1) *It adopts the basic outlook of the marginal product theory of capital and therefore serves to refute it –* 2) it shows the tendency of *r* to fall in the absence of technical invention, and thereby shows the necessity of the latter" (D3/12/34: 5; emphasis added).

Reading Sraffa's comments, one gets the impression that while none of Bortkiewicz's results struck him as true novelties, he perceived the latter's essay as a welcome opportunity to test and sharpen his own argument. Sraffa had thought through similar problems in terms of the different framework of a circular flow of production and was keen to relate Bortkiewicz's unidirec-tional (or "Austrian") analysis to his own. He saw that in important respects Bortkiewicz's essay corroborated his own reconstruction of the classical approach to the theory of value and distribution. However, he also felt that in a number of respects Bortkiewicz had not been faithful to the true problems Ricardo and Marx had been confronted with and the concepts they had forged to solve them, and had therefore arrived at a distorted picture of the issues under consideration. These concerned in particular Ricardo's and Marx's respective demonstrations of the falling tendency of the rate of profits.

The "law of the tendency of the rate of profits to fall": Sraffa's reading of Ricardo and Marx

For a proper understanding of Sraffa's comments on Bortkiewicz's criticism of Marx's law, it is necessary to reconstruct his own reading of Marx's expla-nation of the falling rate of profits. Since there is no single document in which Sraffa set out his understanding of Marx's law, it had to be pieced together from a number of working notes (which are scattered across several folders) and annotations in his books, first and foremost in his copies of *Capital* and the *Theories of Surplus of Value*.[24] Due to space constraints we can here only briefly summarize the argument without providing full details.[25]

According to Sraffa, Marx had developed his law strictly against the back-ground of Ricardo's explanation of a falling tendency of the general rate of profits. As we noted above, Ricardo (1951–73, 1:49), in ascertaining the level of the general rate of profits and its development over time in changing tech-nical conditions, had taken as given "the proportion of the annual labour of the country ... devoted to the support of the labourers." Ricardo's con-cept was subsequently adopted by Marx in terms of a given rate of surplus value. In his observations on the wage-profit relationship, Ricardo typically assumed that the social capital consists only of wages (or can be fully reduced to wages in a finite number of steps), so that the rate of profits, *r*, is given by the ratio of profits, *P*, to wages, *W*,

$$r = \frac{P}{W} = \frac{1-w}{w},$$

where *w* designates proportional wages (i.e., the wage share). Starting from this relationship, Ricardo had then argued that as capital accumulates, proportional wages tend to rise, and the rate of profits tends to fall, because of increasing costs of production due to diminishing returns in agriculture. The rising money prices of agricultural commodities, in particular food, necessitate increases in money wages in order to keep "real," that is, commodity, wages constant. To this Ricardo added the following argument. With the rise in nominal wages and the associated fall in the rate of profits it becomes profitable to introduce known but hitherto unused methods of production ("machinery"). In Ricardo's words, "Machinery and labour are in constant competition and the former can frequently not be employed until labour {i.e., the money wage} rises" (1:395). The introduction of machinery in turn can temporarily check the rise in money wages and the associated fall in the rate of profits. However, with further capital accumulation and a growing population, money wages, and hence also proportional wages, will sooner or later have to start rising again.

In Sraffa's reading, Marx had detected an important error in Ricardo's line of reasoning, which emanated from his neglect of nonwage capital in the analysis of the wage-profit relationship.[26] As Marx ([1861–63] 1989, 73) stressed over and over again, this neglect had serious implications, and in particular had misled Ricardo into focusing attention on the wrong causes in his explanation of a falling tendency of the rate of profits:

> But because for Ricardo the *rate of profit* and the *rate of surplus value* …
> are identical terms, a permanent fall in profit or the tendency of profit
> to fall can only be explained as the result of the *same causes* that bring
> about a permanent fall or tendency to fall in the *rate of surplus value*, i.e.
> in that part of the day during which the worker does not work for himself
> but for the capitalist. What are these causes? If the length of the working
> day is assumed to remain constant, then the part of it during which the
> worker works for nothing for the capitalist can only fall, diminish, if the
> part during which he works for himself grows. And this is only possible
> (assuming that LABOUR is paid at its VALUE) if the *value* of the NECESSAR-
> IES – the means of subsistence on which the worker spends his wages –
> increases. But as a result of the development of the productive power of
> labour, the value of industrial commodities is constantly decreasing. The
> diminishing rate of profit can therefore only be explained by the fact that
> the value of FOOD, the principal component part of the means of subsist-
> ence, is constantly rising.

For Ricardo, the general rate of profits falls if, and only if, proportional wages rise. This proposition was not correct: as Marx had pointed out, it only holds if one disregards the nonwage capital and argues *as if* capital advances consist only of the wages bill. However, once this very restrictive assumption is abandoned, the rate of profits can fall (or rise) even if proportional wages remain constant.

Marx, as Sraffa noted approvingly, had introduced two important concepts into political economy that paved the way to a better understanding of some of the properties of the modern economic system: first, "constant capital," that is, that part of social capital that consists of (produced) means of production; and, second, the "organic composition of capital." The former concept expresses the fact that commodities are produced by means of commodities, a fact that can never be made to disappear completely in a circular system of production. This means that the rate of profits is bounded from above: whereas in Ricardo vanishing wages would be reflected in a rate of profits that tends to infinity, in Marx there is a finite maximum rate of profits, R. The maximum rate corresponds to zero wages and is equal to L/C; it is thus equal to the inverse of the organic composition of the system as a whole. Marx considered the maximum rate of profits to be a purely technological datum of the system as a whole, independent of relative prices and the actual rate of profits. The latter is given by

$$r = \frac{S}{C+V} = \frac{S/L}{C/L+V/L} = \frac{1-w}{1/R+w} = \frac{R(1-w)}{1+Rw}.$$

The expression shows that the actual rate of profits depends on two magnitudes instead of on only one, as Ricardo had contended: on the share of wages, w (or the rate of surplus value, $(1-w)w^{-1}$), and on the maximum rate of profits, R. Differentiating r partially with respect to R gives

$$\frac{\partial r}{\partial R} = \frac{1-w}{(1+Rw)^2} > 0.$$

If the maximum rate of profits falls in the course of economic development, and proportional wages (the rate of surplus value) remain constant, the rate of profits is bound to fall. Even moderately falling proportional wages (a rising rate of surplus value) cannot prevent this fall of the rate of profits.

In Sraffa's reading, Marx had developed his law as a critique of Ricardo's explanation of the falling rate of profits, incorporating major elements of Ricardo's in his own analysis. Thus Marx had argued that an accumulation process without technical change is bound up with a tendency of rising money wages and a falling rate of exploitation (i.e., rising proportional wages) – quite independently of rising costs of food production or the so-called law of population (see Marx [1867] 1954, 581–582).[27] According to Sraffa, Marx had incorporated also another element of Ricardo's doctrine in his own analysis: Ricardo's "machinery substitution argument" recurs in Marx's law of the falling rate of profits in terms of an "increasing organic composition of capital." Moreover, in Sraffa's understanding Marx had based his argument on the same "natural course" scenario as Ricardo had: both had started with an analysis of the case of *accumulation with given technical knowledge*, where known but hitherto unused methods may be introduced in consequence of changes in the distributive variables and relative prices, but technical progress proper is set aside.

It is important to stress that in Sraffa's interpretation, Marx in his theory of the long-run trend of the rate of profits had *not* assumed a constant real wage rate in terms of commodities. Marx is rather taken to have held that real wages in terms of commodities could rise but that due to a lack of organization and strength on the part of workers in the conflict over the distribution of income, workers would typically not obtain a proportionate share of the additional quantities of commodities that are made available by the increase in labor productivity associated with the introduction of machinery. Hence the rate of surplus value would tend to rise and proportional wages fall – and yet, Marx ([1861–63] 1989, 73–74) had maintained, the general rate of profits was bound to fall:

> The rate of profit falls, although the RATE OF SURPLUS VALUE remains the same or rises, because the proportion of variable capital to constant capital decreases with the development of the productive power of labour. The rate of profit thus falls, not because labour becomes less productive, but because it becomes more productive.

What is remarkable is that in interpreting the analyses of Ricardo and Marx, Sraffa distinguished carefully between the case of *capital accumulation* without any technical progress, on the one hand, and the case with "*inventions*" or *technical progress*, on the other. And he related Marx's law of the tendency of the rate of profits to fall exclusively to the former case. This contradicts a widespread interpretation according to which Marx in volume 3 of *Capital* tried to establish a falling tendency of the rate of profits for an economic system in which capital accumulates *and* there is technical progress. More specifically, Sraffa read Bortkiewicz's argument with that part of Ricardo's analysis of the machinery question in mind, in which Ricardo had argued that improved machines can frequently not be employed immediately after they have been invented, because it would not be profitable to do so: they can only be introduced once *nominal* wages have risen in the course of accumulation. However, Sraffa insisted, this case of induced technical change must not be confounded with technical progress. Sraffa had been working on the case of accumulation with induced technical change, the so-called Ricardo effect, since 1942, because he felt that a correct answer to the question at hand had implications for his criticism of marginal productivity theory. This theory, by design, approaches the problem of the explanation (and determination) of the rate of profits in terms of *changes* in known methods of production and in the proportions of factors used (see D3/12/29: 1–7 and D3/12/33: 40 (1–3)). As should have already become clear and will be seen in greater detail below, this earlier work shaped and directed Sraffa's understanding of Bortkiewicz's contribution.

In the following we see the reasons why Sraffa defended Marx against some of Bortkiewicz's criticisms. The essence of his defense turns out always to reside in Marx's understanding (1) that any actual system of production is possessed of a finite maximum rate of profits, and (2) that over time this rate is bound to fall as capital accumulates with *no* technical progress proper, that is, *no* invention.

Sraffa's critical comments on Bortkiewicz's essay of 1906–7

Values and prices: on Bortkiewicz's criticism of Marx's transformation algorithm

The first part of Bortkiewicz's tripartite essay (Bortkiewicz 1906–7) was devoted to a critical summary account of the existing literature on Marx and the transformation problem. Sraffa showed little interest in Bortkiewicz's detailed criticism of Marx's transformation algorithm and excerpted only the following remark: "This objection {that Marx should have recalculated also the constant and variable capital in the various lines of production} foreseen 'to a certain degree by Marx'" (D1/91: 12), together with Bortkiewicz's page reference to chapter 9 in volume 3 of *Capital*.[28] The statement under consideration can be seen as a confirmation of Sraffa's view that Marx was only driven to adopting his erroneous transformation algorithm because he did not have the method of simultaneous equations at his disposal. What interested Sraffa was rather Bortkiewicz's contention that Marx's blunder had serious implications for his law of the falling rate of profits. As Sraffa noted, according to Bortkiewicz the law "rests on this, that Marx establishes a definite (and indeed quite simple and false) arithmetical relation between magnitudes of which one belongs to his 'Value and Surplus-Value Scheme' and the other to his 'Price and Profit Scheme'" (D1/91: 10). Sraffa also excerpted Bortkiewicz's statement that

> Tugan-B. {Tugan-Baranovsky} 'is quite right against Marx' on the two profit rates and that the one based on prices is the correct one. And that this is by no means a subordinate point, appears at its best from the fact that this point is closely connected with the Law of Falling Profit Rate.
> (D1/91: 10)

However, with regard to Bortkiewicz's "'Proof of Error in L. of Fall. R. of Profit" (1906–7, pt. 1, 47–48), Sraffa then only noted drily:

Formula $\dfrac{m}{c+v} = \dfrac{m}{v} \cdot \dfrac{m}{c+v}$ · {m here designates surplus value}

If first factor constant, and second falls, the Law is "obvious." The "error" is that the second factor is expression of the (wrong) "value-profit," not of the "price-profit." That's all!

(D1/91: 11)

Sraffa was apparently not very impressed with this sort of criticism. While he fully agreed that Marx's law had to be formulated in terms of prices rather than labor values, he did not consider this to be all that important and, in particular, he did not consider the validity of the main idea underlying the law to hinge on this. With reference to Bortkiewicz's discussion of the method used by Tugan-Baranovsky in his criticism of Marx, Sraffa stressed the following:

> The whole argument of Tugan and Bortkiewicz is based on assuming widely different Org. Comp. in the production of the three Depts (viz., Means of Prod., Workers-cons.-goods, Capitalists-cons.-goods) from which they get two different rates of profits, reckoning in prices and in values. *Yet they find no difficulty in admitting equal Org. Comp. in the production of the Means of Production used in the three Depts!* See remark on p. 46.

(D1/91: 11; emphasis added)

Actually, in footnote 129 on page 46, Bortkiewicz had drawn the reader's attention to that assumption which underlies Tugan-Baranovsky's method. While Bortkiewicz had been aware that this was a very special assumption, it had not prevented him from adopting it himself in "Zur Berichtigung" (1907a). In Sraffa's view, this assumption was seriously misleading, because it implied that the "Hypothesis" must of necessity be wrong: the hypothesis supposes that the two *social aggregates*, $(V + S)$ and C, could be taken to exhibit approximately the *same* organic composition precisely because each of them is made up of a large number of individual commodities that are produced with possibly vastly *different* organic compositions of capital.

Circular flow vs. unidirectional production: in defense of Marx's concept of "constant capital"

Bortkiewicz's essay (1906–7, pt. 1, 22) continued with the presentation of "a correct solution of the theoretical problem that Marx had set himself." Sraffa was critical of several aspects of Bortkiewicz's analysis. A first criticism concerned the assumption of unidirectional production. Sraffa stressed that Bortkiewicz's reasoning was based on a "Formula of Reduction to labour in {a} *finite* number of steps." He then quoted Bortkiewicz's statement that the analysis of the value of the product has to be carried "up to the point when one reaches a constant capital which is the exclusive product of direct labour," and concluded: "This is the same blunder as Böhm Bawerk!" (D1/91: 12).

In a closely related criticism, Sraffa insisted on the importance of Marx's distinction between *constant* and *variable* capital, a distinction that Bortkiewicz had considered to be superfluous, at best. Sraffa noted that Bortkiewicz had repeatedly blamed "Marx for distinguishing Const, and Var. Cap. and not seeing ('as Ricardo did,' for which B. praises him) that it can be eliminated by reducing all to labour at various times." Sraffa then leveled the following objection at Bortkiewicz's reasoning:

> B. does not see that *all* his argument rests upon making a labour series of a finite number of terms. The consequences of this assumption are:
> 1) The rate of profits can become infinitely large with the fall of wages [which leads to not seeing the cause of the Law of Falling rate of profit].
> 2) With a sufficient fall of wages the value of capital must tend towards 0.
> 3) The idea that Surplus Value "comes out of" Constant and not only Variable Capital.
> 4) The Smith-Ricardo fallacy that "savings are consumed by others."
> 5) The false idea that means of production ("higher stages") *must* have a different organic composition from consumers' goods.
> 6) Another consequence of the finite labour series is that the Value Hypothesis becomes impossible even to be conceived of: the total Const. Cap. *must* change in price in terms of the Product with changes in the rate of profits.
>
> (D1/91: 13–14)

Before we proceed, a few clarifying remarks are apposite. As regards the first consequence mentioned, it should be pointed out that according to Sraffa, Marx's explanation of a falling tendency of the rate of profits had as an important first step the demonstration that the *maximum rate of profits*, R in Sraffa's notation, was bound to fall. In a system in which with regard to the production of each commodity one could always discern a stage with labor "unassisted" (to use Ricardo's phrase) by constant capital, there simply was no maximum rate of profits and hence no falling level of that rate. This implied "not seeing the cause" contemplated by Marx of a falling tendency of the rate of profits. The closely related second consequence stresses the fact that if all capital is supposed to be reducible to advanced wages, then the value of capital is bound to vanish with vanishing wages. Third, if the constant capital can be entirely reduced to advanced wages, that is, variable capital, the distinction between the two types of capital becomes blurred and the idea is close at hand that surplus value "comes out of Constant and not only Variable Capital."

The fourth implication mentioned by Sraffa concerns an erroneous proposition of Adam Smith, which was also adopted by Ricardo, and which was first noticed (and explicated at length in chapters 19 and 20 in volume 2 of *Capital*) by Marx. As is well known, Smith ([1776] 1976, II.iii.18) had contended that

> what is annually saved is as regularly consumed as what is annually spent, and nearly at the same time too; but it is consumed by a different

set of people. ... The consumption is the same, but the consumers are different.

As Marx had pointed out, this proposition is false, because a part of what is annually saved and invested must always consist of means of production which have previously been produced. Smith's error is closely related to his false claim that the portion of the annual gross produce which is devoted to the replacement of the materials used up in the production of the goods which are annually consumed "withdraws no portion of the annual produce from the *neat revenue* of the society" (II.ii.9; emphasis added). Marx had traced this inconsistency in Smith's treatment of (circulating) capital back to his view that the price of every commodity resolves itself entirely, "that is, without leaving any commodity residue, into wage, profit, and rent – a claim which necessarily presupposed the existence of 'ultimate' commodities produced by pure labour without means of production except land" (Sraffa 1960, 94). This is the background to Sraffa's observation that Bortkiewicz's construction, which follows Smith and Ricardo in making a labor series *of a finite* number of terms, gives rise to "the Smith-Ricardo fallacy that 'savings are consumed by others.'"[29] The fifth consequence draws attention to the fact that in an Austrian conceptualization of production, the consumption goods produced by means of intermediate products, that is, capital goods, generally exhibit higher capital-to-labor ratios, or longer periods of production, than the intermediate products. Yet this is not so in circular systems of production.

As regards the sixth consequence, we have already learned that in the early 1940s Sraffa contemplated the conditions to be met in order for the ratio between the value of the product and that of the capital employed in its generation to be invariable with regard to changes in the rate of profits. As we know, the upshot of these considerations was the elaboration of the closely related concepts of Standard commodity, Standard system, and Standard ratio in January 1944. However, at the time of his reading of Bortkiewicz's essay, Sraffa had not yet fully developed these important concepts by means of which he was able to simplify significantly the investigation of the dependence of relative prices on income distribution. What was at his disposal at that time was the concept of the "corn model," which with regard to a single sector at least – the corn sector, in which corn is assumed to be produced by means of seed corn only (and labor) – exhibits a product-to-capital (capital here being seed) ratio that is independent of the level of the rate of profits (and relative prices). This constellation can be said to reflect with regard to a single sector what Marx's "Value Hypothesis" is taken to reflect with regard to the economic system as a whole: according to the latter the ratio between living labor (L), that is, the sum of variable capital (V) and surplus value (S), or value added, on the one hand, and dead labor, or constant capital (C), on the other, *is given independently of the rate of profits*; it actually equals the *maximum rate of profits*, as conceptualized by Marx, L/C, which obtains in the hypothetical case in which $V = 0$ and $S = L$.

The gist of Sraffa's criticism can be summed up as follows: by adopting the "Austrian" device of a reduction series of finite length, Bortkiewicz had focused attention on a special case which is seriously misleading. He did not see that Marx had made an important analytical advance over Smith and Ricardo in the analysis of the wage-profit relationship by recapturing the circularity aspect of production (which had been present in the physiocrats, but was somewhat lost by Smith and Ricardo). Bortkiewicz, Sraffa maintained, by criticizing Marx from the standpoint of Ricardo's "Austrian" construction, had indeed taken the analysis of the wage-profit relationship a step backward from where Marx had left it.

The "essential nature" of the problem under consideration

Sraffa summarized his criticism of the conceptualization of production underlying Bortkiewicz's essay in the following way:

> It is clear, from his context and examples, that B. has always in mind a finite number of terms. When the number is infinite, the description must stop at some point and contain a "residue" term of Const. Capital. Besides, he only sees the production of the particular commodity: he fails to see that, *for Social Capital, the Organic Composition is by far the most important (instructive) aspect – and when the Value Hypothesis holds, the only one that one need use at all.*
>
> (D1/91: 15; emphasis added)

He added:

> The formal objection against B's point of view (reducing all to rotation periods of labour, while neglecting the distinction between Variable and Constant Capital) is that it can only be done by an infinite number of steps [i.e. it can never be done] and the resulting series is not uniformly convergent: in other words, there is always a Residue, and, so long as *r* is variable, it is never negligible.
>
> But the real objection (though somewhat vaguer) is this: That B.'s point of view, for the sake of obtaining absolute exactness in a comparatively trifling matter, sacrifices (by concealing it) *the essential nature of the question* – that is, that *commodities are produced by labour out of commodities.* Suppose that it were true that only corn, besides labour, is used in the production of corn and that this were true of all commodities, i.e. *the relative price of each product and its Const. Cap. were constant with respect to r*: Then, to find the value of, or q{uantity} of labour that produces, a bushel of wheat, we should deduct the seed from the product, and divide the rest ("net product") by the N° of days' labour, and obtain the result. We could also do it by reduction, and the limit of the sum of the infinite series would be the q{uantity} of labour "embodied" in the *gross* product – identical result as before.

But of course we should not dream of doing so – it would be mad; it is only the damned fluctuation of price that drives us to it. It is well to remember (as A. Smith did) that a considerable degree of abstraction is involved in saying that a calf is produced entirely by human labour (rather than by a cow and a bull, as well as labour) on the grounds that the bull and cow are themselves produced by bulls and cows, as well as labour, *and so on*. *The abstraction is useful, but it has its limitations; and it is good to have them well in sight.*

We introduce it as a *correction* to cope with a deviation of price from value (which, note, can be as often on one side as on the other) and *it should retain that character. For, while it supplies exactness, it obscures a fundamental fact.*

(D1/91: 16–17; all emphases added except
for those on *gross, and so on*, and *correction*)

This clarifies neatly Sraffa's point of view on the matter. The appropriate scheme is the one in which commodities are produced by means of commodities, and this was the scheme elaborated by the physiocrats and then reintroduced by Marx in terms of his important distinction between constant and variable capital. The reduction to dated quantities of labor involves a formidable abstraction, "useful" though, but with "limitations." Bortkiewicz had managed to render "absolutely precise" a case that is not really interesting because it "sacrifices the essential nature of the problem": the circular flow of production.

The impact of changes in distribution on relative prices: Bortkiewicz's "monotonic prejudice"

A further criticism of Sraffa's concerned Bortkiewicz's contention that it could safely be presumed that methods of production can generally be ordered monotonically with regard to their capital intensity – a view which we have encountered already in Bortkiewicz's article on Böhm-Bawerk. As Sraffa noted, Bortkiewicz had correctly pointed out, against Böhm-Bawerk, that there is "no 'average period of production'" which could be defined independently of the rate of interest but then had nevertheless put forward the erroneous proposition that "'*im allgemeinen* {in general}' there is lengthening" with a fall in the rate of interest; Sraffa dubbed this opinion "*monotonic prejudice*" (D1/91: 14 and 27 (verso); emphases added). As we saw in the above, Sraffa had criticized this proposition as early as February 1931, and in his working notes he had in fact demonstrated the impossibility of a monotonic ordering of the methods of production long before he came across Bortkiewicz's essay. In one of his notes, commenting on Nicholas Kaldor's "Capital Intensity and the Trade Cycle" (1939), he had pointed out the following:

There is no assurance that, owing simply to a change in the rate of interest, the order is not reversed. Suppose two commodities produced by similar proportions of capital and labour (i.e. which are similarly divided between profits and wages): but one contains more capital in the "early" stages and less in the later ones – i.e. although the total quantity of interest is equal in the two commodities, in this one it is made up to a larger extent of compound interest: it is clear that if the rate of profits rises, the composition of this commodity will come to contain more profits (i.e. capital) than the other.

(D3/12/15: 10)

This finding was one of the results of Sraffa's earlier studies, carried out already in the early 1930s, of the impact of distributional changes on relative prices – a problem that Bortkiewicz addressed in part 2 of his 1906–7 essay. Sraffa scrutinized Bortkiewicz's analysis carefully and excerpted a passage in which the latter had taken the sign of the deviation of the price ratio of two commodities from their ratio of labor values to depend on whether the rotation or turnover period of one of the commodities is generally longer or shorter than that of the other commodity. To this Bortkiewicz had added a remark that Sraffa also excerpted and marked in the margin with two squiggly lines, signaling disapproval: "A more precise formulation of this relationship is not possible." This was not true, Sraffa insisted: things can be made more precise. He approved, however, of Bortkiewicz's following proposition:

It would, for example, not be correct to maintain that as regards the ratio between p_i {the price of commodity i in terms of some other commodity that serves as numéraire} and w_i {the value of commodity i in terms of the standard} it would be decisive whether the average length of the rotation periods is greater with respect to one or the other of the two products. Such a proposition gets pretty close to the truth, at least in those cases in which ρ {the rate of profits, Sraffa's r} is such a small magnitude that one is justified in neglecting the second and higher powers of ρ.

(Bortkiewicz 1906–7, pt. 2, 40)

In part 2 of his essay Bortkiewicz had provided the hitherto most sophisticated analysis of the dependence of relative prices on income distribution. Alas, his analysis was limited to the case of unidirectional production. Moreover, like Kaldor and many others, he had fallen victim to the "monotonic prejudice" in the analysis of the choice-of-technique problem.

Rejecting Bortkiewicz's criticism of Marx's law: "those who deny the tendency always are unaware of the existence of a Max. Rate of Profit"

In Bortkiewicz's understanding, Marx's law of the falling rate of profits stated that with an increase in the organic composition of social capital the rate of profits tends to fall even without a rise in proportional wages. Only a sufficiently strong fall in proportional wages "could paralyze or even overcompensate the falling tendency of the rate of profits" (Bortkiewicz 1906–7, pt. 3, 452). Bortkiewicz had then translated a rising organic composition of capital into a rising average length of the rotation period characterizing the production of the commodities constituting the real wage, δ, and had distinguished between "two modalities" of how a rise in δ can be brought about: "either in one or several of the corresponding lines of production a new preceding stage of production is added or the productivity relations on the different stages of production change" (455). With regard to the first case, on which Sraffa focused attention, Bortkiewicz had explained: "The first case is the one in which a new instrument of labor (e.g., a machine) is introduced where previously only 'manual labor' was used" (456). In this case, Bortkiewicz had stressed, δ may rise, but need not. If there is an increase in δ,

> it is clear that … the amount of labor incorporated in the real wage must decrease, because the introduction of the new instrument of labor is only taken into account, if the productivity of the labor producing the real wage increases.
>
> (456)

However, if this is the case, Bortkiewicz had concluded (457–458), then the rate of profits cannot fall. Sraffa commented on these passages as follows:

> B. tries to disprove Law of Falling Rate of P.
> Represents "increase in Org. Comp. of Social Cap." as lengthening average period of production (δ). p. 456, *he assumes real wage ("corn wage") constant: and his assumption implies (tacitly), not mere accumulation, but the introduction of a new, more profitable method of production*, e.g. a machine, which will of course reduce proportional wage (U) if corn-wage is constant, but (he acknowledges) will not necessarily increase period of production, i.e. Const. Cap.! He quotes an important passage in Kap. IIII p. 247 on how "new" methods of production are introduced, and their effect on lowering profit-rate: but B. *overlooks that "new" here means "known, but not yet used; introduced only after accumulation," from which M's conclusion follows*: he (B.) refutes him on p. 457–8 by an argument which clearly implies that by "new method" he B. understands a "new invention" – and on the basis of this "proves" that rate of profit (r) need not fall!
>
> (D1/91: 22; emphases added)

In Sraffa's view, Bortkiewicz's attempt to disprove Marx's law of the tendency of the rate of profits to fall was marred with two misconceptions. First, in Sraffa's reading Marx had not argued on the basis of a constant "commodity wage," as Bortkiewicz supposed. Second, Bortkiewicz had missed the fact that

Marx's law was meant to apply only to the Ricardian case of capital accumulation with induced technical change: what was allowed for was only the introduction of methods of production that had been discovered in the past but up until now could not be profitably employed. Bortkiewicz had instead discussed the entirely different case of a choice of technique vis-à-vis the discovery of new methods of production, that is, technical progress. In the latter case the problem was whether or not a newly invented method of production will be introduced *at the going real wage rate*. Sraffa then excerpted (in German) the famous passage from volume 3 of *Capital* quoted by Bortkiewicz:

> No capitalist ever voluntarily introduces a new method of production, no matter how much more productive it may be, and how much it may increase the rate of surplus-value, so long as it reduces the rate of profit. Yet every such new method of production cheapens the commodities. Hence, the capitalist sells them originally above their prices of production, or, perhaps, above their value. He pockets the difference between their costs of production and the market-prices of the same commodities produced at higher costs of production. He can do this, because the average labour-time required socially for the production of these latter commodities is higher than the labour-time required for the new methods of production. His method of production stands above the social average. But competition makes it general and subject to the general law. There follows a fall in the rate of profit – perhaps first in this sphere of production, and eventually it achieves a balance with the rest – which is, therefore, wholly independent of the will of the capitalist.
>
> (Marx [1894] 1959, 264–265)

Sraffa commented:

> This is correct, *provided it is understood*:
> 1) that the "new method" was available all the time, but has only become cheaper *after* a rise in proportional wages
> 2) that this rise is consequent on accumulation
> 3) that the various capitals (of different commodities, and of old and new methods) differ *only* in Org. Comp., but not in "rotation period" (so that the relative prices of Const. Capitals don't change with r; and a rise of w *can only* bring in new methods of higher Org. Comp.
>
> (D1/91: 23; first emphasis added)

Hence, in Sraffa's interpretation there is no presumption that Marx's argument above was, and was meant to be, generally valid: it was rather tied to strict requirements. If interpreted along the lines of Ricardo's discussion of accumulation without technical progress proper, Sraffa maintained, Marx was right. In Ricardo's discussion, known but hitherto unused methods of production ("machinery") are eventually adopted, induced, as it were, by an increase in nominal (and proportional) wages and a change in relative prices, which is in turn entailed by the process of accumulation vis-à-vis rising costs of production in agriculture. In Sraffa's reading, Marx had in essence adopted the Ricardian machinery substitution argument, replacing Ricardo's argument of rising costs in agricultural production as the cause of a wage increase by the argument that the increased demand for labor-power due to accumulation per se must raise wages. With constant or even moderately falling proportional wages, w, a fall in the maximum rate of profits, R, is bound to result in a fall in the general rate of profits, r.

In Sraffa's view, Bortkiewicz's criticism in this regard was entirely beside the point. The eminent statistician and theorist had tilted at windmills. This Sraffa attempted to render clear by entering into a detailed criticism of Bortkiewicz's argument. Due to space constraints we can only briefly summarize Sraffa's respective disquisition, which contains a number of tedious numerical examples.[30] Suffice it to say that in a first step he was keen to translate Bortkiewicz's reasoning from the chosen Austrian (unidirectional) scheme of production to the circular flow framework adopted by Marx. Sraffa stressed once again that Bortkiewicz was right in insisting that a proper reasoning had to be in terms of prices of production rather than labor values, but added that Bortkiewicz's respective objection was out of proportion with regard to the importance of the issue under consideration. As Sraffa rendered clear in terms of simple numerical examples, the real issues lay elsewhere and concerned Bortkiewicz's misconceptions as regards the role of constant capital and the maximum rate of profits, on the one hand, and Marx's conceptualization of wages, on the other. This is succinctly stated by Sraffa in a working note of 29 August 1946:

> The idea of a Falling rate of Profit is based on:
> 1) The existence of a Maximum Rate of Profit
> 2) Its identity with the Org. Comp. of Cap.[31]
> 3) The tendency of the Org. Comp. of Cap. to fall with accumulation; and thus a tendency to fall of the Max Rate of Profit.
>   See Marx on "even if workers lived on air."[32]
> Those who deny the tendency always are unaware of the existence of a Max. Rate of Profit: this is due to their belief (on Böhm Bawerk's {*sic*} line) that "ultimately," i.e. in a finite series, goods are made entirely by labour. This is swallowed even by Bortkiewicz (see my notes on his art. II, my p. 2).
> More briefly: Falling rate of Profit is based on
> a) Existence of Maximum rate of Profit
> b) Tendency for Max. R. of P. to fall with accumulation
> Hence, however much wages may fall, they cannot always make up for it. Those who argue against it always say: a sufficient fall in wages can offset any fall in rate of profits (Bortkiewicz, Joan Robinson).[33]
>
> (D3/12/44: 11)

Sraffa's criticism of Bortkiewicz's theory of surplus value: "this is B.'s theory, and a jolly bad one it is"

We now come to a problem with regard to which Sraffa's comments on Bortkiewicz are at first sight rather puzzling: Is the general rate of profits determined by the production conditions of *all industries*, as Marx had maintained, or only by those industries that directly or indirectly contribute to the production of wage goods, as Bortkiewicz had insisted? Readers who are familiar with the modern literature on this issue will probably be surprised to learn that Sraffa is critical of Bortkiewicz's view "that the rate of profit depends *only* on those amounts of labour and those turnover periods which concern the production and distribution of the goods forming the real wage rate" (Bortkiewicz 1952, 32). Yet it is not difficult to see why at the time Sraffa was of this opinion. He marked the passage just quoted with exclamation points in the margin, and stressed:

> It is on the above proposition that B. bases his theory of surplus value: he attributes its origin to Ricardo, and opposes it to the "Falsche Konstruktion" {false construction} of Marx which is based on "Rechenfehler" {errors of calculation} (i.e. the averaging of different rates of profit).
>
> (D1/91: 18)

Sraffa then excerpted Bortkiewicz's following statement:[34]

> If it is indeed true that the level of the rate of profits in no way depends on the conditions of production of those commodities which do not enter into wages, then the origin of profit must clearly be sought in the wage-relationship as such and not in the productivity-enhancing effect of capital. For if this effect were indeed relevant here, it would be inexplicable why certain spheres of production are irrelevant for the determination of the level of profits.
>
> (D1/91: 18)

Sraffa commented on this passage:

> This is B.'s theory, and a jolly bad one it is. It would be easy for the marginalist to reply that this theory is based on the (commodity) real wage being given a priori, and then of course all is determined.[35] – We can add that it is because of this starting point that only wage-goods come into consideration – *that is the only way of changing (what Ricardo calls) proportional wages.*
>
> (D1/91: 18; emphasis added)

Sraffa drew two straight lines beside the remark in the margin. This might be interpreted as indicating his approval, but things appear to be more

complicated. The critical tone at the beginning of the remark suggests that
Sraffa did not endorse Bortkiewicz's criticism of Marx. In the light of what
we have heard above, this is hardly surprising. There is reason to think that
at the time Sraffa was in all probability of the opinion that Marx had a valid
point when he had argued against Ricardo that the rate of profits depends not
only on proportional wages, but also on the organic composition of capital
of the economic system as a whole, and that therefore in the determination
of the rate of profits *all* industries must be taken into account.[36] Sraffa at the
time appears to have been convinced that Marx was right because if wages
were not taken as given in commodity terms but as a share, what was a "wage
good industry" was no longer well defined. As long as it was not known on
which commodities workers spent wages, how could it be known which industries were producing "wage goods"? Bortkiewicz had attacked a straw man –
an attack that had no bearing on Marx's rather different construction.

"Mathematical" vs. "causal-genetic" method

Bortkiewicz, echoing Pareto, had been critical of what he dubbed the "causal-
genetic" method of analysis. This method he had detected in Böhm-Bawerk
and the Austrians who had tried to explain all prices and the distributive variables by tracing them back to the consumers' marginal (expected) estimations
of goods of the first order, that is, consumption goods. A similar method, he
maintained, had been adopted by Marx, who had attempted to explain all
prices and the distributive variables by tracing them back to the quantities
of labor needed directly and indirectly in the production of the various commodities. While strictly opposed in terms of content, both theories employed
the causal-genetic method and thus were concerned with the search for an
ultimate standard of value. This standard was (marginal) utility in one case
and (abstract) labor in the other (see, in particular, Bortkiewicz 1921).

  According to Bortkiewicz, both schools of thought were bound to fail: the
kind of problems they faced could not be mastered in terms of the causal-
genetic method. The phenomenon of ubiquitous interdependence of economic magnitudes necessitated the employment of what Bortkiewicz called
the "mathematical method," that is, the method of simultaneous equations.
Sraffa noted carefully that in Bortkiewicz's view "Value" (i.e., labor value)
was merely a "Hilfsgrösse" – an *auxiliary concept.* To this Bortkiewicz had
added: "Marx has not succeeded in substituting for it a consistent theory.
… Das leistet vielmehr die mathematische Methode {This achieves only the
mathematical method}" (D1/91: 32). Sraffa did not object to this proposition; indeed his work since 1927 confirmed it. However, as we have seen
in the above, adopting the "mathematical method" was not prejudicial as
to the content of the theory advocated. There was no reason to trust the
"forces" contemplated by Walras and Pareto (see, for example, D3/12/3: 4).
As Sraffa observed in a note written in 1942, specifying the meaning of his
own equations,

This paper deals with an extremely elementary problem; so elementary indeed that its solution is generally taken for granted. *The problem is that of ascertaining the conditions of equilibrium of a system of prices and the rate of profits, independently of the study of the forces which may bring about such a state of equilibrium.* Since a solution of the second problem carries with it a solution of the first, that is the course usually adopted in *modern theory.* The first problem however is susceptible of a more general treatment, independent of the particular forces assumed for the second; and in view of the unsatisfactory character of the latter, there is advantage in maintaining its independence.

(D3/12/15: 2; emphases added)

Against this background it is not surprising that Sraffa would take issue with the following statement by Bortkiewicz:

The mathematical method achieves even more than that: it allows one to render the cost of production theory without any difficulties compatible with the law of supply and demand or the determination of relative prices in terms of the subjective value estimations of the buyers (and perhaps also those of the sellers) by incorporating, following Walras's procedure, the cost equations into a comprehensive system of equations, in whose conceptualization also the subjective value estimations are taken into account.

(Bortkiewicz 1906–7, pt. 3, 478)[37]

Sraffa commented:

Thus Bortkiewicz shows that he is an idiot. And that he did not realize the implications of his rule on "methods which are not used have no effect on interest": he applies it strictly only to Böhm {*sic*} and Clark. He does not see it applies to all these things, demand etc. And … he does not see that what Marx says on Demand and Supply is only an extension of it.

(D1/91: 32; the italicized sentence is marked with two straight lines in the margin)

Apparently, Bortkiewicz had forgotten his earlier "dictum" by the time he concluded his essay. How could it otherwise be explained that he now felt that what he called "cost of production theory" was compatible with marginalism? Whereas the former satisfied the dictum, the latter was explicitly designed to explain prices and the distributive variables in terms of hypothetical incremental *changes* of the proportions in which inputs are used and final goods consumed. Hence, both methods of production and of consumption that are *not* used are taken to have an effect on the rate of interest and prices.

In this context Sraffa sided with Marx, who had argued that, in equilibrium, demand and supply do not act anymore and therefore cannot explain value.[38] To this Bortkiewicz had objected that it only reflected Marx's mathematical incompetence and his lack of understanding the by then conventional demand and supply diagram. In Sraffa's view, Marx had instead made exactly the same point as Bortkiewicz himself: in a long-period equilibrium, and given one of the distributive variables, prices and the other distributive variable are fully determined by the methods of production and consumption in use, whereas methods that are not used play no role whatsoever (see D1/91: 33).

Bortkiewicz on Marx and Ricardo: a summing up

Sraffa felt that in important respects Bortkiewicz had forcefully expressed criteria that the theory of value and distribution was to meet that he, Sraffa, fully endorsed and actually, without at the time being aware of his precursor, had managed to translate into an analytically adequate framework. However, he accused Bortkiewicz of not having fully understood the implications of his maxims or of being inconsistent. While Sraffa shared some of Bortkiewicz's criticisms of Marx, he felt that Bortkiewicz had missed the fact that on the whole Marx had been possessed of a deeper understanding of the problems of value and distribution than Ricardo and, as a consequence, also his critic, despite Bortkiewicz's indisputable mathematical skills. Marx had made important progress over and above Ricardo in analyzing the problem of value and distribution in the context of a circular flow of production. Bortkiewicz, following Dmitriev's lead, had instead adopted an Austrian conceptualization of production and had erroneously tried to assess Marx's doctrine in terms of it. No wonder, then, that several of Marx's important achievements escaped his attention. In particular, in a circular flow framework constant capital could not be reduced to variable capital: however far the reduction of the former to the latter was carried out, there always remained some constant capital. This also implied that the maximum rate of profits was finite, not infinite. In terms of his "Value Hypothesis," Marx had been able to establish that this rate was equal to the inverse of the organic composition of capital for the economic system as a whole (that is, the inverse of the economy's average period of production). While Sraffa agreed with Bortkiewicz that Marx's theory of value and distribution was flawed, he did not agree with him as to the magnitude of the flaw involved. He rather credited Marx with having been the first to grasp, albeit in an analytically defective manner, important properties of the interdependent industrial system of production. The fact that the tools at Marx's disposal were not up to his sophisticated economic concepts was no reason to focus attention on the inadequacy of the tools instead of on the fertility of the concepts and how they could be formulated in a logically consistent way. Bortkiewicz with his access to much more refined techniques than Marx fell conceptually back before him. Bortkiewicz was unable to grasp the heuristic importance of Marx's assumption that the value of social capital in terms of the social product is independent of the rate of profits. While Bortkiewicz (in line with Tugan-Baranovsky) insisted on assuming widely different organic composi- tions in the three departments, he found no fault in admitting equal organic compositions in the production of the means of production used in the three departments. It thus of necessity escaped Bortkiewicz's attention that Marx's discussion of the falling tendency of the rate of profits revolved around the development over time of the maximum rate of profits, that is, the inverse of society's organic composition of capital: with given proportional wages, the rate of profits falls if and only if the maximum rate falls.

Concluding remarks

In the course of his work on what was to become his 1960 book, Sraffa repeat- edly referred back to "Bortkiewicz's dictum" and "dogma." In this concluding section we take a brief look at two examples reflecting the continuing impor- tance of Bortkiewicz's propositions for Sraffa's own work. The first example relates to the constructive aspect of it and concerns the elaboration of the concept of the Standard commodity, whereas the second example relates to its critical task of refuting the marginalist theory of production and distribu- tion. A few remarks must suffice.

Removing an "incongruity" in classical analysis

In Bortkiewicz's view, Marx's "theory of exploitation" involved "a definite regress" compared with the "theory of deduction" that Bortkiewicz attrib- uted to Adam Smith and also to Ricardo (Bortkiewicz 1906–7, pt. 3, 447).[39] Sraffa did not agree with this assessment. Things were invariably more com- plex. Both Ricardo and Marx had started from the concept of commodity wages but then had moved on to that of proportional wages, according to which wages, w, could be given as a dimensionless number, $0 \leq w \leq 1$. Alas, every so often both Ricardo and Marx had slipped back to the former con- cept when the latter was appropriate. The coexistence side by side of these two wage concepts in Marx's construction was confusing. This was aggravated by the fact that Marx had made a serious attempt to take into account the circular flow aspect of production in terms of the concepts of constant cap- ital and the organic composition of capital. These difficulties are spelled out with great clarity in Sraffa's following comment on Marx's construction and Bortkiewicz's criticism of it:

> It comes to this. Marx says that as far as Surplus Value, and rate of S.V. are concerned, only wage-good industries come into consideration; but when the rate of profits is concerned all spheres of production, including luxury goods consumed only by capitalists, must be taken into account; for to obtain the rate of profits all the different rates of profit must be averaged out over all capitals. Now this amounts in effect to assuming (as

Marx does) that the mass of profits is equal to the mass of Surplus Value –
i.e. that they represent the same proportion of the Social Revenue. But
this is only true if the Org. Comp. of wage-goods industries is the same
as that of luxury-goods industries; if the org. comp. is different (and that
is the case under consideration) the proportion of Revenue occupied by
Surplus Value is different from that occupied by Profits – the first being
taken in Values, the second in Prices. Thus B. appears justified in concluding that, *given the wages in commodities, and the methods of production of
wage-commodities, the rate of profits is ipso facto determined*, no matter
what happens in luxury-industries.

> (D1/91: 20; emphasis added)

Bortkiewicz's insistence that the luxury-goods industries were unimportant
could obviously not be disputed in the case of given *commodity* wages. Things
were otherwise in the case of given *proportional* wages, even when wages were
still taken to be advanced at the beginning of the production period and thus
reckoned among the capital advanced. With his interpretation Bortkiewicz
had missed the real deficiency of Marx's construction:

> *What Marx does is, on the one hand (1) to take wages as given (inventory)
> in commodities, for subsistence, and on the other (2) to take the mass of
> profits as a given proportion of the product of labour. The two points of view
> are incongruous, and are bound to lead to contradictions.* But B. wants to
> solve the contradiction by bringing (2) into agreement with (1). On the
> contrary, the *correct solution* is to bring (1) into agreement with (2). For
> the point of view of (1) useful as it is as a starting point considers only
> the fodder-and-fuel aspect of wages; it is still tarred with commodity-
> fetishism. *It is necessary to bring out the Revenue aspect of wages;* and this
> is done by regarding them as a *w*, or a proportion of the Revenue. *Thus is
> (1) brought to agree with (2); and the conclusion that all capital must be
> taken into account for the rate of profits becomes true.*

> (D1/91: 20–21; emphases added)

When wages, besides the ever-present element of subsistence, also constitute revenue over and above subsistence, it is no longer possible to identify
a priori which commodities are "wage goods" and thus can be reckoned as a
physically specified part of capital as a whole. It is also no longer possible to
distinguish between "necessaries" and "luxuries": depending on the share of
wages, each and every type of commodity could, in principle, be consumed by
workers. It is from this consideration that Sraffa appears to have concluded
in accordance with Marx that *all* capital and thus *all* industries have to be
taken account of in determining the general rate of profits. In this perspective
(1) had to be brought in line with (2) rather than the other way around, as
Bortkiewicz had (implicitly) suggested.

To the passage cited last Sraffa added in parentheses:

> *Now, what is wanted is a similar step in regard to the "advanced" constant capital, to divest it of its fetish character,* machines (etc), and consider its replacement as a proportion of the gross product.
>
> (D1/91: 21; emphasis added)

As we have seen, as against Ricardo's view that the division of the product between wages and profits is the *only* factor affecting the general rate of profits, Marx had rightly insisted that the proportion between labor (or advanced wages) and means of production – the organic composition of capital – is a *separate*, independent factor (see also Garegnani 1984). The "similar step," referred to by Sraffa, now requested that this second factor be expressed in a form that is congruent with the first one.

With the benefit of hindsight we may say that Sraffa's own attempts in this regard can be traced back to 1931 when he had put forward the Statistical Hypothesis that the actual composition of the net product and that of social capital were such that the price ratio of the two aggregates did not change with changes in the rate of interest (see pp. 155–156). He knew that this hypothesis was wrong, but at the time was not yet possessed of an alternative device that would have allowed him to render the properties of the economic system more transparent. When at the beginning of the 1940s he encountered Marx's parallel "Value Hypothesis," he was clear that it was not generally valid. As we have also seen, he had noted carefully that in Bortkiewicz's interpretation value to Marx was merely a "Hilfsgrösse" – an auxiliary magnitude – employed in order to come to grips with the intricacies of the economic system under consideration. This interpretation Sraffa appears to have endorsed. He therefore must have been struck even more by the parallelism between Marx's and his own approach, because seen from this vantage point the Value Hypothesis and the Statistical Hypothesis served essentially the same purpose. It also had not escaped Sraffa's attention that the latter applied strictly only when the former did as well.

Alas, both hypotheses, useful as they had been in trying to understand value and distribution from a surplus point of view, could not be sustained. Sraffa convinced himself at the latest in the summer and autumn of 1942, if not earlier, in the course of developing, with the help of Abram S. Besicovitch, models with circulating and fixed capital (see Kurz and Salvadori 2004b) that no *actual* system could be expected to satisfy the hypothesis. He therefore, in December 1942, drew the consequence and henceforth sought a solution in terms of an artificial device, a "construction," as he called it (see D3/12/27: 32). However, as he explained in some detail in a working note dated 22 and 27 December 1943, titled "Constant Capital as Proportion. (Cont. from Ring-book, note on Bortkiewicz III)," replacing the inventory with the proportion concept also with regard to social capital was a great deal more difficult:

It has been easy to transform wages in that way; why is this other step so much harder? By transforming wages, we have avoided all the (Bortkiewicz's etc) difficulties as to different Org. Comp. of wage-goods and luxuries; can't we do the same for Const. Cap. (which would amount to dispensing with the necessity of assuming that the Value Hypothesis holds)? The transformation of wages has been done by introducing (in all but in name) money; and taking the Annual Revenue as unit of money (hence the "proportion" = money wage). ...

The root of the trouble is this:

a) Bortkiewicz gets into trouble by considering, with the same "proportions" (i.e. rate of S.V.), values and prices, or different prices. Hence the necessity of puzzling whether, at different prices, the same wage goods can be bought by the same wage; and the necessity of going into the org. comp. of wage goods as opposed to that of luxuries.

I have avoided this, by considering a given proportion *only* in relation to one set of prices – the one that corresponds to it. Hence I never meet the question whether that wage (proportion) can buy the same goods at different prices; for at different prices that wage (proportion) is different, and is not required to buy the same goods. The question does not arise.

Now B.'s case does not arise in reality: commods. do not, in fact, exchange at their values unless $w = 1$; and, whenever $w < 1$, they exchange at the corresponding price, and no other.

The error of B. is to have carried the point of view ("transformation of values into prices") beyond its proper limits, – within which M. kept them.

b) *In considering Constant Capital, I have fallen into the same (a similar, not identical) trap as B.* For I have assumed that as w and r change, it is possible for R (i.e. Const. Cap.) to remain constant. Hence my troubles, the necessity of taking into a/c {account} its Org. Comp., as opposed to that of the product, and of introducing the Value Hypothesis. The comparison may be put thus:

  a) B's fault is that he abstracts from the condition of "equal profits."

  b) My fault is to abstract from the condition of "maximum profits."

(D3/12/35: 9(1–3); emphasis added)

There is no space to enter into a detailed discussion of the path Sraffa followed until, in a set of notes dated 27 January 1944 and interestingly titled "Hypothesis" (see the manuscript D3/12/36: 61–85), he at long last accomplished the task in terms of the construction of the Standard system and Standard commodity (with regard to single-product systems). An important step on the way toward this *Hilfskonstruktion* was the change from *ante* to *post factum* payment of wages: the former, Sraffa had convinced himself, was incompatible with the revenue aspect of proportional wages. However, as soon as wages as a whole were taken to be paid out of the social product rather than out of the social capital, the way was open to replacing the *socioeconomic* distinction of the classical authors between "necessaries" and "luxuries" with the purely *technical* distinction between "basics" and "nonbasics." Basics enter directly or indirectly in the production of all commodities. In the Standard system, nonbasic products are eliminated and the maximum rate of profits, R, is shown to equal the Standard ratio of the Standard system, a ratio of two vectors of commodities that are linearly dependent. The Standard commodity allowed Sraffa to establish the sought-after congruity between wages and capital in the circular flow framework in terms of a linear relation between the rate of profits, r, and proportional wages, w:

$$r = R(1-w).$$

This linear relation applied also to the actual system, provided wages and prices were expressed in terms of the Standard commodity. As Sraffa was to emphasize in his 1960 book, "The same rate of profits, which in the Standard system is obtained as a ratio between *quantities* of commodities, will in the actual system result from the ratio of aggregate *values*" (23).

It is interesting to note that in the moment of his analytical triumph Sraffa was to jot down a nota bene saying:

> That M. {Marx} knew all this is shown by the (otherwise contradictory) applying "simple rule" in reduction of values to prices and *s* to *r*, while elsewhere denying that org. comp. of cons. goods and of means of prod. are equal. Contrast nonsense of Tugan B. and Bortkiewicz.
>
> (D3/12/36: 67 (verso))

Criticizing marginal productivity theory

The second example concerns an element of the grand theme of Sraffa's criticism of marginal productivity theory. As we have seen, Sraffa fully endorsed Bortkiewicz's principle that methods of production (and consumption) that are not actually used can have no effect on the rate of profits and relative prices. In Sraffa's view, marginalist theory violated this principle. In a working note dated 10 October 1943, titled "Bortkiewicz's Dogma," he in this context addressed the problem of cause and effect. Did a given "quantity of capital" determine the rate of profits, as marginalist theory implied, or did a given rate of profits, by deciding the choice of technique by means of which given levels of output were produced, decide the quantity of capital?

Put it like this: We cannot say that *r* is 5% ... because ... these methods are adopted, and so much capital is used. But we can say that these methods were adopted ... because ... *r* was 5%.

The fact is that however much we examine the method of production we cannot discover in it any circumstance that compels a rate of 5% rather than any other ...

It is only when we consider the *alternative possible methods of production*, that we discover a connection between the particular method and the rate of 5%. And the connection is, that at that rate that method is cheaper than any other. But does the reverse connection hold too? Is it true that, "given the quantity of capital," a certain method will be adopted and a certain rate be verified?

We must ask "in what sense '*given*' ... ?

(D3/12/35: 30 (1–2); first emphasis added)

Sraffa denied that the concept of quantity of capital could generally be defined independently of the rate of profits, and, even if it could, that a causal link could be established leading from a given amount of capital via the use of a certain technique to the rate of profits.

We must leave things at that. Suffice it to say that the importance Sraffa attributed to "Bortkiewicz's dictum" for a critique of marginalism is also shown, for example, by the fact that as late as January 1958 he composed a note headed "Margins and margins" (D3/12/46: 52–53) that comprises references to, and quotations from, Bortkiewicz's "Der Kardinalfehler" (1906) and "Zur Zinstheorie" (1907b), a note he originally meant to include in the preface of *Production of Commodities by Means of Commodities* but then did not.

References

Böhm-Bawerk, E. v. [1889] 1902. *Kapital und Kapitalzins*. Vol. 2, *Positive Theorie des Kapitales.* 2nd ed. Innsbruck: Wagner'sche Universitätsbuchhandlung.
——1909–14. *Kapital und Kapitalzins*. 3rd ed. 3 vols. Innsbruck: Wagner'sche Universitätsbuchhandlung. (Sraffa 761, 762, and 763)
——[1889] 1959. *Capital and Interest*. 2 vols. English translation of the fourth edition of *Kapital und Kapitalzins*. South-Holland, Ill.: Libertarian Press.
Bortkiewicz, L. v. 1898. *Das Gesetz der kleinen Zahlen*. Leipzig: B. G. Teubner. (Sraffa 2252)
——1906. Der Kardinalfehler der Böhm-Bawerkschen Zinstheorie. *Schmollers Jahrbuch* 30:943–972.
——1906–7. Wertrechnung und Preisrechnung im Marxschen System. Pts. 1, 2, and 3. *Archiv für Sozialwissenschaft und Sozialpolitik* 23:1–50; 25:10–51, 445–488.
——1907a. Zur Berichtigung der grundlegenden theoretischen Konstruktion von Marx im 3. Band des Kapital. *Jahrbücher für Nationalökonomie und Statistik* 34:319–335.
——1907b. Zur Zinstheorie. II. Entgegnung. *Schmollers Jahrbuch* 31:1288–1307.

———1910–11. Die Rodbertus'sche Grundrententheorie und die Marx'sche Lehre von der absoluten Grundrente. *Archivfür Geschichte des Sozialismus* 1:1–40, 391–434. (Sraffa 2253)

———1921. Objektivismus und Subjektivismus in der Werttheorie. *Ekonomisk tidskrift* 21:1–22.

———1923–24. Zweck und Struktur einer Preisindexzahl. Pts. 1, 2, and 3. *Nordisk statistisk tidskrift* 2:369–408; 3:208–252, 494–516. (Sraffa 2251)

———1925. Böhm-Bawerks Hauptwerk in seinem Verhältnis zur sozialistischen Theorie des Kapitalzinses. *Archivfür die Geschichte des Sozialismus und der Arbeiterbewegung* 11:161–172.

———[1907] 1949. On the Correction of Marx's Fundamental Theoretical Construction in the "Third Volume of Capital." English translation of Bortkiewicz 1907a. In *Karl Marx and the Close of His System*, edited by P. M. Sweezy, New York: Kelley, 199–221.

———1952. Value and Price in the Marxian System. English translation of pts. 2 and 3 of Bortkiewicz 1906–7. *International Economic Papers* 2:5–60.

———1971. *La teoria economica di Marx e altri saggi su Böhm-Bawerk, Walras, e Pareto*. Edited by Luca Meldolesi. Turin: Giulio Einaudi. (Sraffa 2324)

Dmitriev, V. K. [1904] 1974. *Economic Essays on Value, Competition, and Utility*. Edited by D. M. Nuti. Translated by D. Fry. Cambridge: Cambridge University Press. (Sraffa 8304)

Garegnani, P. 1984. Value and Distribution in the Classical Economists and Marx. *Oxford Economic Papers* 36:291–325.

———2004. Di una svolta nella posizione teorica nella interpretazione dei classici in Sraffa nei tardi anni 20. Atti dei Convegni Lincei, no. 200. Rome: Accademia Nazionale dei Lincei.

———2005. On a Turning Point in Sraffa's Theoretical Position and in His Interpretation of the Classical Economists. *European Journal of the History of Economic Thought* 19: 453–497.

Gehrke, C. 2003. Price of Wages: A Curious Phrase. Paper presented at the eighth annual conference of the European Society for the History of Economic Thought at the University of Paris, February.

Gehrke, C., and H. D. Kurz. 2004. The Tendency of the Rate of Profits to Fall in Ricardo and Marx. Paper presented at the conference "Economic Growth and Distribution: On the Nature and Causes of the Wealth of Nations" in Lucca, 16–19 June.

Kaldor, N. 1939. Capital Intensity and the Trade Cycle. *Economica* 6:40–66.

Kurz, H. D. 2002. Sraffa's Analysis of Fixed Capital: Towards an Atomic Analysis. Mimeo, Graz.

———2003. The Surplus Interpretation of the Classical Economists. In *A Companion to the History of Economic Thought*, edited by J. Biddle, J. Davis, and W. Samuels, London: Blackwell, 167–183.

Kurz, H. D., and N. Salvadori. 2001. Sraffa and the Mathematicians: Frank Ramsey and Alister Watson. In *Piero Sraffa's Political Economy: A Centenary Estimate*, edited by T. Cozzi and R. Marchionatti, London: Routledge, 254–284.

———2004a. "Man from the Moon": On Sraffa's Objectivism. *Économies et sociétés* 35:1545–1557.

——2004b. On the Collaboration between Sraffa and Besicovitch: The Cases of Fixed Capital and Non-Basics in Joint Production. Atti dei Convegni Lincei, no. 200. Rome: Accademia Nazionale dei Lincei.

——2005. Representing the Production and Circulation of Commodities in Material Terms: On Sraffa's Objectivism. *Review of Political Economy* 17.3:413–441.

Marx, K. 1900. *Le Capital: Critique de l'économie politique.* Book 2. Paris: Giard & Brière. (Sraffa 3365)

——1901. *Le Capital: Critique de l'économie politique.* Book 3, vol. 1. Paris: Giard & Brière. (Sraffa 3366)

——1902. *Le Capital: Critique de l'économie politique.* Book 3, vol. 2. Paris: Giard & Brière. (Sraffa 3367)

——[1861–63] 1924–25. *Histoire des doctrines économiques.* 8 vols. Edited by K. Kautsky. Translated by J. Molitor. Paris: Alfred Costes. (Sraffa 3699)

——[1867] 1938. *Capital.* Vol. 1. London: Allen &Unwin. (Sraffa 3731)

——[1867] 1954. *Capital.* Vol. 1. Moscow: Progress Publishers.

——[1894] 1959. *Capital.* Vol. 3. Moscow: Progress Publishers.

——[1861–63] 1989. Theories of Surplus Value. Pt. 3. In *Economic Manuscript of 1861–63.* Vol. 32 of Karl Marx and Frederick Engels, *Collected Works.* New York: International Publishers.

Mill, J. [1821] 1826. *Elements of Political Economy.* 3rd ed. Reprint, London: Henry G. Bohn.

Oswalt, H. 1907. Zur Zinstheorie. I. Zuschrift. *Schmollers Jahrbuch* 31:1281–1288.

Pareto, V. 1902. *Les systèmes socialistes.* 2 vols. Paris: Giard & Brière. (Sraffa 1774)

——1906. *Manuale di economia politica con una introduzione alla scienze sociale.* Milan: Società editrice libreria. (Sraffa 699)

Petty, W. [1899] 1986. *The Economic Writings of Sir William Petty.* Edited by C. H. Hull. Reprint, New York: Kelley.

Ricardo, D. 1951–73. *The Works and Correspondence of David Ricardo.* 11 vols. Edited by Piero Sraffa, with the collaboration of M. H. Dobb. Cambridge: Cambridge University Press.

Robinson, J. 1942. *An Essay on Marxian Economics.* London: Macmillan. (Sraffa 3687)

Schefold, B. [1976] 1997. Different Forms of Technical Progress. In *Normal Prices, Technical Change, and Accumulation,* London: Macmillan, 257–275.

Smith, A. [1776] 1976. *An Inquiry into the Nature and Causes of the Wealth of Nations.* Vol. 2 of *The Glasgow Edition of the Works and Correspondence of Adam Smith,* edited by R. H. Campbell, A. S. Skinner, and W. B. Todd. Oxford: Oxford University Press.

Sraffa, P. 1925. Sulle relazioni fra costo e quantità prodotta. *Annali di economia* 2:277–328.

——1951. Introduction to vol. 1 of *The Works and Correspondence of David Ricardo.* Edited by Piero Sraffa, with the collaboration of M. H. Dobb. Cambridge: Cambridge University Press.

——1960. *Production of Commodities by Means of Commodities.* Cambridge: Cambridge University Press.

Stolzmann, R. 1896. *Die soziale Kategorie in der Volkswirtschaftslehre.* Berlin: Puttkamer & Mühlbrecht.

Sweezy, P. M. 1942. *The Theory of Capitalist Development.* New York: Oxford University Press. (Sraffa 1764)

Sweezy, P. M., ed. 1949. *Karl Marx and the Close of His System*. New York: Kelley. (Sraffa 3682)

———ed. 1971. *Economia borghese ed economia marxista: Lefonti dello scontro teorico; Eugen von Böhm-Bawerk, Rudolf Hilferding, Ladislaus von Bortkiewicz*. Florence: La Nuova Italia. (Sraffa 2325)

Vianello, F. 1999. Social Accounting with Adam Smith. In *Value, Distribution, and Capital: Essays in Honour of Pierangelo Garegnani*, edited by G. Mongiovi and F. Petri, London: Routledge, 165–180.

Whitehead, A. N. 1926. *Science and the Modern World*. Cambridge: Cambridge University Press.

Wicksell, K. [1893] 1954. *Value, Capital, and Rent*. Translated by S. H. Frowein. London: George Allen & Unwin.

Notes

1 See folder D1/91: 5–33. Sraffa read Bortkiewicz's articles in the original German and excerpted them either in German or by translating the relevant passages into English. His summaries and comments are in English, except for a few short statements in Italian. Most of the entries are dated and the pages are numbered throughout. The copies of Bortkiewicz's articles that Sraffa used are not in his papers; presumably he used copies from the Marshall Library. This is certainly the case with regard to Bortkiewicz's "Der Kardinalfehler" (1906), because Sraffa noted on the first page of his excerpts from this article, "N.B. Marshall's copy of the offprint in the M.L. {Marshall Library} was unopened till this day, when I cut it" (D1/91: 5). Marshall's offprint copy of "Der Kardinalfehler" is not annotated. (We are grateful to Katia Caldari, who cataloged Marshall's books and articles, for helping us track down this copy.) Unless otherwise stated, translations from German sources are ours.

2 In his notebook Sraffa in one place refers to Sweezy's summary account of Bortkiewicz's argument (see D1/91: 20–21), and the relevant passage is annotated in Sraffa's copy of Sweezy's book. It seems fairly safe to assume that Sraffa first became aware of Vladimir K. Dmitriev's contributions via Bortkiewicz's "Wertrechnung" (1906–7); Bortkiewicz, as is well known, drew heavily on Dmitriev's analysis.

3 Sraffa in January 1943 copied the (German) title of Bortkiewicz's 1907 paper into his notebook (from a reference to it in a footnote in Bortkiewicz's 1906–7 article), which suggests that it was not known to him before. There is no copy of Bortkiewicz's 1907 article in Sraffa's papers, and neither the English translation in Sweezy's *Karl Marx and the Close of His System* (1949) nor the Italian translations in Sweezy's *Economia borghese ed economia marxista* (1971) or in Luca Meldolesi's edition of Bortkiewicz's papers titled *La teoria economica di Marx* (1971) are annotated (see Sraffa 3682, 2324, and 2325).

4 In Sraffa's library are copies of Bortkiewicz's *Das Gesetz der kleinen Zahlen* (1898), "Die Rodbertus'sche Grundrententheorie" (1910–11), and "Zweck und Struktur einer Preisindexzahl" (1923–24); there is also in Sraffa's papers a copy of "Böhm-Bawerks Hauptwerk" (1925).

5 The discussion that follows is based on Garegnani 2004, 2005; Kurz 2002, 2003; and Kurz and Salvadori 2001, 2004a, 2004b, 2005.

6 It deserves mention that Sraffa at first wrote down systems of equations in which apparently heterogeneous things were added up and equated with one another (on this, see Garegnani 2005). To a chemist, for example, this would not necessarily have looked strange or even offensive, because an equation such as "$2H_2O = 2H_2 + O_2$," simply expresses the equality of constituents and compound. Similarly with

regard to Sraffa's equations. However, once the necessary prices – what Sraffa called "absolute values" – were to be determined, it was clear that each quantity had to be expressed by two letters, one being the amount of the commodity, the other its value (in terms of some standard). See the respective comment by Frank Ramsey, with whom Sraffa in the early summer of 1928 discussed his first and "second" (i.e., with-surplus) equations and their solutions (D3/12/2: 28); see also Kurz and Salvadori 2001, sec. 5.

7   As early as the late 1920s Sraffa accused marginal productivity theory of circular reasoning because the concept of "quantity of capital" could not be defined independently of relative prices and thus the rate of interest, which, however, was the unknown to be ascertained.

8   There is a striking similarity between Sraffa's approach and Whitehead's description of the approach generally adopted in physics since the seventeenth century: "Search for measurable elements among your phenomena, and then search for relations between these measures of physical quantities" (Whitehead 1926, 63–64). Sraffa put a vertical line in the margin beside this passage in his copy of the book. For a more detailed account of the issues at hand, see Kurz and Salvadori 2004a, 2005.

9   See also in this context Sraffa's annotations in Pareto's *Les systèmes socialistes* (1902) and *Manuale di economia politica* (1906) and the references to the Lausanne economist in his early papers.

10 Sraffa apparently added the title only later, while preparing the edition of the *Works and Correspondence of David Ricardo*. He had learned that in a parliamentary debate on 30 May 1820 on petitions upon the subject of "agricultural distress," Ricardo had been accused of having "argued as if he had dropped from another planet" (Ricardo 1951–73, 5:56). In a note Sraffa related his metaphor of the "man from the moon" to this incident (see D3/11/227: 48). The metaphor was also referred to by Sraffa when resuming the work on his book in 1955 (see D3/12/49: 10).

11 See Sraffa's annotations in Pareto's *Manuale* (1906).

12 See the excerpts Sraffa took around May 1932 from Mill's *Elements of Political Economy* in D3/12/9: 106–118.

13 For a detailed account of Ricardo's concept of proportional wages, see Gehrke 2003.

14 See also in this context the numerical example in Ricardo 1951–73, 1:50.

15 For Ricardo, it would have been difficult to assume wages paid *post factum* because it would have meant that in many of his observations on profits, capital, which he tended to identify with the wages bill, would have vanished.

16 In Marx's terms, proportional wages are given by $V/(V+S) = [1 + (S/V)]^{-1}$.

17 In Sraffa's own indexes of the French edition of volumes 2 and 3 of *Das Kapital* we find "1st equations 444" and "Equations 440" respectively; see Marx 1900, 1901, 1902. There is every reason to presume that these entries were written in the early 1940s, when Sraffa discovered Marx's achievements as an economist, and not, as has been contended, in the late 1920s.

18 This is why, in our view, Sraffa was to credit Marx, and not Ricardo, with the discovery of the maximum rate of profits in circular systems of production (see Sraffa 1960, 94).

19 There is another reason for his interest in establishing a relationship between r and w. Such a relationship implied that the rate of profits could be ascertained independently of relative prices, which, in turn, could be seen to provide support for Ricardo's dictum that "the great questions of Rent, Wages, and Profits must be explained by the proportions in which the produce is divided," and that the laws of distribution "are not essentially connected with the doctrine of value" (Ricardo 1951–73, 8:194).

20 Bortkiewicz was also critical of the other two grounds and particularly of Böhm-Bawerk's argument in favor of a positive rate of time preference. He insisted that one ought to be "extremely cautious" with any sort of "psychological reasoning" and (as Friedrich von Wieser, Böhm-Bawerk's brother-in-law, had argued before him) that it would have to be shown that a positive time preference exists independently of the phenomenon of interest, because if the latter is positive, the former must necessarily be positive too: a positive time preference would have to be shown to be the *"prius"* relative to the phenomenon of interest (Bortkiewicz 1906, 948). He also attacked the view that a positive time preference follows from the fact that all future possessions are more or less uncertain. Since Böhm-Bawerk was concerned with explaining interest proper, that is, net interest as opposed to gross interest, which includes a risk premium designed to take account of the element of uncertainty just mentioned, myopic behavior due to uncertainty can play no role in his argument. "Taken all together, the purely subjective foundation of Böhm-Bawerk's doctrine turns out to be uncertain and precarious" (950).

21 To the above passage Bortkiewicz appended a footnote in which he stressed that J. B. Clark's theory of marginal productivity also does not satisfy this requirement.

22 Bortkiewicz praised the Russian mathematical economist Vladimir K. Dmitriev for having solved the task under consideration, "provided the technical conditions of production of commodities (including the commodity labor-power) are given" (Bortkiewicz 1906–7, pt. 2, 39). It should be noted, however, that Dmitriev had assumed unidirectional processes of production of finite length and had thus set aside the intricate problem of circular production. Bortkiewicz (1906–7) was to follow Dmitriev in this regard, with negative implications for his understanding of Marx; see the third section.

23 See Böhm-Bawerk 1909–14.

24 See also, however, Sraffa's annotations in his copies of Robinson's *Essay* (1942) and Sweezy's *Theory* (1942).

25 See, therefore, Gehrke and Kurz 2004. For a reconstruction of Ricardo's and Marx's ideas on the falling rate of profit that has some elements in common with Sraffa's reading with regard to the major analytical elements involved, see Schefold [1976] 1997.

26 In order to avoid misunderstandings, it should be stressed that Marx was of course fully aware of the fact that nonwage capital, both circulating and fixed, played a prominent role in Ricardo's analysis of prices and values. What Marx insisted on was that Ricardo had neglected to take into account nonwage capital in his analysis of the wage-profit relationship.

27 Marx ([1867] 1954, 575) had argued in section 1 of chapter 25, "The General Law of Capitalist Accumulation," in book 1 of *Capital* that in the case of accumulation with an unchanging composition of capital, the demand for labourers may exceed the supply, and, therefore, wages may rise. *This must, indeed, ultimately be the case if the conditions supposed above continue.* For since in each year more labourers are employed than in its predecessor, sooner or later a point must be reached, at which the requirements of accumulation begin to surpass the customary supply of labour, and, therefore, *a rise of wages takes place* (emphases added)

28 The reference is especially to the following statement of Marx ([1894] 1959, 161): 'So far as the constant portion is concerned, it is itself equal to the cost-price plus the surplus-value, here therefore equal to cost-price plus profit, and this profit may again be greater or smaller than the surplus-value for which it stands. As for the variable capital, the average daily wage is indeed always equal to the number of hours the labourer must work to produce the necessities of life. But this number of hours is in its turn obscured by the deviation of the prices of production of the necessities of life from their values.'

29 Fernando Vianello (1999, sec. 5) provides a detailed account of Smith's error and Marx's criticism of it.

30 See, in particular, the numerical examples in document D1/91: 27–28 and 27–28 (verso).

31 Here Sraffa implicitly defines the organic composition as L/C.

32 The reference is to the following statement by Marx ([1894] 1959, 247):
'Inasmuch as the development of the productive forces reduces the paid portion of employed labour, it raises the surplus-value, because it raises its rate; but inasmuch as it reduces the total mass of labour employed by a given capital, it reduces the factor of the number by which the rate of surplus-value is multiplied to obtain its mass. Two labourers, each working 12 hours daily, cannot produce the same mass of surplus-value as 24 who work only 2 hours, *even if they could live on air and hence did not have to work for themselves at all.* In this respect, then, the compensation of the reduced number of labourers by intensifying the degree of exploitation has certain insurmountable limits. *It may, for this reason, well check the fall in the rate of profit, but cannot prevent it altogether*' (emphases added)

33 The reference is to Robinson's *Essay* (1942); Sraffa's copy (Sraffa 3687) is heavily annotated.

34 Sraffa quoted this passage in the original German (see Bortkiewicz 1906–7, pt. 3, 446–447); we give a slightly corrected version of the English translation (Bortkiewicz 1952, 33), which contains some inaccuracies.

35 Such a "reply" was indeed put forward by Knut Wicksell ([1893] 1954, 37) with regard to Ricardo's theory: "Since, according to Ricardo, wages represent a magnitude fixed from the beginning …, the cause of capital profit is already settled. It is neither possible nor necessary to explain capital profit in other ways."

36 The two straight lines in the margin Sraffa may have added only later, upon rereading his remarks, that is, after he had developed the concept of *nonbasic* industries, which indeed do not matter when it comes to the determination of the rate of profits in the case in which wages are paid *post factum* (and the standard of value is a basic commodity or a bundle of basics).

37 Sraffa noted that on the same page Bortkiewicz had argued, against Gustav Cassel, that the cost equations could nevertheless be taken out of these relations and treated in isolation.

38 It is interesting to note that such otherwise diverse authors as Marx and Böhm-Bawerk held similar views as to the explanatory power of demand and supply in equilibrium. Marx had pointed out that in classical economics demand and supply were seen to regulate only "market prices," not "natural prices" or "prices of production." He had added: "If demand and supply balance, the oscillation of prices ceases, all other conditions remaining the same. *But then demand and supply also cease to explain anything*" (Marx [1867] 1954, 503; emphasis added). Similarly Böhm-Bawerk ([1889] 1959, 42), who had maintained that demand and supply "offers a *husk for a kernel*" (emphasis added). The authors mentioned, we might say, were interested in analyzing the kernel, not the husk.

39 See also the summary account of Bortkiewicz's criticism of Marx on pages 123–125 of Sweezy's *Theory* (1942), to which Sraffa referred in his notebook.

10 Sraffa's equations 'unveiled'?

A comment on Gilibert

Heinz D. Kurz

In a paper published in 2003, Giorgio Gilibert asks the question: 'Where do [Sraffa's price equations (Sraffa, 1960)] come from? In other words, what is their original source of inspiration?' (p. 28). He adds that having scrutinized Sraffa's hitherto unpublished papers, which are kept in the Wren Library, Trinity College, Cambridge, 'we can suggest some reasonable answers'. Their essence he specifies as follows:

> Let us begin by clearly stating our opinion that Sraffa's source of inspir-ation, as far as the equations are concerned, should not be sought in Marshallian or in Ricardian theory (as is commonly maintained), but in that of Marx. And, more precisely, not in Marx's value-theory (*Capital*, Book I) nor in his price-of-production theory (*Capital*, Book III), but in the reproduction schemes of *Capital*, Book II.
>   We intend to prove [*sic*] ... that the reproduction schemes are the obvi-ous starting point for the analytical path followed by Sraffa.
>
> (p. 28)

In the sequel to his paper Gilibert expresses a surprisingly high degree of confidence in his own reconstruction. We read, for example, that Sraffa's '

This chapter was written in 2003 after the author was given the opportunity to see the galley proofs of Gilibert (2003), which the late Pierangelo Garegnani had sent him. Upon the request of the latter the present chapter was not published, because at the time there was the hope and expectation of bringing out *The Unpublished Papers and Correspondence of Piero Sraffa* on behalf of Cambridge University Press within the following two to three years. This would then have allowed people interested in Sraffa's works to judge the merit or demerit of interpretations put forward against the background of the edited material. Alas, the plan to complete and publish the edition did not materialize for reasons that need not concern us here. I have only mildly revised the 2003 version of the chapter, adding English translations of passages in Italian, giving the details of papers, which at the time were available only as manuscripts, but have since then been published, and carrying out some stylistic changes and corrections. Some of the material presented here has been used in Kurz (2012).

I should like to thank Nerio Naldi for his help, Pierangelo Garegnani, Christian Gehrke, Arrigo Opocher, Neri Salvadori and Ian Steedman for valuable comments and suggestions on the original and Geoff Harcourt on this version of the chapter.

"equations" make sense only' if we interpret them along the lines suggested by him, Gilibert (p. 32); and that 'Our interpretation is confirmed beyond reasonable doubt' (p. 33). To someone who has gone through the huge amount of material several times and has developed some idea of its tremendous complexity, reflecting the working of a remarkably independent and original mind, these bold statements have a ring of irony.

In this chapter I shall argue that Gilibert's reconstruction cannot be sustained, first, because the textual evidence from Sraffa's papers he puts forward does not support his view and, second, because he ignores textual evidence from Sraffa's papers which contradicts it. I conclude that Gilibert has not succeeded in 'unveiling' the origin of Sraffa's equations. He has given no compelling evidence that Marx's schemes of reproduction were Sraffa's 'starting point'; and, I should like to add, to the best of my knowledge no such evidence exists.

Since the issue is very difficult and would require a long and intricate story to be unravelled, this comment is not the place to give what I consider to be a more satisfactory answer to the questions posed by Gilibert. Therefore the aim of this comment is purely negative. However, as I go along I shall provide a few hints as to where, I think, such an answer ought to be sought.

The composition of the chapter is the following. In the first section, I remark on the difficulty of the task of reconstructing the intellectual development of Sraffa in view of the highly complex and occasionally fragmented material and on how to proceed in such a way that the probability of misinterpretation is minimized. In the second section I scrutinize the three pieces of textual 'evidence' put forward by Gilibert in support of his view and conclude that the evidence does not show what Gilibert purports it shows. In the third section I comment briefly on selected aspects of his reading of Sraffa's 'equations' through the lens of Marx's schemes of reproduction. In the fourth section I draw the readers' attention to a few documents (out of many) which, I surmise, Gilibert has seen and which he has put on one side without further explanation. Alas, these documents (and many others) fly in the face of his interpretation. In the final section I conclude that it is not good enough to find 'reasonable answers' vis-à-vis a judicious selection from Sraffa's papers: one rather has to find reasonable answers vis-à-vis the relevant material as a whole.

With respect to one aspect of his interpretation Gilibert maintains: 'The reconstruction offered here is largely speculative [*sic*], but it has at least [*sic*] the advantage of offering a plausible and consistent interpretation of the papers concerned' (p. 36). This is a dangerous argument, because if one arrives at an allegedly 'plausible and consistent interpretation' by restricting the textual domain of one's investigation then there is no reason to presume that the reconstruction is faithful to the author under consideration. In the present instance, I am afraid to say, this is indeed the case.

On the 'question of method'

In his *Studies in Words*, C. S. Lewis describes vividly the danger of misinterpreting:

> The highly intelligent and sensitive reader will, without knowledge, be most in danger of [committing errors]. His mind bubbles over with possible meanings. He has ready to hand un-thought-of metaphors, highly individual shades of feeling, subtle associations, ambiguities – every manner of semantic gymnastics – which he can attribute to the author. Hence the difficulty of 'making sense' out of a strange phrase will seldom be for him insuperable. Where the duller reader simply does not understand, he misunderstands – triumphantly, brilliantly. *But it is not enough to make sense. We want to find the sense the author intended.*
>
> (Lewis, 1960, pp. 4–5; emphasis added)

Indeed, the only thing that matters is to find the sense Sraffa intended. It hardly needs to be mentioned that this is an extremely difficult task and that there is no golden rule, which, if followed, would invariably lead us to an answer that stands the test of close scrutiny. However, some precautions can and ought to be taken in order not to misunderstand and misinterpret all too easily, brilliantly or otherwise. From what we know, after having been appointed to the Ricardo edition by the Royal Economic Society in January 1930 Sraffa, via Tatiana Schucht, discussed some of the editorial problems he faced with his friend Antonio Gramsci.[1] Perhaps partly as a reflection of their discussions Gramsci wrote the following passage on the 'question of method', which is directly pertinent to the present case:

> *Quistione di metodo.* Se si vuole studiare la nascita di una concezione del mondo che dal suo fondatore non è stata mai esposta sistematicamente (e la cui coerenza essenziale è da ricercare non in ogni singolo scritto o serie di scritti ma nell'intiero sviluppo del lavoro intellettuale vario in cui gli elementi della concezione sono impliciti) *occorre fare preliminarmente un lavoro filologico minuzioso e condotto col massimo scrupolo de esattezza, di onestà scientifica, di lealtà intellettuale, di assenza di ogni preconcetto ed apriorismo o partito preso.* Occorre, prima di tutto, ricostruire il processo di sviluppo intellettuale del pensatore dato, per identificare gli elementi divenuti stabili e "permanenti", cioè che sono stati assunti come pensiero proprio, diverso e superiore al "materiale" precedentemente studiato e che ha servito di stimolo; solo questi elementi sono momenti essenziali del processo del sviluppo. ...
>
> (Gramsci, 1948, p. 76; second emphasis added)[2]

Gramsci's book is in Sraffa's library (for short, Sr.L.) (see Sr.L. 3979) and it is annotated. In the margin of the paragraph quoted Sraffa added a straight line, whereas in the margin of the italicized passage (which in the book is underlined by Sraffa) there are two straight lines. Sraffa's own editorial work has rightly been praised for its philological meticulousness, its maximum scrupulousness as to exactness, its scientific honesty, its intellectual loyalty and the absence of any preconceptions and apriorisms or position taken. It has also rightly been praised for Sraffa's identification of elements in Ricardo's thought, which in the course of time became stable and permanent, that is, especially his reconstruction of the development of Ricardo's theory of value and distribution.

Compared to the Ricardo editorial project the Sraffa project is a great deal, in fact: incomparably, more difficult. Sraffa published very little during his lifetime, but he wrote a lot. There are several thousand pages in his unpublished papers that contain preparatory notes, explorations of specific ideas, elaborations of particular points, alternative approaches to a problem, early drafts of sections and whole chapters, etc., which eventually culminated in the publication of *Production of Commodities by Means of Commodities* (1960). His respective work extended over a long period of time, from the mid 1920s to 1959, interrupted twice, each time for a decade or so (roughly during the 1930s and from the mid 1940s to the mid 1950s). Sraffa was a most attentive student of the old and contemporary economics literature, but his intellectual curiosities and interests went far beyond it, including recent developments in the natural sciences, especially physics, chemistry and biology, and in philosophy. His studies and manuscripts reflect impressively his comprehensive intellectual concerns and the numerous and diverse sources he tapped. In private conversation, Sraffa is reported to have called his notes and papers the 'iceberg', the tip of which is his published work. Hence, what is needed is an investigation of that iceberg – the materialization of the inspirations he derived from multiple sources, of the process of his intellectual development, and of the progress of his analytical work. The papers ought to be studied together with the sources to which he explicitly refers in them, many of which are to be found in his library: his books and other pieces of literature, several of which are annotated and contain indexes prepared by Sraffa himself on the fly-leaves at the end of the items or on their inside back covers. The annotations and the indexes of his books frequently exhibit a complex age structure. They were apparently composed at different times reflecting Sraffa's progressing analytical preoccupations, which in turn are echoed in his notes and manuscripts. On the basis of his handwriting, which changed over time, and of echoes in his notes and papers, his annotations and entries in his indexes can often with a reasonable degree of confidence be ascribed to one of the three main periods of his constructive work (broadly: 1927–1931, 1942–1946, 1955–1959) and in some cases even to particular years within those periods. Then there are Sraffa's diaries, which contain several valuable hints as to which problems he was working on when, which literature he consulted and with whom he discussed the problems. Finally, there is Sraffa's correspondence and exchange of notes with other scholars (most notably his 'mathematical friends' and Keynes) and observations by others on the progress of Sraffa's work (especially Keynes in the early period).

Hence, in order to avoid as much as possible the pitfalls of misunderstanding and misinterpreting, which are particularly numerous in the case of Sraffa, a first and obvious precaution is to take into account *all* the information at our disposal: (i) Sraffa's papers, (ii) his library and annotations and personal indexes in his books, (iii) his diaries and (iv) his correspondence and exchange of notes with other scholars and their remarks on Sraffa's work. It is much too risky to base one's interpretation only on some of the available sources to the neglect of others.

However, given the sheer mass of material at hand, this does not do away with the necessity of proceeding in terms of working hypotheses, or 'speculations', to use Gilibert's term, of how the material might reasonably be interpreted. As soon as one feels entitled to put forward such a working hypothesis, and has collected the documents which, after careful scrutiny, philological and other, appear to support it, one ought to go over the material once again deliberately on the look-out for documents that *contradict* the hypothesis or that might be incompatible with it. Since, as has been mentioned, Sraffa tried out many ideas and concepts, some of which he kept, while others he abandoned, documents can be set aside which reflect ideas or concepts jettisoned by him: they can safely be assumed not to have contributed to what became 'stable and permanent' in Sraffa's analysis. However, if there are documents, which are neither compatible with the interpretation suggested nor can be put on one side on the grounds just mentioned, one has to face the fact that one's working hypothesis is either entirely or partly wrong and therefore has to be abandoned or amended.

In the case of Gilibert's interpretation I fear that the conclusion will be that it has to be abandoned.

Gilibert's three elements of 'documental evidence'

Gilibert rests his case on three elements of 'documental evidence':

> First, Sraffa consistently labels his price equations without surplus as '1st equations'. The same expression ('1st equations') can be found written in the margin of his copy of *Capital* to designate the scheme of simple reproduction. Second, in a document (D3/12/16) dated 7 August 1942, he writes: '1st equations (simple reproduction)'. Finally, a few days before (30 July 1942) Sraffa, commenting on Rosa Luxemburg's opinion, according to which the reproduction schemes can be considered as an up-to-date version of the *Tableau Économique*, writes: 'Equations = Tableau Economique'.
>
> (p. 28)[3]

Sraffa, as has been noted by several authors including Gilibert, began to develop his systems of equations, starting with the no-surplus or 'first equations', in November 1927. Confronting this fact with Gilibert's three elements gives the following picture. First, while elements two and three are dated by Sraffa himself as 1942, that is fifteen years *after* he had for the first time composed his first equations, with regard to element one Gilibert does not specify at around what time he believes Sraffa had written in his copy of the French edition of volume II of *Das Kapital*, *Le Capital* (Marx, 1900), the expression he, Sraffa, had coined in November 1927: 'first equations'. Below I shall argue that there is reason to think that Sraffa's jotting on a fly-leaf (and not in the margin, as Gilibert writes) dates also from the 1940s. Second, *none* of the documents contains a clear statement by Sraffa expressing beyond doubt that he had started from Marx's schemes of reproduction.

Then there are the following questions, which one ought to answer.

First, Sraffa throughout his work was careful to indicate the sources he used and the authors of concepts he discussed or explored. Had Marx's schemes of reproduction been 'the obvious starting point for the analytical path followed by Sraffa', as Gilibert contends (p. 28), why is this fact not at all obvious right from the beginning of Sraffa's constructive work? Why is there a need to 'prove' the obvious (p. 28)? Why does the 'original draft of the "first equations"' appear to be 'cryptic and obscure', as Gilibert opines (p. 28)? It is certainly somewhat of a riddle that Sraffa in this crucial case, writing for himself, would deviate from his usual habit of meticulously documenting the sources of concepts he adopted and of inspirations he got, is it not?

Second, and closely related, why did Sraffa in the winter of 1927–1928 invoke the new concepts of 'first' and 'second equations' and repeatedly called them '*my* equations' (emphasis added)? Why did he not dub his first equations, for example, 'Marx's equations' or 'simple reproduction without surplus', as would have been natural had he started from Marx's schemes of reproduction?

Third, what weight do Gilibert's three pieces of 'documental evidence' carry with regard to the interpretation put forward? More specifically, assume for a moment that Sraffa had developed his first equations entirely independently of Marx's reproduction schemes and had only afterwards discovered the latter. Is there anything in Gilibert's three cited elements that would rule out this possibility? Obviously no. There is nothing in them that would prevent us from entertaining the view that Sraffa jotted down in his copy of *Le Capital* 'first equations', after having discovered that his approach had to some extent been anticipated by Marx. In fact, in this case Sraffa's jotting could even be said to be more plausible: Had Marx's schemes been Sraffa's starting point, why should he have noted the obvious in *Le Capital* instead of noting it in his papers? What speaks against the view that Sraffa's jotting is an expression of his surprise when discerning that Marx had adopted a somewhat similar point of view, a fact of which Sraffa had been unaware when elaborating his equations in the winter of 1927–1928?

Fourth, one cannot escape the question: Are there any indications as to the date of the jotting? There is evidence that Sraffa did not always read the books he consulted in a single go from front to back cover. Typically he proceeded selectively as to which parts or chapters of a book to read, and which not, guided by the particular analytical problems he was struggling with at the time and his expectation as to what he might find in a particular work. Sraffa annotated many of his books, including his copies of the various editions of *Das Kapital*, especially the French and English ones, and the French edition of *Theorien über den Mehrwert*. In addition they contain in some cases very detailed indexes composed by Sraffa himself. Sraffa's annotations and indexes frequently exhibit a complex age structure. This applies especially to books he would consult repeatedly, such as, for example, Marshall's *Principles* or Marx's *Das Kapital* and *Theorien*. The age structure reflects neatly, as has already been emphasized, Sraffa's changing analytical preoccupations as his constructive work evolved.

Can one be a bit more precise with regard to the case under consideration? In 1935 a French translation of Rosa Luxemburg's *Die Akkumulation des Kapitals* was published (Luxemburg, 1935). Sraffa acquired the book and appears to have read it in the early 1940s. He annotated especially those passages in which Luxemburg pointed out that Marx's schemes of reproduction derived from the *Tableau économique* and in which she dealt with Marx's two-sectoral scheme of simple reproduction as it is to be found in volume II of *Das Kapital*.[4] The reference in the French edition of Luxemburg's book is to the second French edition of *Das Kapital*, translated by J. Molitor and published in 1893 (which is not in Sraffa's library). Surprisingly, in the margin of Luxemburg's reproduction of Marx's scheme (Luxemburg, 1935, p. 75) Sraffa put three straight lines! Still more surprisingly, he also put three straight lines in the margin of the footnote in which Luxemburg (or rather the editor) gives as the source of the scheme p. 371 of the edition of *Le Capital* used! The following questions are close at hand: Had Sraffa in 1927 indeed started from Marx's schemes of reproduction and had he been working on them and their reformulation at great intensity for some four years, how can it be explained that several years later he would find it worth annotating – emphatically![5] – the passage in Luxemburg's book in which the alleged starting point of his entire enterprise and its source were given? Had he forgotten from where he had taken off? Or could this not be interpreted, and perhaps with greater plausibility, as indicating that Sraffa had studied Marx's *schemes* of reproduction only *after* his initial period of constructive work in the winter of 1927–1928 and possibly as late as the early 1940s?

Let us now have a closer look at Sraffa's own index in Marx (1900). There is reason to assume that the index was composed in (at least) two different periods of time. The index can be subdivided in two parts. The first part refers exclusively to pages of the book up to p. 122, which is the first page of chapter VI in part I.[6] The second part of the index begins with '1st equations 444' and refers especially to pages in part III of the book, which contains the schemes of reproduction, plus several additional references to earlier pages.[7]

We may also take a brief look at the French edition of volume III of *Das Kapital*, which is in two volumes (Marx, 1901–1902). In Sraffa's own index to volume II of the edition we find in a handwriting that is clearly different from the handwriting of the preceding notes:

Hypothesis 433
Equations 440

Now we know that the term 'Hypothesis' Sraffa began to use in his papers only in the 1940s, reflecting his recent intensive reading of Marx, especially *Capital*.[8] Hence it can safely be assumed that also the item 'Equations' was added only in the second period and not in the first.

We conclude that the three pieces Gilibert singled out from Sraffa's papers render *no* support to his interpretation. While two of the documents belong definitely to the 1940s, there are strong reasons to presume that also the third document was composed that late.[9] It is worth mentioning that in *none* of them does Sraffa state explicitly that the starting point of his equations in November 1927 was Marx's reproduction schemes. Therefore Gilibert's three elements provide *no* 'documental evidence' at all in support of his interpretation. They could be employed at least as well, if not more effectively, in an attempt to establish the *opposite* point of view that Marx's schemes of reproduction were *not* the 'original source of inspiration' of Sraffa's first equations; that Sraffa had elaborated his equations quite *independently* of Marx's schemes, either from scratch or inspired by some other sources; and that only *after* he had done so had he come across Marx's schemes and had seen certain similarities (but also differences) between his own analysis and Marx's.[10]

The rest of Gilibert's paper presupposes the validity of his basic contention, which as we have seen has not been established. Therefore there is no real need to enter into a discussion of his subsequent analysis: whatever its merits or demerits, it cannot, *as a matter of principle*, patch over the fact that his contention is not even supported by the very limited material put forward. In fact, Gilibert's subsequent argument consists essentially of a set of speculations on the origin of the 'first equations', on how the first draft of them ought to be interpreted, and on the analytical path that led to their published version. His speculations are skilful and some even ingenious, but speculations nevertheless. Finally, Gilibert puts forward what he himself explicitly considers a 'speculation' concerning the relationship between what Sraffa at some stage of his work called 'My Hypothesis' and his elaboration of the 'Standard system' and 'Standard commodity'.

Hence, while there is no need to embark on a critical discussion of the rest of Gilibert's argument, a few comments on some aspects of his speculations might contribute to a further clarification why his reconstruction does not 'unveil' Sraffa's equations, and indicate where to look in order to get closer to an answer that is less unsatisfactory.

A 'fundamental document'

Gilibert refers to two documents, which he calls 'fundamental' (p. 29), one taken from a notebook dated July 1928, the other composed in August 1942. The two documents serve him as 'guides' for his subsequent reasoning (p. 29). Here we limit our attention to the first document about which Gilibert writes: 'The first is a working research programme, a sort of strategic plan for the future book.' The piece is indeed of interest because it bears testimony to the fact that several months *after* Sraffa had elaborated his first systems of equations he acknowledged some similarities, but also differences, between what he was in the process of doing and what Marx had done in his analysis of reproduction, *as Sraffa perceived it at the time*. The document under consideration is D3/12/9: 11 (reproduced by Gilibert on p. 29) in which Sraffa mentions the French edition of volume II of *Das Kapital* (Marx, 1900).

The reader's attention should focus (a) on precisely which part of that volume Sraffa refers to and (b) on the exact wording of the note. Sraffa refers to

Marx, Cap. vol. 2°, cap. I-III della Pte 1ª.

(D3/12/9: 11)

Chapter III of part I in that edition ends on p. 87.[11] It is worth noting that the three chapters do *not* contain any *schemes* of reproduction. In these chapters Marx discusses the circuit of money capital (chapter I), of productive capital (chapter II) and of commodity-capital (chapter III) – yet without any reference to the schemes of reproduction. The introduction of the scheme of simple reproduction has to wait until part III of the volume, more precisely, until p. 444 (see also Gilibert, p. 30). This may strike the reader as a trite observation; it is made because after having quoted in full the document under discussion Gilibert immediately moves on to 'the well-known *scheme* of simple reproduction, as presented in *Capital*, Book II' (p. 30; emphasis added). When well known to whom?

This brings us to Sraffa's wording in the document under discussion. Interestingly, nowhere does Sraffa use the expression 'schema' (scheme) of reproduction. This expression is indeed not to be found in chapters I–III of part I of that volume. Hence, from a strictly philological point of view even this document, dated July 1928, and despite its reference to volume II of *Le Capital*, cannot be seen as clearly indicating that Sraffa was referring to Marx's *schemes* of reproduction.[12]

Yet to Gilibert this is an indisputable fact and to him the document even contains 'a sort of strategic plan for the future book'. Therefore, after having presented the 'well-known scheme of simple reproduction' and having

stressed that in it all magnitudes are expressed in 'money terms' (p. 31) he
begins to interpret Sraffa's equations and the development of his respective
analysis against the background of the 'guide' provided by D3/12/9: 11 (and
the other one mentioned earlier).

Here it suffices to turn immediately to Gilibert's interpretation of a system of Sraffa's with three equations, dated winter 1927 (D3/12/5: 2), in terms
of Marx's (three-sector) scheme of simple reproduction.[13] For reasons that
will become clear below, I reproduce the document in full and italicize parts
of it:

No surplus –

$$A = a_1 + b_1 + c_1$$
$$B = a_2 + b_2 + c_2 \quad \text{where} \quad$$
$$C = a_3 + b_3 + c_3$$

$$A = \Sigma a$$
$$B = \Sigma b$$
$$C = \Sigma c$$

These are homogeneous linear equations. They have infinite sets of solutions, but the solutions of each set are proportional. These proportions
are *univoche* [unique].

These proportions we call ratios of Absolute values. They are purely
numerical relations between the *things A, B* ... They are not necessarily the ratios, in which exchange will actually take place in any community in which *the quantities of things respectively used in production (i.e.
consumed) and produced* satisfy those equations: such actual ratios of
exchange are also conditioned by such things as legal institutions, etc.
which vary in different organisations of society and which are 'arbitrary',
i.e. irrelevant, from our present point of view.

(D3/12/5: 2; italics added)

Gilibert's first reaction to it is:

this is a rather disconcerting way of writing. Equations without unknowns?
Equations where heterogeneous quantities are summed up? Sraffa's formal education (classic high school and faculty of jurisprudence) had
indeed a strong humanist basis, but it is also true that his papers attest,
from the 1920s on, a good acquaintance with algebra. And we cannot
reasonably suspect him of having committed such trivial errors.

(p. 32)

I leave aside whether already from the 1920s on Sraffa had a 'good acquaintance with algebra' and whether he was not also occasionally committing
'trivial errors' in his manuscripts. Instead, I immediately turn to Gilibert's
suggested way out of the impasse. He insists:

In fact, these 'equations' *make sense only* if we interpret them as a simple algebraic transcription (with letters substituted by numbers) of a

Marxian scheme with three industries (simple reproduction is attested by the Σ conditions), and without surplus.

The quantities summed are homogeneous, all being measured in money terms.

(p. 32; emphases added)

Before I comment on his reasoning let me first recall how in *Production of Commodities by Means of Commodities* Sraffa tabulated the conditions of production of an industry. We find, for example, on the first page of the main text of his book the expression

280 qr. wheat + 12 t. iron → 400 qr. wheat

(Sraffa, 1960, p. 3)

What is the difference between this expression and any one of those in document D3/12/5: 2 above? Here it suffices to note that from a purely formal point of view Sraffa employs in both expressions the algebraic sign '+', whereas in the former compared with the latter he uses the symbol '→' instead of the algebraic sign '='. Now, the meaning of Sraffa's 1960 tabulation of production processes has generally been considered as crystal clear, and as far as I know nobody has ever seriously objected that by using the algebraic sign '+' Sraffa is guilty of having committed the trivial error of summing up heterogeneous quantities.

The uncertainty as to the meaning of the expressions in the note of winter 1927 therefore appears to have a great deal to do with Sraffa's use of the equality sign and his speaking in fact of equations. However, if his abstract expressions were simply read as tabulations of productive operations, giving the physical amount of the output of a process on one side of the equality sign and the physical amounts of the different things used up in the course of its production on the other, then some of the uncertainty would effectively be removed. Yet are we entitled to read the above expressions in the way suggested? Gilibert implicitly says no, because in his view the above expressions 'make sense only' if all quantities involved are interpreted as 'being measured in money terms'.

This dictum comes as a surprise in view of the text Sraffa appended to his system which, unfortunately, Gilibert quotes only in part (p. 33).[14] In that text the reference is explicitly to 'the *things A, B, …*'. However, still more explicitly but, alas! not quoted by Gilibert, the reference is to '*the quantities of things respectively used in production (i.e. consumed) and produced*'.[15] In view of this one cannot escape the impression that if Gilibert's contention was correct, Sraffa must have been an author who tried to play tricks on the future readers of his unpublished papers (and thus also on himself): Not only did he not say that he had conceptualized his above expressions in terms of quantities measured in money terms, he even said something different, namely, that the magnitudes under consideration were 'quantities of things respectively used in production (i.e. consumed) and produced'.

Sraffa, as is evidenced by several of his papers (see also below), was particularly afraid of 'small errors' because they have a tendency to grow into big ones. (Small errors, one might add, are less easy to discover and therefore have a potential of hidden effectiveness.)

I now turn to some pieces of evidence from Sraffa's papers and library, which Gilibert does not refer to but which contradict his interpretation or are incompatible with it. I discuss three areas of evidence. The first refers to Sraffa's study of the natural sciences, the second to his early studies of Marx and the classical economists, and the third to his study of marginalist authors and especially Paretian general equilibrium theory.

Evidence not referred to by Gilibert

Sraffa's approach and the natural sciences: a few observations

Gilibert has in all probability come across what can safely be considered the companion document of the one just discussed, but surprisingly he does not refer to it: D3/12/11: 87.[16] It is entitled 'Value without surplus' and is contained in a folder dated by Sraffa 'end of November, 1927'. There is reason to presume that it predates the document used by Gilibert (D3/12/5: 2). It is apposite to reproduce it in full:

$$A = a_1 + b_1 + c_1$$
$$B = a_2 + b_2 + c_2$$
$$C = a_3 + b_3 + c_3$$

Questo è un *determinante*. Inoltre, le somme verticali sono uguali alle somme orizzontali.

$$\overline{\quad \quad \quad \quad}$$
$$\;\;'' \quad '' \quad ''$$
$$A \quad B \quad C$$

Vedere se a questo determinante è possibile applicare il metodo di Volterra (Chini, p. 35) per trovare il numero dei 'componenti indipendenti' del sistema. Questo forse servirebbe: a) quando non tutti i beni entrassero come fattori di ciascuno. b) quando ci sia surplus, cioè considerando i vari surpluses come merci diverse (supponendo cioè che appena sorge il surplus, si continua a produrre la stessa quantità di 'grano' di prima, e le risorse residue vengon tutte dedicate a produrre gioielli e altre cose 'improduttive').

(D3/12/11: 87)[17]

The reference is to a book by Mineo Chini entitled *Corso speciale di matematiche con numerosi applicazioni ad uso principalmente dei chimici e dei naturalisti* (1923, sixth edn). The book is in Sraffa's library and has a few annotations. In the above document Sraffa draws explicitly attention to p. 35 of that book. On this page he annotated a passage dealing with substances of determinate chemical composition and systems of such substances. This discussion is immediately followed by Chini's investigation of the solutions of the corresponding linear systems (ibid., pp. 36 *et seq*), which is also annotated by Sraffa. The passage reads:

> Quando si abbia un certo numero di <u>sostanze di determinata composizione chimica</u>, ciascuna delle quali possa prendersi in quantità arbitraria, è chiaro che i vari corpi semplici che entrano a far parte di un tale sistema non sempre potranno a loro volta prefissarsi <u>tutti</u> in quantità arbitraria, ma in generale sarà possibile ciò soltanto per <u>un certo numero di essi</u>. Le quantità (masse) dei rimanenti elementi resteranno invece pienamente determinate da quelle prestabilite per i primi; i quali vengono perciò detti i *<u>componenti independenti</u>* del sistema. [The underlinings are by Sraffa and there is an arrow pointing from the last underlined item to the last but one; in the margin of the passage Sraffa put two straight lines. The text runs on:] Per ottenere il numero di questi componenti (del quale si fa uso per es. quando si voglia applicare ad un complesso eterogeneo la cosidetta *regola delle fasi*), il prof. Volterra, in una delle sue pubblicazioni (*Atti della R. Accademia dei Lincei* – Seduta del 22 novembre 1903), ha indicato il metodo sequente.
>
> (Chini, p. 35; emphases in the original. Subsequently Chini expounds Volterra's method.)[18],[19]

What to make of all this? A few observations must suffice.

First, it is worth emphasizing that right at the beginning of his work on the 'equations', in November 1927, Sraffa consulted a book on mathematics, and, perhaps significantly, not a book on pure mathematics, but on mathematics for chemists and natural scientists.[20] This is fully in accordance with a fact which up till now appears to have largely escaped the attention of many commentators on Sraffa: his vivid interest in contemporary developments in the natural sciences and his attempt to develop an approach in economics in full recognition of these developments. He was particularly fascinated by quantum physics and thermodynamics. This met with his materialist and objectivist orientation which he had brought to Cambridge not least as a fruit of his long discussions with Antonio Gramsci, and which, he felt, was corroborated by recent developments in the sciences.[21] He studied meticulously such authors as Heinrich Hertz, Jules Henri Poincaré, Alfred N. Whitehead and A. S. Eddington.[22] He excerpted, for example, the following passage on the physicist Werner Heisenberg from an essay on 'The quantum theory' by H. S. Allen published in *Nature* in 1928:

> Heisenberg put forward the demand that only such quantities as are observable should be represented in the mathematical formulation of *atomic theory*. ... This led to the development of the matrix mechanics,

every term in a matrix corresponding to something which is, at least ideally, observable.

(Allen, 1928, p. 891, emphasis added; cited in D1/9: 13)[23]

In summer 1929 Sraffa explicitly stated that he was keen to elaborate an 'atomic analysis' (D3/12/13: 16 (9)); and in August 1931, in a critical retrospect, he characterized his previous analytical efforts *explicitly* as having been concerned with developing 'an entirely objective point of view' which is 'the natural science point of view' (D3/12/7: 161 (3)). This view implied that

we must start by assuming *that for every effect there must be sufficient cause, that the causes are identical with their effects, & that there can be nothing in the effect which was not in the causes: in our case, there can be no product for which there has not been an equivalent cost, and all costs (= expenses) must be necessary to produce it.*

(D3/12/7: 161 (3); emphasis added)

Sraffa saw this kind of view foreshadowed in the writings of such authors as William Petty, the Physiocrats and especially Anonymous (1821).

Second, in view of what has just been said, and more particularly in view of Sraffa's reference to Chini (1923) above, there is reason to think that Sraffa wrote his above 'first equations' as chemists do since Lavoisier who in the late eighteenth century presented chemical reactions first as a balance sheet and then as an algebraic equation, with the name of a substance expressing the equality of constituents and compound, e.g. '$2H_2O = 2H_2 + O_2$'.[24] From a perspective revolving around the concept of balancing, the analogy between a product that obtains as the result of the 'destruction' of necessary quantities of means of production and means of subsistence, on the one hand, and a chemical reaction conceived of as a balance of the weights of inputs and outputs is close at hand. In both cases the balance expresses conservation of mass. Seen in this way, there appears to be nothing 'cryptic or obscure' about Sraffa's first equations. This is indirectly confirmed by Sraffa's text of D3/12/11: 87. He stresses that into the quantities of the substances – which he calls 'beni' or 'merci' (i.e. goods or commodities) – on the left hand side of the equality sign 'enter' the quantities of the substances – which he calls 'beni' or 'fattori' (i.e. goods or factors) – on the right hand side of the equality sign. Hence there can be no doubt that in the identical production schemas contained in the twin documents, D3/12/11: 87 and D3/12/5: 2, the reference is *directly* to physical quantities of goods, or commodities, or factors, and *not*, as Gilibert claims, to quantities in terms of money. Notice also that Sraffa uses a term familiar in marginalist theory ('factors'), but no Marxian one.

Third, and closely connected with what has just been said, an expression of the type '$2H_2O = 2H_2 + O_2$' may even be regarded as a proper algebraic equation when interpreted as follows: 'the mass of two molecules of water is equal to the mass of two molecules of hydrogen plus the mass of one molecule of oxygen'. In this interpretation H_2O is not just a symbol for water, but has a quantitative aspect: it is the mass of a molecule of water. Similarly, an expression of the type '$11A = 3A + 9B$' (D3/12/11: 17) could be interpreted both as a tabulation of a production process (and in this case it is not an algebraic equation) or as an algebraic equation saying: 'The value of 11 units of A equals the sum of the value of 3 units of A and 9 units of B.' Obviously, in this interpretation A and B assume the true meaning of values or prices, but a system of such algebraic equations is non-contradictory only in the case in which there is no surplus, as Sraffa kept stressing (see, for example, D3/12/6: 16 and D3/12/2: 32–35). Finally, it deserves mention that more recently chemists use two symbols: '$=$' when the reaction is reversible, and '$\rightarrow$' when it is not. Since single economic productive processes are never reversible, one might wonder whether it is for this reason that in his book Sraffa switched to the latter symbol.[25]

Fourth, we have seen that Sraffa characterized his own approach as belonging to the tradition established by Petty and the Physiocrats who are said to have had the right concept of 'cost'. In this context it is worth mentioning that in a document of some fifty pages composed in the summer of 1929 Sraffa explained in some detail why at the time he thought that labour was not a 'quantity' that could be taken as a datum in value theory (see also the reflection of his argument in D3/12/13: 2 and footnote 35 below). He expounded that his objection to the approach in terms of labour quantities 'è basata sulla veduta essenzialmente fisiocratica, che il *valore* sia una quantità intrinseca degli oggetti, quasi una *qualità fisica o chimica*' (D3/12/12: 7; emphases added).[26] This characterization is fully in accordance with the evidence laid out here.

Fifth, the text of D3/12/11: 87 above also 'unveils', if we may use Gilibert's word, another important and closely related aspect of Sraffa's early work. In the late 1920s he was keen to stay analytically within the realm of *necessities*. The latter obtains in an unadulterated way in the no-surplus or 'natural' economy and is reflected in the first equations. The no-surplus case, Sraffa insisted, 'would exhibit the true absolute costs' (D3/12/6: 11) of the different commodities and the corresponding 'absolute values' of them. Interestingly, he also used the term 'physical value' of products and insisted that it '*is* equal to what has been consumed' (D3/12/1: 5; see also D3/12/10: 54). He showed that the sought ratios, or (relative) values, are uniquely determined by the socio-technical conditions of production and can be ascertained by solving a set of linear homogeneous production equations.[27]

Yet what about the with-surplus case? The 'natural science point of view' Sraffa had assumed implied: 'We shall have to adopt *that definition which makes the scale of absolute values identical with what it was when there was no surplus*' (D3/12/6: 14; emphasis added). In this way the logic applying to values in the case of production for subsistence was taken to carry over to the with-surplus case.[28] This necessitated reducing the surplus, or interest – an 'effect' for which there had to be 'sufficient cause' – to some 'cost' or other. Interest, Sraffa insisted, reflects some objective necessity, rooted in some objective 'social' as opposed to 'natural' obstacles that have to be overcome:

> Interest appears thus as the necessary means of overcoming an obstacle to production. It is a social necessity as distinguished from the material necessity of, say, putting coal into a locomotive that it may do its work.
> (D3/12/18: 11; see also ibid.: 3–6)[29]

Interest has to be paid, Sraffa argued, in order to prevent capitalists from 'withdrawing' their (circulating) capital, thus thwarting the 'self-replacement' of the economy.[30] More precisely, Sraffa conceived of the surplus product, typically a composite commodity, as the physical input into an artificial industry producing 'luxuries' or 'gioielli e altre cose "improduttive" ' (as we read in the above document) for capitalists (see also D3/12/8: 29). By construction, luxuries satisfy the condition mentioned in a) above: 'quando non tutti i beni entrassero come fattori di ciascuno'. These artificial goods are 'unproductive' in the sense that, while produced, they are not themselves employed in production. They serve only a single purpose: they are the incentive needed to make capitalists refrain from withdrawing their (circulating) capital. These goods are thus envisaged to perform with regard to capital what workers' means of subsistence perform with regard to labour: the payment of the former are a *social*, that of the latter a *natural* prerequisite for production to go on unhampered.

As Sraffa noted in the document of August 1931 already referred to above, in this way the surplus was made to 'disappear' or 'melt away' (D3/12/7: 161 (3)). This 'where there is an effect there must be sufficient cause' point of view is confirmed by a document from winter 1927–1928. In it Sraffa concluded with respect to the new equations he had elaborated: 'These absolute values *with* surplus are no more what is necessary to *enable* to produce *A*, but what is necessary to *induce* to produce *A*' (D3/12/6: 10). By introducing an artificial (composite) commodity hypothetically generated by consuming the surplus product of the actual system as an input, Sraffa sought to assimilate the with-surplus case to the no-surplus one. By tucking away the surplus in an artificial industry, the resulting equations would be rendered non-contradictory and solvable in the conventional way, just like his first equations.[31]

The physical interpretation is corroborated beyond a shadow of doubt by a document entitled 'Physical costs & value', contained in a folder 'Nov. [1927]', which reads:

> When I say that the value of a product is 'determined' by the physical volume of commodities used up in its production, it should *not* be understood that it is determined by the value of those commodities. This would be a vicious circle, because the value of the product is equal to the value of the factors [!] *plus* the surplus produced.

What I say is simply that the numerical proportions between amount of factors [!] and amount of product *is*, by definition, the absolute value of the product.

(D3/12/11: 101; 'not' is underlined twice in the original)

And in a document contained in the same folder he talked of 'physical value' (D3/12/11: 75). *In this context he nowhere talked of quantities in terms of money or labour values, and he nowhere used Marxian terms.* Vis-à-vis this evidence, how could Marx's schemes of reproduction possibly be 'the obvious starting point for the analytical path followed by Sraffa', as Gilibert contends?

As Whitehead had remarked on the success of seventeenth century science:

Science was becoming, and has remained, primarily *quantitative. Search for measurable elements among your phenomena, and then search for relations between these measures of physical quantities.*

(Whitehead, 1926, pp. 63–4, emphasis added; annotated by Sraffa)

I conclude by remarking that in Sraffa's work on and around his 'first equations' I did not spot a single atom emanating from a source, which could undoubtedly be identified as Marx's schemes of reproduction.

Early readings of Marx and the classical economists

We know that Sraffa read the French edition, or rather parts of it, of *Theorien über den Mehrwert* (Marx, 1924–1925) when in the spring and summer of 1927 he prepared the lectures on 'Advanced Theory of Value' which he was originally supposed to give beginning with Michaelmas term 1927–1928 (but which were then postponed on his request by one year). One question we ought to ask is: Are there any annotations in Sraffa's copy indicating disapproval of or critical comments on some of Marx's propositions that shed some light on the approach he, Sraffa, took in his first systems of equations? There are indeed, I think. In particular, in his copy of the eight volumes of the *Histoire* Sraffa noted carefully passages in which Marx distanced himself explicitly from an approach to the theory of value that proceeds directly in terms of quantities of *use values*, or commodities. Right at the beginning of the *Histoire*, in volume I, Marx took issue with Petty who had singled out food, not labour, as the measure of value. In the margin Sraffa placed a wrinkled line along a passage in which Marx contended that any such physical input 'n'est pas la mesure immanente des valeurs' (is not the immanent measure of value) (Marx, 1924, vol. I, p. 3, fn), signalling disagreement. See also the fly-leaf with Sraffa's own index regarding Petty and the Physiocrats' reference to the food of workers. Indeed, as we shall see in a moment, Sraffa for a considerable time followed Petty's approach in his own analysis and equations and tried to reduce the values of commodities to 'food' or an 'absolutely necessary commodity'.[32]

And in a document composed in November 1927, mirroring his readings, he stressed with reference to the *Histoire*, vol. I (p. 3): 'Petty had foreseen the possibility of being misunderstood' (D3/12/11: 36). In fact, according to Sraffa, Marx himself can be said to have misunderstood Petty (see also D3/12/4: 4). In addition, in his own index to volume III Sraffa noted 'Quantités de produits (non de travail) comme mesure 278, 287–9, 306–7' (Marx, 1925, vol. III, fly-leaf at end of book).[33] And then again, in volume VI, we find in Sraffa's own index the entry 'Marx against physical costs 122' (Marx, 1925, vol. VI, fly-leaf at end of book), the reference being to an argument by Robert Torrens concerning the generation of a surplus product of corn appropriated as profits. Apparently Sraffa did not agree with Marx's objection. Also, in his copy of *A Contribution to the Critique of Political Economy* (Marx, 1904, pp. 20–1), Sraffa took issue with Marx's claim that 'use-value as such lies outside the sphere of investigation of political economy'.

These and numerous other documents indicate that already from an early time on Sraffa had the intuition that a satisfactory theory of value could be elaborated by starting from *physical real costs* (as opposed to Marshall's 'real costs'). Understandably, therefore, when in November 1927 Sraffa finally succeeded in demonstrating, in terms of his first and second equations, that his intuition had not led him astray, he was at a pitch of excitement.[34] The intuition under discussion guided his early constructive work and is reflected in numerous documents and especially in

(a) a set of altogether 71 pages called 'Notes: London/Summer 1927 (Physical real costs, etc.)' (D3/12/3); and
(b) a set of 24 notes written at about the same time or shortly afterwards, entitled 'Physical real costs' (D3/12/42: 33–56).

These notes document in detail Sraffa's attempts to escape from the received and well-entrenched Marshallian mode of thought in terms of demand and supply within a partial, or rather 'particular', equilibrium framework and to move in the direction of an objectivist approach to the theory of value and distribution centred on the concept of physical real costs within a *general* framework of the analysis. For a while Sraffa appears to have thought that this was possible by starting from Marshall and purging his analysis of its subjectivist elements (see below). However, it did not take him long to see that this was not possible and that a more radical break with marginalist analysis was needed. At the same time his studies of the classical authors, partially inspired by his readings of the *Histoire*, made it clear to him that the approach of Petty, the Physiocrats and then the English classical political economists was not just an early and rude version of demand and supply analysis, as Marshall and contemporary commentators had contended. It was rather a fundamentally different approach. Alas, the details of its analytical structure and its content had yet to be re-discovered from under thick layers of (mis)interpretation – a task to which Sraffa dedicated much of his energy from mid 1927. His efforts were soon to bear fruit.

Against Marshall Sraffa stressed: 'the sort of "costs" which determines values is the collection of material things used up in production and not a "sum of efforts and sacrifices"' (D3/12/7: 106). And against Smith, Ricardo and Marx he emphasized that physical real costs do away 'with "human energy" and such metaphysical things' (D3/12/42: 33) and that 'A. Smith & Ricardo & Marx indeed began to *corrupt* the old idea of cost, – from food to labour. But their notion was still near enough to be in many cases equivalent' (D3/12/4: 2; emphasis added).[35] Yet, as we have already heard, Sraffa feared that small errors have a tendency to grow into large ones (see, for example, D3/12/11: 36). How could Sraffa have started from labour (values), which he qualified as a 'corruption' of the right concept of cost?

These and several other documents bear witness to the fact that according to the Sraffa of summer 1927 and winter 1927–1928 a probing into the vexed question of value had to start directly from physical quantities of materials or 'things' – one of Sraffa's favourite terms at the time – used up in production. However, echoing Petty's view, Sraffa at the time at first felt that 'the various things entering into real cost' had to be reduced to 'a common measure' or 'an absolutely necessary commodity' (Petty's 'food'). If such a commodity could be found, the cost 'of all the other things' could be expressed

> in terms of the necessary one and thus by going back enough in the genealogy of production … we might find exactly the total amount of corn (if this were the ideal necessary commodity, which [it] is not) that has *actually* entered into the production of, say, this book, and covers *entirely* its cost of production at the exclusion of any other commodity.
> (D3/12/3: 37–8)

This concern with reducing physical real costs to some such commodity is reflected in numerous calculations accompanying some of Sraffa's first equations.[36] However, approaching the problem of value from a rigorous physical real cost point of view, he soon found out that in the extreme each of the things used up in production or produced could serve as a common measure of commodities in the sense that all other things or commodities could be reduced to it. There was not just one 'common measure', there were many since in the no-surplus economy each and every commodity enters into each and every commodity.[37]

To stress what by now should be obvious: Sraffa started directly from *things*, that is, goods or commodities, which of necessity are destroyed in the production of other *things*. This is clearly evidenced also by document D3/12/5: 2, dubbed 'fundamental' by Gilibert and discussed in the third section above. In the light of this evidence one can only wonder how Sraffa in November 1927 could have felt the need to first algebraically transcribe a Marxian scheme with monetary magnitudes in order then to arrive via some sophisticated argument, explained to us by Gilibert, at a purely physical scheme in terms of which he would eventually approach the problem of value and distribution. There can be no doubt that Sraffa did not follow such a roundabout route, but started directly from physical magnitudes.

Readings of marginalist authors: Marshall and general equilibrium theorists

There is another source Sraffa examined critically in his early work, which has not yet been adequately taken into consideration in the literature. Again, a few remarks must suffice. First, the reader will have noticed that Sraffa's equations are systems of *simultaneous equations* and were explicitly called so by him. Sraffa, as is well known, had concluded his 1926 article with the observation that 'the process of diffusion of profits throughout the various stages of production and of the process of forming a normal level of profits throughout all the industries of a country' (Sraffa, 1926, p. 550) had been beyond the scope of his investigation. Yet this task was now on his agenda. Obviously it could not be accomplished in a partial framework of the analysis, such as Marshall's: a *general* framework was badly needed. Authors such as Léon Walras, Irving Fisher, Vilfredo Pareto and Gustav Cassel had elaborated general frameworks. The question was close at hand whether they had managed to come up with a satisfactory theory of value, and if not, why not, and whether Sraffa could learn from them for his own project. Sraffa had studied some of their contributions at an early stage of his work, that is, well before November 1927, and some even when still in Italy. Sraffa at any rate had every reason to explore carefully the concept of 'general equilibrium'. This he did.

In his struggle to escape from received Marshallian modes of thought, Sraffa in a document titled 'Marginal uses', presumably composed in early or mid 1927, took issue with an argument in § 5 of chapter VIII of book V of Marshall's *Principles* ([1890] 1949, pp. 339–40).[38] There Marshall discussed 'The part played by the net product at the margin of production in the modern doctrine of Distribution', which 'is apt to be misunderstood' (ibid., p. 339). To the claim that the marginal use of a thing is 'governing' the value of the whole Marshall objected: '*It is not so*; … we must *go to the margin to study the action of those forces which govern* the value of the whole: and that is a very different affair' (quoted by Sraffa in D3/12/3: 20; the second emphasis is in the original). Sraffa disagreed:

> *No*: the fundamental force is *physical real cost* – but as this does not cover the whole (chiefly *not* cover margins) we go at the margin to see how a different force (disutility) governs the details of value.
>
> Besides, what of cost (utility) being the loss of utility from not using it in 'alternative uses', if this is not *only* so at the margin? Except at the margin this is nonsense.

Besides, at the margin, we are justified in ignoring quantities of the second order; such as what happens in other commodities, when we are considering the particular equilibrium of one [v. 'alternative uses']: but *the governing ultimate forces are seen only in general equilibrium.*

> (D3/12/42: 46; the square brackets are
> in the original; the last emphasis is mine)

Here we encounter once again the major intuition guiding Sraffa's work at the time. Going directly to the main point, he insisted that the 'fundamental force' that governs both values and the net product (interest) is physical real cost. This fact, however, can be seen 'only in general equilibrium'.

As his studies progressed, Sraffa became more and more convinced that the earlier economists, especially Petty and the Physiocrats, had been possessed of essentially sound concepts, but suffered from a 'primitive, rudimentary technique', whereas marginalist economists suffered from dubious concepts, yet were possessed of a 'refined' and 'highly perfected' technique (see, for example, D3/12/4: 10). As regards technique, this applied to Marshall but even more so to Pareto. Sraffa's library and papers show that he had carefully studied especially two works of Pareto – the latter's essay, in German, on 'Anwendungen der Mathematik auf Nationalökonomie' (Applications of mathematics to economics) (Pareto, 1902) and the *Manuale di economia politica* (Pareto, 1906).[39] His copy especially of the *Manuale* has numerous annotations and a rich index in his hand. He approved of Pareto's attack on cardinal utility theory and admitted that the ordinal concept, expressed in terms of indifference curves, appeared to be logically unassailable (see also D1/23). However, he did not think that it offered a reliable guide to the main determinants of consumer behaviour, which Sraffa saw essentially grounded in income distribution, conventions, habits, institutions and generally the social group to which a person belonged. However, disenchanted with Marshallian partial analysis he now left no doubt that general equilibrium was of potential interest because it attempted to envisage the 'system as a whole' and to study the interconnectedness of its parts. In a document contained in a folder dated '1927' Sraffa remarked: 'Explain the notion of *equilibrium*, and its relation to *causes*: much to be found in Pareto ...' (D3/12/3: 1).

Sraffa had annotated the passage in which Pareto had pointed out that the concept of equilibrium defined in terms of a set of simultaneous equations, in order to be solvable, requires that the number of independent equations equals the number of dependent variables to be ascertained. He had also noted approvingly a number of points of substance with regard to which Pareto had expressed views he, Sraffa, considered valid. These included, for example, Pareto's opinion that production is concerned with overcoming 'obstacles', which, Sraffa noted, was essentially the same view as the one entertained by the classical economists (see D3/12/5: 17). Now, in the pre-Lectures, in which Sraffa distinguished between two types of theories of value[40] he at first appears to have hesitated as to how to classify Pareto's theory:

> Should Pareto's doctrine of general equilibrium be classed as belonging to the first or to the second theory of value? It surely is mainly concerned with the mechanism through which equilibrium is reached, and is not in quest of an ultimate standard. But on the other hand, could it be denied that it may legitimately be used in *challenging the existence of any such standard?*
>
> (D3/12/3: 20; emphasis added)

The background to this observation appears to be the following. In his 1902 treatise (see also Pareto, 1906, p. 235) Pareto had argued that the prices of commodities and their costs of production are ascertained simultaneously. Therefore, he had concluded, sentences such as 'the costs of production determine the selling price' may lead to 'false inferences and sophisms'.[41] Non-mathematical economists, he had insisted, ask themselves questions such as: 'What is the "cause" of value? What is the cause of interest? etc.' However,

> such problems are indeterminate, because they are based on arbitrary hypotheses. It is not possible to indicate *that* parameter which 'determines', for example, p_1 [the price of commodity 1], and it is a sterile controversy when someone claims that it is parameter a_1 [the coefficient of production concerning the use of commodity 1 in its own production], whereas others claim that it is a_2 [the coefficient of production concerning the use of commodity 2 in the production of commodity 1] etc.
>
> (Pareto, 1902, p. 1115)

The simultaneous determination of relative prices (and the rate of interest) in fact did away, or so it seemed, with the old quest for the 'common measure' of value.

Sraffa, as has already been stressed, did not approve of Pareto's individualistic approach with its emphasis on the choice of individual consumers (see, for example, D3/12/13: 2–5). He saw his scepticism in this regard partly confirmed by Pareto's own qualification, repeated time and again, that 'if we wish to consider the phenomenon in all its aspects, theory will no longer be possible' (Pareto, 1906, p. 247). Exemplified in terms of consumer choice: 'the ophelimity of any consumption depends on all the circumstances in which the consumption takes place', which obviously could never be taken into account.[42] Therefore, Pareto insisted, 'it is absolutely necessary to separate the main parts of [the system] and to disentangle, from the complete and complex phenomenon, *the ideal and simple elements which can provide the subject matter of theories*' (ibid.; emphasis added) Yet Sraffa felt that Pareto had not been fully aware of the difficulties involved. With reference to the works of Alfred Marshall, Henry Cunynghame, Francis Y. Edgeworth and Arthur C. Pigou he pointed out that the existence of external economies undermined the strictly individualistic point of view. Hence, received general equilibrium theory was not only confronted with the phenomenon of great complexity, as Pareto had maintained, it was also confronted with a kind of complexity which, as a matter of principle, could not be captured in terms of the individualistic approach. As regards the problem of externalities and demand, Sraffa stressed 'that it is not sufficient to make utility of one commodity [a] function of all others consumed by [an] individual', but it had also to be made dependent on the consumption of the 'community' as a whole – obviously a Herculean, if not outright impossible task. Sraffa drew the following parallel: 'It would be as if in astronomy we said the movement of each star depends upon all the others, but we have not the faintest idea of the shape of the functions!' (D3/12/3: 63).

This raised the question whether the part should be considered as constitutive of the whole, as marginalist authors had assumed, or vice versa. Sraffa, for reasons that should by now be obvious, sided with the latter methodological standpoint (see, in particular, D3/12/3: 45–8) and found himself in agreement with the 'objectivism' of contemporary natural sciences (see, in particular, Whitehead, 1926). The view that the whole is constitutive of the part is reflected, inter alia, in Sraffa's assumption of given gross outputs. To take gross outputs as given was dictated by the ubiquitous nature of externalities and increasing returns that are external to the industry, as they had been investigated by Adam Smith in his analysis of the division of labour.[43]

Against this background, Sraffa's own analytical scheme, as it gradually began to emerge with the '1st equations', may be envisaged as a radical response to Pareto's above maxim to focus attention on 'the ideal and simple elements which can provide the subject matter of theories'. As Sraffa clarified in a note written in 1942 shortly after he had resumed his constructive analytical work:

> This paper [i.e. the book he was about to write] deals with an extremely elementary problem; so elementary indeed that its solution is generally taken for granted. The problem is that of ascertaining the conditions of equilibrium of a system of prices & the rate of profits, independently of the study of the forces which may bring about such a state of equilibrium. Since a solution of the second problem carries with it a solution of the first, that is the course usually adopted in modern theory. The first problem however is susceptible of a more general treatment, independent of the particular forces assumed for the second; & in view of the unsatisfactory character of the latter, there is advantage in maintaining its independence.
>
> (D3/12/15: 2)[44]

Concluding remarks

It is argued that Gilibert's reconstruction of the origin of Sraffa's price (or production) equations and their 'original source of inspiration' cannot be sustained. More precisely, there is no presumption that Marx's 'reproduction schemes are the obvious starting point for the analytical path followed by Sraffa' (p. 28). Scrutiny shows that the chosen items from Sraffa's papers on which Gilbert rests his case do not support it; they may even be said to support the opposite case, namely that Sraffa did not start from Marx's schemes of reproduction. More important, a considerable amount of textual evidence can be provided which contradicts Gilibert's interpretation. Some of this evidence is referred to in this comment.

References

Allen, H. S. (1928). The quantum theory, *Nature*, Supplement, No. 3084, 8 December.

Anonymous (1821). *An inquiry into those principles respecting the nature of demand and the necessity of consumption, lately advocated by Mr Malthus, from which it is concluded, that taxation and the maintenance of unproductive consumers can be conducive to the Progress of Wealth*, London, R. Hunter. (Sr.L. 1488). Reprinted in a reprint of S. Bailey, *A Critical Dissertation on the Nature, Measure and Causes of Value*, first published in 1825, London, R. Hunter, New York, 1967, Augustus M. Kelley.

Bonar, J. (1911). *Disturbing Elements in the Study and Teaching of Political Economy*, Baltimore, John Hopkins Press. (Sr.L. 539)

Bortkiewicz, L. v. (1906–1907). Wertrechnung und Preisrechnung im Marxschen System, *Archiv für Sozialwissenschaft und Sozialpolitik*, 23 (1906), 1–50, 25 (1907), 10–51 and 445–88. (The first two instalments of Bortkiewicz's essay were translated into English and published in 1951 as 'Value and Price in the Marxian System', *International Economic Papers*, 2, 5–60.)

Chini, M. (1923). *Corso speciale di matematiche con numerosi applicazioni ad uso principalmente dei chimici e dei naturalisti* (1923, 6th edn), Livorno, Raffaello Giusti. (Sr.L. 3204)

Chrystal, G. (1889). *Algebra*, Edinburgh, A. and C. Black.

Garegnani, P. (2005). On a turning point in Sraffa's theoretical and interpretative position in the late 1920s, *European Journal of the History of Economic Thought*, 12(3), 453–92; reprinted in Kurz, H. D., Pasinetti, L. L. and Salvadori, N. (eds), *Piero Sraffa: The Man and the Scholar – Exploring his Unpublished Papers*, London, Routledge, pp. 79–118.

Gehrke, C. and Kurz, H. D. (2006). Sraffa on von Bortkiewicz: reconstructing the Classical theory of value and distribution, *History of Political Economy*, 38(1), 91–149.

Gentile, G. (1899). *La filosofia di Marx: studi critici*, Pisa, Enrico Spoerri. (Sr.L. 3363)

Gilibert, G. (2003). The equations unveiled: Sraffa's price equations in the making, *Contributions to Political Economy*, 22, 27–40.

Gramsci, A. (1948). *Il materialismo storico e la filosofia di Benedetto Croce, papers 1929–1934*, Milano, Einaudi. (Sr.L. 3979)

Gramsci, A. and Schucht, T. (1997). *Lettere (1926–1935)*, edited by A. Natoli and C. Daniele, Torino, Einaudi.

Kurz, H. D. (2002). Sraffa's contributions to economics: some notes on his unpublished papers, in *Competing Economic Theories. Essays in Memory of Giovanni Caravale*, edited by S. Nisticò and D. Tosato, London, Routledge.

Kurz, H. D. (2012). Don't treat too ill my Piero! Interpreting Sraffa's papers, *Cambridge Journal of Economics*, 36(6), 1535–69.

Kurz, H. D. and Salvadori, N. (2001). Sraffa and the mathematicians: Frank Ramsey and Alister Watson, in *Piero Sraffa's Political Economy. A Centenary Estimate*, edited by T. Cozzi and R. Marchionatti, London, Routledge, 187–216.

Kurz, H. D. and Salvadori, N. (2005). Representing the production and circulation of commodities in material terms: on Sraffa's objectivism, *Review of Political Economy*, 17(3), 69–97; reprinted in Kurz, H. D., Pasinetti, L. L. and Salvadori, N. (eds), 2008, *Piero Sraffa: The Man and the Scholar – Exploring his Unpublished Papers*, London: Routledge, pp. 249–77.

Labriola, A. (1922). *Il valore della scienza economica: introduzioni a una critica dell'economia politica*, Napoli, Alberto Morano. (Sr.L. 3577)

Lewis, C. S. (1960). *Studies in Words*, Cambridge, Cambridge University Press.

Luxemburg, R. (1935). *L'accumulation du capital. Contribution a l'explication économique de l'impérialisme*, translated from German and introduced by M. Ollivier, Paris, Librairie du Travail. (Sr.L. 3282)

Marshall, A. (1922). *Principles of Economics*, 8th edn 1920 (1st edn. 1890), reprint, London, Macmillan. (Sr.L. 2591)

Marshall, A. (1949). *Principles of Economics*, 8th edn 1920 (1st edn. 1890), reset and reprinted 1949. (Sr.L. 2591)

Marx, K. (1900). *Le Capital. Critique de l'économie politique*, Livre II, *Le procès de circulation du capital*, translated by J. Borchardt and H. Vanderrydt, Paris, V. Giard & E. Brière. (Sr.L. 3365)

Marx, K. (1901–1902). *Le Capital. Critique de l'économie politique*, Livre III, *Le procès d'ensemble de la production capitaliste*, in two volumes. Volume I, translated by J. Borchardt and H. Vanderrydt, Paris 1901, V. Giard & E. Brière. (Sr.L. 3366) Volume II, same translators, Paris 1902, same publisher. (Sr.L. 3367)

Marx, K. (1904). *A Contribution to the Critique of Political Economy*, translated from the second German edition (edited K. Kautsky 1859 (1st edn), 1897 (2nd edn)) by N. I. Stone, Chicago, Charles H. Kerr & Company. (Sr.L. 3739)

Marx, K. (1924–1925). *Oeuvres complètes de Karl Marx. Histoire des doctrines économiques*, translated by J. Molitor, eight vols, Paris, Alfred Costes. (Sr.L. 3699)

Marx, K. (1938). *Capital*, vol. I, London, Allen & Unwin. (Sr.L. 3731).

Marx, K. (1956). *Capital*, vol. II, Moscow, Progress Publishers.

Marx, K. (1961). *Teorie del plusvalore*, vol. I, in *I classici del marxismo*, translation and preface by Giorgio Giorgetti, Editore Riuniti. (Sr.L. 3248)

Pareto, V. (1902). Anwendungen der Mathematik auf Nationalökonomie, in *Encyklopädie der mathematischen Wissenschaften*, vol. I, No. 7, Leipzig, Teubner. (Sr.L. 4536)

Pareto, V. (1906). *Manuale di economia politica con una introduzione alla scienza sociale*, Milan, Società editrice libreraria. (Sr.L. 699)

Petty, W. (1986). *The Economic Writings of Sir William Petty*, two vols, edited by C. H. Hull. Originally published in 1899, Cambridge: Cambridge University Press. Reprinted in one volume (1986). New York: Kelley.

Poincaré, J. H. (1902). *La Science e l'Hypothèse*, Paris, Ernest Flammarion. (Sr.L. 3137)

Predella, P. (1915). *Algebra ed aritmetica: ad uso dei licei*, Turin, G. B. Paravia. (Sr.L. 3203)

Sraffa, P. (1926). The laws of returns under competitive conditions, *The Economic Journal*, 36, December, 535–50.

Sraffa, P. (1960). *Production of Commodities by Means of Commodities*, Cambridge, Cambridge University Press.

Sraffa, P. (1991). *Lettere a Tania per Gramsci*, edited by V. Gerratana, Rome, Editori Riuniti.

Whitaker, A. C. (1904). *History and Criticism of the Labor Theory of Value in English Political Economy*, New York, Columbia University Press. (Sr.L. 1095)

Whitehead, A. N. (1926). *Science and the Modern World*, Lowell Lectures 1925, Cambridge, Cambridge University Press. (Sr.L. 662)

Notes

1 See the respective correspondence between Sraffa and Schucht and Schucht and Gramsci in Sraffa (1991) and Gramsci and Schucht (1997).
2 English translation:

> *Question of method.* If one wants to study the birth of a conception of the world that has never been exposed systematically by its founder (and whose essential coherence is not to be established in each single manuscript or set of manuscripts, but in the entire development of the multifaceted (vario) intellectual work in which the elements of the conception are implicit) *it is necessary first to make a philologically meticulous work, carried out with a maximum of scrupulousness as to exactness, of scientific honesty, of intellectual loyalty, of the absence of any preconception and apriorism or position taken.* It is necessary, first of all, to reconstruct the intellectual process of development of the given thinker in order to identify the elements that became stable and 'permanent', that is those that have been assumed as his proper thoughts, different from and superior to the 'material' previously studied, which served as a stimulus; only these elements are essential moments of the process of development.

3 Throughout his paper Gilibert gives only the class mark of the folder in which a document he refers to is contained (following the catalogue of Sraffa's papers prepared by Jonathan Smith, archivist), but not the details of the document within the folder. For the reader's convenience I provide the full information on where to find the three documents mentioned. They are, respectively, Sr.L. 3365, fly-leaf; D3/12/16: 13 (3) (in the original we find '1st Equations (simple reproduction)'); and D3/12/16: 7.
4 See the reference to the book in Gilibert's third element (D3/12/16: 7), dated 30 July 1942. The full document reads:
Equations = Tableau Èconomique [*sic*]
See Akk. d. Kap., pp. 28, 60, 75 = (Pt. I, Ch. 2, 3, 4).
The pages given in the document refer precisely to the corresponding annotations in Sraffa's copy of Luxemburg (1935); see Sr.L. 3282.
5 As far as I can see, three pencilled straight lines in the margin of Sraffa's books and papers are perhaps only topped, in terms of the emphasis intended, by bold lines in blue or red pencil and remarks in boxes.

6   In the table of contents that chapter is wrongly numbered chapter IV.

7   In the third section below I draw the attention to the fact that the first part of the index covers first and foremost those chapters (i.e. chapters I–III of part I of Marx, 1900) that are referred to in document D3/12/9: 11, which, as we shall see, plays an important role in Gilibert's argument.

8   The concept described in this way, but not the term, can, however, be traced back to early 1931; see D3/12/7: 157 (1–8), 158 und 159 (1–3). For a discussion of some of the issues at hand, see Gehrke and Kurz (2006). Here it suffices to draw the reader's attention to the following facts. By the end of the 1930s the Ricardo edition was basically ready (with a single important exception: the missing letters of Ricardo to James Mill) and in the course of its preparation Sraffa had acquired a thorough and deep understanding of the classical economists. Since he considered Marx as the last great representative of that school before marginalism rose to dominance, the questions that apparently bothered Sraffa a great deal were essentially two. First, how did Marx's analysis relate to the analysis especially of Ricardo – did it involve analytical progress or, as some commentators maintained, regress? Second, what had gone wrong – why had demand and supply theory, which Sraffa considered to be inherently flawed, managed to prevail over classical theory? This explains why in September 1940 Sraffa would study with utmost care the recently published reprint of the English version of volume I of *Das Kapital* (Marx, 1938) while he was in an internment camp on the Isle of Man (see Sr.L. 3731, first page). Back in Cambridge he then carefully scrutinized also volumes II and III of *Le Capital*, or at least parts of them, which is reflected in several notes and references in Sraffa's papers and in annotations in his books. In early 1943 Sraffa then came across writings of Ladislaus von Bortkiewicz, especially a paper on value and price in Marx, in which Bortkiewicz (1906–1907) had claimed that in important respects Marx's work involved substantial regress compared with Ricardo's. Sraffa had to find answers to these questions and to Bortkiewicz's claim, which explains why from the 1940s on Marx's analysis became a major point of reference of Sraffa's own work, which it had not been in the late 1920s and early 1930s. (Not surprisingly, therefore, with a few exceptions the documental evidence put forward by Gilibert stems from the 1940s.)

9   Gilibert refers to the 'period 1940–1943' as one of the periods 'in which Sraffa focused his attention on the price equations' (p. 29). It should however be mentioned that the period under consideration extended well into the mid 1940s, with the main work done from 1942 on, and that a few documents were composed as late as 1948.

10 In his comment on this chapter Geoff Harcourt put the following query to me: Could Sraffa not have come across Marx's schemes of reproduction at an earlier time, but then did not see their significance, and only after he had worked out his equations did the over lapse occur to him? Harcourt added that someone might unconsciously 'pinch' parts of the argument from someone else's writing, which he has read some years beforehand, but obviously has neither fully understood or perhaps absorbed. While for obvious reasons this cannot be excluded, I am not aware of any *déjà vu* experience in this regard reflected in Sraffa's papers.

11 Recall what in the above (footnote 7) has been said about Sraffa's own index in the book.

12 Sraffa, as will be argued in the fourth section below, at the beginning of his constructive work assumed an objectivist – in the sense of a natural science – point of view. This implied, as he wrote in retrospect in August 1931, that 'we must start by assuming that for every effect there must be sufficient cause' (D3/12/7: 161 (3)). This is fully corroborated by his attempts right from the beginning of his work on the with-surplus equations, in the winter of 1927–1928, to conceive of 'interest',

the term Sraffa used at the time, as some 'necessary cost', or, in other words, to subject it to some 'objectivisation'. For reasons that cannot be explained here (see, therefore, Kurz and Salvadori, 2005, and Kurz, 2012, section 4), this led him swiftly to the question whether interest should be reckoned on circulating capital only or also on fixed capital. At first he was of the opinion that the surplus should only be reckoned with regard to the 'physical real costs' of production. These he identified with circulating capital, that is, the means of production 'destroyed' or used up in the course of production, including the physical real costs incurred in order to make good the wear and tear of fixed capital, and the means of subsistence needed in order to 'enable' workers to perform their task. This is reflected in his respective equations by the fact that no surplus, or 'interest', is paid on aged fixed capital. However, he soon got doubts as to the legitimacy of this approach and in the spring and summer of 1928 consulted the works of several authors to see how they had gone about this problem. These included in addition to writings by Marshall, Jannaccone and Sismondi, to mention just a few, the French edition of volumes II and III of *Das Kapital*. One of Sraffa's predominant analytical interests at the time is well reflected in point 3) of his note D3/12/9: 11 which is reproduced here in full:

3) riproduz. con accumulaz. totale (necessità di interesse su cap. fisso: se no, non è possibile accumulaz. proporzionale in tutte le industrie. Chi presterebbe a un'industria che non rende abbastanza per riprodursi? Ma le macchine usate valgon meno delle nuove: però se l'accumulaz. è avvenuta sempre nel passato, la media delle macchine è più nuova del normale e quindi riceve più ammortamento di quel che spenda: è ciò esattamente uguale al richiesto?) (English translation: '3) reproduction with total accumulation (necessity of interest on fixed capital: if no, a proportional accumulation in all industries is not possible. Who would lend to an industry that does not obtain enough to reproduce itself? But the used machines are worth less than the new ones: if however the accumulation has always happened in the past, the medium of the machines is newer than normal and therefore receives more amortisation than what it pays: and thus is exactly equal to what is requested?)'

For a reference to the French edition of volume III of *Das Kapital*, which belongs to the same period when Sraffa worked on the treatment of fixed capital in the equations, see D3/12/7: 103.

13 Gilibert gives as reference D3/12/5 (p. 32); there can be no doubt that he means D3/12/5: 2.

14 I take this opportunity to point out a slip in document D3/12/2: 31 as reproduced by Gilibert (p. 33). (Again he gives only the class mark of the folder in which the document is to be found, but there is no doubt that he refers to item 31 in it.). Sraffa stated (correctly) that '$B = 2/3C$' and not, as in Gilibert's reproduction, that '$B = 1/3C$'. I should also like to point out that the document under consideration was not 'revisited by Sraffa on the 20th February 1955', as Gilibert claims, but was in all probability composed on that day. (This follows from Sraffa's handwriting and the kind of paper he used.)

15 Sraffa used the term 'things' as a *terminus technicus* in his early works, meaning items 'bearing a label "private", according to law' (D3/12/6: 5). In the Italian economics literature he consulted, especially, Pareto (1906) and Pantaleoni, Sraffa annotated the term 'cose' (things); see, for example, Sr.L. 699.

16 The above system served as a kind of workhorse in much of Sraffa's early analysis. For example, the same set of first equations is also to be found at the beginning of document D3/12/11: 77–8, titled 'With surplus equations', which is also not

mentioned by Gilibert and which squarely contradicts his interpretation. In the document Sraffa refers to the surplus of iron as 'the *physical* difference between the iron consumed by all industries and the iron produced by the iron industry' (ibid.: 77; emphasis added). See also D3/12/9: 45 in which the with-surplus equations are discussed and Sraffa distinguishes between 'productive' and 'unproductive' industries (the latter being identified with the surplus-using, luxuries-producing industries).

17 The translations of the remark next to the tabulation and the following text read: 'This is a *determinant*. Moreover the vertical sums are equal to the horizontal sums.' (This is, of course, not a determinant. Ramsey in all probability mentioned the concept during their discussion since the system of equations is square and the corresponding matrix therefore has a determinant. After the meeting Sraffa probably jotted down on the sheet with the equations what he had learned from Ramsey, as he did generally after discussions with his mathematical friends.) And:

> It is to be seen whether one can apply to this determinant the method of Volterra (Chini, p. 35) in order to find the number of 'independent components' of the system. This might perhaps help: a) when not all goods entered as factors into each one. b) when there is a surplus, that is considering the various surpluses as different commodities (assuming therefore that as soon as the surplus emerges, one continues to produce the same quantity of 'corn' as before, and the residual resources are all going to be dedicated to produce jewellery and other 'unproductive' things).

18 The English translation reads:

> When one has a certain number of substances of determinate chemical composition, each one of them may be taken in an arbitrary quantity, then it is clear that the various simple elements that enter and are a part of such a system cannot themselves be all prefixed in arbitrary quantities, but this will generally be possible only for a certain number of them. The quantities (masses) of the remaining elements will instead be completely determined by those fixed already of the first ones; these will be called the *independent components* of the system.

And:

> In order to obtain the number of these components (of which one can make use, for example, when one wants to apply to a heterogeneous complex the so-called *phase rule* [of Gibbs]), Prof. Volterra, in one of his publications ... has indicated the following method.

19 Interestingly, there are two markers in Chini's book relating to pp. 80–1 and 132–3. While these markers may have been left purely accidentally in the places indicated, it deserves to be mentioned that on the pages under consideration Chini discusses how a *given* physical system – a piece of metal or a gas – responds to a rise or fall in temperature: the metal will expand or shrink, the pressure and volume of the gas will increase or decrease. However, there are limits to these induced changes. Analogously, the properties of a with-surplus economy with a *given* system of production are not fully determinate independently of the state of the distribution of the surplus (or, if we may use the metaphor, the 'heat' created in the conflict over the distribution of income). In some of his notes Sraffa had recourse to this analogy.

20 He consulted also other mathematics books.
21 As Sraffa's papers and his library show, he was also widely read in philosophy.
22 At the time the works of physicists (and other natural scientists) were widely read also by social scientists and Sraffa was no exception to the rule. He may well have come across, for example, the works of Hertz and Helmholtz when reading Labriola (1922, p. 326). Sraffa's annotations in his copy of the book (Sr.L. 3577) are most interesting not least because of his remarks in his own index at the end of the book. For example, with reference to E. Picard's *La Science moderne et son état actuel* (Paris, 1905), he stressed: 'gli econ. mat. [the reference is to the mathematical economists like Walras and Pareto] hanno negligés des masses cachées 326' (The mathematical economists have neglected the hidden masses). Hertz and other physicists and chemists are also mentioned in Poincaré (1902; see Sr.L. 3137).
23 On atomic theory in contemporary biology, chemistry and physics, see also Sraffa's annotation in his copy of Whitehead (1926, p. 141). On the materialist conception of history, see Sraffa's annotations in his copy of Gramsci (1948, p. 161). In economics Bonar (1911, p. 11; see Sraffa's annotation in Sr.L. 539) had already used the term 'atomic theory', but with the very different meaning of 'atomistic' as in marginalist theory.
24 As is well known, in his preface to volume II of *Das Kapital* Engels had written: 'Marx stands in the same relation to his predecessors in the theory of surplus-value as Lavoisier stood to Priestley and Scheele' in chemistry (Marx, 1956, p. 16). See also the inside back cover of Marx (1961; Sr.L. 3248), where Sraffa refers to Engels's comparison and adds: 'cioè *fecondità* di un ipotesi'. Sraffa's relation to his predecessors will have to be re-assessed in the light of his position with regard to the natural sciences.
25 When Sraffa in 1942 resumed work on his systems of equations he also specified the notation adopted; in a note composed in August of that year he stressed that in the equations '+' means 'with' and '=' means 'produce'; see D3/12/20: 4. And on 20 October 1942 he introduced the symbol '→' to describe production; see D3/12/23: 1.
26 English translation: 'is based on the essentially physiocratic point of view that value is a quantity that is intrinsic to the objects, almost a physical or chemical quality'.
27 In Sraffa (1960, p. 3) we will eventually read that 'such values spring directly from the methods of production'. That the solution of a set of linear homogeneous equations is at stake is clearly spelled out in the first of the twin documents (D3/12/5: 2), the only one Gilibert discusses (see the third section above), which, chronologically, comes later than the one reproduced at the beginning of this section.
28 In a document contained in 'Notes' dated 'Michaelmas Term, 1928' Sraffa related his above approach of making the surplus disappear to the ' "Method of exhaustion" v. E.B., 14, 535d' (D3/12/10: 41). The reference is apparently to the entry 'Infinitesimal calculus' by A. E. H. Love in *The Encyclopædia Britannica*, 11th edition, vol. XIV, p. 535, right hand column (d = destra). The passage Sraffa appears to have in mind concerns 'Greek methods' and reads:

The Greek geometers made little progress with the problem of tangents, but they devised methods for investigating the problem of quadratures. One of these methods was afterwards called the 'method of exhaustions', and the principle on which it is based was laid down in the lemma prefixed to the 12th book of Euclid's *Elements* as follows: 'If from the greater of two magnitudes there be taken more than its half, and from the remainder more than its half, and so on, there will at length remain a magnitude less than the smaller of the proposed magnitudes.' The method adopted by Archimedes was more general.

See also Sraffa's reference to Archimedes in an entry in his *Cambridge Pocket Diary* on 9 December 1927 (E 1). (See also the closely related issue whether the reduction of the value of a commodity to dated quantities of labour or to some commodity converges to a limit in D3/12/7: 3, 27–32 and 126–30.)

29 It deserves mentioning that this idea was still present when in summer 1942 Sraffa jotted down a list of topics (or the planned contents of the book he was to write) in D3/12/15: 1. It contains, among other things: '2) With profits – everything a necessity.'

30 Notice that Sraffa spoke of self-replacement and not of simple reproduction. See in the above context also a note left in Sraffa's copy of volume I of *Capital* containing a quotation from a paper by John Maurice Clark published in 1924. In the paper Clark maintained that in the last instance profits are due to private property in the means of production: the 'power to produce cannot exist apart from the power to withhold'; see Sr.L. 3731. As Sraffa noted elsewhere, Pareto held a similar view.

31 However, he soon found out that this was not the case. He overcame the impasse in which he found himself by introducing a new variable, the 'rate of surplus' or 'rate of interest' (or rather the interest factor), which was then determined simultaneously with the values of commodities; see, for example, D3/12/6: 17.

32 For a detailed discussion of this aspect in Sraffa's early work, see Garegnani (2005).

33 See also Sraffa's respective excerpts from the *Histoire* in D3/12/11: 88 and his quotation from Gentile (1899) in D3/12/10: 40. In the former Sraffa noted that Marx had commented on Petty's approach: 'C'est bien la théorie des physiocrats'. And in the latter he stated: 'Il Feuerbach disse, come espressione ultima e tipica del suo materialismo: *l'uomo è nè più nè meno di ciò che mangia* (der Mensch sei nur das, was er esse).' (Feurbach says, as an ultimate and typical expression of his materialism: man is neither more nor less than what he eats.) (Sraffa's emphasis). See also Sraffa's annotation in Whitaker (1904, pp. 66–7; Sr.L. 1095).

34 This is testified to by Keynes who on 28 November 1927 wrote to his wife, Lydia:

Sraffa is in so much intellectual ferment and excitement about his ideas since I said that I thought there was something in them that he walks very fast up and down his room all day thinking about them. It is impossible for him to write them down, because as soon as he thinks about them, he has to start walking again. He is now inclined to give up his Christmas visit to Italy so that he can be able to continue in these courses for several weeks more.

(JMK/PP/45/190/3/268–9)

35 It is not clear, which 'cases' Sraffa had in mind and whether at the time he had a clear understanding, when the labour theory of value applied, and when not. For a considerable time Sraffa was in fact of the opinion that human labour was 'a non measurable quantity, or rather not a quantity at all' (D3/12/11: 64. As D3/12/7: 93 shows, this was partly based on a misinterpretation of Ricardo.) As late as the second half of 1929 he still had doubts as to whether quantities of labour could be taken as data of the theory. In a document dealing with 'The quantities involved in econ. Theory' he stressed with regard to those quantities that have

an objective, independent existence at every or some instants of the natural (i.e. not interfered with by the experimenter) process of production and distribution; they can therefore be measured physically, with the ordinary instruments for measuring number, weight, time, etc.

He added:

> Such are quantities of various materials used or produced, of lands[,] quantities
> of labour (?), lengths of periods (?), etc. These are the *only* quantities which must
> enter as constants in economic theory, i.e. which can be assumed to be 'known'
> or 'given'.
>
> (D3/12/13: 2; the question marks in brackets are in the original)

(When Sraffa moved on from the concept of wages as an inventory of commodities to that of a share of the product, that is, Ricardo's 'proportional wages',
labour had to be treated as a measurable quantity; for this shift, see, in particular
D3/12/16: 13 (1–3) dated 7 August 1942.) The above document provides a neat
blending of two sources of inspiration of Sraffa: Petty's point of view ('to express
my self in Terms of *Number, Weight* or *Measure*'; see Petty, [1899] 1986, p. 244),
which Sraffa had endorsed, and quantum physics (see the reference to the 'experimenter' whose role was discussed at length by Heisenberg, Schrödinger and others
championing the new theory). It was as late as August 1931, in a document titled
'Surplus product' (D3/12/7: 161 (1–5)), to which I referred already several times,
that he reformulated the aims of his research. The reason for this was that his
attempts at objectivising 'interest' as some sort of necessary social cost had caused
him insuperable difficulties and had in the end not allowed him to escape from the
problem of 'incentives' – a subjective concept – the grand theme of marginalism.

36 Sraffa was also clear from an early time onwards that the process of reduction (at
first to dated quantities of some other commodity, much later to dated quantities
of labour) had nothing to do with a historical regress, but simply involved solving
a system of simultaneous equations. He stressed:

> The objection that thus we go back for centuries and that what happened cen-
> turies ago is irrelevant to present values is met by the fact that, although we
> talk of going back in time, *we simply go up the simultaneous equations which all
> apply to the present time* (i.e. all the different stages of production are carried on
> simultaneously)
>
> (D3/12/7: 30; emphasis added; see also D3/12/6: 4)

As early as December 1927 Sraffa noted that (in the case in which labour is rendered explicit as an input) the methods of ' "substitution" in equations' and of
'reduction', which he took from Predella (1915, pp. 49–51), show 'that *all* values
are "due" to labour, *or* to wheat *or* to any other thing *that enters in the production
of every of them*' (D3/12/10: 71; emphasis added). There was no need to embark
on Hegelian metaphysics as in the case of Marx, Petty's political arithmetic was all
that was needed (at least to begin with).

37 In the terminology of Sraffa (1960, p. 8), every commodity is a *basic*. Sraffa in 1928
also noted that in the equations with surplus a 'serious trouble' arises (D3/12/7:
31), because now at any step of the reduction one encounters not only commodities but also (the rate of) interest. Only if the latter can be conceived of in commodity terms, could the reduction to a common measure be continued. See again
what has been said on Sraffa's attempt to reduce interest to some socially necessary
cost in the fourth observation on D3/12/11: 87 on p. 207 above.

38 Sraffa's working copy of Marshall's *Principles* was the reprint of the eighth edition
(Marshall, [1890] 1922); the page reference in D3/12/3: 20 is accordingly to p. 410.

39 Here we cannot enter into a discussion of Sraffa's studies of other contributions
to general equilibrium theory, especially Wicksell's temporal, or 'Austrian', variant
of it.

40 The two types are 'simultaneous' or 'geometrical' theories, which focus on the determination of values in given conditions, and 'mechanical' theories which focus on the determinants of changes in the values of commodities (see D3/12/7: 115–21). (On the concept of geometrical theory see also D3/12/8: 1, where Sraffa refers to Chrystal (1889).) Marshall's analysis was considered to be a typical representative of the latter type whereas the theory of the classical economists was considered to belong to the first type.

41 See in this context Sraffa's remark in his 1960 book that 'the term "cost of production" has been avoided in this work', because this term (as well as that of 'capital') has come 'to be insuperably linked with the supposition that they stand for quantities that can be measured independently of, and prior to, the determination of the prices of the products' (Sraffa, 1960, p. 9).

42 This is reflected in Sraffa's 1926 paper. There he writes about 'simultaneous equilibrium in numerous industries' that this is 'a well-known conception, whose complexity, however, prevents it from bearing fruit, *at least in the present state of our knowledge*' (1926, p. 541; emphasis added).

43 In this context, see especially the document 'Why I neglect Incr. + Dim. Ret. in equations' (D3/12/7: 85–7).

44 In this context, see also Sraffa's comments on Pareto's theory in D3/12/9: 93 and D3/12/10: 39 and his remark:

The dictum of Edgeworth, that 'to treat *variables* as *constants* is the characteristic vice of the unmathematical [*sic*] economist', might to-day be reversed: the mathematical economists have gone so far in correcting this vice that they can no longer conceive of a constant except as the result of the compensation of two equal and opposite variables.

(Sraffa, 1926, p. 541 n.)

11 On the beginnings of Sraffa's path to *Production of Commodities by Means of Commodities*

A comment on De Vivo

Heinz D. Kurz and Neri Salvadori

In a paper published in 2003, Giancarlo de Vivo (2003: 1) aimed 'to reconstruct as far as possible the path [Sraffa] followed in the research which led him to reach the remarkable results' published in his 1960 book (Sraffa, 1960). De Vivo was one of the first scholars venturing to publish his findings and interpretation of some of the highly complex material under consideration.[1] He deserves credit for having provided others with some guidance on how the material might perhaps be interpreted and how its different pieces might hang together, even though parts of what he has written might eventually turn out to be untenable. There would be nothing surprising in this in view of a subject matter as difficult as the one under consideration. To De Vivo's credit it has also to be mentioned that he is careful to express his uncertainty and reservation as to the interpretation put forward by him. He even claims that 'work like the present one can never aim at being definitive' and 'that others may provide a partially or entirely different reconstruction of that path'. He adds:

> The writing of a paper like this must necessarily be like the piecing together of a jigsaw puzzle, with the added difficulty that many of the pieces must be left out. It is therefore by no means impossible that using different pieces, a partly or entirely different picture may be put together.
>
> (p. 2)

This chapter is based on a paper that was written in 2004. We then refrained from publishing it for the reasons given in the introductory chapter of this volume. The main argument put forward is the same. We have only rewritten some passages and have inserted references to the literature on the theme published since then. Together with other scholars the authors are in charge of editing Piero Sraffa's papers and correspondence. The other editors are, of course, not implicated and there is no presumption that they share the views expressed here. We are grateful to Geoff Harcourt for useful suggestions on this version of the chapter.

This non-dogmatic attitude and openness towards alternative interpretations are, of course, welcome. At the same time the reasoning given in their support points toward a serious problem. Since there is the one and only Sraffa whose intellectual development is to be reconstructed, as a matter of logic there can be only a single path Sraffa followed, and not several. The fact that alternative stories can be told by using different selections from the available material does not contradict this. Some stories can be expected to swiftly turn out to be unsustainable, if confronted with the material put on one side. Since we are interested in *the* path, whose endpoint was Sraffa's 1960 book, one has to focus attention on what became 'stable and permanent' (Gramsci, 1948) as his thoughts developed. All material containing ideas and views Sraffa entertained at some point in time, but then abandoned, while reflecting moments in his intellectual development, are of secondary importance and cannot form the basis of an interpretation that commands validity. A minimum requirement of any serious reconstruction is therefore that *all* material available to us is taken into consideration and subjected to careful scrutiny. There can hardly be any disagreement on this. Therefore it is remarkable that De Vivo rests his case of a plurality of reconstructions explicitly on the possibility of basing any one of them on special selections from the whole set of available evidence. While this is in fact the case, what matters is to find the picture that comes closest to the true one, the correct interpretation, the sense Sraffa intended. This is a difficult task, no doubt, but according to our experience it is not a mission impossible. And should the elaboration of a completely right interpretation turn out to be impossible, this does not mean that one cannot clearly identify interpretations that are partially or entirely wrong.

As a scholar who has variously demonstrated his meticulousness as regards textual exegesis, De Vivo is surely aware of the dangers of a selective approach to historical material. These dangers have been vividly described in the relevant literature. For example, in Ernst Bernheim's *Lehrbuch der Historischen Methode* we read that if one's interpretation is not 'guided by methodical discipline' (*durch methodische Disziplin paralysiert*) the enterprise is in danger of degenerating to an exercise of safeguarding one's preconceived opinions and prejudices:

> One then hears and reads from the sources what in the sense of an already assumed position one has hoped and expected to hear and read in them; one closes one's apprehension entirely or partially with regard to those data that contradict the preliminarily elaborated opinion or that request its revision.
>
> (Bernheim, 1894: 468–9)

Bernheim even discusses the possibility of a set of mutually incompatible interpretations, each based on a different subset of the respective material under consideration and (seemingly) compatible with it, and yet *each one* missing the sense of the material taken as a whole.

We insist that any serious reconstruction has to be subjected to what Bernheim called 'methodical discipline'. This involves, first, scrutinizing the interpretation suggested against the pieces of evidence put forward in its support in order to find out whether there is indeed the alleged correspondence between the two. It involves, second, confronting the subset of the material on which a particular reconstruction is based with the complementary set of material in order to see whether the interpretation given involves an illusion due to the selected material on which it is based.

This will be done in this comment with regard to De Vivo's interpretation. In order to show that his reconstruction does not stand up to close scrutiny it suffices (i) to establish that he has not reasoned correctly vis-à-vis the documents he used and (ii) to draw the attention to evidence not used by him that contradicts his reconstruction. This we do.

Unfortunately, De Vivo does not tell the reader why he has selected some material instead of some other material. Is it because the pieces left out are unimportant, and if so, why? Is it because they make no sense to him, are cryptic or mysterious? Is it because in them Sraffa committed blunders or followed ideas he was later to abandon? Or is it because they would disturb the (alleged) harmony of the interpretation given? Since selecting pieces of evidence from the material and reconstructing Sraffa's intellectual path amount almost to one and the same thing, one could, of course, attempt to infer the criteria De Vivo applied in referring to particular pieces of evidence. Since this is not possible without at least some speculation, we refrain from engaging in it. We rather focus on what he has written. It is shown that important elements of De Vivo's reconstruction cannot be sustained. Hence another reconstruction is not only possible, but necessary, in order to arrive at a less unsatisfactory view of Sraffa's path to his book.

The composition of the comment is the following. The first section deals with De Vivo's contention, echoed by Gilibert (2003), that with the systems of equations Sraffa began to elaborate from November 1927 he started from Marx's scheme of simple reproduction. Apparently, De Vivo is himself not sure about whether this is correct, because after having stated his interpretation he quickly adds two different ones, which are not compatible with the former. His reservation with regard to his original interpretation is well taken. In fact we show that the latter meets with serious difficulties.

Sraffa's first equations: 'things'!

In the abstract of his paper De Vivo contends:

> The starting point of Sraffa's research was the formulation of his cost-price equations, which surprisingly enough appear to have been derived ... from Marx's reproduction schemes, published in volume II of *Capital* ...
>
> (p. 1)

In the text he adds:

> It can safely be assumed that Sraffa's shift of emphasis, in 1926–27, from his critique of Marshall to his 'equations', was mainly due to his (re-) reading of Marx.
>
> (p. 6)

And later in his paper, following a discussion of document D3/12/5: 2–3 in Sraffa's papers kept at Trinity College Library in Cambridge, UK, he contends that 'this is consistent with seeing the two sets of equations [contained in the document] as deriving from Marx's reproduction schemes' (p. 10).

Surprisingly, De Vivo does not see the need, or possibility, of establishing the correctness of these propositions beyond any reasonable doubt. On the contrary, he even opines that 'The above interpretation of the meaning of the variables in the equations has, however, at least [!] two stumbling blocks' (p. 10), to which we turn below. In the end the reader is left with three alternative interpretations, none of which De Vivo himself considers as entirely convincing. He concludes by drawing the attention to a discussion Sraffa had with his colleague and friend Frank Plumpton Ramsey about his equations:

> I think, however, that this hermeneutic problem should not detain us too much. Whether it was Frank Ramsey or not to suggest it, Sraffa got to write the equations in the correct way …
>
> (p. 11)

We now turn to De Vivo's first interpretation, that is the one he appears to favour compared with the other two.

First interpretation

De Vivo's argument starts with his reading of document D3/12/5: 2–3. The folder D3/12/5 consists of some 35 pages taken from a ring book plus one extra sheet. Sraffa dated the folder 'Winter 1927–28' and gave it the title 'Notes on "looms" ', and indeed all the sheets except four refer to the problem of fixed capital ('looms'). The material that interests us here consists exactly of these four sheets. Two of them De Vivo reproduces extensively (but not fully) (with a misprint though). They include two sets of symbols: The first one is:

$$
\left.\begin{array}{l}
A = a_1 + b_1 + c_1 \\
B = a_2 + b_2 + c_2 \\
C = a_3 + b_3 + c_3
\end{array}\right\} \quad \text{where} \quad
\begin{array}{l}
A = \Sigma a \\
B = \Sigma b \\
C = \Sigma c
\end{array}
$$

The second one is:[2]

$$aA = a_1A + b_1B + c_1C \quad a = \sum a?$$
$$bB = a_2A + b_2B + c_2C$$
$$cC = a_3A + b_3B + c_3C$$

If the two sets were to correspond to the same thing, the meaning of the symbols could not be the same. More precisely, what is indicated as 'A' in the first set is indicated by 'aA' in the second: what is indicated by 'a_1' in the first is indicated by 'a_1A' in the second; and so on. This means that the information, which in the second set is indicated by two symbols in the first is indicated by just one. As an example, 'a_1' in the second set means just an amount or a number, like 5 or 6, whereas 'a_1' in the first set means an amount of something that can be represented by A, like 5 of A or 6 of A, and the reader is supposed to understand that 'a_1' refers to an amount of A and not to an amount of B, because the letter 'a' is used in 'a_1'.[3] The fact that the notation is not consistent should not be a problem: Sraffa was writing for himself and was looking for an appropriate notation with which to express what he had in mind. The former notation was soon to be abandoned by him, whereas the latter was used also later. This emerges clearly from the following sheet:

> The above equations imply a reversible process. I.e., if $A = a_1 + b_1 + c_1$, this means that we can get A by compounding a, b, c, and that we can get back a, b, c by splitting up A. Suppose that in a weeks [sic] work we build up a motor car, using timber, coal to feed machines, iron, corn to feed the labourers: surely on the motorcar trying to get out of it the corn, the trees, the coal, etc. used in producing it we shall not succeed. *The process does not seem reversible.* But this is so only if we remain within the single enterprise or industry that has produced the car. *If we consider the aggregate of industry as a whole, however, reversion will be possible.* If exchange is carried out at the natural ratios of value, we shall be able to get out of the car, through exchange, the corn, coal, etc. that have been used in its production; and simultaneously every other industry will be able to get out of its undifferentiated product the exact amounts of different things it had at the beginning of the period.
>
> (D3/12/5: 4; emphases added)[4]

Sraffa leaves no doubt that the upper case letters (A, B, C) refer to material outputs of certain products (e.g. a motor car), whereas the lower case letters (a, b, c) to material inputs (e.g. timber, coal, etc.), needed in the production of the respective output.

De Vivo comments that the first set of equations 'is very similar to Marx's equations of simple reproduction' (p. 9), which he then reproduces. (Sraffa used the 1900 French edition of volume II of *Das Kapital* – see Marx (1900) – where the scheme is to be found on p. 444.) De Vivo observes that 'Marx explicitly assumes that commodities exchange at their "values" (embodied labours) …, or – we may add – simply embodied labours' (p. 10). He adds:

> Marx's are not even equations strictly speaking (indeed, they contain no unknowns): they can be seen as accounting identities.
>
> Sraffa instead speaks of his own relations as equations, with unknowns to which solutions have to be found. *This has a meaning* if we take the a_is, b_is, and c_is of the first set of equations as meaning the total value of each commodity input for the production of A, B, and C – the latter also interpreted as *the total values, not the quantities*, of the commodities produced.
>
> (p. 10; first emphasis added)

The weak claim De Vivo puts forward, namely that his suggested reading of Sraffa's equations 'has a meaning', cannot be disputed. The question is: Is it the meaning Sraffa intended? De Vivo is not sure about it and discerns 'at least two stumbling blocks' (p. 10) in the way of his interpretation. Before we turn to them the following observation is apposite. In his papers Sraffa typically noted scrupulously any concept he had encountered in the literature he consulted and found worth scrutinizing or even adopting himself. Had Marx's schemes of reproduction been the 'starting point' of his systems of equations, as De Vivo contends, then Sraffa could be expected to have explicitly said so. Yet he did not. And he used terms ('self-replacing system' and 'interest' rather than 'simple reproduction' and 'profits' or 'surplus value', etc.) that also do not point in the direction of the alleged Marxian origin of his equations. De Vivo's second interpretation corroborates this and emphasizes elements that contradict his first interpretation. Interestingly, they contain the key to what we consider to be the most convincing interpretation of Sraffa's equations. Had De Vivo rigorously attempted to get to the bottom of things, he would have seen the role 'things' play in Sraffa's highly original work.

Second interpretation

The first stumbling block relates to the different notations used in Sraffa's two sets of equations and how to render them intelligible in terms of a single interpretation. Since 'a_1' has been interpreted as a (labour) value magnitude in the first set, De Vivo opts in favour of interpreting '$a_1 A$' as a quantity ('a_1') multiplied by a price ('A'). 'The second obstacle' or stumbling block, De Vivo stresses, 'is more worrying' (ibid.). This is so, he argues, because there is a document dated June 1928 (D3/12/2: 28), that is, more than half a year *after* the above equations had been composed, which reports on a discussion Sraffa had with the mathematician and philosopher Frank Ramsey. In this discussion Ramsey apparently had insisted that in his equations without a surplus Sraffa ought to express 'each quantity … by *two* letters, one being the number of units, the other the unit of the commodity' (D3/12/2: 28). De Vivo concludes that contrary to his own interpretation of the equations in terms of *value* magnitudes

> This appears to suggest that in the first set of equations above, the *A*'s, *B*'s, and *C*'s stand for *quantities*, not values ...

To this he significantly adds in brackets:

> this is perhaps also reinforced by Sraffa's referring to them as 'things'.
>
> (p. 10)

Things! While there is no doubt that the document of June 1928 is of great importance,[5] the reader may wonder whether the document containing the above equations, D3/12/5: 2–3, is not already crystal clear as to the meaning of the magnitudes involved. In fact, the interpretation of the equations in terms of *quantities* instead of values is not only 'perhaps' reinforced by Sraffa's reference to 'things' in the text accompanying the equations (D3/12/5: 2; the full text is given in Kurz, 2004, section III). Sraffa himself leaves not the slightest doubt about the meaning of the symbols. Alas, De Vivo (and, following him, Gilibert, 2003) only partially reproduces Sraffa's explanation that comes with the above equations. Strangely enough they leave out precisely the passage that leaves no doubt about the meaning of the symbols. In addition to 'the *things A, B, ...*', Sraffa referred explicitly to

> the *quantities of things* respectively *used in production (i.e. consumed) and produced.*
>
> (D3/12/5: 2; emphases added)[6]

Can there be any doubt that the reference is to physical amounts of products productively consumed and produced and *not* to values? Hence, the meaning De Vivo at first attributed to Sraffa's equations cannot be sustained. De Vivo seems to sense this, but what would be an alternative interpretation? He apparently perceives only the following option, which appears to strike him as even less satisfactory than his original reading of the equations:

> There is no doubt that the easiest way out of these difficulties would be to read the equations as simply making the mistake of summing heterogeneous things.
>
> (p. 10)

But could Sraffa possibly be accused of committing such an elementary error – an error besides, which, according to De Vivo, he had previously criticized in marginalist authors?[7] To De Vivo the 'easiest way out' cannot sensibly be taken. Instead he suggests 'a third, "intermediate", but I am afraid not precise [*sic*], interpretation of the above equations' (ibid.). Before we turn to it, let us stress the obvious: vis-à-vis the uncertainties, which in de Vivo's view, cloud the meaning of the above equations, he is able to muster only lukewarm support for his interpretation that they derive from Marx's reproduction schemes.

Third interpretation

Let us now have a closer look at his third interpretation. He points out, rightly we think, that Sraffa at the time was keen to reduce commodities to some common measure,[8] with the result, De Vivo contends, that 'prices and quantities of commodities were perhaps in some sense interchangeable (or confused?) in his [Sraffa's] mind' (p. 11). This statement came as a surprise to us, because De Vivo at first strictly rejected the idea that Sraffa might have committed the error of summing heterogeneous things but now is inclined to consider the possibility of Sraffa 'confusing' prices and quantities 'in his mind'. De Vivo refers to a sample of documents which are meant to somehow support his third way of reading the equations but does not get very far and after half a page gives up: 'Whether it was Frank Ramsey or not to suggest it, Sraffa got to write the equations in the correct way ... ' (p. 11).

Yet contrary to De Vivo's view it is not difficult to get a clear idea of what Sraffa had in mind when jotting down his equations. Most importantly, Sraffa explicitly and surprisingly did *not* consider it an 'error' to sum heterogeneous things. On the contrary. In a comment on Whitaker's (1904) criticism of Torrens he wrote:

> Torrens knew that the (absolute)[(1)] value of the product is determined by (in fact, is) the amount of things that have been destroyed for its production. But he did not see his way through without finding a 'common measure' of them: he probably felt a repulsion to, or thought that it could not be done, *to sum together quantities of heterogeneous things measured in different units. This was of course fatal: he started to find something common in them, upon which to base his measurement: the labour theory was ready at hand ... The result was of course absurd.*
>
> (D3/12/5: 26; emphasis added)

De Vivo appears to have felt essentially the same repulsion when trying to make sense of Sraffa's first equations. And as in the case of Torrens this was 'fatal' for his reading of them. Very much like Torrens he had recourse to the labour theory of value, which, in Sraffa's view, was 'of course absurd'. The similarity between Torrens' approach and De Vivo's interpretation is indeed striking. And the criticism Sraffa levelled at Torrens applies equally to De Vivo's reconstruction.[9]

Sraffa's point of view as it is expressed in his equations is supported by his reflection on the concepts of interdependence, in the present case between different lines of production, and causality:[10] 'Interdependence is equivalent to causality as opposed to causation: it holds between categories' (D1/9: 2). With reference to his equations Sraffa stressed that 'there is a causal connection (*causa essendi*) between the two sets of quantities' – that is, physical real costs and values – and that 'the theory reproduces as a logical relation between two concepts ... the concrete causal relation between the two facts' (D1/9: 10). There is a remark in the margin: '(Sono "indici"; v. Marx, 1924–25, VI, 244)'.

Things

Let us pause for a moment and take stock of what has been said. De Vivo provides three alternative interpretations of the above equations. He admits that his first and apparently favourite one in terms of (labour) *value* magnitudes – the one on which his contention as to the derivation of Sraffa's equations from Marx's scheme of reproduction rests – is contradicted by Sraffa's explicit reference to 'things'. He also admits that his third interpretation is 'not very precise' and presupposes that Sraffa confused prices and quantities in his mind. His second reading is in terms of 'quantities of things'. It has the tremendous advantage of being fully in accordance with what Sraffa *actually* wrote in the document containing the equations under consideration. However, it seems to have the drawback of implying that Sraffa had committed the blunder of summing heterogeneous things.

Before we continue, it is necessary to reflect a bit more on what Sraffa meant by 'things'. Actually, the term was used by natural scientists such as Hertz or Whitehead, whose contributions Sraffa read at the time. In fact it assumed the character of a *terminus technicus* in Sraffa's papers. In a document contained in a folder dated 'Winter 1927–28' Sraffa defined:

> 'Things': but what things? why not water, which has been consumed in definite quantity, (rain) and would thus have a value? 'Limited things'? no, everything is limited: or else, we must add 'according to needs', a meaningless phrase, and we dont [*sic*] deal in utilities.
>
> Therefore, simply, 'appropriated things': as they are in a given historical phase. May be slaves, may be land. We do'nt [*sic*] enquire here about reasons: simply things bearing a label 'private', [']according to law'.

> (D3/12/6: 5)

The things referred to in what Sraffa called 'my equations' (and not schemes of reproduction) are products or rather privately owned commodities: motor cars, timber, coal, etc. In a document stemming from November 1927 he stressed that the unit of production he has taken is 'typified by the uniformity of product', and that 'a collection of things is used as circ.[ulating] cap.[ital.] and "fused" into a single product' (D3/12/11: 35).

We conclude from our critical examination that De Vivo's first interpretation cannot be sustained. He has not argued correctly and has overlooked elements in the documents he cites from Sraffa's papers that contradict his reconstruction. In particular there is no evidence whatsoever that in Sraffa's equations the reference is to '*the total values, not the quantities*, of the commodities produced' (p. 10). There is rather compelling and indeed exclusive evidence to the contrary.

We may now ask whether there are documents in Sraffa's papers not cited by De Vivo that support his case. Alas, we are not aware of any such documents. There are, however, many documents that provide further evidence to the contrary. We mention here just a few of them.

Evidence not referred to by De Vivo

There is no sign that Sraffa ever felt to have committed a blunder when writing his above equations. He wrote them, we think, as chemists use to write chemical reactions, that is, as an algebraic equation, with the name of a substance expressing the equality of constituents and compound, e.g. '$2H_2O = 2H_2 + O_2$'. From a perspective revolving around the concept of balancing, the analogy between a product that obtains as the result of the 'destruction' of necessary quantities of means of production and means of subsistence, on the one hand, and a chemical reaction conceived of as a balance of the weights of inputs and outputs is close at hand. In both cases the balance expresses the conservation of mass (and energy).[11]

This is indirectly confirmed by a companion document to D3/12/5: 2, which was written at about the same time (in all probability earlier) and which contains the *same* set of equations as those reproduced above: D3/12/11: 87. (The document is given in full in Kurz, 2004: subsection IV.1.) Interestingly, De Vivo mentions the document in passing (p. 12), but apparently has difficulties in relating properly to it.[12] (Below we shall come back to his treatment of it.) In it Sraffa refers to a book by Mineo Chini (1923) on mathematics for chemists and natural scientists and stresses with regard to the *identical* set of equations as the first set reproduced above that into the quantities of the substances – which he explicitly calls 'beni' or 'merci' (i.e. goods or commodities) – on the left hand side of the equality sign 'enter' the quantities of the substances – which he calls 'beni' or 'fattori' (i.e. goods or factors) – on the right hand side of the equality sign. Hence in the *identical* sets of equations contained in the twin documents, D3/12/11: 87 and D3/12/5: 2, the reference is *directly* to physical quantities of goods, or commodities, or factors, and *not*, as De Vivo claims in his first interpretation, to labour values.

Closely connected to what has just been said, an expression of the type '$2H_2O = 2H_2 + O_2$' may even be regarded as a proper algebraic equation when interpreted as follows: 'the mass of two molecules of water is equal to the sum of the mass of two molecules of hydrogen plus the mass of one molecule of oxygen'. In this interpretation H_2O is not just a symbol for water, but has a quantitative aspect: it is the mass of a molecule of water. Similarly, an expression of the type '$A = a_1 + b_1 + c_1$', or better: '$aA = a_1A + b_1B + c_1C$', could be interpreted both as a tabulation of a production process (and in this case it is not an algebraic equation) or as an algebraic equation stating the equality of two masses. Obviously, in this interpretation A, B and C assume the true meaning of prices. Finally, it deserves mentioning that more recently chemists use two symbols: '=' when the reaction is reversible, and '→' when it is not.[13] Since single economic productive processes are never reversible, one might want to ask whether it is for this reason that in his book Sraffa switched to the latter symbol. But there is something more. If we consider just the no surplus case – the 'first equations', as Sraffa called them at the time – we see that Sraffa paid much attention to the problem of reversibility (see the passage from D3/12/5: 4 quoted above).

Sraffa in the 1920s (and also later) had a vivid interest in contemporary developments in the natural sciences and attempted to develop an approach in economics in full recognition of these developments. This is documented by several notes and papers, books in his library and annotations in them and by his diaries. This concern met with his materialist and objectivist philosophical orientation. Actually, in summer 1929 he explicitly specified the aim of his work as elaborating an 'atomic analysis' (D3/12/13: 16 (9)); and in August 1931, looking back at his previous efforts, he spoke of his 'entirely objective point of view', which, he emphasized, was 'the natural science point of view' (D3/12/7: 161 (3)).[14]

In the light of this evidence we wonder whether Sraffa's above equations can be interpreted differently from what emerges clearly from the twin documents D3/12/11: 87 and D3/12/5: 2. They can surely *not* be read as De Vivo (in his first alternative) (and Gilibert, 2003) suggests.

We come now to Sraffa's second equations, that is, those relating to a with-surplus economy and a given inventory (or commodity) wage.

Sraffa's second equations: more 'things'!

We have mentioned that De Vivo referred to document D3/12/11: 87 only in passing, but without apparently being able to make sense of it. So let us see whether things look differently in the light of what has just been said. He quotes the following extract from Sraffa's text of D3/12/11: 87 accompanying the *above* equations:

> considera i vari surpluses come merci diverse (supponendo cioè che appena sorge il surplus, si continua a produrre la stessa quantità di 'grano' di prima, e le risorse residue vengon tutte dedicate a produrre gioielli e altre cose 'improduttive')[15]

Yet, interestingly, De Vivo relates this text to a *different* set of equations, one with a surplus, contained in a *different* document, namely, in D3/12/10: 67 (see its reproduction on p. 12). He opines: 'The logic of this kind of equations is not fully clear' (p. 12). The passage he quotes from D3/12/11: 87 also refers to a with-surplus economy, and the treatment of the latter is indeed Sraffa's concern. What, then, is in all probability the 'logic' behind Sraffa's argument in the with-surplus case?

As is explained in some detail in Kurz (2004: subsection IV.1; see also Kurz and Salvadori, 2005a, 2005b and Kurz, 2012), Sraffa's 'natural science point of view' implied that for every 'effect' there had to be 'sufficient cause'. This means that any surplus must have a sufficient cause and cannot but reflect some objective 'social' as opposed to 'natural' obstacles that have to be overcome: it has to correspond to some social 'cost'. The surplus, or 'interest' as Sraffa was soon to call it, has to be paid in order to prevent capitalists from 'withdrawing' their (circulating) capital.[16] Similarly, wages have to be paid in order to 'enable' workers to perform their task and preserve their capacity to work. More precisely, Sraffa conceived of the surplus product as the physical input into an artificial industry producing 'luxuries' or 'gioielli e altre cose "improduttive"' for capitalists. In this way the surplus was made to vanish and we would be back in a quasi-natural economy. Sraffa thus thought to be able to carry over the logic applying to his first (no surplus) equations also to his second (with surplus) equations. The equations in D3/12/10: 67, to which De Vivo refers (p. 12), reflect precisely the concept of the surplus Sraffa held at the time, namely as reflecting a 'social' cost: the payments to capital owners in terms of 'unproductive goods' are the price to be paid by society to prevent them from 'withdrawing' their circulating capital. This 'logic' follows from the 'entirely objective point of view' Sraffa had embraced at the time.

Yet the document D3/12/10: 67 (compared with D3/12/11: 87 from which the above passage is taken) is interesting also for the following reason. Sraffa was now aware of the fact that his device of re-interpreting the surplus as a physical real 'cost' incurred in the production of luxuries was no solution to the problem he had encountered with his second equations. The problem consisted in the following: As soon as there is a surplus the original system of equations becomes *contradictory*. Did the device Sraffa invoked render them consistent again? Obviously no. This is what Sraffa acknowledged in the passage taken from D3/12/10: 67 and quoted by De Vivo (p. 12): The new set of equations that obtained by adding a surplus-consuming artificial industry producing luxuries had not removed the contradictory character of the system. Hence the sought solution was none or at least incomplete. Something was missing.

After some deliberation Sraffa eventually found a way out of the impasse. The route he adopted allowed him to preserve the conceptualization of interest as a necessary social cost and yet arrive at a non-contradictory system of equations. With free competition a uniform rate of interest would be paid on all *circulating* capital.[17] The introduction of this new variable allowed Sraffa to overcome the impasse. In document D3/12/8: 29 dated 'Lent 1928' he put down the following tabulation of production processes

$$18A = 4A + 3B + 9C$$
$$25B = 1A + 8B + 1C$$
$$13C = 7A + 10B + 2C$$

Here a number apparently gives the amount of a commodity produced or used up and the associated capital letter the kind of commodity under consideration. The above system exhibits a physical surplus product, S, which Sraffa tabulated accordingly

$$S = 6A + 4B + 1C$$

He then turned to the determination of relative values with 'the ratio of surplus (on circ. cap. only)'. As De Vivo points out (p. 13), Sraffa at the time called 'seed' the use of any commodity in its own production and considered it a 'fixed capital' which receives no interest.[18] Denoting the value of one unit of commodity A and C, expressed in terms of commodity B, by α and γ, respectively, the value of the surplus by δ, and the surplus ratio by r[19], Sraffa then established the following equations

$$18\alpha = 4\alpha + (3 + 9\gamma)r$$
$$25 = (1\alpha + 1\gamma)r + 8$$
$$13\gamma = (7\alpha + 10)r + 2\gamma$$
$$\delta = (6\alpha + 4 + 1\gamma)r$$

The important thing to note is that r, α and γ can be determined exclusively in terms of the first three equations, whereas the fourth equation is purely passive and only needed in order to determine δ. However, although Sraffa had found a way out of the impasse and had arrived at a non-contradictory system, he still clung to the old idea of reducing the surplus or anything that stood for it to some ultimate measure of value or necessary commodity. This is why we see him raise the question whether r – the interest factor – could be reduced to commodity A. Yet he soon got doubts as to the 'legittimità' (legitimacy) of this procedure.[20]

He also soon got doubts as regards the assumption of paying no interest on 'seed' (and, more generally, durable instruments of production) and reformulated his above price system applying r also to the quantities of own inputs.

'A very early and brief mood'?

De Vivo opines:

At the beginning [Sraffa's] heroes seem to have been William Petty and the Physiocrats – 'it was only Petty & the Physiocrats who had the right notion of cost as "the loaf of bread" ' [D3/12/4: 4] – he writes. But this, I believe, was only a very early and brief mood, perhaps a sort of remnant from the Marshall period ... Early enough [*sic*] however his appreciation of Marx changed.

(p. 7)

This view cannot be sustained. The 'physical real cost' approach to the theory of value and distribution was most certainly not 'only a very early and brief mood' of Sraffa's. He rather unswervingly clung to it throughout his first and second equations, which form the very foundation of his entire analysis. The approach is encountered again in an undiluted form in Chapter I and §§ 1–8 of Chapter II of his 1960 book. There wages are explicitly regarded 'as consisting of the necessary subsistence of the workers and thus entering the system on the same footing as the fuel for the engines or the feed for the cattle' (Sraffa, 1960: 9). In this context it is worth mentioning that Sraffa up until shortly before the publication of his book thought of giving it the title 'Production of Commodities by Commodities', which reflects well his objectivist and materialist perspective on the problems under consideration (see D3/12/80: 2).

It is not clear what De Vivo wants to say when he writes 'Early enough however his [Sraffa's] appreciation of Marx changed'. It looks as if with this formulation he tries to express a transition from Sraffa's earlier physical real cost approach to a new one, more in the spirit of Marx. In support of his view he then refers to three documents: D3/12/4: 15 and 17 and D3/12/11: 55. The first document discusses the possibility of 'a restatement of Marx' in the sense of 'simply a translation of Marx into English, from the forms of Hegelian metaphysics to the forms's of Hume's metaphysics' (D3/12/4: 15). This statement taken in isolation has no clear meaning. The third document mentioned is more illuminating in regard to what Sraffa may have had in mind. In it he argues that the history of economic thought should be written backwards: 'stato attuale dell'ec.; come vi si è giunti, mostrando la differenza e la superiorità delle vecchie teorie'.[21] Only after this task has been accomplished, was his own theory to be expounded: 'Poi, esporre la teoria.' (Then explain the theory.) He concluded:

> Il mio scopo è: I esporre la storia, che è veramente l'essenziale{;} II farmi capire: per il che si richiede che io vada dal noto all'ignoto, da Marshall a Marx, dalla disultilità al *costo materiale*.
>
> (D3/12/11: 55; emphasis added)[22]

Here Sraffa reckoned Marx explicitly as belonging broadly to the 'material' or 'physical real cost' tradition inaugurated by Petty and developed by the Physiocrats.[23] Alas, his Hegelian metaphysics had led Marx astray and contributed to shunting this tradition on a track, which involved a 'corruption' of the old idea of cost, but was still near enough to be in some cases equivalent. On Sraffa's premise that Marx had been the last of the great classical economists, who had elaborated on their doctrine, the idea is close at hand that a resumption of the classical approach and its consequent elaboration was eventually bound to result in a 'restatement of Marx', purged of its Hegelian metaphysics and corrupting influence. Looking at Marx through the lens of this approach did not involve, as De Vivo appears to imply, that Sraffa distanced himself from the physical real cost perspective – quite the contrary: Sraffa rather saw the need to rigorously reformulate Marx's theory in terms of material costs and purge it from labour values.

Sraffa and Ramsey

De Vivo refers to Sraffa's report of a discussion he had on his first and second equations and their solvability with his colleague and friend Frank Plumpton Ramsey on 26 June 1928 (D3/12/2: 28). De Vivo writes:

> Frank Ramsey had told Sraffa that approximate solutions could probably be found for his systems of equations, with any number of equations, and that 'It can probably be proved that, whatever the number of equations[,] only *one* set of solutions is significant' [D3/12/2: 28]

He adds:

> There is no clue as to the basis of Ramsey's statements, made at such an early state.
>
> (p. 14)

Apparently it has escaped De Vivo's attention that the next note in the same folder has in all probability come out of the same meeting (D3/12/2: 29) and provides the missing 'clue'. This note has been discussed in detail in Kurz and Salvadori (2000: 196–8) and the reader is asked to consult our paper. Here it suffices to remark that Ramsey had reformulated the original system of linear homogeneous equations (with a surplus and a uniform rate of interest), which is in Sraffa's hand, by first putting the system in its canonical form and then by setting the determinant of coefficients equal to zero in order to obtain a non-trivial solution. The conclusions Ramsey drew from this Sraffa then summarized for his own use in terms of three statements.

The meeting with Ramsey must have confirmed Sraffa in his conviction that there was something interesting in what he was doing. After all, his main intuition that both relative prices and the rate of interest could be ascertained exclusively in terms of physical real costs by solving the corresponding system of simultaneous equations had proved to be right.

Conclusion

In this chapter we have critically examined the interpretation put forward by De Vivo on Sraffa's path to his 1960 book. De Vivo deserves credit for having opened up the discussion on this highly complex issue and for having put forward stimulating ideas, which at first sight might look convincing. However, a close examination of them shows that many of them cannot be sustained. In particular, there is no compelling evidence that Sraffa derived the systems of equations he began to develop in November 1927 from Marx's schemes of reproduction in volume II of *Capital*. There is rather compelling evidence that he started from the concept of physical real cost, as it had been advocated by William Petty and the Physiocrats. With this concept Sraffa confronted Alfred Marshall's concept of 'physical cost', which despite its name took all costs to be explicable in subjectivist terms (disutility, abstinence, etc.). In the first period of his reconstructive work, extending from late 1927 to mid 1931, Sraffa stated explicitly that he was keen to elaborate an 'atomic analysis' (D3/12/13: 16), using a *terminus technicus* encountered in the natural sciences. And in August 1931, in a critical retrospect, he characterized his previous analytical efforts as having been concerned with developing 'an entirely objective point of view', which is 'the natural science point of view' (D3/12/7: 161 (3)). To Sraffa political economy was, or rather ought to be, a 'science of things' rather than a science of motives (as in the marginalist authors), where he left no doubt that the 'things' referred to in his equations were physical quantities of commodities used up or produced and not labour values, as De Vivo contended. In fact, at the time Sraffa was highly critical of the labour theory of value and chastised Smith, Ricardo, Torrens and Marx for having 'corrupted' the 'right notion of cost as "the loaf of bread"' and other material inputs, which are necessarily destroyed in the course of the production of the outputs. This concern with physical real costs was not a 'passing mood' of Sraffa's, as De Vivo opined, but permeates his entire reconstructive work, including its endpoint: his 1960 book. We also clear up the meaning of a number of propositions in Sraffa's papers that De Vivo found puzzling.

References

Bernheim, E. (1894). *Lehrbuch der Historischen Methode. Mit Nachweis der wichtigsten Quellen und Hülfsmittel zum Studium der Geschichte*, 2nd edn, Leipzig, Duncker & Humblot.

Cannan, E. (1929). *A Review of Economic Theory*, London, P. S. King & Son. (Sr.L. 1146)

Chini, M. (1923). *Corso speciale di matematiche con numerosi applicazioni ad uso principalmente dei chimici e dei naturalisti* (1923, 6th edn), Livorno, Raffaello Giusti. (Sr.L. 3204)

De Vivo, G. (2000). Produzione di merci a mezzo di merci: note sul percorso intellettuale di Sraffa, in M. Pivetti (ed.), *Piero Sraffa. Contributi per una biografia intellettuale*, Rome, Carocci.

De Vivo, G. (2003). Sraffa's path to *Production of Commodities by Means of Commodities*: an interpretation, *Contributions to Political Economy*, 22(1), 1–25.

Gilibert, G. (2003). The equations unveiled: Sraffa's price equations in the making, *Contributions to Political Economy*, 22, 27–40.

Gramsci, A. (1948). *Il materialismo storico e la filosofia di Benedetto Croce, papers 1929–1934*, Milano, Einaudi. (Sraffa 3979)

Hertz, H. (1899), *Principles of Mechanics*, London, Macmillan.

Kurz, H. D. (2004). *Sraffa's Early Studies of the Production of Commodities by Commodities. Towards an 'Atomic Analysis'*, unpublished manuscript, Graz.

Kurz, H. D. (2012). Don't treat too ill my Piero! Interpreting Sraffa's papers, *Cambridge Journal of Economics*, 36(6), 1535–69.

Kurz, H. D. and Salvadori, N. (2000). Sraffa and the mathematicians: Frank Ramsey and Alister Watson, in T. Cozzi and R. Marchionatti (eds), *Piero Sraffa's Political Economy. A Centenary Estimate*, London, Routledge.

Kurz, H. D. and Salvadori, N. (2005a). Representing the production and circulation of commodities in material terms: on Sraffa's objectivism, *Review of Political Economy*, 17(3), 413–41.

Kurz, H. D. and Salvadori, N. (2005b). Removing an 'insuperable obstacle' in the way of an objectivist analysis: Sraffa's attempts at fixed capital, *European Journal of the History of Economic Thought*, 12(3), 493–523.

Kurz, H. D. and Salvadori, N. (2009). Sraffa and the labour theory of value: a few observations, in J. Vint, J.S. Metcalfe, H. D. Kurz, N. Salvadori and P. A. Samuelson (eds), *Economic Theory and Economic Thought: Festschrift in Honour of Ian Steedman*, London, Routledge, 187–213.

Marx, K. (1900). *Le Capital. Critique de l'économie politique*, Livre II, *Le procès de circulation du capital*, translated by J. Borchardt and H. Vanderrydt, Paris, V. Giard & E. Brière. (Sr.L. 3365)

Marx, K. (1924–1925). *Oeuvres complètes de Karl Marx. Histoire des doctrines économiques*, translated by J. Molitor, eight vols, Paris, Alfred Costes [ancienne librairie Schleicher]. (Sr.L. 3699)

Naldi, N. (1998). Piero Sraffa's early approach to political economy: from the gymnasium to the beginning of his academic career, in T. Cozzi and R. Marchionatti (eds), *Piero Sraffa's Political Economy. A Centenary Estimate*, London, Routledge.

Pantaleoni, M. (1894). *Principii di economia pura*, 2nd edn (1st edn 1889), Florence, G. Barbera. (Sr.L. 2302 and 2889)

Sraffa, P. (1960). *Production of Commodities by Means of Commodities*, Cambridge, Cambridge University Press.

Whitaker, A. C. (1904). *History and Criticism of the Labor Theory of Value in English Political Economy*, New York, Columbia University Press. (Sr.L. 1095)

Whyte, L. L. (1928). *Archimedes or The Future of Physics*, London, Kegan, Paul, Trench, Trubner & Co.; New York, E. P. Dutton & Co.

Notes

1 See, in particular, the paper on which the main text of the present paper is based: De Vivo (2000).

2 In De Vivo (p. 9) we read 'B' instead of 'bB' in the second equation of the second system.

3 In his essay 'The Foundations of Mathematics', published in 1925, Sraffa's 'math-ematical friend' Frank Ramsey defined what he called an 'atomic proposition' in the following way:

this is one which could not be analysed in terms of other propositions and could consist of names alone without logical constants. For instance, by joining 'ϕ', the name of a quality, to '*a*' the name of an individual, and writing 'ϕa', we have an atomic proposition asserting that the individual has the quality. (See Sraffa's library (for short Sr.L.), item 2389, p. 5.)

4 Sraffa's observation on the reversibility appears to have been prompted by reading Whyte (1928).
5 We shall come back to it in the third section; see also Kurz and Salvadori (2000: 262–4).
6 In the above we have also seen that in the explanation accompanying the first set of equations under consideration Sraffa had explicitly referred to the output of one of the processes as a 'motor car' and to its inputs as 'timber, coal to feed machines, iron, corn to feed the labourers' (D3/12/5: 4). In this context it is also worth mentioning that a few pages earlier in his paper (p. 7, n. 3) De Vivo quotes Sraffa who had insisted that 'P.[olitical] E.[conomy] was a *science of things*' (D3/12/10: 61; emphasis added).
7 De Vivo does not say what he has in mind in this regard.
8 For some details, see Kurz (2004, subsections IV.2 and IV.3).

(1)   To this Sraffa appended the following footnote: 'Torrens calls it natural, as opposed to market, price, Cannan, 208.' The reference is to Cannan (1929).

9 It deserves to be mentioned that at the time Sraffa apparently did not see yet that the solution of his system of production equations without a surplus reflected the labour theory of value. To see this, one has to (i) explicitly bring in the labour performed in the various lines of production and (ii) render heterogeneous labours commensurable. This can be done by assessing the different quantities of subsistence corresponding to different kinds of labour in terms of the prices that obtain when solving the system and then using the resulting scale to reduce 'any difference in quality ... to equivalent differences in quantity' (Sraffa, 1960: 10). See also Kurz and Salvadori (2009).
10 The following considerations reflect upon Sraffa's absorption of some considerations he encountered in Hertz (1899) on the concepts of cause and interdependence; see Kurz and Salvadori (2005a, section 4).
11 At the time John Dalton's 'atomic theory' was widely discussed and referred to also in contributions to political economy. The theory is based on two Laws: (i) the Law of the Conservation of Mass and (ii) the Law of Definite Proportions: in a given chemical compound, the elements are always combined in the same proportion by mass. See, for example, the discussion of the second law in Pantaleoni ([1889] 1894: 99–102). Sraffa can safely be assumed to have started to think about the relationship between economics and chemistry as early as in the period 1923–1925. He was critical of the application of the second law to economic production processes as is evidenced, *inter alia*, by lectures given in Perugia. As Naldi (1998: 109) observed, the title of one of Sraffa's lectures in March 1925 was 'Critica della teoria delle proporzioni definite'. And in Sraffa's papers on decreasing returns there is a note in which he stresses that in economics there is no such a thing as a ' "law of definite proportions" as there is in chemistry' (D1/4: 38). (We are grateful to Nerio Naldi for having drawn our attention to this fact.) An important aspect of Sraffa's criticisms of the second law recurred in his pre-Lectures of summer 1927 when he discussed the fact that the vector of the means of subsistence needed to 'enable' a worker to perform his productive activity is not strictly given. See, in particular, D3/12/3: 44, where he observes: 'so soon as there are substitutes, there is an *infinite* number of combinations of the different commodities which satisfy the condition of maintaining life and efficiency of the producers'. Hence with regard to subsistence there are no given definite proportions. (Later, when dealing with the problem of alternative methods of production from which cost-minimising producers can

choose – the so-called choice of technique problem – Sraffa observed that also in production there are no given definite proportions.)

12 By the time Gilibert (2003) wrote his paper, he either had not seen the piece or did not find it worth discussing.

13 When Sraffa in 1942 resumed work on his systems of equations he also specified the notation adopted. In a note composed in August of that year he stressed that in the equations '+' means 'with' and '=' means 'produce'; see D3/12/20: 4. And on 20 October 1942 he introduced the symbol '→' to describe production; see D3/12/23: 1. By that time the notation then used in his 1960 book was at hand.

14 Sraffa's natural science point of view becomes particularly clear in his treatment of fixed capital. From the late 1920s on he was asking himself whether the concept of 'transfer of physical substance' carries over from circulating to fixed capital. This problem caused him a lot of headache until in the winter of 1942–1943 he eventually adopted the joint products approach to durable instruments of production. See Kurz and Salvadori (2005a, section IV).

15 English translation:
Regard the various surpluses as different commodities (thus assuming that as soon as the surplus emerges, one continues to produce the same quantity of 'corn' as before, and the residual resources are all dedicated to produce jewelry and other 'unproductive' things)

16 It deserves to be stressed again that, significantly, Sraffa used the term 'interest' and not 'surplus value' or 'profit', which would have been the natural thing to do, had his starting point been Marx's schemes of reproduction.

17 The payment of interest only to circulating capital and not to aged fixed capital Sraffa motivated by the fact that in the short run capitalists as a class cannot withdraw (i.e. consume) the latter. This they can do only in the long run by spending total gross revenue on consumption and thus refraining from making good the wear and tear of fixed capital.

18 There is reason to presume that Sraffa followed Adam Smith in this regard, who had argued that seed was a fixed capital because it did not change hands, i.e. circulate. See on this Kurz and Salvadori (2005b: section 2).

19 While Sraffa did not explicitly say so, it is clear that here r represents the surplus or interest factor (= 1 + interest rate), not the surplus or interest rate.

20 The attempt to reduce interest, conceived as 'a necessary cost', to some (composite) commodity led Sraffa to the following consideration. The sought commodity would have to satisfy the condition that it enters into the production of each commodity 'in the same proportion as interest: if therefore we regard interest as a necessary cost (entirely consumed, not saved), the "luxuries", i.e. the "food of the capitalist" would be the commodity that satisfies this condition' (D3/12/7: 32).

21 English translation: 'actual state of economics; how we got there, showing the difference and the superiority of the old theories'.

22 English translation: 'My task is: I expound the history, which is truly the essential{;} II make myself understood: this requests me to go from the known to the unknown, from Marshall to Marx, from disutility to material cost.'

23 This view is foreshadowed in the pre-Lectures where Sraffa wrote: 'if the physical interpretation or real cost is accepted, quantity of labour is the best measure of cost' (D3/12/3: 40). As to the origin of the physical real cost concept Sraffa was sure that this could be traced back even farther than Petty, to the canonists, in particular, with their doctrine of 'just price'.

Part IV
Growth and distribution

12 Endogenous growth in a stylised 'classical' model[*]

Heinz D. Kurz and Neri Salvadori

Introduction

Interpreters from Adolph Lowe (1954) to Walter Eltis (1984) have stressed that economic growth and socio-economic development in the classical authors from Adam Smith to David Ricardo and Karl Marx were considered endogenous phenomena. In their writings, the behaviour of agents, their creativity and need for achievement and distinction, and social rules and institutions defined the confines within which the process of the production, distribution and use of social wealth unfolded. The concept of exogenous growth, as it was introduced by Gustav Cassel and then made central in Robert Solow's growth model (Solow 1956), was totally extraneous to the way the classical economists thought. In their view the main problem the social sciences were confronted with consisted of the fact, in the words of Smith's teacher Adam Ferguson, that history is 'the result of human action, but not of human design'. What was needed was to come to grips, as best as one could, with the consequence of purposeful human actions, both intended and unintended.

In this chapter we consider a very small and highly stylised aspect of the endogenous character of economic growth as envisaged by the classical authors. To keep the argument within limits, we set aside problems that cannot be dealt with in a short chapter. In particular, we do not deal with the development aspect of economic growth, the technical, social, structural and institutional changes involved, the availability of an ever greater variety and quality of goods, the erosion of received patterns of consumption, of cultural styles and of social relations, and the establishment of new ones, and so forth. These themes play an important role in work of authors such as Smith and Marx. We also set aside analytical complications due to the factual intricacies of an ever more sophisticated system of the social division of labour and an ever more complex network of interdependent sectors of production.

[*] Reproduced with permission from George Stathakis and Gianni Vaggi (eds), *Economic Development and Social Change*, London: Routledge, 2006.

The chapter assumes essentially a one-sector economy in which 'corn' is produced by means of doses of labour-cum-capital, where capital consists only of corn and each dose of labour-cum-capital exhibits the same proportion of labour to corn. This means that labour-cum-capital can be treated as if it were a single factor of production. This bold simplification of the 'classical' approach to the problem of economic growth can only be justified if it does not misrepresent an important aspect of at least a variant of that approach. One generally engages in such simplifications only for heuristic reasons, and the heuristic perspective underlying this chapter is to prepare the ground for a comparison with prominent contributions to the so-called 'new' growth literature (see Kurz and Salvadori 1996, 1998a, 1998b, 1999, 2003).

Many of the models elaborated in the new growth literature are essentially one-sector models and know only a single capital good, just as our model does. By highlighting certain ideas found in the classical approach in the simplest form possible, we provide similes of some ideas found in modern contributions to growth theory. This allows us to raise the question, and provide elements of an answer to it, of continuity and change in growth theory from the classical to the modern authors. We believe that the stylised classical model elaborated in this chapter following a well-known literature (see Kaldor 1955–56, Samuelson 1959, Pasinetti 1960), despite some valid criticisms that can be forwarded against it, is able to capture a number of elements of at least an important thread in classical thinking.

The following analysis will be exclusively *long period.* That is, attention will focus on positions of the economic system characterised, in competitive conditions, by a uniform rate of profit throughout the system, a uniform real wage rate, and a uniform rate of rent for each quality of land.

The composition of the chapter is as follows. In the second section we outline the stylised 'classical' or rather Ricardesque theory of growth, and use Kaldor's well-known diagram to illustrate the endogeneity of the rate of growth. We deal both with the case in which the real wage is given and independent of the rate of growth of the workforce, and the case in which a higher rate of growth requires a higher real wage rate, reflecting a kind of Malthusian population dynamics. It is argued that the introduction of the latter does not affect the basic logic of the classical point of view, namely, that in normal conditions the pace at which capital accumulates regulates the pace at which the labouring population grows. In other words, labour is considered as generated within the process of capital accumulation and economic growth.

The third section deals with neoclassical models of economic growth. It is first argued that for reasons that have partly to do with its analytical structure, which takes the initial endowments of the economy of 'factors of production' as given, the marginalist approach starts naturally from a long-term rate of growth that equals some exogenously given rate of growth of the factor(s) of production. This is exemplified in terms of the contributions of Alfred Marshall, Gustav Cassel and Robert Solow.

Next, it is argued that the endogenisation of the growth rate in a class of models belonging to the so-called 'new' growth theory is carried out in a manner reminiscent of classical economics. While in the Solow growth model, for example, labour is treated as a non-producible and non-accumulable factor of production whose fixed rate of growth constrains the long-term expansion of the economic system, in some new growth models this factor is replaced by 'human capital' or 'knowledge', which are taken to be producible and even accumulable (or costlessly transferable among subsequent generations of the population). Very much like the classical assumption of a given real wage rate this is equivalent to the assumption that there is a mechanism generating 'labour'. The final section contains some concluding remarks.

Endogenous growth in the 'classical' economists

Accumulation vis-à-vis diminishing returns in agriculture

We begin our discussion with a selection of some stylised analytical elements – and their interaction – that figure prominently in David Ricardo's work, and that are often considered to represent the building blocks of the classical position *tout court*. This invariably involves a bold reduction of the fascinating richness and diversity of classical analyses. It does not adequately represent Ricardo's much more analytically focused contribution to the problem under consideration. However, it captures some of the ideas that permeate much of his work, and this is one of the reasons why we embark on the following Ricardesque model.

The focus of our attention is on what Ricardo called the 'natural' course of the economy. By this he meant an economic system in which capital accumulates, the population grows, but there is no technical progress. Hence the argument is based on the (implicit) assumption that the set of (constant returns to scale) methods of production from which cost-minimising producers can choose is given and constant. Assuming the real wage rate of workers to be given and constant, the rate of profits is bound to fall. Due to extensive and intensive diminishing returns on land, 'with every increased portion of capital employed on it, there will be a decreased rate of production' (Ricardo [1817] 1951: 98).

Profits are viewed as a residual income based on the surplus product left after the used up means of production and the wage goods in the support of workers have been deducted from the social product (net of rents). The 'decreased rate of production' thus involves a decrease in profitability. On the premise that there are only negligible savings out of wages and rents, a falling rate of profits involves a falling rate of capital accumulation. Hence, as regards the dynamism of the economy, attention should focus on profitability. Assuming that the marginal propensity to accumulate out of profits, s, is given and constant, a 'classical' accumulation function can be formulated

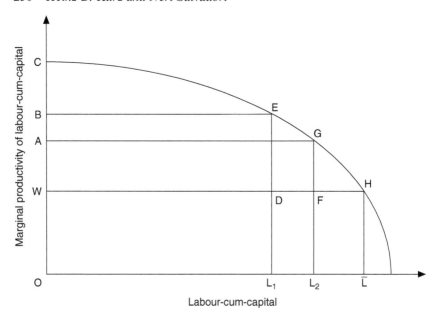

Figure 12.1 Land as an indispensable resource

$$g = \begin{cases} s(r - r_{min}) & \text{if } r \geq r_{min} \\ 0 & \text{if } r \leq r_{min} \end{cases}$$

where $r_{min} \geq 0$ is the minimum level of profitability which, if reached, will arrest accumulation (ibid: 120). Ricardo's 'natural' course will necessarily end up in a stationary state.[1]

Clearly, in Ricardo the rate of accumulation is endogenously determined. The demand for labour is governed by the pace at which capital accumulates, whereas the long-term supply of labour is regulated by some 'Malthusian Law of Population'.[2]

Assuming for simplicity a given and constant real wage rate, Ricardo's view of the long-run relationship between profitability and accumulation and thus growth can be illustrated as in Figure 12.1 (see Kaldor 1955–56). The curve CEGH is the marginal productivity of labour-cum-capital; it is decreasing since land is scarce. When labour-cum-capital increases, either less fertile qualities of land must be cultivated or the same qualities of land must be cultivated with processes which require less land per unit of product, but are more costly in terms of labour-cum-capital. Let the real wage rate equal OW. Then, if the amount of labour-cum-capital applied is L_1, the area $OCEL_1$ gives the product, $OWDL_1$ gives total capital employed and BCE total rent. Profits are determined as a residual and correspond to the rectangular WBED. As a consequence, the *rate* of profits can be determined as the ratio of the areas of two rectangles that have the same basis and, therefore, it equals the ratio WB/OW.

If in the course of capital accumulation and population growth the amount of labour-cum-capital rises to the level of L_2, then OCGL$_2$ gives the product, OWFL$_2$ the capital, ACG the rent and WAGF profits. The rate of profit has fallen to WA/OW. Obviously, if a positive profit rate implies a positive growth rate (i.e. $r_{min} = 0$), the economy will expand until labour-cum-capital has reached the level $\bar{L}$. At that point, the profit rate is equal to zero and so is the growth rate. The system has come to a standstill; the engine of growth, profitability, has run out of steam.

In this bold simplification the required size of the work force is considered as essentially generated by the accumulation process itself. In other words, labour power is treated as a kind of producible commodity. It differs from the other commodity, corn, in that it is not produced in a capitalistic way by a special industry on a par with the corn-growing sector, but is the result of the interplay between the generative behaviour of the working population and socio-economic conditions. In the most simple conceptualisation possible, labour power is seen to be in elastic supply at a given real (that is, corn) wage rate. Increasing the amount of corn available in the support of workers involves a proportional increase of the work force.

In this view the rate of growth of labour supply adjusts to any given rate of growth of labour demand without necessitating a variation in the real wage rate.[3] Labour can thus place no limit on growth because it is 'generated' within the growth process itself. The only limit to growth can come from other non-accumulable factors of production. As Ricardo and others made clear, these factors are natural resources in general and land in particular. In other words, there is only endogenous growth in the classical economists. This growth is bound to lose momentum as the scarcity of natural resources makes itself felt in terms of extensive and intensive diminishing returns. (Technical change is of course seen to counteract these tendencies.)

The assumption of a given and constant real wage rate which is independent of the rate of growth of the demand for 'hands' can, of course, only be justified as a first step in terms of its simplicity. In fact, in some of his discussions with Thomas Robert Malthus, Ricardo appears to have adopted this assumption precisely for the sake of convenience. There is clear evidence that he did not consider it a stylised historical fact of long-term economic development. Reading his works, one gets the impression that the relationship between the expansion of the economic system as a whole and the wage and population dynamics is far from simple, and actually differs both between different countries in the same period and between different periods of the same country, depending on a variety of historical, cultural and institutional factors.

For example, Ricardo stressed that 'population may be so little stimulated by ample wages as to increase at the slowest rate – or *it may even go in a retrograde direction*' (Ricardo, *Works*, VIII: 169, emphasis added). And in his *Notes on Malthus* he insisted that 'population and necessaries are not necessarily linked together so intimately'; 'better education and improved habits' may break the population mechanism (Ricardo, *Works*, II: 115).

However, we encounter also the following view expressed in his letter to Malthus of 18 December 1814:

> A diminution of the proportion of produce, in consequence of the accumulation of capital, does not fall wholly on the owner of stock, but is shared with him by the labourers. The whole amount of wages paid will be greater, but the portion paid to each man, will in all probability, be somewhat diminished.
>
> (Ricardo, *Works*, VI: 162–3)

In what follows, we formalise the idea that higher rates of capital accumulation, which presuppose higher rates of growth of the workforce, correspond to higher levels of the real wage rate.[4] We shall see that the basic logic of the argument which we have illustrated by means of the assumption of a fixed real wage rate remains essentially untouched: in normal conditions the pace at which capital accumulates regulates the pace at which labour grows.

Assume that higher growth rates of the labouring population require higher levels of the corn wage paid to workers. Higher wages, the usual argument goes, give workers and their families access to more abundant and better nutrition and medical services. This reduces infant mortality and increases the average length of life of workers. Let $\bar{w}$ be the wage rate that must be paid in order to keep the labouring population stationary, and let $w = \bar{w}(1+g)$ be the wage rate to be paid in order for the labouring population to grow at the rate g. Further, let the marginal productivity of labour-cum-capital (the CEGH curve of Figure 12.1) be the function $f(L)$. Then the rate of profits r turns out to be

$$r = \frac{f(L) - \bar{w}(1+g)}{\bar{w}(1+g)}.$$

Hence, on the simplifying assumption that $r_{min} = 0$,

$$g = s\frac{f(L) - \bar{w}(1+g)}{\bar{w}(1+g)},$$

from which we obtain a second degree equation in g:

$$\bar{w}g^2 + (1+s)\bar{w}\,g - s[f(L) - \bar{w}] = 0,$$

which, for $f(L) > \bar{w}$, has a positive and a negative solution. The negative solution is insignificant from an economic point of view because it is less than

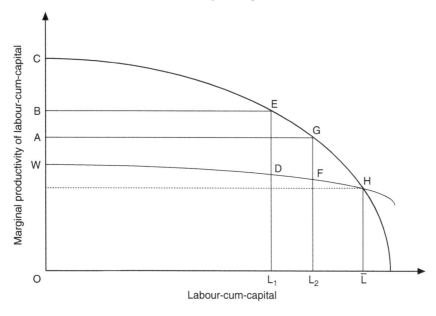

Figure 12.2 The wage rate as a function of the growth rate

-1 and would thus be associated with a negative real wage rate. The positive solution is

$$g = \frac{\sqrt{(1-s)^2\,\bar{w}^2 + 4sf(L)\bar{w}} - (1+s)\bar{w}}{2\bar{w}}.$$

The result of this simple exercise is that the WDFH curve (see Figure 12.2), which in Figure 12.1 was a horizontal straight line, becomes a decreasing curve:

$$\bar{w}(1+g) = \frac{\sqrt{(1-s)^2\,\bar{w}^2 + 4sf(L)\bar{w}} + (1-s)\bar{w}}{2}.$$

Note that if $f(L) > \bar{w}$, then $f(L) > \bar{w}(1+g) > \bar{w}$, whereas if $f(L) = \bar{w}$, then $f(L) = \bar{w}(1+g) = \bar{w}$. To conclude, the resulting modifications of Figure 12.1 do not change the substance of the 'classical' point of view expounded above.[5]

Production with land as a free good

We may now briefly turn to the hypothetical case in which the economy can grow without ever experiencing the constraint of scarce land(s). This amounts to setting land aside in Ricardo's doctrine, which might strike the reader as something like Hamlet without the prince. However, Ricardo himself contemplated this case. In his letter to Malthus already referred to, he wrote:

> Accumulation of capital has a tendency to lower profits. Why? Because every accumulation is attended with increased difficulty in obtaining food, unless it is accompanied with improvements in agriculture, in which case it has no tendency to diminish profits. If there were no increased difficulty, profits would never fall, because there are no other limits to the profitable production of manufactures but the rise of wages. *If with every accumulation of capital we could tack a piece of fresh fertile land to our Island, profits would never fall.*
>
> (Ricardo, *Works*, VI: 162, emphasis added)

Similarly, in his letter to Malthus of 17 October 1815 he stated that

> [P]rofits do not *necessarily* fall with the increase of the quantity of capital because the demand for capital is infinite and is governed by the same law as population itself. They are both checked by the rise in the price of food, and the consequent increase in the value of labour. If there were no such rise, what could prevent population and capital from increasing without limit?
>
> (Ricardo, *Works*, VI: 301)

If land of the best quality were abundant (and its ownership sufficiently dispersed), it would be a free good. From an economic point of view, land can therefore be ignored like the air or the sunlight. Then the graph giving the marginal productivity of labour-cum-capital would be a horizontal line and, therefore, the rate of profits would be constant whatever the amount of labour-cum-capital. This case is illustrated in Figure 12.3. As a consequence, the growth rate would also be constant over time: the system could expand without end at a rate that equals the given rate of profits times the propensity to accumulate. As we have seen, Ricardo was perfectly aware of this implication.

In this case, if we take into account the possibility contemplated in the above that a higher rate of growth of the work force might require a higher level of the real wage rate, then the WDF curve in Figure 12.3 would be higher, but it would still be a horizontal straight line below the CEG and above the WDF straight lines.

Production with a 'backstop technology'

However, to assume that there is no land at all, or that it is available in given quality and unlimited quantity, is unnecessarily restrictive. With the system growing without end, and setting aside land-saving technical progress as contemplated by Ricardo (*Works*, I, Chapter II; see also Gehrke *et al.* 2003),

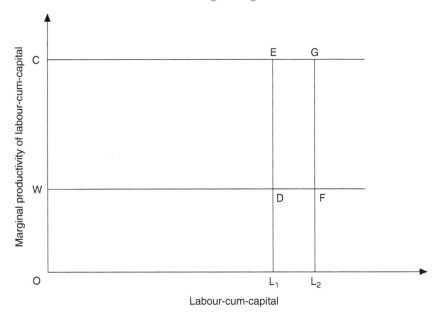

Figure 12.3 Land as a free good

the point will surely come when land of the best quality will become scarce. This brings us to another constellation in which the rate of profits need not vanish as capital accumulates. The constellation under consideration bears a close resemblance to a case discussed in the economics of 'exhaustible' resources: the existence of an ultimate 'backstop technology'. For example, some exhaustible resources are used to produce energy. In addition, there is solar energy that may be considered a non-depletable resource. A technology based on the use of solar energy defines the backstop technology mentioned. Let us now translate this assumption into the context of a Ricardian model with land.

The case under consideration would correspond to a situation in which 'land', although useful in production, is not indispensable. In other words, there is a technology that allows the production of the commodity without any 'land' input; this is the backstop technology. With continuous substitutability between labour-cum-capital and land, the marginal productivity of labour-cum-capital would be continuously decreasing, but it would be bounded from below. This case is illustrated in Figure 12.4, with the dashed line giving the lower boundary. In this case, the profit rate and thus the growth rate would be falling, but they could never fall below certain – positive – levels. The system would grow indefinitely at a rate of growth which would asymptotically approach the product of the given saving rate times the value of the (lower) boundary of the profit rate. In Figure 12.4 the latter is given by WR/OW.

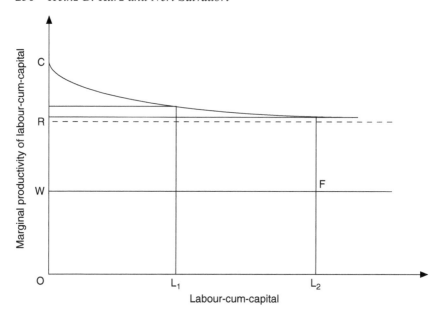

Figure 12.4 A backstop technology

Also in this case we may take into account the possibility contemplated in the above that a higher rate of growth of the work force might require a higher level of the real wage rate. In an expanding system the level of the real wage rate will therefore exceed the level required to keep the work force stationary. The WF curve that in Figure 12.4 is a horizontal straight line becomes a decreasing curve with the horizontal asymptote passing through the point

$$R' = \left(0, \frac{\sqrt{(1-s)^2 \, \bar{w}^2 + 4s\bar{w}\mathrm{OR}} + (1-s)\bar{w}}{2} \right)$$

not in the figure, where $\bar{w}$ < OR' < OR if and only if $\bar{w}$ < OR. The rate of profits would be bounded from below at a positive level.

To conclude, it must be stressed again that the Ricardesque paths of endogenous growth illustrated in Figures 12.1–12.4 depend on the fact that labour is considered as a commodity that is (in some sense) 'produced' by means of corn and nothing else. In this conceptualisation the real wage rate is dealt with 'on the same footing as the fuel for the engines or the feed for the cattle', as an attentive interpreter of the classical economists remarked. Using neoclassical terminology, the straight line WF might be interpreted as the 'marginal cost function' related to the 'production' of labour. If the wage rate depends on the growth rate and thus on the amount of work employed, then the marginal cost function ceases to be a straight line.

However, this does not affect the substance of the argument. Put in a nut-shell, the 'secret' of the endogeneity of growth in classical authors consists in the assumption that there is a built-in mechanism producing labour, where the rate of production is attuned to the needs of capital accumulation. In this way the non-accumulable factor 'labour' is deprived of the capacity to bring the growth process to a halt.

Classical and neoclassical approaches

Contributions to the classical theory of value and distribution, notwith-standing the many differences between authors, share a common feature: when investigating the relationship between the system of relative prices and income distribution, they start from the same set of data or independent variables. These are:

(C1)   the technical conditions of production of the various commodities,
(C2)   the size and composition of the social product,
(C3)   one of the distributive variables: either the wage rate or the rate of profits, and
(C4)   the available quantities of natural resources, in particular, land.

In correspondence with the underlying long-period competitive position of the economy, the capital stock is assumed to be fully adjusted to these data. Hence the 'normal' desired pattern of utilisation of plant and equipment would be realised, and a uniform rate of return on its supply price obtained.

This analytical structure is also reflected in the simple one-sector models presented in the previous section. Data (C1) and (C4) determine the curve which links the marginal productivity of labour-cum-capital to the amount of labour employed, data (C2) specifies a point on that curve and finally data (C3) determines the distribution of the product. Once the latter is ascertained, growth is determined by the saving-alias-investment or accumulation func-tion (in the case under consideration by equation $g = sr$).

By contrast, the marginalist theories of value and distribution typically start from the following data or independent variables:

(M1)   the set of technical alternatives from which cost-minimising produ-cers can choose,
(M2)   the preferences of consumers, and
(M3)   the initial endowments of the economy and the distribution of prop-erty rights among individual agents.

It is easily checked that (M1) is not very different from (C1), whereas (C2) could be thought of as reflecting (M2). What makes the two theories really different are the data (C3) and (M3). However, in the special case in which there is no labour in the economy – and therefore (C3) is automatically deleted because the rate of profits would be endogenously determined and could not be given from outside the system – (M3) would not be very different from (C4).

It will be shown that it is a characteristic feature of some of the most prominent contributions to the modern literature on endogenous growth that they eliminate labour from the picture and put in its stead 'human capital' or 'knowledge', that is, something that a twentieth century audience can accept as a producible (and accumulable) factor of production. However, the conditions of production of this *surrogate of labour* play exactly the same role played in the classical analysis by the assumption of a given real wage rate. This chapter attempts first and foremost to provide a clear statement of this fact.

A theory based on the typical marginalist set of data (M1)-(M3) is hardly able to determine growth endogenously. It would presumably not be much of an exaggeration to claim that the majority of neoclassical authors have been concerned with developing theories that revolved around the concept of an *exogenously* given long-term rate of economic growth. It suffices to recall the efforts of some of the leading advocates of marginalism. Thus, in Chapter V of Book V of his *Principles of Economics*, Alfred Marshall first introduced the 'famous fiction of the stationary state' and then tried to weaken the strong assumptions required by it:

> The Stationary state has just been taken to be one in which population is stationary. But nearly all its distinctive features may be exhibited in a place where population and wealth are both growing, provided they are growing at about the same rate, and there is no scarcity of land: and provided also the methods of production and the conditions of trade change but little; and above all, where the character of man himself is a constant quantity. For in such a state by far the most important conditions of production and consumption, of exchange and distribution will remain of the same quality, and in the same general relations to one another, though they are all increasing in volume.
>
> (Marshall [1890] 1977: 306)

The resulting economic system grows at a constant rate that equals the exogenous rate of growth of population.[6] Income distribution and relative prices are the same as in the stationary economy. In modern parlance: the system expands along a steady-state growth path.

We encounter essentially the same idea in Gustav Cassel's *Theoretische Sozialökonomie* (Cassel [1918] 1932). The model of exogenous growth delineated by Cassel can be considered the proximate starting point of the development of neoclassical growth theory. In Chapter IV of Book I of the treatise, Cassel presented two models, one of a stationary economy, the other one of an economy growing along a steady-state path.

In his first model, Cassel assumed that there are z (primary) factors of production. The quantities of these resources and thus the amounts of services provided by them are taken to be in given supply. The *n* goods produced in the economy are pure consumption goods, that is, there are no produced means of production or capital goods contemplated in the model. Goods are produced exclusively by combining primary factor services at fixed technical coefficients of production. There are as many single-product processes of production as there are goods to be produced; hence there is no choice of technique. General equilibrium is characterised by the following sets of equations: (1) equality of supply and demand for each factor service; (2) equality of the price of a good and its cost of production, that is, the sum total of factor service payments incurred in its production, and thus the absence of what in this literature is called profit; (3) equality of supply and demand for each good produced, where the demand for each good is conceived as a function of the prices of all goods. The resulting sets of equations constitute what is known as the 'Walras-Cassel model' (Dorfman *et al.* 1958: 346). It satisfied the then going criterion of completeness: there are as many equations as there are unknowns to be ascertained.[7]

Cassel then turned to the model of a uniformly progressing economy (which he described only verbally). He introduced it as follows:

> We must now take into consideration the society which is progressing at a uniform rate. In it, the quantities of the factors of production which are available in each period … are subject to a uniform increase. We shall represent by [g] the *fixed rate of this increase*, and of the uniform progress of the society generally.
>
> (Cassel [1918] 1932: 152, emphasis added)

In Cassel's view this generalisation to the case of an economy growing at an exogenously given and constant rate does not cause substantial problems. The previously developed set of equations can easily be adapted to it, 'so that the whole pricing problem is solved' (ibid: 153). Cassel thus arrived at basically the same result as Marshall.

The method which marginalist economists, including those just mentioned, generally adopted up till the 1930s was the long-period method inherited from the classical authors. However, with their fundamentally different kind of analysis – demand and supply theory – they encountered formidable problems. These originated with their concept of capital. The sought determination of income distribution in terms of the demand for and the supply of the different factors of production – labour, land and capital – necessitated that they specify the capital endowment of the economy at a given point in time in terms of a 'quantity of capital' that could be ascertained independently of, and prior to, the determination of relative prices and the rate of profits.

Yet, as Erik Lindahl and others understood very well, this was possible only in the exceptionally special case of a corn model in which there was but a single capital good. In order to apply the demand and supply approach to all economic phenomena, neoclassical authors were thus compelled to abandon long-period analysis and develop in its stead intertemporal (and temporary) equilibrium analysis.

Here is not the place to enter into a detailed discussion of these developments (see therefore, for example, Kurz and Salvadori 1995, Chapter 14). We rather jump several decades and turn immediately to the reasons for the recent resumption of (some special form of) long-period analysis in 'new' growth theory. Until a few decades ago, the number of commodities and, as a consequence, the time horizon in intertemporal general equilibrium theory was assumed to be finite and, therefore, arbitrary.

> The principal objection to the restriction to a finite number of goods is that it requires a finite horizon and there is no natural way to choose the final period. Moreover, since there will be terminal stocks in the final period there is no natural way to value them without contemplating future periods in which they will be used
>
> (McKenzie 1987: 507)

The introduction of an *infinite* horizon turned out to be critical (see also Burgstaller 1994: 43–8). It pushed the analysis inevitably towards the long period, albeit only in the very special sense of *steady state.*[8] This was clearly spelled out, for instance, by Robert Lucas in a contribution to the theories of endogenous growth. He observed that

> [F]or *any* initial capital $K(0) > 0$, the optimal capital-consumption path $(K(t), c(t))$ will converge to the balanced path asymptotically. That is, the balanced path will be a good approximation to any actual path 'most' of the time [and that] this is exactly the reason why the balanced path is interesting to us.
>
> (Lucas 1988: 11)

Lucas thus advocated a *(re-)switching* from an intertemporal analysis to a steady-state one. Since the balanced path of the intertemporal model is the only path analysed by Lucas, in the perspective under consideration the intertemporal model may be regarded simply as a step toward obtaining a rigorous steady-state setting.

Moreover, Lucas abandoned one of the characteristic features of all neoclassical theories, that is, income distribution is determined by demand and supply of factors of production. If we concentrate on the balanced path, capital in the initial period *cannot* be taken as given along with other 'initial endowments'. Since distribution cannot be determined by demand and supply of capital and labour, in Lucas's model it is determined in the following way. Labour is considered the vehicle of 'human capital', that is, a producible factor. Hence all factors are taken to be producible and the rate of profits is determined as in Chapter II of *Production of Commodities by Means of Commodities* (Sraffa 1960). At the beginning of that chapter (§§ 4–5), wages are regarded as entering the system 'on the same footing as the fuel for the engines or the feed for the cattle'. In this case the rate of profits and prices are determined by the socio-technical conditions of production alone – the 'methods of production and productive consumption' (Sraffa 1960: 3). The introduction of several alternative processes of production does not change the result.

The similarity between the determination of the rate of profit in Lucas's model and at the beginning of Chapter II of Sraffa's book is not surprising, since the assumption of a given real wage rate, put in a growth framework, is formally equivalent to the assumption that there is a technology producing 'labour'. The 'human capital' story could be seen as simply a rhetorical device to render the idea of a given real wage more palatable to modern scholars. As regards their basic analytical structure (as opposed to their building blocks), some of the so-called 'new' growth theories can therefore be said to exhibit a certain resemblance to 'classical' economics. In particular, in the free competition versions of the theory, the 'technology' to produce 'human capital' (or, alternatively, 'knowledge' in some approaches) plays the same role as the assumption of a given real wage rate in 'classical' economics.

From the end of Chapter II of *Production of Commodities by Means of Commodities* to the end of the book, workers may get a part of the surplus. As a consequence, the quantity of labour employed in each industry has to be represented explicitly, and the rate of profits and prices can be determined only if an extra equation determining income distribution is introduced into the analysis. The additional equation generally used by advocates of neoclassical analysis is the equality between the demand for and the supply of 'capital', which requires the homogeneity of this factor.[9] But no extra equation is required in the class of 'new' growth theories under consideration, since as in the Ricardo we dealt with here there is a mechanism attuning the size of the workforce – dubbed 'human capital' or 'knowledge' in the literature under consideration – to the requirements of an expanding economic system.

Concluding remarks

We have argued that in the classical economists economic growth and development of a nation were considered genuinely endogenous. This is exemplified with respect to a highly stylised version of one aspect encountered in the writings of the classical authors, especially Ricardo: The 'natural' course an economy would follow in the hypothetical case in which capital accumulates and the population grows but there is no technical change.

The respective argument is expounded in terms of a simple 'corn' model. In the constellation under consideration, decreasing returns will sooner or later make themselves felt due to the scarcity of land(s). With the real wage rate given and constant the rate of profits is bound to fall and the rents of land will increase. The falling tendency of the rate of profits entails a deceleration of capital accumulation and growth until the system comes to a standstill (setting aside depletable resources). Essentially the same holds true in the case in which a higher rate of growth of the workforce requires a higher real wage rate, reflecting some kind of Malthusian population mechanism. It is argued that the latter does not affect the basic logic of the classical point of view, namely, that in the conditions contemplated, the pace at which capital accumulates regulates the pace at which the labouring population grows. In other words, labour is considered as generated within the process of capital accumulation and thus cannot bring growth to a halt. Growth might, however, be suffocated by the scarcity of natural resources, especially land.

Next we dealt briefly with neoclassical models of growth whose natural starting point was a system in which the long-term rate of growth equals some exogenously given rate of growth of the factor(s) of production. It is then argued that the endogenisation of the growth rate in a class of 'new' growth models is effected in a way that is reminiscent of classical economics. In the Solow model labour is treated as a non-producible and non-accumulable factor of production whose fixed rate of growth constrains the long-term expansion of the economic system. In contradistinction, in some new growth models this factor is replaced by 'human capital' or 'knowledge', which are taken to be producible, accumulable or costlessly transferable among subsequent generations of the population. Very much like the classical assumption of a given real wage rate this is equivalent to the assumption that there is a mechanism generating 'labour'.

Acknowledgements

This chapter uses some of the material contained in some earlier papers by us on the so-called 'new' growth theory; see, in particular, Kurz and Salvadori (1996, 1998a, 1998b, 1999). We thank Christian Gehrke, Mark Knell and Rodolfo Signorino for useful comments.

References

Burgstaller, A. (1994) *Property and Prices. Toward a Unified Theory of Value*, Cambridge: Cambridge University Press.
Cassel, G. (1932) *The Theory of Social Economy*, revised English translation of the 5th German edition of Cassel (1918), *Theoretische Sozialökonomie*, by L. Barron, New York: Harcourt Brace.
Dorfman, R., Samuelson, P. A. and Solow, R. M. (1958) *Linear Programming and Economic Analysis*, New York, Toronto and London: McGraw-Hill.
Eltis, W. (1984) *The Classical Theory of Economic Growth*, London: Macmillan.
Garegnani, P. (1976) 'On a Change in the Notion of Equilibrium in Recent Work on Value and Distribution', in M. Brown, K. Sato and P. Zarembka (eds), *Essays in Modern Capital Theory*, Amsterdam: North Holland.
Gehrke, C, Kurz, H. D. and Salvadori, N. (2003) 'Ricardo on Agricultural Improvements: A Note', *Scottish Journal of Political Economy*, 50: 291–6.

Hicks, J. and Hollander, S. (1977) 'Mr. Ricardo and the Moderns', *Quarterly Journal of Economics*, 91: 351–69.

Kaldor, N. (1955–56) 'Alternative Theories of Distribution', *Review of Economic Studies*, 23: 83–100.

Kurz, H. D. and Salvadori, N. (1995) *Theory of Production. A Long-period Analysis*, Cambridge, Melbourne and New York: Cambridge University Press.

Kurz, H. D. and Salvadori, N. (1996) 'In the Beginning All the World Was Australia ...', in M. Sawyer (ed.), *Festschrift in Honour of G. C. Harcourt*, London: Routledge, vol. II: 425–43.

Kurz, H. D. and Salvadori, N. (1998a) 'The "New" Growth Theory: Old Wine in New Goatskins', in F. Coricelli, M. Di Matteo and F. H. Hahn (eds), *New Theories in Growth and Development*, London: Macmillan, and New York: St. Martin's Press: 63–94.

Kurz, H. D. and Salvadori, N. (1998b) ' "Endogenous" Growth Models and the "Classical" Tradition', in H. D. Kurz and N. Salvadori, *Understanding 'Classical' Economics*, London: Routledge: 66–89.

Kurz, H. D. and Salvadori, N. (1999) 'Theories of "Endogenous" Growth in Historical Perspective', in Murat R. Sertel (ed.), *Contemporary Economic Issues. Proceedings of the Eleventh World Congress of the International Economic Association, Tunis. Volume 4, Economic Behaviour and Design*, London: Macmillan, and New York: St. Martin's Press: 225–61.

Kurz, H. D. and Salvadori, N. (2003) 'Theories of Economic Growth – Old and New', in Neri Salvadori (ed.), *The Theory of Economic Growth: A 'Classical' Perspective*, Cheltenham (UK): Edward Elgar: 1–22.

Lowe, A. (1954) 'The Classical Theory of Growth', *Social Research*, 21: 127–58.

Lucas, R. E. (1988) 'On the Mechanisms of Economic Development', *Journal of Monetary Economics*, 22: 3–42.

Marshall, A. (1977) *Principles of Economics*, reprint of the 8th edn (1920), 1st edn 1890, London and Basingstoke: Macmillan.

McKenzie, L. W. (1987) 'General Equilibrium', *The New Palgrave. A Dictionary of Economics*, edited by J. Eatwell, P. Newman and M. Milgate, London: Macmillan, vol. II: 498–512.

Pasinetti, L. L. (1960) 'A Mathematical Formulation of the Ricardian System', *Review of Economic Studies*, 27: 78–98.

Ricardo, D. (1951–72) *The Works and Correspondence of David Ricardo*, edited by Piero Sraffa with the collaboration of M. H. Dobb, Vols I, II, VI and VIII, Cambridge: Cambridge University Press.

Samuelson, P. A. (1959) 'A Modern Treatment of the Ricardian Economy: I. The Pricing of Goods and of Labor and Land Services; II. Capital and Interest Aspects of the Pricing Process', *Quarterly Journal of Economics*, 73: 1–35; 79: 217–31.

Solow, R. M. (1956) 'A Contribution to the Theory of Economic Growth,' *Quarterly Journal of Economics*, 70: 65–94.

Sraffa, P. (1960) *Production of Commodities by Means of Commodities*, Cambridge: Cambridge University Press.

Stirati, A. (1994) *The Theory of Wages in Classical Economics. A Study of Adam Smith, David Ricardo, and their Contemporaries*, Aldershot: Edward Elgar.

Notes

1 This path must, of course, not be identified with the actual path the economy is taking because technical progress will repeatedly offset the impact of the 'niggardliness of nature' on the rate of profits.

2 Real wages may rise, that is, the 'market price of labour' may rise above the 'natural' wage rate. This is the case in a situation in which capital accumulates rapidly, leading to an excess demand for labour. As Ricardo put it, 'notwithstanding the tendency of wages to conform to their natural rate, their market rate may, in an improving society, *for an indefinite period*, be constantly above it' (ibid: 94–5, emphasis added). If such a constellation prevails for some time it is even possible that 'custom renders absolute necessaries' what in the past had been comforts or luxuries. Hence, the natural wage is driven upward by persistently high levels of the actual wage rate. Accordingly, the concept of 'natural wage' in Ricardo is a flexible one and must not be mistaken for a physiological subsistence minimum. See Stirati (1994) and Kurz and Salvadori (1995, Chapter 15).

3 In the more sophisticated conceptualisations underlying the arguments of Smith and Ricardo, higher rates of growth of labour supply presuppose higher levels of the real wage rate. But as we shall see below, the basic logic remains the same: In normal conditions the pace at which capital accumulates regulates the pace at which labour grows.

4 The parallel tendency of the rate of profits and the real wage rate to fall contemplated in the cited passage has recently gained some prominence in the so-called 'New View' of the long-run trend of wages. See, in particular, Hicks and Hollander (1977). These interpreters of Ricardo (and of the classical economists at large) feel entitled to superimpose onto Ricardo's analysis the marginalist concept of a 'labour market', conceived of in the conventional way in terms of the confrontation of a demand and a supply function. It should be noted, however, that this concept is extraneous to classical thinking.

5 If $r_{min} > 0$, then $\bar{w}(1+g) = \dfrac{\sqrt{\left[1 - s(1 + r_{min})\right]^2 \bar{w}^2 + 4sf(L)\bar{w}} + \left[1 - s(1 + r_{min})\right]\bar{w}}{2}$

6 It should be noted that Marshall saw reason to suppose that the growth of population depended, among other things, on socio-economic factors and thus could not sensibly be treated, other than in a first step of the analysis, as exogenous (Marshall [1890] 1977, Book IV, Chapter IV).

7 The approach to the theory of general equilibrium in terms of equations was criticised by Knut Wicksell, Hans Neisser, Heinrich von Stackelberg, Frederick Zeuthen, Karl Schlesinger and Abraham Wald and led to the development of the neoclassical theory of general equilibrium in terms of inequalities coupled with the introduction of the Rule of Free Goods (or free disposal assumption); see Kurz and Salvadori (1995, Chapter 13, Section 7).

8 It should be stressed that, contrary to some neoclassical interpreters, in the classical economists the long-period method was not limited to steady states. Indeed, in their analyses (as well as in early marginalist authors such as Knut Wicksell, who still shared to a considerable extent the concerns of the classical economists) the steady state played no essential role whatsoever. See on this the penetrating study of Garegnani (1976).

9 This is the famous critique of that theory put forward in the 1960s; for a review of that critique, see, for example, Kurz and Salvadori (1995, Chapter 14).

13 Pasinetti versus Rebelo: two different models or just one?*

Simone D'Alessandro and Neri Salvadori

Introduction

Pasinetti (1960) reformulated the Ricardian theory of accumulation in terms of a two-sector model involving three social classes: workers, capitalists, and landlords. Rebelo (1991)[1] introduced *another* model in order to show that increasing returns are not necessary to obtain endogenous growth and that it is enough to assume that the capital goods that are indispensable in production can themselves be produced without the direct or indirect contribution of factors that cannot be accumulated, such as land. In this chapter, we start from the model introduced by Pasinetti and show that small changes concerning the assumed pattern of consumption of the three mentioned social classes are able to obtain Rebelo's model.

The main motivation of this analysis concerns the interpretation of much of what is known as the "new growth theory." In a number of papers Kurz and Salvadori (1998a, 1999; see also Kurz, 1997; Salvadori, 1998) have argued that the structure of some of the models developed within this theory is substantially "Classical" rather than "Neo-Classical" since it does not determine the rate of profit in terms of the demand and supply of capital, but in terms of a "technology" producing, in the different approaches, "human capital" or "knowledge," a procedure that is analytically equivalent to the assumption of a given real wage rate adopted by Classical economists, most notably Adam Smith and David Ricardo. This claim concerns the structure of the theory and not the tools adopted to obtain the results, which are typical of the modern neoclassical toolbox (representative agent, utility maximization, rational expectations, and so on). Take the example of intertemporal equilibrium. In many contributions to "new growth theory" it is introduced just in order to obtain a rigorous steady-state setting. The consequence is that capital cannot be considered as given in the long period and exactly the same results could be obtained with no reference to any intertemporal equilibrium by assuming a long-period setting in which, as for Classical economists, the amounts of capital goods and labor are not given, but are adapted to the requirements of

* Reproduced with permission from *Journal of Economic Behavior & Organization*, 65(3), 2008.

society. The analysis presented in this chapter confirms the claim put forward by Kurz and Salvadori, since the Classical derivation of the model investigated by Pasinetti is undisputed.[2]

Another reason to perform the analysis provided in this chapter is derived from the literature on the descriptive value of the AK model. Whereas authors such as Jones (1995) and Whelan (2003) have argued that the traditional one-sector model of economic growth provides a poor description of the long-run behavior of industrial economies, Felbermayr and Licandro (2005) have maintained that the two-sector AK model explains important stylized facts[3] about the different behaviors of the sectors producing investment and consumption goods since the end of World War II. The consumption patterns depicted in the Ricardian two-commodity model can then be considered as reflecting the fact that in the eighteenth century workers consumed mainly agricultural commodities whereas the consumption patterns depicted in Rebelo's model may reflect the fact that workers in industrial countries, since the mid twentieth century, have consumed mainly industrial commodities. Therefore Pasinetti's and Rebelo's models, having the same structural framework, can be interpreted as two different phases of the transition of the economy from the early Industrial Revolution to mature capitalism.

Following Ricardo and using Occam's razor, Pasinetti assumed that (i) workers consume all their wages in necessary goods (that is, agricultural commodities produced by using land), (ii) capitalists do not consume: they invest all their profits, (iii) landlords consume all their rents in terms of luxury goods (that is, industrial commodities produced without using land). The model is a two-commodity model, and the two commodities are called "corn" and "gold." These evocative names remind us that corn, the agricultural commodity, is intended as a necessary good and that the industrial commodity, gold, is intended as a luxury good. In this chapter, we reverse the consumption patterns: the industrial commodity is a necessary good that is consumed by workers, whereas the agricultural commodity is consumed by landlords *and* capitalists. Consumption by capitalists is a necessary ingredient of our manipulation of Pasinetti's model: if the agricultural commodity were consumed only by landlords, it would never be produced since there would be no demand for it. Readers can readily understand that we had difficulties using the labels "corn" and "gold" for the agricultural and the industrial commodity, respectively. A solution would have been to use two other names, like "champagne" and "bread," differing from those used by Pasinetti. In the end, we decided to leave the names used by Pasinetti, alerting readers that they must disregard the evocative meanings of such names and, therefore, must not be confused by the fact that workers consume "gold" and capitalists and landlords consume "corn": a name is just a name. What is important is that this simple manipulation transforms Pasinetti's model into Rebelo's model.

The chapter is organized in the following way. The second section starts with the description of technology used by Pasinetti. By introducing into it the assumption that workers consume only gold and that the wage rate is fixed in terms of gold instead of corn, the description of technology depicted by Rebelo is obtained. The third section determines prices and distribution variables. A comparison with the results obtained by Pasinetti and Rebelo is also provided. The fourth section deals with dynamical systems, and the equivalence among the models studied by Pasinetti and Rebelo is obtained. The final section concludes.

Technology

Pasinetti describes technology with two simple production functions. The physical quantity of corn produced, X_1, is a function of the number of workers employed in corn production, N_1:[4]

$$X_1 = f(N_1), \quad f(0) \geq 0, \quad f'(0) > \bar{x}, \quad f''(N_1) < 0, \tag{1}$$

where $\bar{x}$ is the natural wage-rate in terms of corn (since workers are assumed to consume only corn in Pasinetti's model), which in a simplified formulation of the model is considered as given.[5] The physical quantity of gold produced, X_2, is proportional to the number of workers employed in corn production N_2:

$$X_2 = aN_2. \tag{2}$$

Obviously

$$N = N_1 + N_2,$$

$$K = W = \bar{x}N,$$

where N is the total number of workers, W the total wage-bill, and K is the physical stock of capital (both measured in terms of corn). The role of "capital" may appear peculiar in this model. From a purely technological point of view there is no technical capital in the model, in the sense that there is no material input needed to produce either corn or gold; corn is produced by means of labor and land and gold is produced by means of labor alone. However, wages need to be anticipated to laborers, so capital consists in the anticipation of wages and a profit is obtained since production requires time.

Contrary to Pasinetti's original formulation, in the present chapter we assume that workers consume only gold. Hence we can define

$$Z_1 := \bar{x}N_1 = \phi Z$$

$$Z_2 := \bar{x}N_2 = (1 - \phi)Z$$

$$Z_1 + Z_2 = Z,$$

where $\bar{x}$ is the (given) natural wage-rate in terms of *gold* (since workers are assumed to consume only *gold* in our manipulation of Pasinetti's model); Z_1, Z_2, and Z are the amounts of capital used in the production of corn, in the production of gold, and in the whole economy, respectively. The change of symbols from K to Z to indicate "capital" is justified by the desire to use the symbols used by Rebelo. Then Eqs. (1) and (2) become

$$X_1 = F(Z_1) := f\left(\frac{Z_1}{\bar{x}}\right), \quad F(0) \geq 0, \quad F'(0) > 1, \quad F''(Z_1) < 0,$$

$$X_2 = AZ_2,$$

(3)

where $A = a/\bar{x} > 1$. The reader can easily check that these are exactly the production functions used by Rebelo, the only difference being that Rebelo uses a Cobb-Douglas form of Eq. (3). In the following we will follow Rebelo in assuming that the production function of corn is of the Cobb-Douglas type:[6]

$$X_1 = BZ_1^\alpha T^{1-\alpha} = \beta Z_1^\alpha,$$

where T is the fixed amount of land and B is a positive constant.

Prices, rent, and rate of profit

Following Ricardo, and Pasinetti, the rent in terms of corn R equals the net gain of the owners of the more fertile lands with respect to the owners of the marginal land. That is

$$R = f(N_1) - N_1 f'(N_1) = F(Z_1) - Z_1 F'(Z_1) = \beta Z_1^\alpha - \alpha \beta Z_1^\alpha.$$

(4)

Then prices are determined taking into account that, under the usual assumption of perfect competition in capital market, the rate of profit on the use of gold as capital, r_2, is uniform among all its employments:

$$X_1 p_1 = Rp_1 + (\delta + r_2)Z_1 p_2$$

$$X_2 p_2 = (\delta + r_2)Z_2 p_2,$$

(5)

where δ is the depreciation rate of gold.[7] Setting corn as the numeraire ($p_1 = 1$), we obtain[8]

$$r_2 = A - \delta$$

$$p_2 = \frac{F'(Z_1)}{A} = \frac{\alpha \beta}{A} Z_1^{\alpha-1}.$$

(6)

The rate of profit r_2 is determined only by the conditions of production of gold, whereas the conditions of production of corn concur only to determine the price of corn in terms of gold.

If we compare this with the results obtained by Pasinetti, we see that relative prices are the same, but the rate of profit is determined only by the conditions of production of corn, whereas the conditions of production of gold concur only to determine the price of corn in terms of gold. Pasinetti was aware of the reason why the rate of profit is independent of the conditions of production of the luxury good:

> The independence of the rate of profit from the conditions of production of luxury-goods is a property of all the theoretical models which use the distinction between wage- and luxury-goods. In plain words, it is due to the peculiarity that wage-goods are necessary to produce any type of goods, while luxury-goods are not. Mr. Sraffa pointed out to me that the property was first discovered by Ladislaus von Bortkiewicz.
>
> (pp. 85f)

He was also conscious of the fact that if there is no physical capital, then prices are proportional to labor inputs and since labor inputs are invariant regarding changes in the consumption patterns, it should not come as a surprise that relative prices are here the same as those found by Pasinetti. Another important difference is that when workers consume only gold, the rate of profit on capital invested (gold) is constant over time, whereas when workers consume only corn the rate of profit on capital invested (corn) is a decreasing function of invested capital. We will see that this is the reason why Pasinetti, following Ricardo's perspective, predicts a decreasing growth rate until the stationary state is reached, whereas in this chapter we predict, with Rebelo, that the economy grows forever and if appropriate assumptions on saving and investment hold, it does so at a constant rate. Hence the differences between the model here presented and that presented by Pasinetti are clearly comprehensible within the logic of Pasinetti's model.

If we compare the above results with the results derived by Rebelo, there is no difference between his equations and ours. Rebelo makes also an interesting remark concerning the rates of profit:

> Given that $[p_2]$ is not constant, the real interest rate for loans denominated in capital goods ($[r_2]$) is different from that of consumption-denominated loans ($[r_1]$).
>
> (p. 504)

Obviously the Fisher formula applies and therefore,

$$r_1 = r_2 + g_p, \tag{7}$$

where g_p is the growth rate of price p_2:

$$g_p := \frac{\dot{p_2}}{p_2} = \frac{Z_1 F''(Z_1)}{F'(Z_1)} \frac{\dot{Z_1}}{Z_1} = (a-1)\frac{\dot{Z_1}}{Z_1}. \tag{8}$$

Dynamical properties

All but the last relations we found among variables are static in the sense that they do not refer to changes of variables over time. As mentioned in a foot-note above, in the paper by Pasinetti two kinds of dynamics are considered: the dynamics of population and that of capital. The former affects the real wage rate, which we have considered as given and constant here, and will, as a consequence, be ignored. The latter is represented by Pasinetti by assuming that the derivative of capital with respect to time is a known increasing func-tion of total profits. In our formalism,

$$\dot{Z} = \Phi(r_2 Z), \quad \Phi'(r_2 Z) > 0.$$

Obviously function $\Phi(r_2 Z)$ can only be interpreted as a consequence of capi-talists' preferences with regard to investment. Pasinetti does not attempt to determine this function. At that time the concept of microfoundation was not popular. What he considered relevant was the fact that net investment is positive (and therefore the growth rate is positive) when profits are larger than a known threshold. In a footnote Pasinetti also refers to "a minimum rate of profit ... necessary in order to induce capital accumulation" (p. 14), but he never puts this relationship in terms of rates instead of absolute values. Otherwise he would have put this relationship as

$$\frac{\dot{Z}}{Z} = \varphi(r_2), \quad \varphi'(r_2) > 0. \tag{9}$$

A function of this type does not change the structure of Pasinetti's model and is certainly more suitable for a comparison with modern literature. Indeed this is the relationship we will use in the following.

Rebelo, on the other hand, assumes a constant population composed of identical agents who seek to maximize utility. The result of this maximizing problem is that the growth rate of consumption, g_1, equals a function of the interest rate for consumption-denominated loans r_1:

$$g_1 = \frac{r_1 - \rho}{\sigma}, \tag{10}$$

where ρ is the intertemporal discount rate and $\sigma > 0$ is a parameter of the instantaneous utility function. Since in our presentation workers and landlords are not assumed to save, only capitalists have to choose between saving-investment and consumption.

In order to clarify that the two models are different sides of the same coin, let us first determine investment, $\dot{Z}$, and consumption by capitalists, C, by taking account of the facts that the gold industry produces the only capital good (that is wage good) and the corn industry produces only consumption goods for capitalists and landlords. Therefore in equilibrium we must have

$$C = X_1 - R = Z_1 F'(Z_1) = \alpha \beta Z_1^\alpha,$$
$$\dot{Z} + \delta Z = X_2 = A Z_2.$$

From the former we get

$$g_1 := \frac{\dot{C}}{C} = \left[1 + \frac{Z_1 F''(Z_1)}{F'(Z_1)}\right]\frac{\dot{Z}_1}{Z_1} = \alpha \frac{\dot{Z}_1}{Z_1}, \tag{11}$$

and from the latter we obtain that

$$\frac{Z_2}{Z} = \frac{1}{A}\frac{\dot{Z}}{Z} + \frac{\delta}{A},$$

so that in steady state Z_2/Z is constant and therefore

$$g_2 := \frac{\dot{Z}}{Z} = \frac{\dot{Z}_1}{Z_1} = \frac{\dot{Z}_2}{Z_2}. \tag{12}$$

Hence from (6)–(8) and (10)–(12) we obtain

$$\alpha g_2 = g_1 = \frac{A - \delta + (\alpha - 1)g_2 - \rho}{\sigma};$$

that is,[9]

$$g_2 = \frac{A - \delta - \rho}{1 - \alpha(1 - \sigma)} \tag{13}$$

$$g_1 = \alpha\frac{A - \delta - \rho}{1 - \alpha(1 - \sigma)} \tag{14}$$

which coincide with the results obtained by Rebelo. Finally, it is easily checked that the same outcome is obtained if instead of Eq. (10) we use Eq. (9) with the special form[10]

$$\frac{\dot{Z}}{Z} = \frac{r_2 - \rho}{1 - \sigma(1 - \sigma)},$$

(15)

which is increasing in r_2 since $0 < \alpha < 1$ and $\sigma > 0$. In fact, Eqs. (6), (15), (11), (12) determine again Eqs. (13) and (14). This remark completes the proof of the equivalence between the modified Pasinetti's model here presented and Rebelo's model. Rebelo's model can be interpreted as a modified Pasinetti's model in which workers consume gold instead of corn, both landlords and capitalists consume only corn, and, further, the production function in the corn sector is a Cobb-Douglas and the investment function (9) has the form (15).

Concluding remarks

In this chapter, we have compared Pasinetti's model formalizing Ricardian growth theory and Rebelo's model, which is one of the simplest models developed within the "new" growth literature. We have shown that both models share the same structure in the sense that they consist of the same set of equations, even if the interpretation given to these equations and to the symbols involved may be different. We have argued that this is an important result for the interpretation of the recent literature on growth since it renders some support to the thesis that many endogenous growth models have a 'Classical' flavour since they abandoned one of the characteristic features of all neoclassical theories, that is, income distribution is determined by demand and supply of factors of production. Moreover, the switch from Pasinetti's to Rebelo's framework may also be interpreted as reflecting the change in the consumption pattern of workers from early to late industrial societies.

Acknowledgement

We thank Davide Fiaschi, Giuseppe Freni, Heinz D. Kurz, and two referees of the *Journal of Economic Behavior and Organization* for comments on previous versions of this chapter. The usual disclaimer applies.

References

Felbermayr, G.J., Licandro, O., 2005. The underestimated virtues of the two-sector AK model. *Contributions to Macroeconomics* 5, art. 9.

Freni, G., 1991. Capitale tecnico nei modelli dinamici ricardiani. *Studi Economici* 44, 141–159.

Hahn, F.H., 1975. Revival of political economy: the wrong issues and the wrong argument. *Economic Record* 51, 360–364.

Hahn, F.H., 1982. The Neo–Ricardians. *Cambridge Journal of Economics* 6, 353–374.

Kurz, H.D., 1997. What could the "new" growth theory teach Smith or Ricardo? *Economic Issues* 2, 1–20.

Kurz, H.D., Salvadori, N., 1992. Morishima on Ricardo: a review article. *Cambridge Journal of Economics* 16, 227–247.

Kurz, H.D., Salvadori, N., 1995. *Theory of Production*. Cambridge University Press, Cambridge.

Kurz, H.D., Salvadori, N., 1998a. Endogenous growth models and the "classical" tradition. In: Kurz, H.D., Salvadori, N. (Eds.), *Understanding "Classical" Economics. Studies in the Long-Period Theory*. Routledge, London and New York, pp. 66–89.

Kurz, H.D., Salvadori, N., 1998b. Morishima on Ricardo: a rejoinder. *Cambridge Journal of Economics* 22, 227–239.

Kurz, H.D., Salvadori, N., 1999. Theories of "endogenous" growth in historical perspective. In: Sertel, M.R. (Ed.), Contemporary Economic Issues. Proceedings of the Eleventh World Congress of the International Economic Association, Tunis, vol. 4, Economic Behaviour and Design. Macmillan, London, pp. 225–261.

Jones, C.I., 1995. Time series tests of endogenous growth models. *Quarterly Journal of Economics* 110, 495–525.

Morishima, M., 1996. Morishima on Ricardo: two replies. *Cambridge Journal of Economics* 20, 91–109.

Pasinetti, L.L., 1960. A mathematical formulation of the Ricardian system. *Review of Economic Studies* 27, 78–98.

Rebelo, S., 1991. Long run policy analysis and long run growth. *Journal of Political Economy* 99, 500–521.

Salvadori, N., 1998. A linear multisector model of "endogenous" growth and the problem of capital. *Metroeconomica* 49, 319–335.

Whelan, K., 2003. A two-sector approach to modeling US NIPA data. *Journal of Money, Credit, and Banking* 35, 627–656.

Notes

1 More precisely, we refer to the basic model of Rebelo's article that is analyzed in Section 2 of that paper.

2 Hahn (1975, 1982) suggested that the classical approach addresses a special case of neoclassical general equilibrium theory. Following Hahn, it could be argued that it is not surprising that in the investigation of a single topic the two approaches (one of which is a special case of the other) produce the same model. However the "special case" argument supported by Hahn does not stand up to close scrutiny (see, for instance, Kurz and Salvadori, 1995, pp. 451–455): the two approaches are founded on two sets of data none of which includes the other. On the contrary, many of the models of "new growth theory," and certainly the model by Rebelo, use a set of data which can be shown to be analogous to the set of data used by the Classical approach.

3 Following Felbermayr and Licandro (2005), since World War II (i) the price of investment goods continuously declined with respect to the price of consumer goods, (ii) nominal series of consumption and investment have a similar trend with respect to nominal output so that the consumption and investment shares in

nominal output are stationary, and (iii) the ratio of real investment to real output is non-stationary. Indeed, the growth rate or real investment has been greater than that of real consumption.

4   The construction of this production function has been the subject of an exchange between Kurz and Salvadori (1992, 1998b) and Morishima (1996). See also Freni (1991).

5   Pasinetti considered two dynamical processes: one concerning the wage rate and the other concerning the rate of profit. See also the fourth section below. Pasinetti considered the former process quicker than the latter. This allowed him to consider a model in which the former process has obtained its steady state, whereas the latter has not. Also in this chapter we take account of the latter process only. If we considered also the former, the analysis would be slightly more complex since the wage rate would be an increasing function of the growth rate.

6   The function $X_1 = BZ_1^\alpha T^{1-\alpha}$ is that used by Rebelo. Since T is constant and given, we can just set $X_1 = BZ_1^\alpha$. However we want to emphasize that the Cobb-Douglas function is not able to capture extensive rent, which presupposes a number of different qualities of land, the possibility that some qualities of land are not used in production, and the possibility that a quality of land is used only partially.

7   A $\delta \neq 1$ is unreasonable in the Pasinettian interpretation of the model in which capital consists only in advanced wages, which themselves consist of gold. But it is not unreasonable in the Rebelian interpretation in which capital consists just of gold.

8   Eq. (5) can also be written $F'(Z_1)p_1 = (\delta + r_2)p_2$; that is, formula (4) can be interpreted as a consequence of the optimizing behavior of the firms producing corn: capital is paid its marginal product.

9   If the production function of corn is not of a Cobb-Douglas type, then there is endogenous growth since $g_2 + g_p = g_1 = (A - \delta + g_p - \rho)/\sigma$ but no steady state exists. In fact, if g_p and g_2 are constant over time, then we obtain from Eq. (8) that $F'(Z_1) = EZ_1^\theta$, where $\theta = g_p/g_2$ and E is a constant of integration.

10   If the investment function (9) has not the form (15), then there is endogenous growth provided that $\varphi(A - \delta) > 0$.

Part V

Exhaustible resources

14 Ricardo on exhaustible resources, and the Hotelling Rule[*]

Heinz D. Kurz and Neri Salvadori[1]

Introduction

Modern contributions to the economics of exhaustible natural resources, such as oil or coal, generally start from one form or another of the famous 'Hotelling Rule', first put forward by Harold Hotelling (1931). The Hotelling Rule is an application of the concept of a competitive (uniform) rate of profits to all processes in the economy, whether these are conservation or production processes. In the classical economists this rule is not yet to be found. Does this mean that their analyses are of necessity defective, incomplete or inferior? Or does it only mean that their argument relates to a world characterized by conditions that are different from those contemplated by the Hotelling Rule? Or is the rule implicit in their analyses and what is missing is only an explicit reference to royalties as something different from profits?

This chapter answers these questions. As regards the classical economists we will focus attention on David Ricardo, the most 'classical' of all classical authors, and deal with Adam Smith only in passing. Takashi Negishi, in the introduction to a collection of essays devoted to the history of economic thought, stressed that 'it is necessary to study theories that are regarded as past ones from the point of view of other research programmes' (Negishi 1994: xi). Alternatively, one might study theories that are regarded as incorporating the most recent vintages of economic knowledge from the point of view of earlier approaches to the problem at hand. Comparing old and new can be expected to shed new light on both and improve our understanding on what is truly novel, what is only an old result in a new garb and on what has been lost sight of in the course of time. As Negishi put it succinctly in another contribution:

> The history of our science should be used as a mirror in which the current theory reflects the knowledge of how it failed to succeed in the past. To learn from past theories does not impede the progress of our science. Progress often means, however, sacrificing something old. To make

* Reproduced with permission from Aiko Ikeo and Heinz D. Kurz (eds), *A History of Economic Theory: Essays in Honour of Takashi Negishi*, London: Routledge, 2009.

sure that we are going in the right direction, it is always necessary to see whether we have sacrificed something in error.

(Negishi 1992: 228)

The Hotelling Rule, as it is typically presented, concerns the fact that the prices of resources *in situ* need to increase over time at a rate that is equal to the competitive rate of profits. This fact seems in turn to imply another fact, namely, that *all* prices need to change over time. As mentioned in the above, the first fact follows from the requirement that the conservation of a resource is an economic activity which ought to yield to the proprietors of deposits of the resource the same rate of profit as is obtained from any productive activity. The second fact is not immediately obvious.

The contribution of this chapter may thus be summarized in the following way. While it is commonly thought that Ricardo's treatment of exhaustible resources is to be found first and foremost in the barely three pages of Chapter III of the *Principles*, 'On the Rent of Mines', this is actually not so. This chapter is in fact confined to a discussion of the rents of differently fertile mines in complete analogy to the rents of differently fertile lands. These rents arise because the exploitation of mines is typically subject to capacity constraints which imply that mines with different costs of extraction have to be operated at the same time. Ricardo develops an analysis of exhaustible resources rather in the context of a discussion of the difference between rent and profits. He begins this discussion in Chapter II, 'On Rent', in which he also criticizes Smith's cavalier and confusing use of the two concepts. Then, in Chapter XXIV, 'Doctrine of Adam Smith concerning the Rent of Land', he elaborates on his criticism of Smith's doctrine. He illustrates the fecundity of his own, Ricardo's, rigorous conceptualizations of these two important analytical categories in political economy and shows that Smith's analysis is bound to end in a muddle. As usual, Ricardo is 'desirous only to elucidate the principle' at work (Ricardo 1951: 121), as he stresses in another context, and therefore bases his argument on strong assumptions. These assumptions, which we will explicate below, imply that the exhaustion of each and every deposit of an exhaustible resource will nevertheless leave the prices of all produced commodities unaffected over time. In this way Ricardo manages to isolate a particular phenomenon at hand and put it into sharp relief. In the context we are interested in, this refers to the distinction between differential rent and profits, where what Ricardo calls profits comprises what we nowadays call royalties. Hence royalties are there in Ricardo's analysis, but they are not easily identifiable as such.

The composition of the chapter is as follows. In the next section we specify the two fundamental assumptions required in order to be able to establish the fact that all prices need to change over time because of the Hotelling Rule. We then confront these assumptions with alternative ones which, it will be argued, are characteristic of the analyses of Smith and Ricardo. The following section, on Ricardo, provides some evidence in support of this proposition in terms of passages taken from Ricardo's *Principles*. The main differences between the world in which all prices need to change over time because of the Hotelling Rule and the world about which Ricardo wrote are the following: (i) While Smith and Ricardo were aware of the exhaustibility of each and every deposit of a resource, they did not yet contemplate the case of the exhaustibility of the resource as a whole, (ii) Ricardo assumed that in order to meet the effectual demand for a resource, several deposits typically have to be worked simultaneously, because with regard to each deposit there is a capacity constraint that limits the time rate of raising the resource. The following section provides a mathematical formulation of the Ricardian point of view which allows one to compare the latter with the one underlying the Hotelling Rule. It concludes that Ricardo may have well come up with the modern interpretation of the Hotelling Rule had he considered the case of the exhaustion of a resource in its entirety as a realistic possibility, which apparently he did not. Hence, a modern formulation of Ricardo's view may complement the view expressed by the Hotelling Rule and thus render the overall argument about exhaustible resources more complete. The final section contains some concluding remarks.[2]

Different assumptions – different worlds

The modern interpretation of the Hotelling Rule presupposes that the following two assumptions hold:

(H1)   The resource is available in homogeneous quality and in an overall quantity that is limited and that at any moment of time is known with certainty.

(H2)   The amount of the resource that can be extracted in a given period of time, a year, for example, is only constrained by the amount of it left over from the preceding period.

(H stands, of course, for Hotelling.) In case one of these assumptions, or both, is not met, the Hotelling Rule has to be modified according to circumstances. It portrays a bold case of a resource whose exhaustion is actually foreseeable with certainty. The Rule does not rigidly fit many cases in the real world. Yet it expresses an important principle at work that contributes to our understanding of what is going on in the latter. It can be objected that despite the fact that today we have a much clearer idea of what is still there of certain resources at a given moment of time and are possessed of much improved techniques to discover hitherto unknown deposits of resources, assumption (H1) is typically not met with regard to any single exhaustible resource. It is also not clear whether knowing precisely what is still there would mean much, because technical progress typically affects the economic importance of a resource. The discovery of new ways to use known substances as well as the discovery of the useful properties of hitherto unused substances may lead to substitution processes and in the extreme replace some given resource entirely by new ones. Also assumption (H2) is never strictly met. Typically, there are capacity constraints that limit the time rate of exploiting a deposit. These constraints are very often binding with regard to any single deposit of the resource, so that many deposits have to be exploited simultaneously in order to meet effectual demand.

We might go to the opposite extreme and postulate instead of assumptions (H1) and (H2) the following:

(Rl)   For each exhausted deposit of the resource, another one with exactly the same characteristics is discovered and the cost of the search, in terms of labour and commodities, is always the same.

(R2)   The working of each deposit is subject to a capacity constraint that limits the amount of the resource that can be extracted in a given period of time.

(R stands, of course, for Ricardo.) If assumptions (Rl) and (R2) replace assumptions (H1) and (H2), we are in a world that is much closer to that of the classical economists. Its properties are obviously different from those invoked in modern interpretations of the Hotelling Rule and therefore it should come as no surprise that Ricardo came up with a view which at first sight sits uncomfortably with modern interpretations of Hotelling's analysis. However, the reason is not that one of the analyses is right and the other wrong, but that they cover vastly different cases.

It goes without saying that there are intermediate cases between the two extremes: (H1) may be combined with (R2) or (H2) with (Rl). Many additional cases could be studied which would take into account, for example, that the discovery costs of new deposits are not constant or that the capacity constraint may depend on the amount of the resource that is still *in situ*.

We shall refrain from elaborating a richer typology of cases followed by a comparative investigation of them all. We focus attention rather on the case that was most probably at the back of Ricardo's mind. For this purpose we discuss, in the following section, what Ricardo wrote about exhaustible resources, the distinction between profits and rent and his criticism of Adam Smith's views on the matter.

Ricardo on exhaustible resources

In the *Principles* Ricardo defines rent rigorously in the following way:

> Rent is that portion of the produce of the earth, *which is paid to the landlord for the use of the original and indestructible powers of the soil.*
>
> > (Ricardo 1951: 67, emphasis added)

He continues:

> It is often, however, confounded with the interest and profit of capital, and, in popular language, the term is applied to whatever is annually paid by a farmer to his landlord. If, of two adjoining farms of the same extent,

and of the same natural fertility, one had all the conveniences of farming buildings, and, besides, were properly drained and manured, and advantageously divided by hedges, fences and walls, while the other had none of these advantages, more remuneration would naturally be paid for the use of one, than for the use of the other; yet in both cases this remuneration would be called rent. But it is evident, that a portion only of the money annually to be paid for the improved farm, would be given for the original and indestructible powers of the soil; the other portion would be paid for the use of the capital which had been employed in ameliorating the quality of the land, and in erecting such buildings as were necessary to secure and preserve the produce.

(Ricardo 1951: 67)

Adam Smith, Ricardo goes on to argue, did not stick to a rigorously defined concept when using the word rent. In Part II of Chapter XI of Book I of *The Wealth of Nations (WN)*, 'Of the Produce of Land which sometimes does, and sometimes does not, afford Rent', Smith gives an example of the timber business, timber clearly being a reproducible resource, in which he confounds the concepts of profits and rent (*WN* I.xi.c.5):

He [Smith] tells us, that the demand for timber, and its consequent high price, in the more southern countries of Europe, caused a rent to be paid for forests in Norway, which could before afford no rent. Is it not, however, evident, that the person who paid what he thus calls rent, paid it in consideration of the valuable commodity which was then standing on the land, and that he actually repaid himself with a profit, by the sale of the timber? If, indeed, after the timber was removed, any compensation were paid to the landlord for the use of the land, for the purpose of growing timber or any other produce, with a view to future demand, such compensation might justly be called rent, because it would be paid for the productive powers of the land; *but in the case stated by Adam Smith, the compensation was paid for the liberty of removing and selling the timber, and not for the liberty of growing it.*

(Ricardo 1951: 68, emphasis added)

Ricardo's criticism extends to Smith's discussion of coal mines and stone quarries:

He [Smith] speaks also of the rent of coal mines, and of stone quarries, to which the same observation applies – that the compensation given for the mine or quarry, is paid for the value of the coal or stone which can be removed from them, and has no connection with the original and indestructible powers of the land.

(Ricardo 1951: 68)

In Ricardo's view the distinction between profits and rent is crucial, because as capital accumulates and the population grows the two component parts of the social surplus are typically affected differently:

> This is a distinction of great importance, in an enquiry concerning rent and profits; for it is found, that *the laws which regulate the progress of rent, are widely different from those which regulate the progress of profits, and seldom operate in the same direction.* In all improved countries, that which is annually paid to the landlord, partaking of both characters, rent and profit, is sometimes kept stationary by the effects of opposing causes; at other times advances or recedes, as one or the other of these causes preponderates. In the future pages of this work, then, whenever I speak of the rent of land, I wish to be understood as speaking of that compensation, which is paid to the owner of land for the use of its original and indestructible powers.
>
> (Ricardo 1951: 68–9, emphasis added)

Hence what Smith called 'rent' of coal mines or stone quarries is to Ricardo profits and not rent. But does Ricardo not contradict himself by giving Chapter III of the *Principles* the title 'On the Rent of Mines'? Scrutiny shows that this is not so. Chapter III is actually devoted to the rent of mines precisely in the sense Ricardo intended. The problem is the following: Why are mines possessed of different 'fertilities' operated simultaneously? Why is not the most 'fertile' mine exploited in full first, followed by the second fertile mine, and so on? The answer is straightforward: Several mines have to be worked at the same time because each one is typically subject to a capacity constraint that limits the amount of the coal or ore that can be extracted per unit of time. This constraint itself is seen to depend typically also on the amount already extracted. Effectual demand cannot be satisfied in the given circumstances by operating exclusively the most 'fertile' mine, because the required rate of output in order to meet effectual demand cannot be generated in this way. The amount of the resource 'which can be removed' (Ricardo 1951: 68) will generally fall short of the resource *in situ* at the beginning of the extraction period. The same argument applies in the case in which there are several equally fertile mines. Yet,

> If there were abundance of equally fertile mines, which any one might appropriate, they could yield no rent; the value of their produce would depend on the quantity of labour necessary to extract the metal from the mine and bring it to market.
>
> (Ricardo 1951: 85)

This is generally not the case and differently fertile mines will have to be wrought simultaneously. The situation may change due to innovations, as Ricardo emphasizes with regard to coal: 'by new processes the quantity should be increased, the price would fall, and some mines would be abandoned' (Ricardo 1951: 331).

The absence of an abundance of equally fertile mines and the presence of a capacity constraint limiting the yearly output of any single mine in general necessitate the utilization of mines of different fertility in order to meet the effectual demand for the resource. In such circumstances, Ricardo stresses, it is the 'relative fertility of mines [which] determines the portion of their produce, which shall be paid for the rent of mines' (ibid.: 330). Ricardo concludes that 'the whole principle of rent is here ... as applicable to land as it is to mines' (ibid.: 330). When mines of different fertilities need to be wrought simultaneously, then this makes room for the emergence of (extensive) rents, exactly as in the case of the agricultural cultivation of land. This is rent in the true sense of the word and has nothing whatsoever to do with what nowadays we call 'royalties'. What we call 'royalties', Ricardo actually calls 'profits'.

Ricardo's use of the concept of profits for 'the compensation ... paid for the liberty of removing and selling the timber' is not surprising: timber can be sown and grown again, it is clearly not an exhaustible resource, but a reproducible good, and to the extent to which it is used as a produced means of production it is capital. But the use of the word profits for the compensation paid for the liberty of removing and selling coal or stones may be surprising; coal cannot be reproduced by men, neither can stones. However, new coal pits can always be expected to be discovered and the cost of the search is equal to the value of the mine, a value that decreases with the amount of the resource that has been removed. In other words, Ricardo did not need the word royalties since the minerals and ores, etc., as such were *not* considered to be fully exhaustible in the foreseeable future. Both in Ricardo and in Smith we encounter time and again references to the finding of new deposits with no serious consideration given to the fact that such deposits, taken as a whole, are limited. This is the reason why Ricardo did not need a new concept in order to be able to deal with the case under consideration. The concept of profits was all that was required.

The fact that Ricardo did not elaborate what now is called the Hotelling Rule cannot therefore be considered an expression of a failure and a lack of analytical profundity on his part. It simply expresses a concern with a world in which the total exhaustion of certain resources was not yet considered a possibility worth studying.

What we now call royalties are a sub-category of profits. Profits are proportional to the value of capital invested or possessed, and in conditions of free competition the rate of profits obtained in order to conserve the mineral in the ground has to be equal to the rate of profits obtained from any other production or conservation process.

If assumption (R1) held true, while each deposit would be exhaustible, the resource as such would not; and each deposit could in fact be treated as if it were a (reproducible) machine: the price of the new machine equals the cost of the search and the price of an old machine of age *t* equals the value of the deposit after t periods of utilization (see Kurz and Salvadori 1995: 359–60). The price of the resource *in situ* would change as predicted by the Hotelling Rule, but the price of the extracted mineral would be constant over time.[3] In the next section we assume that (HI) and (R2) apply. We will show that also in this case the changes in the prices of the resources *in situ* may not need the introduction of intertemporal equilibria. But the model elaborated is more general and is of some interest in itself. It consists essentially of a modified version of a model we put forward in Kurz and Salvadori (2000). The novelty in the new formalization compared with the original one is to be seen first and foremost in the introduction of capacity constraints with respect to the exploitation of each single deposit of a resource.

A formalization

The formalization suggested here is based on the following simplifying assumptions. A finite number n of different commodities, which are fully divisible, are produced in the economy and a finite number m ($>n$) of constant returns to scale processes are known to produce them. Let $\mathbf{p}_t$ be the vector of prices of commodities available at time $t \in \mathbb{N}_0$; let $\mathbf{x}_t$ be the vector of the intensities of operation of processes at time $t \in \mathbb{N}$; let $\mathbf{y}_t$ be the vector of royalties earned with respect to the various natural resources at time $t \in \mathbb{N}$; let $\mathbf{q}_t$ be the vector of rents obtained in exploiting the different deposits of them at time $t \in \mathbb{N}_0$; let z_t be the vector of the amounts of the resources available at time $t \in \mathbb{N}_0$. A process or method of production is defined by a quadruplet ($\mathbf{a}$, $\mathbf{b}$, $\mathbf{c}$, l), where $\mathbf{a} \in \mathbb{R}^n$ is the commodity input vector, $\mathbf{b} \in \mathbb{R}^n$ is the output vector, $\mathbf{c} \in \mathbb{R}^s$ is the exhaustible resources input vector, and l is the labour input, a scalar; of course $\mathbf{a} \geq 0$, $\mathbf{b} \geq 0$, $\mathbf{c} \geq 0$, $l \geq 0$. The production period is uniform across all processes. It is important to remark that the inputs referred to in vector $\mathbf{c}$ are inputs of the resources *as they are provided by nature*; for example, extracted oil is *not* contained in $\mathbf{c}$, but in $\mathbf{b}$, if ($\mathbf{a}$, $\mathbf{b}$, $\mathbf{c}$, l) is an extraction process, or in a, if ($\mathbf{a}$, $\mathbf{b}$, $\mathbf{c}$, l) is a process that uses it, unless the extraction costs are nil. The m existing processes are defined by quadruplets

$$(\mathbf{a}_j, \mathbf{b}_j, \mathbf{c}_j, l_j). \, j = 1, 2, ..., m$$

Then define matrices $\mathbf{A}$, $\mathbf{B}$, $\mathbf{C}$ and vector l as follows:[4]

$$\mathbf{A} = \begin{bmatrix} \mathbf{a}_1^T \\ \mathbf{a}_2^T \\ \vdots \\ \mathbf{a}_m^T \end{bmatrix}, \quad \mathbf{B} = \begin{bmatrix} \mathbf{b}_1^T \\ \mathbf{b}_2^T \\ \vdots \\ \mathbf{b}_m^T \end{bmatrix}, \quad \mathbf{C} = \begin{bmatrix} \mathbf{c}_1^T \\ \mathbf{c}_2^T \\ \vdots \\ \mathbf{c}_m^T \end{bmatrix}, \quad l = \begin{bmatrix} l_1^T \\ l_2^T \\ \vdots \\ l_m^T \end{bmatrix}.$$

Assume that the annual consumption of commodities by profit (and royalty) recipients is proportional to a vector $\mathbf{d}$, which, for simplicity, is assumed to be given and constant over time, that is, independent of prices and quantities, including the quantities of the exhaustible resources left over at the end of each production period; the actual consumption δ is determined endogenously. In addition, the real wage rate, defined by a commodity vector $\mathbf{w}$, is taken to be given and constant over time. Technical innovations of any kind are set aside. All exhaustible resources are private property. In conditions of free competition there will be a uniform nominal rate of profits γ_t across all production activities in the economy. This implies that, for each time $t \in \mathbb{N}_0$, the following inequalities and equations are to be satisfied:

$$\mathbf{Bp}_{t+1} \leq (1+\gamma_t)(\mathbf{Ap}_t + \mathbf{Cy}_t + \mathbf{Cq}_t) + \mathbf{lw}^T \mathbf{p}_{t+1} \tag{1}$$

$$\mathbf{x}_{t+1}^T \mathbf{Bp}_{t+1} = \mathbf{x}_{t+1}^T \left[(1+\gamma_t)(\mathbf{Ap}_t + \mathbf{Cy}_t + \mathbf{Cq}_t) + \mathbf{lw}^T \mathbf{p}_{t+1} \right] \tag{2}$$

$$\mathbf{y}_{t+1} \leq (1+\gamma_t)\mathbf{y}_t \tag{3}$$

$$\mathbf{z}_{t+1}^T \mathbf{y}_{t+1}^T = (1+\gamma_t)\mathbf{z}_{t+1}^T \mathbf{y}_t \tag{4}$$

$$\mathbf{x}_{t+1}^T \left(\mathbf{B} - \mathbf{lw}^T \right) \geq \mathbf{x}_{t+2}^T \mathbf{A} + \delta \mathbf{d}^T \tag{5}$$

$$\mathbf{x}_{t+1}^T \left(\mathbf{B} - \mathbf{lw}^T \right) \mathbf{p}_{t+1} = \left(\mathbf{x}_{t+2}^T \mathbf{A} + \delta \mathbf{d}^T \right) \mathbf{p}_{t+1} \tag{6}$$

$$\mathbf{z}_t^T \geq \mathbf{x}_{t+1}^T \mathbf{C} + \mathbf{z}_{t+1}^T \tag{7}$$

$$\mathbf{z}_t^T \mathbf{y}_t = \left(\mathbf{x}_{t+1}^T \mathbf{C} + \mathbf{z}_{t+1}^T \right) \mathbf{y}_t \tag{8}$$

$$\mathbf{z}_t^T \leq \mathbf{z}_{t+1}^T + \mathbf{t}^T \tag{9}$$

$$\mathbf{z}_t^T \mathbf{q}_t = \left(\mathbf{z}_{t+1}^T + \mathbf{t}^T \right) \mathbf{q}_t \tag{10}$$

$$\delta > 0, \ \mathbf{p}_t \geq 0, \ \mathbf{y}_t \geq 0, \ \mathbf{q} \geq 0, \ \mathbf{z}_t \geq 0, \ \mathbf{x}_{t+1} \geq 0. \tag{11}$$

Inequality (1) means that nobody can get extra profits by producing commodities available at time $t+1$. Equation (2) implies, because of inequalities (1) and (11), that commodities available at time $t+1$ will only be produced if the ruling nominal rate of interest is obtained. Inequality (3) means that nobody can get extra profits by storing exhaustible resources from time t to time $t+1$. Equation (4) implies, because of inequalities (3) and (11), that exhaustible resources will be stored from time t to time $t+1$ only if the ruling nominal rate of interest will be obtained by this storage activity. Inequality (5) implies that the amounts of commodities produced are not smaller than the amounts of commodities required, and equation (6) implies that if an amount is larger, then the price of that commodity is zero. Inequality (7) implies that the amounts of exhaustible resources available at time t are not smaller than the amounts of exhaustible resources available at time $t+1$ plus the amounts of exhaustible resources utilized to produce commodities available at time $t+1$, and equation (8) implies that if an amount is larger, then the price of that exhaustible resource is zero. Inequality (9) implies that at each time t extraction of resource j cannot be larger than $\mathbf{t}^T \mathbf{e}_j$, and equation (10) implies that if it is smaller, then the rent obtained by the owner of the deposit of resource j is zero. The meaning of inequalities (11) is obvious.

The difference with a world in which there are no capacity constraints in the extraction of resources is close at hand; the elements of vector $\mathbf{t}$ are so high that inequality (9) is always satisfied as a strict inequality, then equation (10) implies that $\boldsymbol{q}_t = \mathbf{0}$: in this case the model collapses to that analysed in Kurz and Salvadori (2000).

Despite the changes introduced in this model, the procedure to prove the existence of a solution to the model in Kurz and Salvadori (2000). In the presence of a 'backstop technology' can be applied also here. More precisely, let the processes $(\bar{\mathbf{A}}, \bar{\mathbf{B}}, \mathbf{0}, \bar{\mathbf{I}})$ be obtained from $(\mathbf{A}, \mathbf{B}, \mathbf{C}, \mathbf{I})$ by deleting all the processes using directly some natural resource (i.e. process $(\mathbf{e}_i^T \mathbf{A}, \mathbf{e}_i^T \mathbf{B}, \mathbf{e}_i^T \mathbf{C}, \mathbf{e}_i^T \mathbf{I})$ is in the set of processes $(\bar{\mathbf{A}}, \bar{\mathbf{B}}, \mathbf{0}, \bar{\mathbf{I}})$ if and only if $\mathbf{e}_i^T \mathbf{C} = \mathbf{0})$ and let us assume that there is a scalar r^* and there are vectors $\mathbf{x}^*$ and $\mathbf{p}^*$ which solve the system

$$\mathbf{x}^T \left(\bar{\mathbf{B}} - \bar{\mathbf{A}} - \bar{\mathbf{I}} \mathbf{w}^T \right) \geq \mathbf{d}^T$$

$$\mathbf{x}^T \left(\bar{\mathbf{B}} - \bar{\mathbf{A}} - \bar{\mathbf{I}} \mathbf{w}^T \right) \mathbf{p} = \mathbf{d}^T \mathbf{p}$$

$$\bar{\mathbf{B}} \mathbf{p} \leq (1 + r^*) \bar{\mathbf{A}} \mathbf{p} - \bar{\mathbf{I}} \mathbf{w}^T \mathbf{p}$$

$$\mathbf{x}^T \bar{\mathbf{B}} \mathbf{p} \leq \mathbf{x}^T \left[(1 + r^*) \bar{\mathbf{A}} \mathbf{p} - \bar{\mathbf{I}} \mathbf{w}^T \mathbf{p} \right]$$

$$\mathbf{x} \geq \mathbf{0}, \mathbf{p} \geq \mathbf{0}, \mathbf{d}^T \mathbf{p} = 1.$$

Let us assume, further, that the processes corresponding to positive elements of vector $\mathbf{x}^*$, $(\hat{\mathbf{A}}, \hat{\mathbf{B}}, \mathbf{0}, \hat{\mathbf{I}})$, are exactly n and that in the absence of exhaustible resources the economy would converge to these processes. Then the procedure used by Kurz and Salvadori (2000) is able to construct a solution also for system (1)–(11) despite the introduction of capacity constraints on the extraction of resources. Such a proof follows exactly the same lines and we will not provide it here.

What we want to stress here, on the contrary, is that the introduction of capacity constraints on the extraction of resources may introduce a further reason in support of the view that whereas the prices of resources *in situ* are bound to change at a rate equal to the rate of profits, all other prices will remain constant. We do not wish to assert that this will in fact happen, but that it *may* happen. This is so because the owners of deposits of resources get not only royalties, but also rents. The sum of royalties and rents for a given deposit may be constant even if royalties are changing, since rents are changing in equal amounts but in the opposite direction. To see this, consider an economy where capacity constraints are so high that production of consumption **d** requires the operation of the backstop technology and therefore processes $(\hat{\mathbf{A}}, \hat{\mathbf{B}}, 0, \hat{\mathbf{l}})$ are activated. As a consequence, vector **p** is determined and it may also be constant over time (it is so in the long run). This does not mean that production goes on in the same way year after year. Not at all: production changes potentially every year since the use of the resources reduces their availability. But the reduction in the availability of resources also reduces the rents and, since the price of the extracted mineral is constant over time, the rent is reduced by exactly the same amount in which royalties are increased, because of Hotelling's Rule.

Concluding remarks

The world to which the Hotelling Rule applies in its modern interpretation and the world to which the classical, especially Ricardian, analysis applies are rather different. While the Hotelling Rule presupposes that a scarce natural resource is available in a known quantity and its extraction is not subject to any capacity constraints, Ricardo's treatment of exhaustible deposits does not contemplate the case of the exhaustion of the resource as a whole and allows for capacity constraints that limit extraction per unit of time with respect to each deposit actually known at a given moment of time. Both types of analyses are valuable and improve our understanding of the properties of economic systems that make use of wasting assets. It is then argued in terms of a model with exhaustible resources that incorporates what we think are the premises from which Ricardo begins his reasoning, that the Hotelling Rule can be considered to be implied by it: the Rule concerns the resources *in situ* and requests their prices to change at a rate that is equal to the competitive rate of profits. However, these changes need not affect the prices of the other commodities, including the prices of the resources that are actually extracted. Hence, in Ricardo's argument the Hotelling Rule may be said to be effective, but its effects may be limited to changing prices of the conserved amounts of exhaustible resources only. The owners of deposits will obtain both royalties and rents; in the course of time rents will fall and royalties rise, and the sum of both may remain constant. If this condition is met, then these price changes will not affect any other prices in the economic system. Ricardo's argument may be said to implicitly correspond to this case.

References

Hotelling, H. (1931) 'The economics of exhaustible resources', *Journal of Political Economy*, 39: 137–75.

Kemp, M.C. and H.V. Long (1984) 'The role of natural resources in trade models', in R.W. Jones and P.B. Kenen (eds), *Handbook of International Economics*, Vol. I (International Trade), Amsterdam: Elsevier, pp. 367–417.

Kurz, H.D. and N. Salvadori (1997 [1995]) *Theory of Production. A Long-period Analysis*, rev. p/b edn, Cambridge: Cambridge University Press.

Kurz, H.D. and N. Salvadori (2000) 'Economic dynamics in a simple model with exhaustible resources and a given real wage rate', *Structural Change and Economic Dynamics*, 11: 167–79.

Negishi, T. (1992) 'Comment. Minisymposium on "The History of Economics and the History of Science" ', *History of Political Economy*, 24(1): 227–9.

Negishi, T. (1994) *The Collected Essays of Takashi Negishi, Vol. II The History of Economics*, Aldershot: Edward Elgar.

Ricardo, D. (1951 [1817]) *On the Principles of Political Economy and Taxation*, in P. Sraffa (ed.) with the collaboration of M.H. Dobb, *The Works and Correspondence of David Ricardo*, Vol. I, Cambridge: Cambridge University Press. (P/b edn 2004, Indianapolis, IN: Liberty Fund.)

Smith, A. (1976 [1776]) *An Inquiry into the Nature and Causes of the Wealth of Nations*, in R.H. Campbell, A.S. Skinner and W.B. Todd (eds), *The Glasgow Edition of the Works and Correspondence of Adam Smith*, Vol. I, Oxford University Press, Oxford. (In the text quoted as *WN*, book number, chapter number, section number, paragraph number.)

Notes

1 Neri Salvadori thanks Francesco Chioni for the discussions they had while Chioni worked on his Laurea Thesis under Salvadori's supervision.

2 Aiko Ikeo has drawn our attention to the interesting paper by Kemp and Long (1984), who in the context of a discussion of the conventional 2 x 2 Heckscher–Ohlin trade model replaced the usual assumption of two non-depletable original factors of production ('Ricardo's indestructible powers of the soil') and allowed instead for one or two exhaustible resources ('Hotelling's destructible power of the soil'). They thus also combined ideas of Ricardo and Hotelling. However, their overall set-up differs markedly from the present one. In particular, they adopted a partial equilibrium framework by taking relative world market prices of final goods as given to the small open economy. In the case of exhaustible resources it is assumed that their exhaustion affects only production conditions in the economy under consideration, but not world market prices. They were also concerned only with homogeneous factors of production and thus not with extensive differential rent. The problem of whether Hotelling's fundamental idea is somewhere hidden in Ricardo's argument is not touched upon by them.

3 Adam Smith wrote about the discovery of new mines:

> In this search [for new mines] there seem to be no certain limits either to the possible success, or to the possible disappointment of human industry. In the course of a century or two, it is possible that new mines may be discovered more fertile than any that have ever yet been known; and it is just equally possible that the most fertile mine then known may be more barren than any that was wrought before the discovery of the mines of America. (*WN* I.xi.m. 21)

4 Transposition of a vector or a matrix is denoted by superscript T.

15 Exhaustible resources[*]

Rents, profits, royalties and prices

Heinz D. Kurz and Neri Salvadori

Introduction

Bertram Schefold was keen to extend the classical approach to the theory of value and distribution, as it had already been reformulated and generalized earlier by Piero Sraffa (1960), to exhaustible resources (see the collections of essays in Schefold, 1989, 1997). A start had been made by Parrinello (1983) and then Schefold, who opened up a new field of research to those who adopted the approach under consideration and applied it to many questions not dealt with in Sraffa's classic contribution.[1] These efforts brought about a rich harvest of works, including contributions to the problem of 'wasting assets', as Sraffa called the case of exhaustible resources in the preparatory notes of his book (see Kurz and Salvadori, 2001: 290–3). Inspired by the works of these authors, we also entered into a discussion of exhaustible resources in some of our contributions (see Kurz and Salvadori, 2000, 2001, 2009).

In a recent paper (Kurz and Salvadori, 2009) we compared the approaches to exhaustible resources of David Ricardo, on the one hand, and of Harold Hotelling, on the other. We argued that the fact that in the classical economists, and especially Ricardo, the famous Hotelling Rule is not yet to be found does not mean that their analyses are of necessity defective, incomplete or inferior. It rather means that their arguments relate to a world characterized by conditions different from those contemplated by the Hotelling Rule. The latter may, however, be said to be implicit in Ricardo's analysis. What is missing is only an explicit reference to 'royalties' as something distinct and different from profits.

The Hotelling Rule implies that the prices of resources *in situ* need to increase over time at a rate that is equal to the competitive rate of profits. This follows from the requirement that in competitive conditions the conservation of a resource is an economic activity which ought to yield to the proprietors of deposits of the resource the same rate of profits as is obtained from any productive activity.[2] This seems in turn to imply that in the presence of

---

[*] Reproduced with permission from Volker Caspari (ed.), *The Evolution of Economic Theory: Essays in Honour of Bertram Schefold*, London: Routledge, 2011.

exhaustible resources, and assuming a general framework of the analysis,[3] *all* prices are bound to change over time. However, this need not be the case.

In this chapter we illustrate in terms of a numerical example our previous argument which was designed to clarify the relationship between Ricardo's approach to the problem of mines in terms of differential rent theory and Hotelling's approach to the problem of exhaustible resources in terms of royalties. For this purpose we develop a simple model that allows us to incorporate both points of view and the underlying leading principles in a single scheme and discuss its mathematical properties. A main outcome of the analysis is a clear distinction between three different types of property income: rents, profits and royalties. As Ricardo stressed in his criticism of Adam Smith's doctrine (Smith, 1976) with regard to the difference between the rent of land and profits, a clear distinction between the two is crucial, because as capital accumulates, the population grows and less and less fertile land has to be cultivated, the two component parts of the social surplus are typically affected differently: while rent rates increase, the competitive rate of profits falls.[4] In Ricardo land is treated as a renewable resource that is actually renewed all the time, that is, its quality does not deteriorate in the course of its utilization in the production of corn (or other crops). It thus differs markedly from exhaustible resources. The latter are gradually depleted each time parts of them are actually removed for productive (or consumptive) purposes from given stocks. However, Ricardo's finding that rents and profits move in different directions is corroborated with regard to different kinds of exhaustible resources (or, alternatively, differently fertile deposits of one such resource). As will be shown, royalties, which are a special kind of profits, may move in the opposite direction of rents. In well specified circumstances this may imply that whereas the prices of exhaustible resources *in situ* are bound to change at a rate equal to the rate of profits, all other prices remain constant. This is so because the owners of deposits of resources receive both royalties and rents. The sum of royalties and rents for a given deposit may be constant even if royalties are changing, since rents are changing in equal amounts but in the opposite direction.

The composition of the chapter is as follows. In the next section we stress the fact that the worlds Ricardo and Hotelling contemplated in their analyses differ in important respects. The third section presents the model which serves as our work-horse for the following investigation and puts forward the assumed numerical specification. The fourth section provides a number of examples constructed in order to illustrate different possibilities as to whether the prices of produced commodities will or will not change as time goes by and some of the natural resources are actually gradually exhausted. The final section contains some concluding remarks.

Different approaches to the problem of exhaustible resources

In modern interpretations of the Hotelling Rule it is typically assumed that the following two conditions are met: (H1) the resource is available in homogeneous quality and in an overall quantity that is limited and that at any moment of time is known with certainty; (H2) the amount of the resource that can be extracted in a given period of time, a year, for example, is only constrained by the amount of it left over from the preceding period.[5]

In case one of these assumptions, or both, are not met, the Hotelling Rule has to be modified accordingly. The Rule portrays the bold case of a resource whose exhaustion is actually foreseeable with certainty. Alas, it does not fit (m)any cases in the real world![6] Yet it expresses an important principle at work that contributes to our understanding of what is going on in the real world. It can be objected that despite the fact that today we have a much clearer idea of what is still there of certain resources at a given moment of time and are possessed of much improved techniques to discover hitherto unknown deposits of resources, assumption (H1) is typically not met with regard to any single exhaustible resource. It is also not clear whether knowing precisely what is still there would mean much, because technical progress typically affects the economic importance of a resource. The discovery of new ways to use known substances as well as the discovery of the useful properties of hitherto unused substances may lead to substitution processes and in the extreme replace some given resource entirely by new ones. Also, assumption (H2) is never strictly met. Typically, there are *capacity constraints* that limit the time rate of exploiting a deposit. These constraints are very often binding with regard to any single deposit of the resource, so that many deposits have to be exploited simultaneously in order to meet effectual demand.

We may go to the opposite extreme and postulate the following: (R1) for each exhausted deposit of the resource another one with exactly the same characteristics is discovered and the cost of the search, in terms of labour and commodities, is always the same; (R2) the working of each deposit is subject to a capacity constraint that limits the amount of the resource that can be extracted in a given period.[7]

The world contemplated by assumptions (R1) and (R2) is much closer to the one the classical economists experienced. As the evidence provided in Kurz and Salvadori (2009) shows, they were aware of the principal exhaustibility of some resources, but they did not think that this was an imminent problem. New deposits of such resources were discovered all the time as old ones were exhausted. In addition, technical progress continuously changed the conditions of production. John Stuart Mill expressed well the classical point of view in this regard. He argued that (i) the working of exhaustible resources is similar to the working of land (a resource that is taken to be inexhaustible); (ii) in both kinds of activities there are two antagonistic forces at work – diminishing returns and improvements (technical progress); (iii) the potential for such improvements is larger in the mining and other extraction processes than in agriculture (see Mill, 1965: 495).[8]

In this contribution we set aside technical progress. Nevertheless, the properties of a world that is subject to assumptions (R1) and (R2) are markedly different from those invoked in modern interpretations of the Hotelling Rule. Therefore it should come as no surprise that the Hotelling Rule appears to contradict Ricardo's view. However, the reason is not that one of the analyses is right and the other wrong, but that they deal with vastly different cases.

Intermediate cases between the two extremes can also be investigated: (H1) may be combined with (R2) or (H2) with (R1). In this chapter (as well as in Kurz and Salvadori, 2009) we focus attention on the first possibility which combines Hotelling's assumption of given stocks of exhaustible resources with Ricardo's assumption that the exploitation of each stock is subject to a capacity constraint that limits the amount of the resource that can be extracted in a given period. In order to avoid the 'end of the world' scenario, we add to assumption (H1) and (R2) the assumption that in addition to methods of production that use exhaustible resources, there are methods that do not. These are known as 'backstop' methods or techniques (see Kurz and Salvadori, 1995: 360).

The model and its numerical specifications

The model employed in this chapter is a simplified version of the model elaborated in Kurz and Salvadori (2009). One of its characteristic features is that it distinguishes between *production* processes (or methods), *extraction* processes and *conservation* processes. In order to put the features of the model in which we are interested most into sharp relief, we assume that there is only a single consumption good, corn. Three methods of producing corn are known. It can be produced either:

- by means of corn, extracted oil and labour;
- by means of corn, extracted methane and labour;
- or by means of corn and labour only.

While each of the first two methods mentioned uses an exhaustible resource, oil or methane, the last one does not: it represents a backstop process. In Table 15.1, process (1) gives the last one, process (2) the one that uses oil and process (3) the one that uses methane. There are constant returns to scale with regard to each single process. Obviously, because of the backstop process the system is not doomed to extinction once all the available amounts of oil and methane happen to have been used up: it can survive without them – provided the backstop process is sufficiently productive, which we take for granted.[9] In this case only process (1) will be operated. If we take the wage rate w as the standard of value or numéraire, $w = 1$, then the price of corn in terms of labour (or, to use Smith's concept, in terms of 'labour commanded') will be:

$$p_c = \frac{4}{3 - r}$$

(where the subscript stands for 'corn' (c)). This would be the *long-period* solution of the system.

Table 15.1 The available processes

Processes	Material inputs					Labour	Products				
	Corn	Oil under the ground	Methane under the ground	Extracted oil	Extracted methane		Corn	Oil under the ground	Methane under the ground	Extracted oil	Extracted methane
(1)	1/4	–	–	–	–	1	1	–	–	–	–
(2)	1/10	–	–	1	–	1	1	–	–	–	–
(3)	1/4	–	–	–	1	1/10	1	–	–	–	–
(4)	–	1	–	–	–	c	–	–	–	1	–
(5)	–	–	1	–	–	d	–	–	–	–	1
(6)	–	1	–	–	–	–	–	1	–	–	–
(7)	–	–	1	–	–	–	–	–	1	–	–

But what will be the prices during the transition towards the depletion of natural resources? Obviously the input–output information given up until now is not sufficient to answer this question. We need a lot of additional pieces of information. First, we need to know which extraction processes are available in order to remove oil and methane from the ground. Second, we need to know how much of these resources is available at the beginning of our investigation, that is, at time 0. Third, we need to know which conservation processes are available. Fourth, we need to know whether and which capacity constraints apply to the extraction of oil and methane, respectively. Fifth, we need to know how much of the only consumption good, corn, is consumed per period. (The reference is to pure consumption and not to the use of corn as a means of production.) Finally, we need to know the amounts of produced inputs (including corn) available at time 0, since the analysis is not a long-period one.

Clearly, depending on the whole set of data postulated, or givens, the model will generate different paths of quantities, prices and the distributive variables. Some of these will be illustrated in the following.

The extraction of oil and methane is represented by processes (4) and (5), respectively. It is for simplicity assumed that only labour is needed, and no other inputs. In order to extract one unit of oil, c units of labour are required, and in order to extract one unit of methane, d units of labour. (Varying the input magnitudes of labour per unit of output will be shown to generate different behaviours of the model.) Processes (6) and (7) give the conservation processes. It is for simplicity assumed that no costs are involved in keeping oil and methane in their *in situ* deposits.

Reflecting (H1), it is assumed that the total amount of oil available in oil fields is 2,500 units, and the total amount of methane in gas fields is 1,900 units, each expressed in its own technical unit. Reflecting (R2), if the extraction of oil and methane is subject to capacity constraints then it is assumed that no more than 400 units of oil and no more than 400 units of methane can be extracted per period (year).

We also have to specify the amount of corn that is consumed per year in addition to what is being used up, directly and indirectly, as a material input in its own production. It will be assumed that total (net) consumption amounts to 1,000 units (tons) of corn.

Finally we need to specify the amounts of commodities available on the ground at time 0 destined to be used as inputs. Further we need to know whether such commodities are perishable within a single period of time or partially perishable; in the latter case we would need to know also the rate at which they perish. This is so, since the analysis to be carried out is an intertemporal one. For instance, if there was only process (1), we know, as mentioned in the above, that the long-period price of corn in terms of labour is $p_c = 4/(3-r)$. But in an intertemporal analysis this is so only if the amount of corn available for production at time 0 happens to be equal to 1,000/3 units, so that the corn produced is 4,000/3 units, which means that one period later, at time 1, 1,000 units of corn are available for consumption and 1,000/3 units are available for production. If the amount of corn available at time 0 happens instead to be larger than 1,000/3, and corn perishes during a single period and therefore cannot be saved and carried over to the next period, there is at time 0 more corn available than what can be used. In competitive conditions the owners of corn will bid down the price of corn at time 0 to zero. As a consequence, the price of corn at time 1 will be unity, whatever is the rate of profits. It follows that the price of corn at time 2 will be:

$$p_{c2} = \frac{5+r}{4}$$

and in general the price of corn at time t will be:

$$p_{ct} = \frac{4}{3-r} - \frac{4}{3-r}\left[\frac{1+r}{4}\right]^t,$$

which effectively tends to $4/(3-r)$ as t approaches infinity.

In order not to confound the problem of arbitrarily given initial endowments and their implications for the quantity and price dynamics of the system under consideration with the problem of exhaustible resources, we assume throughout the following argument that the amounts of commodities available at time 0 for production are exactly those needed to have constant prices from time $\bar{t}$ onwards, whenever a time $\bar{t}$ with this property exists. (In the following it is shown that in the circumstances stated the property will always hold good.)

Examples

We may now construct a few numerical examples that illustrate different cases in which the prices of produced commodities will, or will not, change over time. The emphasis will be on cases in which the prices of commodities available on or above the ground may be constant over time even in the transition period. It will be seen that this is the result of the requirement, for which there exist different motivations, that the backstop process is employed.

The backstop technology is cost-minimizing since the beginning

In the above we have seen that the backstop process may be used only after the natural resources have been exhausted and processes (1) and (2) can no longer be operated. However, there is also the (abstract) possibility of the backstop technology being cost-minimizing right from the beginning of our considerations. For a given rate of profits, r, it all depends on how the technical characteristics of the processes by means of which oil or methane are extracted *and* then used up in the production of corn, on the one hand, compare to the technical characteristics of the backstop process, on the other. Assuming given production processes (1) and (2), it all depends on extraction processes (4) and (5). A little calculation shows that if $c > 3/5(3–r)$ and if at the same time $d > 9/10(1+r)$, then neither oil nor methane would be extracted in order to be used in producing corn, because it would not be profitable to do so. The technology that extracts and employs oil and methane would be dominated by the backstop technology. In this case neither oil nor methane would be productive resources. The important lesson to be drawn from this little example is that whether some substance in the ground is, or is not, a resource *cannot generally be defined independently of the rate of profits and the technical alternatives that are available in the system.*

It goes without saying that in the case in which the strict inequality sign applies to only one of the labour coefficients, but not the other one, one of the substances will be a resource that can and in certain conditions will be extracted and then employed.

All production processes can be employed simultaneously

Assume now that $c > 3/5(3–r)$ and $d > 9/10(1+r)$. In this case all three processes producing corn are equiprofitable and the price of corn has to meet the conditions defining the backstop process (see the section on 'The model and its numerical specifications' above). In this case there is neither room for royalties on oil and methane nor for rents on oil and methane fields: the price of extracted oil at time t is given by:

$$P_{eot} = c = \frac{3}{5(3-r)}$$

(the subscripts stand for 'extracted' (*e*), 'oil' (*o*) and 'time' (*t*)), and the price of extracted methane is given by:

$$p_{emt} = d = \frac{9}{10(1+r)}$$

(the subscript stands for 'methane' (*m*)). Capitalists producing corn will be indifferent as to whether to produce corn by means of corn alone (and, of course, labour), or by means of corn and oil, or by mean of corn and methane. In the following we assume that

$$d = c < \frac{3}{5(3-r)} < \frac{9}{10(1+r)}.$$

Hence the two exhaustible resources can be expected to be actually exploited and used, and in order to do so either royalties on the resources or rents on the fields, or both, need to be paid. This brings us to a new set of examples.

Extraction with capacity constraints

We now employ the assumptions mentioned in the third section above, namely, first, that the economy consumes (net) 1,000 units of corn per year and, second, that the extraction of oil and methane from given fields (containing a total of 2,500 and 1,900 units respectively) is subject to capacity constraints: only a maximum of 400 units of oil and a maximum of 400 units of methane can be extracted per year from the respective deposits.

Since the extraction of oil and methane are constrained, the owners of the oil or methane fields are able to get a rent except when the extraction of oil or methane is smaller than 400 units per year. At the same time the capacity constraints have been chosen in such a way that it is impossible to supply the needed amount of corn only in terms of process (2), or only in terms of process (3) or even in terms of employing processes (2) and (3) conjointly. Without also operating backstop process (1), effectual (net) consumption demand could not be met. As a consequence:

$$p_{ct+1} = (1+r)\frac{1}{4}p_{ct} + w_t \tag{1}$$

Hence if $p_{ct+1} = p_{ct}$ and $w_t = 1$, then $p_{ct+1} = p_{ct} = 4/(3 - r)$. In case processes (2) and (3) are operated, then:

$$p_{ct+1} = (1+r)\left[\frac{1}{10}p_{ct} + p_{eot}\right] + w_t \tag{2}$$

$$p_{ct+1} = (1+r)\left[\frac{1}{4}p_{ct} + p_{emt}\right] + \frac{1}{10}w_t \tag{3}$$

and, as a consequence,

$$p_{eot} = \frac{3}{5(3-r)} \quad \text{and} \quad p_{emt} = \frac{9}{10(1+r)}.$$

In this case some oil and methane need to be extracted and the rest conserved. Denoting the rent paid per unit of extracted oil (methane) by q_o (q_m), the corresponding price of oil (methane) by p_{eo} (p_{em}), and the price per unit of conserved or unextracted oil (methane) by p_{uo} (p_{um}), and keeping in mind that the extraction of oil and methane require the same amount of labour per unit of each resource $(c = d)$, we have:

$$p_{eot+1} = (1+r)p_{uot} + q_{ot} + cw_t \tag{4}$$

$$p_{emt+1} = (1+r)p_{umt} + q_{mt} + cw_t \tag{5}$$

$$p_{uot+1} = (1+r)p_{uot} \tag{6}$$

$$p_{umt+1} = (1+r)p_{umt} \tag{7}$$

Note that processes (6) and (7) are operated in any case, as long as the two resources have not been fully exhausted. Equations (6) and (7) imply that

$$p_{uot} = (1+r)^t p_{uo0} \quad \text{and} \quad p_{umt} = (1+r)^t p_{um0}$$

which is, of course, the Hotelling Rule. Further, $q_{m4} = 0$ and $q_{o6} = 0$, since for $t = 4$ only 300 units of methane are still available and no rent can be obtained on gas fields, and at $t = 6$ only 100 units of oil are still available and no rent can be obtained on oil fields. This implies that

$$p_{uo6} = \frac{3 - 5c(3-r)}{5(3-r)(1+r)} \quad \text{and} \quad p_{um4} = \frac{9 - 10c(1+r)}{10(1+r)^2};$$

and therefore

$$p_{uot} = \frac{3 - 5c(3-r)}{5(3-r)(1+r)^{7-t}} \quad \text{and} \quad p_{umt} = \frac{9 - 10c(1+r)}{10(1+r)^{5-t}}$$

The important point to be emphasized is the following. Although the Hotelling Rule applies to the prices of the *in situ* stocks of the two resources, *the prices of the commodities above the ground, including extracted oil and methane, are constant.* This is so because the rent rates that result from the capacity constraints with regard to the extraction of the two resources change over time in a particular way: they start falling as soon as royalties on oil and methane start rising, and they do so in such a way that their fall just compensates the rise in royalties:

$$q_{ot} = \frac{[3 - 5c(3-r)]\left[1 - (1+r)^{6-t}\right]}{5(3-r)(1+r)^{6-t}}, \quad q_{mt} = \frac{[9 - 10c(1+r)]\left[(1+r)^{4-t} - 1\right]}{10(1+r)^{4-t}}$$

No capacity constraint with regard to oil extraction

In order to understand better the role played by capacity constraints on extraction, consider a case that is identical to the previous one, except that there is no capacity constraint limiting the extraction of oil, whereas there is one with regard to the extraction of methane.

This implies, first, that process (1) will not need to be activated at time 0: the entire effectual demand can be met without it. Further, no rent will be paid to the proprietors of oil fields. Hence, equations (2) and (6) hold, whereas instead of equation (4) we have:

$$p_{eot+1} = (1+r)p_{uot} + cw_t \tag{8}$$

If $w_t = 1$, equations (2), (6), and (8) determine:

$$p_{uot} = (1+r)^t p_{uo0}$$
$$p_{eot} = (1+r)^t p_{uo0} + c \tag{9}$$
$$p_{ct+1} = \frac{1+r}{10}p_{ct} + (1+r)^{t+1}p_{uo0} + (1+r)c + 1$$

Equation (9) in turn determines:

$$p_{ct} = A\left[\frac{1+r}{10}\right] + \frac{10}{9}p_{uo0}(1+r)^t + \frac{10[(1+r)c+1]}{9-r},$$

where A is a constant (to be ascertained) such that

$$p_{ct+1} \le (1+r)\frac{1}{4}p_{ct} + 1,$$

otherwise capitalists would prefer to use process (1) instead of process (2) to produce corn.

Let T be the time at which oil is almost entirely exhausted, that is, $T = 2$ in the case in which it is never profitable to produce corn with methane, i.e. use process (3). Otherwise either $T = 3$ or $T = 4$, in the case in which it is profitable to produce corn with methane for a positive number of years smaller or larger than 3, respectively, before oil is exhausted. Hence

$$p_{cT+1} = (1+r)\frac{1}{4}p_{cT} + 1$$

and therefore

$$A\left[\frac{1+r}{10}\right]^{T+1} + \frac{10}{9}p_{uo0}(1+r)^{T+1} + \frac{10\left[(1+r)c+1\right]}{9-r}$$
$$= \frac{1+r}{4}\left\{A\left[\frac{1+r}{10}\right]^{T} + \frac{10}{9}p_{uo0}(1+r)^{T} + \frac{10\left[(1+r)c+1\right]}{9-r}\right\} + 1.$$

That is,

$$A = \frac{5\cdot 10^{T+1}}{9}p_{uo0} + \frac{\left[5c(3-r)-1\right]10^{T+1}}{(9-r)(1+r)}$$

and

$$p_{ct} = \frac{10\left(1+5\cdot 10^{T-1}\right)}{9}(1+r)^{r}p_{uo0}$$
$$+ \frac{10}{9-r}\frac{c\left[5\cdot 10^{T-t}(3-r)+(1+r)^{T+1-t}\right]-10^{T-t}+(1+r)^{T-t}}{(1+r)^{T-t}}.$$

Note that only if

$$p_{uo0} = \frac{3(9-r)-15c(5-r)(3-r)}{5(3-r)(9-r)(1+r)^{T}}$$

$p_{cT+1} = 4/(3 - r)$ and the price of corn is constant for $t \geq T+1$.

It will be profitable to produce corn by methane for at least one year if

$$p_{ct+1} > (1+r)\left[\frac{1}{4}p_{ct} + c\right] + \frac{1}{10} \tag{10}$$

for some t. It is easily checked that inequality (10) holds if $c = 0$ and $t = T$. Then there is a $\gamma > 0$ such that inequality (10) holds for $0 \leq c < \gamma$ and $0 \geq t \geq T$. Let us assume that c is in this interval and therefore $T = 4$. Moreover, equations (3) and (5) hold and $q_{m4} = 0$. Since equation (7) always holds if methane is not exhausted,

$$p_{umt} = (1+r)^{t}p_{um0}$$

This example shows that if the extraction capacity of one resource is not limited and therefore the backstop process does not need to be operated since the beginning, the interplay of rent and royalties is not sufficient to keep prices of corn and of extracted resources constant over time.

Higher capacity constraints with regard to oil and methane

While the absence of any capacity constraint with regard to one resource and the presence of a constraint with regard to the other one refers already, in an extreme way, to the role of *differences in constraints* on the behaviour of the system, some further examples might contribute to our understanding of the phenomena at hand. Here it suffices to draw attention to the following case. Assume that the two resources are subject to positive, but different capacity constraints: no more than 700 units of oil can be extracted per year and no more than 600 units of methane. In this case, the backstop process (1) will not be operated at time 0 and rent will be paid only on one of the two fields of exhaustible resources. The exercise is clear enough, and interested readers can carry it out themselves.

Concluding remarks

The chapter argues that in well specified circumstances the prices of produced commodities need not change, although the *in situ* prices of exhaustible resources that are actually exhausted over time will change. In order to show this, we start from the observation, to be found, for example, in the writings of the classical economists from Adam Smith to David Ricardo, that the exploitation of fields or deposits of exhaustible resources is typically subject to capacity constraints that limit the amount of the resource that can be extracted during a given time period from each field or deposit. As a consequence, several deposits of resources with different unit costs of extraction are exploited side by side. This implies that rents will have to be paid to the owners of fields that are more 'fertile', to use Ricardo's expression in chapter 3 of the *Principles*. Finally, if the backstop process is operated, this implies that the prices of commodities available on the ground are constant despite the fact that the prices of resources *in situ* vary over time according to the Hotelling Rule. This is made possible by an inverse movement of rents on the one hand and royalties on the other.

A little model in which corn can be produced by means of corn alone or by means of corn and oil or corn and methane, two exhaustible resources, is then elaborated and numerically specified. The findings of our analysis are illustrated by means of judiciously chosen examples. While the analytical structure of the model is quite simple, one gets a fairly rich typology of cases, each of which is associated with different time paths of the quantity of corn produced, the amounts of two kinds of exhaustible resources extracted or conserved in the ground, the prices of corn and the resources in and above the ground, and income distribution. The analysis allows one to distinguish clearly between three different types of property income: rents, profits and royalties. It also provides some reasons that help us to explain why the Hotelling Rule does not perform all that well in empirical studies.

References

Hotelling, H. (1931). The economics of exhaustible resources, *Journal of Political Economy*, 39: 137–75.

Krautkraemer, J. A. (1998). Nonrenewable resource scarcity, *Journal of Economic Literature*, 36(4): 2065–107.

Kurz, H. D. and Salvadori, N. (1995). *Theory of Production: A Long-Period Analysis*, rev. edn 1997, Cambridge: Cambridge University Press.

Kurz, H. D. and Salvadori, N. (2000). Economic dynamics in a simple model with exhaustible resources and a given real wage rate, *Structural Change and Economic Dynamics*, 11: 167–79.

Kurz, H. D. and Salvadori, N. (2001). Classical economics and the problem of exhaustible resources, *Metroeconomica*, 52(3): 282–96.

Kurz, H. D. and Salvadori, N. (2009). Ricardo on exhaustible resources, and the Hotelling Rule, in Aiko Ikeo and Heinz D. Kurz (eds), *The History of Economic Theory: Festschrift in Honour of Takashi Negishi*, London: Routledge, pp. 68–79.

Mill, J. S. (1965). *Principles of Political Economy with Some of Their Applications to Social Philosophy*, 1st edn 1848, edited by J. M. Robson. Toronto: University of Toronto Press.

Parrinello, S. (1983). Exhaustible natural resources and the classical method of long-period equilibrium, in J. Kregel (ed.), *Distribution, Effective Demand and International Economic Relations*, London: Macmillan, pp. 186–99.

Ricardo, D. (1951). *On the Principles of Political Economy and Taxation*, first edn 1817, in *The Works and Correspondence of David Ricardo*, Vol. I, edited by Piero Sraffa with the collaboration of Maurice H. Dobb, Cambridge: Cambridge University Press.

Schefold, B. (1989). *Mr Sraffa on Joint Production and Other Essays*, London: Macmillan.

Schefold, B. (1997). *Normal Prices, Technical Change and Accumulation*, London: Macmillan.

Smith, A. (1976). *An Inquiry into the Nature and Causes of the Wealth of Nations*, 1st edn 1776, in *The Glasgow Edition of the Works and Correspondence of Adam Smith*, Vol. II, edited by R. H. Campbell, A. S. Skinner and W. B. Todd, Oxford: Oxford University Press.

Sraffa, P. (1960). *Production of Commodities by Means of Commodities*, Cambridge: Cambridge University Press.

Notes

1 In his book, Sraffa (1960: 74) mentions exhaustible resources only in passing and on a par with land: 'Natural resources which are used in production, such as land and mineral deposits.' A separate paragraph that he had originally planned to publish, he deleted at the proofreading stage.

2 Empirical studies have shown that the Hotelling Rule does not perform all that well; see Krautkraemer (1998). Some of the reasons for this will hopefully become

clear in the sequel. (Other important reasons, especially technical progress, will be mentioned only in passing.)

3 As is well known, Hotelling (1931) assumed a partial equilibrium framework in which the rate of interest (or profits) was given from outside the system. Ricardo's analysis may on the contrary be characterized as concerned with the system as a whole, in which the rate of profits will typically change as the scarcity of resources makes itself felt ever more severely.

4 Ricardo took the soil to be possessed of 'original and indestructible powers' (Ricardo, 1951: 67). For an elaboration of the classical theory of extensive and intensive rent, see Kurz and Salvadori (1995: ch. 10).

5 H stands, of course, for Hotelling.

6 This is confirmed by Krautkraemer (1998). He maintains, among other things: 'For the most part, the implications of this basic Hotelling model have not been consistent with empirical studies of nonrenewable resource prices and *in situ* values' (p. 2066). 'Other factors have overshadowed finite availability of the resource as determinants of the observed dynamic behavior of nonrenewable resource prices and *in situ* values' (p. 2087). And: 'It does seem to be a recurring tendency *to overestimate the imminence of nonrenewable resource exhaustion*' (p. 2103; emphasis added).

7 R stands, of course, for Ricardo.

8 Mill even contended boldly that the exhaustibility of each single resource is not really a problem: 'the almost inevitable progress of human culture and improvement *... forbids us to consider [it] as probable*' (p. 496; emphases added). This is perhaps the strongest statement put forward in the history of political economy up until then that the exhaustion of natural resources (and, implicitly, the Hotelling Rule) need not concern us much: technical progress renders the problem of exhaustion improbable.

9 There is, of course, the possibility that the backstop process might become cost-minimizing before all the oil and methane have been used up.

16 The 'classical' approach to exhaustible resources

Parrinello and the others

Heinz D. Kurz and Neri Salvadori

Introduction

Sergio Parrinello is to be credited with having pioneered the extension of Piero Sraffa's analysis at least in two important directions.[1] First, in 1970 he reformulated the pure theory of international trade within a 'classical' framework of the analysis in which capital consists of heteregeneous produced means of production (Parrinello 1970). This was the starting point of a number of contributions by Steedman, Metcalfe, Mainwaring and others who showed that several of the traditional trade theorems, derived within the Heckscher-Ohlin-Samuelson trade model, do not carry over to a framework with a positive rate of profits and heterogeneous capital goods. Second, in 1983 Parrinello turned to the problem of exhaustible resources, such as oil or gas, and asked critically whether the long-period method Sraffa had adopted can also deal with this case or whether it has to be abandoned in favour of some other method (Parrinello 1983). Also this paper triggered a number of contributions taking up the challenge.

In this short intervention we focus attention on the second case. We proceed in the following way. The next section deals with Sraffa's discussion of exhaustible resources in his hitherto unpublished papers and their reflection in his 1960 book (Sraffa 1960). In the third section we summarize briefly Parrinello's argument in his 1983 paper against the background of Sraffa's considerations. The fourth section provides a short account of the main issues raised and competing answers given in the discussions that followed Parrinello's paper, and Parrinello's revision of his earlier view in Parrinello (2004). The fifth section turns to our own more recent contributions to the issue at hand which focus attention on the explanatory power of David Ricardo's approach to exhaustible resources on the one hand and Richard Hotelling's approach on the other. The final section concludes.

Sraffa on exhaustible resources

When in 1983 Parrinello published his paper he had to rely exclusively on Sraffa's published works. Therefore he could not yet know what is there in Sraffa's manuscripts and papers kept at Trinity College, Cambridge, regarding the problem of exhaustible resources. Today, we are in a much better position because we have access to Sraffa's literary heritage. We take this opportunity to recall some of the documents dealing with the case under consideration.

First, it is to be noted that the problem of exhaustible resources, or 'wasting assets', as Sraffa used to call them, was on his mind from an early time of his (re)constructive work, which started in the second half of the 1920s, and the problem remained there until his respective work culminated in the publication of his 1960 book. And Sraffa was also aware from an early time onwards that the problem caused difficulties for the long-period method. In a note dated 25 March 1946 he counterposed the difference between the *physical real cost* approach to the problem of value and distribution, which he had endorsed, and the classical-Marxian *labour theory of value*. He actually insisted that the former was able to deal with exhaustible resources, whereas the latter was not:

> The difference between the 'Physical real costs' and the Ricardo-Marxian theory of 'labour costs' is that the first does, and the latter does not, include in them the natural resources that are used up in the course of production (such as coal, iron, exhaustion of land) – [Air, water etc. are not used up: as there is an unlimited supply, no subtraction can be made from ∞]. This is fundamental because it does away with 'human energy' and such metaphysical things.

He added with regard to the natural ingredients of production:

> But how are we going to replace these natural things? There are 3 cases: a) they can be reproduced by labour (land properties, with manure and so on); b) they can be substituted by labour (coal by hydroelectric plant: or by spending in research and discovery of new sources and new methods of economising) c) they cannot be either reproduced nor substituted – and in this case they cannot find a place in a theory of continuous production and consumption: they are dynamical facts, that is a stock that is being gradually exhausted and cannot be renewed, and must ultimately lead to the destruction of the society. But this case does not satisfy our condition of a society that just manages to keep continuously alive.
>
> (Sraffa Papers, D3/12/42: 33)

In Sraffa's view exhaustible resources thus constitute 'dynamical facts' which cannot be studied rigorously in a framework in which prices and income distribution do not change. A dynamic theory is needed. However, Sraffa was sceptical that a reliable dynamic theory could be elaborated. At any rate, the task was intrinsically difficult, as Sraffa emphasized in another note:

> It is 'a fatal mistake' of some economists that they believe that by introducing complicated dynamic assumptions, they get nearer to the true reality; in fact they get further removed for two reasons: a) that the system is

much more statical than we believe, and its 'short periods' are very long, b) that the assumptions being too complicated it becomes impossible for the mind to grasp and dominate them – and thus it fails to realize the absurdity of the conclusions.

(Sraffa Papers, D3/12/11: 33)

Interestingly, this warning did not prevent Sraffa from undertaking probing steps into the as yet unchartered territory. An echo of his respective attempts is actually to be found in the introductory passage of Chapter XI of his book, which is entitled 'Land'. Parrinello (1983) cites the passage referred to:

Natural resources which are used in production, such as land and mineral deposits, and which being in short supply enable their owners to obtain a rent, can be said to occupy among means of production a position equivalent to that of 'non-basics' among products. Being employed in production, but not themselves produced, they are the converse of commodities which, although produced, are not used in production.

(Sraffa 1960: 74)

What the early readers of *Production of Commodities by Means of Commodities* did not know is that up until the final proof stage of his book Sraffa kept a passage in the text of what is paragraph 91 of his book designed to deal with the specific character of wasting assets (as opposed to non-depletable natural resources including, by assumption, land).[2] The paragraph under consideration deals with machines of an obsolete type, and Sraffa draws a parallel between them and exhaustible resources. We first reproduce the paragraph as it has actually been published:

Machines of an obsolete type which are still in use are similar to land in so far as they are employed as means of production, although not currently produced. The quasi-rent (if we may apply Marshall's term in a more restricted sense than he gave it) which is received for those fixed capital items which, having been in active use in the past, have now been superseded but are worth employing for what they can get, is determined precisely in the same way as the rent of land. And like land such obsolete instruments have the properties of non-basics and are excluded from the composition of the Standard product.

(Sraffa 1960: 78)

The passage he deleted at the proof-reading stage reads:

On the other hand, as in the case of other wasting assets (such as mineral deposits) the annual depletion must be taken into account, which gives rise to as many separate processes as are the years of the asset's prospective residual life, on the same general principle as was done in Chapter X for 'live' fixed capital.

(Sraffa Papers: folder D3/12/96)

Let us now discuss Parrinello's 1983 paper against the background of Sraffa's above considerations.

Parrinello's 1983 paper

Parrinello gave his paper on the occasion of a Conference held in early September 1981 in Villa Manin di Passariano, Udine, which actually marked the official beginning of the Trieste Summer School at the Centro di Studi Economici Avanzati. It was organized by Sergio Parrinello, Pierangelo Garegnani and Jan Kregel, but the man who really was responsible for its success over many years was Parrinello.

In the paper Parrinello stressed that 'a problem of compatibility' existed between the long-period method revived by Sraffa and the case of exhaustible natural resources (Parrinello 1983: 188). He went on to interpret the intro-ductory passage of Chapter XI of Sraffa's book (quoted above) and con-cluded that 'Sraffa seems, in his theory of value, to equate land with mineral resources' (188–9). While it is true that Sraffa considered both non-depletable and exhaustible resources as occupying among means of production a pos-ition equivalent to that of non-basics among products, he compared gradual depletion of exhaustible resources with that of machines of an obsolete type. Therefore, with the benefit of hindsight we may agree with Parrinello 'that the assimilation of mineral deposits to land, if taken too far, may become misleading' (190). At the same time it is not clear that the implied criticism applies to Sraffa's approach.

Starting from Sraffa's production equations and seeking a way to preserve the classical approach as much as possible and yet cope with the problem of exhaustible resources, Parrinello then counterposes 'two ways in which exhaustible natural resources can be treated in the theory of value' (190). According to the *first* option there is a given 'number of mines of a certain type and the "mine" [is] equated with a machine which exists but is no longer reproduced' (191). This coincides essentially with the approach taken by Sraffa in the passage he deleted at the proofreading stage of his book. According to the *second* option the natural resource is considered

as an inventory of goods no longer produced. The availability of the resource is in this case measured by the quantity under ground or on the surface and this quantity is considered to be divisible into inputs which can belong to distinct processes of two kinds: extractive processes and conservation processes.

(191)

He then provides formalizations of what he considers to be the characteristic features of the two alternatives and emphasizes their differences. He maintains that in dealing with the second method (*resources as an inventory*) the problem emerges that conserving the resource, i.e. not extracting it, must earn its proprietor the same rate of return as when it is extracted. Therefore conservation processes and extraction processes must explicitly be distinguished. In conditions of free competition this implies, however, that the price of the *in situ* stock of the resource must rise, following the Hotelling Rule (Hotelling 1931) (197). Parrinello then compares this case to the case of 'beans' in Sraffa's book (1960: 91), which are assumed to exhibit a very low rate of own reproduction. The case can only be dealt with in terms of a difference between the price of beans at the beginning of the production period and the price at its end, just as in the Hotelling case. This fact is said to spell trouble for the long-period method, because 'the choice of the system of production is not independent of the quantity of the natural resource in short supply'. Parrinello concludes: 'It therefore becomes impossible, in the absence of particular hypotheses, to maintain the thesis that long-term prices can be explained solely on the basis of the distribution and methods of production used in a self-contained period of time.' (196) To this he adds that this seems to 'lead the theory of value founded on the concept of surplus towards positions close to the neo-classical approach' (196–7). He insisted, however, that the two theories still exhibit a 'substantial difference' (197) as regards the manner in which the rate of interest is determined – whether by time preference or surplus.

As regards the first method (*resources as mines*), 'the extraction of the mineral and its conservation below the ground cannot be considered as two separate processes' (197): they must rather be combined into a single process in which 'the quantity of the mineral extracted and the quantity which remains in the ground at the end of the period are treated as joint products' (198). Parrinello then draws the attention to the special case in which the natural rate of growth of the resource happens to be such that whatever is extracted in a given period is exactly replenished during the same period. In this case, he insists, 'the royalty [defined as the "user cost of the mine" (190)]' would be zero: '*we would have before us a renewable resource which, with respect to the system of production activated, is equal to land*' (198; emphasis in the original).[3]

Parrinello concludes his paper with 'some critical remarks'. He argues 'that the approach in terms of mines would be preferable to that in terms of inventories, in those cases in which the exhaustion of the mine would be so slow as to equate them, as Sraffa suggests, with land' (199). Having said this, he expresses doubts as to 'an analytical treatment which assimilates it [the problem] to the Ricardian concept of land. ... [T]o assume that the resources in question are "practically" inexhaustible is begging the question' (199). The classical method is said to be

> *not compatible* ... with too rapid an historical process of decreasing productivity of 'extensive' or 'intensive' nature, associated with a progressive

increase of products obtained from land or a progressive exhaustion of other natural resources which receive rents or royalties.

(199)

Parrinello rightly draws the attention to some open questions in the classical approach, as it had been reformulated by Piero Sraffa, and indicates the directions in which a solution may be found. In the following years others took up the challenge and provided analyses dealing with the case of exhaustible resources. Parrinello deserves the merit for having started the debate and having put forward ideas which were then further developed by other authors. In the following section we provide a brief summary account of the debate under consideration. The unifying element of all contributions dealt with is that they started from Sraffa (1960).

The debate that followed

Parrinello's paper triggered a rich literature to which contributed, among others, Salvadori (1987), Schefold (1989: ch. 19b, 2001), Kurz and Salvadori (1995, 1997, 2001, 2002, 2009, 2011), Bidard and Erreygers (2001a, 2001b), Lager (2001), Parrinello (2001), Ravagnani (2002) and Hosoda (2001). In addition there were contributions dealing with the problem at hand from a classical point of view, but which were not directly related to Parrinello's paper, including Roncaglia (1983, 1985), Gibson (1984), Pegoretti (1986, 1990) and Quadrio Curzio (1983, 1986). Here we focus attention only on some of the former.

Schefold (1989) took up Parrinello's invitation to consider the case of exhaustile resources and argued that the theory of such resources 'is of practical relevance only under exceptional circumstances' and concluded 'that the classicists may be excused for having ignored it by subsuming the incomes of mine owners to the general theory of rent' (1989: 228). He felt justified in his defence of the classical authors in terms of four sets of facts: (i) the uncertainty concerning the future course of prices; (ii) the unpredictability of the impact of technical progress on the system; (iii) the relatively slow change of the royalty of any one mine; and (iv) the great importance of cost differentials between mines.

Prior to him Salvadori (1987) had provided a formalization of the problem which was then further developed in Kurz and Salvadori (1995: ch. 12, sec. 4). Notice that the title of the chapter in which the case was dealt with is 'On limits to the long-period method', echoing somewhat Parrinello's concern with an incompatibility between the problem at hand and the long-period method. The model elaborated is a dynamic input–output model which allows one to trace the time paths of the state variables of the system, including the prices of commodities. The model is based on a given and constant real wage rate and a given net output vector (of consumption goods); in order to avoid the end of the world scenario it is assumed that there is an ultimate 'backstop technology', based on the use of solar (or geothermal) energy. In Kurz and Salvadori (1997) an aspect of their previous argument has been corrected and in Kurz and Salvadori (2000) a still more elaborate version of the analysis has been put forward. An aspect of the solution of the model is stressed concerning the structural change of the economy over time, that is, the change in the processes of production adopted to satisfy effectual demand and the intensities with which the processes are operated, the overall level and composition of employment, etc.

The analysis put forward by Kurz and Salvadori was criticized by Bidard and Erreygers in a paper first given in Graz in 2000 on the occasion of a conference of the *European Society for the History of Economic Thought* (*ESHET*). The scholars mentioned were then invited to bring the debate into the open in a special issue of *Metroeconomica* published in August 2001 entitled 'Symposium on exhaustible natural resources and Sraffian analysis'. To the symposium contributed apart from those just mentioned Eiji Hosoda (2001), Christian Lager (2001), Sergio Parrinello (2001) and Bertram Schefold (2001); the issue was introduced and edited by Ian Steedman. The symposium started with a revised version of the paper by Bidard and Erreygers mentioned above, in which they put forward a model – the 'corn-guano model' – that may be considered a simple extension of the famous 'corn model' (Bidard and Erreygers 2001a). In the model there is a single produced commodity, corn, and a single exhaustible resource, guano. The model was meant to expose in as simple terms as possible the difficulties the long-period method faces when allowing for exhaustible resources. In a second paper Bidard and Erreygers (2001b) added further reflections on their model and put forward the following propositions: (i) the long-period method is barren when it is applied to the problem of exhaustible resources; (ii) the Hotelling Rule is but an expression of competitive conditions ruling in the system; (iii) the trajectories of the prices of the two commodities depends on the chosen numeraire.

In their reply to Bidard and Erreygers Kurz and Salvadori argued instead (i) that under well-specified conditions Ricardo's (and Sraffa's) treatment of exhaustible resources is correct and the long-period method useful; (ii) the approaches of Ricardo and Hotelling are not incompatible with one another, but complementary; (iii) the properties of an economic system must not depend on the numeraire chosen by the theorist; if there is such a dependence then this is a sign that something in the argument is wrong.

Parrinello (2001) argued in terms of a different model that the presence of exhaustible resources 'does not *add* insurmountable difficulties for the development of the [classical] approach itself' (314), which he considers to reside in the assumption of free competition 'combined with one exogenous distributive variables' (314). Taking one distributive variable as given implies determining the others residually, or rather, that income distribution is not settled in the usual marginalist way.

Schefold (2001) insisted that the Bidard-Erreygers model suffers from not distinguishing between the resource *in situ* and the extracted resource and the respective prices of the resource. In addition he reiterated his earlier argument that the model is too simple and does not take account of important facts of the real world, such as technical progress, etc.

Interestingly, Parrinello later changed his earlier view and argued 'that we can use Sraffa's equations to deal with the existence of exhaustible natural resources without modifying the form of equations, after an important reinterpretation' (2004: 319). The important reinterpretation referred to concerns the given quantities in Sraffa (1960). These must include, Parrinello argued, 'a flow of the resource, instead of its total stock left in the ground' (Parrinello 2004: 320). The flow is taken to correspond to the 'effectual supply' of the resource at the prices of production determined by Sraffa's equations. Hence there is no need to refer to the total stock of the resource *in situ* – an unknown magnitude anyway – and thus to the growing relative scarcity of the resource, reflected in the Hotelling Rule. In this interpretation the classical approach to exhaustible resources is seen to be fundamentally different from the neoclassical intertemporal equilibrium approach.

Our recent work

In our view the problem failed to be settled for good by the *Metroeconomica* symposium. In more recent papers (Kurz and Salvadori 2009, 2011) our attention focused on the proposition that the approaches of Ricardo and Hotelling can be integrated into a single model. This necessitated, however, first to get a clearer idea of Ricardo's position on the matter. In order to accomplish this one has to scrutinize his critique of Adam Smith's views on the distinction between rents and profits. Ricardo insists that rent is often 'confounded with the interest and profit of capital, and, in popular language, the term is applied to whatever is annually paid by a farmer to his landlord' (*Works*, vol. I: 67). Then, with a reference to *WN* I.xi.c.5, where Smith gives an example of the timber business and calls rent the payment to the land owner as a compensation of the right to get the timber grown on the land, Ricardo comments: 'in the case stated by Adam Smith, the compensation was paid for the liberty of removing and selling the timber, and not for the liberty of growing it' (68). Finally, Ricardo compared mineral deposits to timber:

> He [Smith] speaks also of the rent of coal mines, and of stone quarries, to which the same observation applies – that the compensation given for the mine or quarry, is paid for the value of the coal or stone which can be removed from them, and has no connection with the original and indestructible powers of the land.
>
> (Ibid.)

Hence what Smith called the 'rent' of coal mines or stone quarries is to Ricardo profits and not rent. These remarks by Ricardo do not contradict the content of Chapter 3 of the *Principles* whose title is 'On the Rent of Mines'.

The chapter is actually devoted to the rent of mines precisely in the sense Ricardo intended. The problem is the following: Why are mines that are possessed of different 'fertilities' operated simultaneously? Why is not the most fertile mine exploited in full first, followed by the second fertile mine, and so on? The answer is straightforward: Several mines have to be worked at the same time because each one is typically subject to a capacity constraint that limits the amount of the coal or ore that can be extracted per unit of time. This constraint itself is seen to depend typically also on the amount already extracted. Effectual demand cannot be satisfied in the given circumstances by operating exclusively the most fertile mine, because the required rate of output in order to meet effectual demand cannot be generated in this way. The amount of the resource 'which can be removed' (ibid.: 68) of any one deposit will generally fall short of the resource *in situ* at the beginning of the extraction period.

In Kurz and Salvadori (2009) we explored extensively Ricardo's views on mines and compared the approaches to exhaustible resources of David Ricardo and of Harold Hotelling. We argued that the fact that in the classical economists, and especially Ricardo, the famous Hotelling Rule is not yet to be found does not mean that their analyses are of necessity defective, incomplete or inferior. While their arguments relate to a world characterized by conditions different from those contemplated by the Hotelling Rule, the latter may, however, be said to be implicit in Ricardo's analysis. What is missing is only an explicit reference to 'royalties' as something similar to and yet different from profits.

It then emerges that the different worlds Ricardo and Hotelling contemplated in their analyses can be characterized as follows:

Ricardo:

(R1) For each exhausted deposit of the resource another one with similar characteristics is discovered and the cost of the search, in terms of labour and commodities, is approximately the same.
(R2) The working of each deposit is subject to a *capacity constraint* that limits the amount of the resource that can be extracted in a given period of time.

Hotelling:

(H1) The resource is available in homogeneous quality and in an overall quantity that is limited and that at any moment of time is known with certainty.
(H2) The amount of the resource that can be extracted in a given period of time, a year, for example, is only constrained by the amount of it left over from the preceding period.

These sets of different premises give rise to different constellations, with the emphasis on *differential rent* in Ricardo and on *royalties* in Hotelling. In all models we elaborated we assumed that there is a *backstop process* that prevents the system from dwindling away.

The Hotelling Rule implies that the prices of resources *in situ* need to increase over time at a rate that is equal to the competitive rate of profits. This follows from the requirement that in competitive conditions the conservation of a resource is an economic activity which ought to yield to the proprietors of deposits of the resource the same rate of profits as is obtained from any productive activity.[4] This seems in turn to imply that in the presence of exhaustible resources, and assuming a general framework of the analysis,[5] *all* prices are bound to change over time. However, this need not be the case.

A main purpose of our paper was to develop a simple model that allows us to incorporate both points of view and the underlying leading principles in a single scheme and discuss its mathematical properties. A main outcome of the analysis is a clear distinction between three different types of property income: *rents*, *profits* and *royalties*. Ricardo's finding that rents and profits move in different directions is corroborated with regard to different kinds of exhaustible resources (or, alternatively, differently fertile deposits of one such resource). Royalties, which turn out to be a special kind of profits, may move in the opposite direction of rents. In well-specified circumstances this may imply that whereas the prices of exhaustible resources *in situ* are bound to change at a rate equal to the rate of profits, all other prices remain constant. This is so because the owners of deposits of resources receive both royalties and rents. The sum of royalties and rents for a given deposit may be constant even if royalties are changing, since rents are changing in equal amounts but in the opposite direction.

In a follow-up paper which was published in a Festschrift in honour of Bertram Schefold (Kurz and Salvadori 2011) we illustrate these findings in terms of a simple numerical example. We argue that in well-specified circumstances the prices of produced commodities need not change, although the *in situ* prices of exhaustible resources that are actually exhausted over time will change. In order to show this, we start from the observation to be found, for example, in the writings of the classical economists from Adam Smith to David Ricardo, that the exploitation of fields or deposits of exhaustible resources is typically subject to capacity constraints that limit the amount of the resource that can be extracted during a given time period from each field or deposit. As a consequence, several deposits of resources with different unit costs of extraction are exploited side by side. This implies that rents will have to be paid to the owners of fields that are more 'fertile', to use Ricardo's expression in Chapter 3 of the *Principles*. Finally, if the backstop process is operated, this implies that the prices of commodities available on the ground are constant despite the fact that the prices of resources *in situ* vary over time according to Hotelling's Rule. This is made possible by an inverse movement of rents on the one hand and royalties on the other.

Concluding remarks

In this chapter we provide a summary account of the discussions of the problem of exhaustible resources within a classical framework of the analysis triggered by Serio Parrinello. It is argued that the classical approach as it was formulated by Piero Sraffa is capable of dealing with the problem in a satisfactory way. In particular, it is shown that the analysis of Ricardo in terms of profits and that of Hotelling in terms of royalties are not incompatible with one another, but capture different aspects of the problem at hand. These aspects can be jointly studied in terms of a single formalization of the problem of exhaustible resources.

References

Bidard, Ch. and Erreygers, G. (2001a). 'The Corn–Guano Model', *Metroeconomica*, 52(3), pp. 243–53.

Bidard, Ch. and Erreygers, G. (2001b). 'Further Reflections on the Corn–Guano Model', *Metroeconomica*, 52(3), pp. 254–67.

Gibson, B. (1984). 'Profit and Rent in a Classical Theory of Exhaustible and Renewable Resources', *Zeitschrift für Nationalökonomie*, 44, pp. 131–49.

Hosoda, E. (2001). 'Recycling and Landfilling in a Dynamic Sraffian Model: Application of the Corn–Guano Model to a Waste Treatment Problem', *Metroeconomica*, 52(3), pp. 268–81.

Hotelling, H. (1931). 'The Economics of Exhaustible Resources', *Journal of Political Economy*, 39, pp. 137–75.

Krautkraemer, J. A. (1998). 'Nonrenewable Resource Scarcity', *Journal of Economic Literature*, 36(4), pp. 2065–107.

Kurz, H. D. and Salvadori, N. (1995). *Theory of Production. A Long-Period Analysis*, Revised paperback edition 1997, Cambridge, UK: Cambridge University Press.

Kurz, H. D. and Salvadori, N. (1997). 'Exhaustible Resources in a Dynamic Input-Output Model with 'Classical' Resources', *Economic Systems Research*, 9(3), pp. 235–51.

Kurz, H. D. and Salvadori, N. (2000). 'Economic Dynamics in a Simple Model with Exhaustible Resources and a Given Real Wage Rate', *Structural Change and Economic Dynamics*, 11(1–2), pp. 167–79.

Kurz, H. D. and Salvadori, N. (2001). 'Classical Economics and the Problem of Exhaustible Resources', *Metroeconomica*, 52(3), pp. 282–96.

Kurz, H. D. and Salvadori, N. (2002). 'On the Long-period Method. A Comment on Ravagnani', a reply to 'Produced Quantities and Returns in Sraffa's Theory of Normal Prices: Textual Evidence and Analytical Issues', by Fabio Ravagnani, in S. Böhm, Ch. Gehrke, H. D. Kurz and R. Sturn (eds.), *Is there Progress in Economics? Knowledge, Truth and the History of Economic Thought*, Cheltenham: Edward Elgar.

Kurz, H. D. and Salvadori, N. (2009). 'Ricardo on Exhaustible Resources, and the Hotelling Rule', in Aiko Ikeo and Heinz D. Kurz (eds.), *The History of Economic Theory. Essays in Honour of Takashi Negishi*, London: Routledge, pp. 68–79.

Kurz, H. D. and Salvadori, N. (2011). 'Exhaustible Resources: Rents, Profits, Royalties, and Prices', in Volker Caspari (ed.), *The Evolution of Economic Theory, Essays in Honour of Bertram Schefold*, London: Routledge.

Lager, Ch. (2001). 'A Note on Non-Stationary Prices', *Metroeconomica*, 52(3), pp. 297–300.

Parrinello, S. (1970). 'Introduzione ad una teoria neoricardiana del commercio internazionale', *Studi Economici*, 25, pp. 267–321.

Parrinello, S. (1983). 'Exhaustible Natural Resources and the Classical Method of Long-period Equilibrium', in J. Kregel (ed.), *Distribution, Effective Demand and International Economic Relations*, London: Macmillan, pp. 186–99.

Parrinello, S. (2001). 'The Price of Exhaustible Resources', *Metroeconomica*, 52(3), pp. 301–15.

Parrinello, S. (2004). 'The Notion of Effectual Supply and the Theory of Normal Prices with Exhaustible Resources', *Economic Systems Research*, 16(3), pp. 319–30.

Pegoretti, G. (1986). *Risorse, produzione, distribuzione*, Milan: Franco Angeli.

Pegoretti, G. (1990). 'Offerta di risorse non riproducibili, scelta della tecnica e struttura produttiva', in A. Quadrio Curzio and R. Scazzieri (eds.), *Dinamica economica e strutturale*, Bologna: Il Mulino, pp. 81–121.

Quadrio Curzio, A. (1983). 'Primary Commodity Prices, Exhaustible Resources and International Monetary Relations: Alternative Explanations', in J. Kregel (ed.), *Distribution, Effective Demand and International Economic Relations*, London: Macmillan, pp. 142–52.

Quadrio Curzio, A. (1986). 'Technological Scarcity: An Essay on Production and Structural Change', in M. Baranzini and R. Scazzieri (eds.), *Foundations of Economics*, Oxford: Basil Blackwell, pp. 311–38.

Ravagnani, F. (2002). 'Produced Quantities and Returns in Sraffa's Theory of Normal Prices: Textual Evidence and Analytical Issues', in S. Böhm, Ch. Gehrke, H. D. Kurz and R. Sturn (eds.), *Is there Progress in Economics? Knowledge, Truth and the History of Economic Thought*, Cheltenham: Edward Elgar.

Ricardo, D. (1951–1973). *The Works and Correspondence of David Ricardo*, 11 volumes, edited by Piero Sraffa with the collaboration of M.H. Dobb, Cambridge: Cambridge University Press.

Roncaglia, A. (1983). 'The Price of Oil', *Journal of Post Keynesian Economics*, 5, pp. 557–78.

Roncaglia, A. (1985). *The International Oil Market*, London: Macmillan.

Salvadori, N. (1987). 'Les ressources naturelles rares dans la théorie de Sraffa', in G. Bidard (ed.), *La rente, acutalité de l'approche classique*, Paris: Economica, pp. 161–76.

Schefold, B. (1989). *Mr Sraffa on Joint Production and Other Essays*, London: Macmillan.

Schefold, B. (2001). 'Critique of the Corn-Guano Model', *Metroeconomica*, 52(3), pp. 316–28.

Smith, A. [1776] (1976). *An Inquiry into the Nature and Causes of the Wealth of Nations*. Vol. 2 of *The Glasgow Edition of the Works and Correspondence of Adam Smith*, edited by R.H. Campbell, A.S. Skinner and W.B. Todd, Oxford: Oxford University Press.

Sraffa, P. (1960). *Production of Commodities by Means of Commodities. Prelude to a Critique of Economic Theory*, Cambridge: Cambridge University Press.

Notes

1 The other fields with regard to which he suggested generalizations of Sraffa's analysis are the inclusion of services and their specific characteristics and monopoly.

2 Sraffa drafted Chapter XI in January 1958. While this was not yet the final version, it came very close to it with the exception of the passage on wasting assets.
3 Another special case has been pointed out by Kurz and Salvadori (1995: 359–60): for each deposit or mine of the resource that is being exhausted another one with the same characteristics is discovered, where the cost of the search (in terms of labour and means of production) is always the same. In this case the resource would never be exhausted and each deposit could be treated as if it were a machine: the price of the new machine equals the cost of the search and the price of an old machine of age t equals the value of the deposit after t periods of working it.
4 Empirical studies have shown that the Hotelling Rule does not perform all that well; for some of the reasons why this is so, see Krautkraemer (1998).
5 As is well known, Hotelling (1931) assumed a partial equilibrium framework in which the rate of interest (or profits) was given from outside the system. Ricardo's analysis may on the contrary be characterized as concerned with the system as a whole, in which the rate of profits will typically change as the scarcity of natural resources makes itself felt ever more severely.

Index

For Product Safety Concerns and Information please contact our EU
representative GPSR@taylorandfrancis.com
Taylor & Francis Verlag GmbH, Kaufingerstraße 24, 80331 München, Germany